THE LONGMAN HANDBOOK OF
TWENTIETH-CENTURY EUROPE

Also by Chris Cook and John Stevenson

British Historical Facts: 1760–1830
The Longman Handbook of Modern European History 1763–1997
British Historical Facts: 1688–1760
The Longman Companion to Britain since 1945
Britain in the Depression: Society and Politics, 1929–39, 2nd edn
The Longman Handbook of the Modern World
The Longman Handbook of Modern British History, 1714–2001

Other books by Chris Cook

Post-war Britain: a Political History (*with Alan Sked*)
The Age of Alignment: Electoral Politics in Britain, 1922–1929
A Short History of the Liberal Party, 1900–2001
By-elections in British Politics (*ed. with John Ramsden*)
The Politics of Reappraisal, 1918–1939 (*ed. with Gillian Peele*)
The Decade of Disillusion (*ed. with David McKie*)
Crisis and Controversy: Essays in Honour of A. J. P. Taylor (*ed. with Alan Sked*)
Trade Unions in British Politics (*ed. with Ben Pimlott*)
The Dictionary of Historical Terms
The Facts on File World Political Almanac
The Longman Guide to Sources in Contemporary British History (*2 vols with David Waller et al.*)

Other books by John Stevenson

Popular Disturbances in England, 1700–1870, 2nd edn
British Society, 1914–1945
Order and Disorder in Early Modern England (*with A. J. Fletcher*)
The Working Class and Politics in Britain and America, 1929–1945 (*ed. with S. Salter*)
Third Party Politics since 1945
The Longman Companion to Britain in the Eighteenth Century (*with J. Gregory*)
A History of Europe

THE LONGMAN HANDBOOK OF

TWENTIETH-CENTURY EUROPE

Chris Cook and John Stevenson

PEARSON
Longman

London • New York • Toronto • Sydney • Tokyo • Singapore
Hong Kong • Cape Town • Madrid • Paris • Amsterdam • Munich • Milan

Pearson Education Limited

Head Office:
Edinburgh Gate
Harlow CM20 2JE
Tel: +44 (0)1279 623623
Fax: +44 (0)1279 431059

London Office:
128 Long Acre
London WC2E 9AN
Tel: +44 (0)20 7447 2000
Fax: +44 (0)20 7447 2170
Website: www.history-minds.com

_____

First published in Great Britain in 2003

© Chris Cook and John Stevenson 2003

The right of Chris Cook and John Stevenson to be identified as Authors
of this Work has been asserted by them in accordance with the Copyright,
Designs and Patents Act 1988.

ISBN 0 582 23508 1

British Library Cataloguing in Publication Data
A CIP catalogue record for this book can be obtained from the British Library

Library of Congress Cataloging in Publication Data
A CIP catalog record for this book can be obtained from the Library of Congress

10 9 8 7 6 5 4 3 2 1

Typeset in 10/12pt New Baskerville by Graphicraft Limited, Hong Kong
Printed and bound in Malaysia

The Publishers' policy is to use paper manufactured from sustainable forests.

CONTENTS

Naval strength of major European Powers in 1914

	Britain	Germany	France	Italy	Russia	Austria–Hungary	Turkey
Dreadnoughts	24	13	14	1	4	3	1
Pre-Dreadnoughts	38	30	9	17	7	12	3
Battle cruisers	10	6	0	0	1	0	0
Cruisers	47	14	19	5	8	3	0
Light cruisers	61	35	6	6	5	4	2
Destroyers	228	152	81	33	106	18	8
Submarines	76	30	67	20	36	14	0

Naval losses of major European Powers, 1914–18

	Britain	Germany	France	Italy	Russia	Austria–Hungary	Turkey
Dreadnoughts	2	0 (18)*	0	1	2	2	0
Pre-Dreadnoughts	11	1 (0)	4	3	2	1	1
Battle cruisers	3	1 (6)	0	0	0	0	0
Cruisers	13	6 (0)	5	1	2	0	0
Light cruisers	12	17 (23)	0	2	0	3	1
Destroyers	67	66 (92)	12	8	20	6	3
Submarines	54	199 (all)	14	8	20	14	0

* Figures in brackets indicate vessels surrendered.

VERSAILLES, THE LEAGUE OF NATIONS AND INTER-WAR DIPLOMACY

1918

8 Jan.	Wilson issues Fourteen Points as a basis for peace.
3 Mar.	Germany signs the Treaty of Brest-Litovsk with the Russian Bolshevik government, making huge territorial gains in the East and releasing fresh troops for an offensive in the West.
21 Mar.	Germany launches final offensive in the West, but fails to achieve a decisive breakthrough.
9 Apr.	Renewed German offensive in Flanders against the British also fails to achieve a knock-out blow.
18 June	Assisted by recently arrived American reinforcements, the Allies begin a counter-attack.
8 Aug.	With German armies in retreat, Ludendorff refers to this as the 'Black Day' of the German army.

11 Aug.	Ludendorff offers his resignation to the Kaiser but is refused, but he calls for an end to the war.
26 Sept.	Foch launches massive offensive against the German lines with 126 divisions.
28 Sept.	Hindenburg and Ludendorff say that Germany must seek an armistice as military victory is impossible.
30 Sept.	Bulgarians sign armistice with Western allies.
3–4 Oct.	The new German Chancellor, Prince Max of Baden, appeals to President Wilson for an armistice based on the Fourteen Points.
9 Oct.	Wilson's First Note. Without consulting his allies, Wilson asks if Germany accepts the Fourteen Points unconditionally, and is prepared to evacuate all occupied territory.
12 Oct.	Prince Max sends a non-committal but favourable reply to Wilson, but simultaneously a U-boat sinks the liner *Leinster* with the loss of 200 lives, outraging Allied politicians and public.
14 Oct.	Wilson's Second Note demands an immediate end to submarine warfare, and immediate evacuation of occupied territory. It also calls for guarantees of 'constitutional change' implying that peace depends on the removal of the Kaiser. The High Command and the Kaiser reject this and suggest that Germany can fight on, but Prince Max replies to Wilson promising to stop attacks on civilian vessels and assures him that Germany now has a parliamentary government.
15 Oct.	Czech Republic proclaimed as Austro–Hungarian Empire begins to disintegrate.
17 Oct.	Hungary declares independence from the Austro–Hungarian Empire.
23 Oct.	Wilson's Third Note demands a promise that Germany will not resume hostilities after the armistice and says that Wilson will deal only with 'representatives of the German people'.
27 Oct.	Emperor Charles (Karl) of Austria tells the Kaiser he intends to sue for peace.
30 Oct.	Turks sign armistice.
31 Oct.	War in the Middle East officially ends.
3 Nov.	Austria–Hungary requests an armistice. Mutiny breaks out in Kiel where the sailors refuse to put to sea, elect a soviet and take over the port.
7 Nov.	Revolution breaks out in Munich with organisation of soldiers' and workers' councils which proclaim a Bavarian Socialist Republic. In Berlin, the majority Socialist Party calls for the Kaiser's abdication. Unrest spreads throughout Germany.

1935

6 Jan.	Franco–Italian agreement concerning colonies and Austria.
2 May	Alliance between France and Russia providing for mutual aid against aggression.
18 June	Anglo–German Naval Agreement.

1936

7 Aug.	Non-intervention agreement between Britain, France, Germany, Italy, Russia and others, regarding the Spanish Civil War.
25 Nov.	Anti-Comintern Pact between Germany and Japan.

1937

6 Nov.	Italy joined the Anti-Comintern Pact.

1938

29 Sept.	Munich Agreement between Britain, France, Germany and Italy forced Czechoslovakia to cede territory to Germany, Hungary and Poland.

1939

31 Mar.	France and Britain guaranteed Polish integrity.
22 May	'Pact of Steel' between Germany and Italy formalised the Rome–Berlin 'Axis'.
23 Aug.	German–Soviet Pact promised Russian neutrality in war involving Germany.

The League of Nations

1919

28 Apr.	Draft Covenant of the League approved by a plenary session of the Paris Peace Conference. Headquarters of the League to be in Geneva.
19 Nov.	Vote in the US Senate rejects Versailles Treaty and American membership of the League.

1920

10 Jan.	League of Nations formally comes into existence. Joined by almost all European states as well as more than 22 extra-European states.
Feb.	First meeting of its Council held in London which appoints High Commissioner to administer Danzig, now a 'free city' under League of Nations authority.
19 Mar.	Vote by US Senate confirms US rejection of the League.

Apr.–Oct.	Vilna seized from Lithuania by Poland in contravention of the League's wishes. Russo–Polish War decides the eastern boundary of Poland without reference to the League and confirmed in the Treaty of Riga (Mar. 1921).
Nov.	First meeting of the Assembly of the League.
1921	League settles Aaland Islands dispute between Finland and Sweden.
	Permanent Court of International Justice set up at the Hague.
1922	Mussolini defies the League with his absorption of Fiume into Italy.
	Hungary joins the League.
	League sanctions Polish possession of Vilna.
1923	French occupy the Ruhr without reference to League, and the League is unable to prevent the Italian occupation of Corfu.
	Disarmament Commission of the League proposes a Treaty of Mutual Assistance in which countries would offer mutual protection to each other. Accepted by France and Czechoslovakia, it is rejected by other states as too binding.
1925	League resolves border dispute between Bulgaria and Greece.
1926	Germany joins the League.
	League successfully arbitrates between Britain and Turkey over Mosul.
	International disarmament conference meets and prepares a report for future discussion.
1930	Disarmament commission agrees a draft convention but is opposed by Germany and the USSR.
1931	Japanese invade and overrun Manchuria; China appeals to the League for support. League sends fact-finding mission under Lord Lytton.
1932	Sixty nations meet at disarmament conference (Feb.) chaired by Arthur Henderson, British Foreign Secretary. It fails to reach mutually acceptable conclusions.
	Lytton Report on Manchuria condemns Japanese aggression but no action is taken.
1933	Following the accession of Hitler, Germany withdraws from the disarmament conference and also from the League.
	Japan leaves the League.

6 Aug.	The draft law on the establishment of the Consultative State Duma published.
5 Sept.	The Treaty of Portsmouth ends the Russo–Japanese conflict.
Oct.	The Constitutional Democratic Party (the Kadets) is formed.
7 Oct.	Nationwide political strikes begin.
13 Oct.	The St Petersburg Soviet of Workers' Deputies holds its first session.
17 Oct.	Tsar issues 'October Manifesto' promising a constitution and an elected parliament with genuine legislative power. The Tsar also grants freedom of the press, free speech and religious toleration.
20 Oct.	Political demonstrations in Moscow.
24–28 Oct.	Armed forces revolt at Kronstadt.
Oct.–Dec.	Formation of Workers' Soviets in major Russian cities and towns.
Nov.	Rise of the moderate Octobrist Party.
11–15 Nov.	Rising in Sevastopol.
21 Nov.	First sitting of the Moscow Soviet.
Nov.–Dec.	The Bolshevik daily newspaper *New Life*, edited by Lenin, is published in St Petersburg.
23 Dec.	Moscow Soviet stages uprising; widespread armed risings in Russia.
Dec. 1905– Jan. 1906	Moscow rising crushed. Punitive expeditions by Tsarist forces near Moscow, in the Baltic and Siberia.

1906

Apr.	Elections boycotted by Social Democrats and Social Revolutionaries; Constitutional Democrats ('Kadets') win largest number of seats.
6 May	Tsar issues Fundamental Law of the Empire by which the Tsar retains most of his autocratic power. Legislative power is to be divided between the Duma and the upper house, half the members of which are to be appointed by the Tsar. When the Duma is not in session the government may legislate by decree.
10 May	First Duma assembles; votes no confidence in the government.
June	Stolypin becomes Prime Minister.
July	Soldiers and sailors rise in Skeaborg and Kronstadt. The Russian economy is bolstered by a series of enormous loans.
21 July	Deadlock over the constitutional issue leads to the dissolution of the Duma. Kadet leaders issue Vyborg Manifesto calling

	for a refusal to pay taxes and enter military service, but no response.
25 Aug.	Stolypin makes large tracts of land available to the peasants.
1 Sept.	In an attempt to suppress the revolutionary movement, the government introduces Field Courts Martial; as a result over six hundred people are executed.
Oct.	Peasants are allowed to leave their village communes or to join others. Stolypin also removes the restrictions on the election of peasants to the zemstvos. Peasants also become eligible for any rank in government service.
22 Nov.	Stolypin's Agrarian Reform Act ends communal system of land-holding. Peasants are allowed to leave the commune at will and claim their share of land in private property.

1907

5 Mar.	The Second Duma meets, dominated by opposition to the autocracy.
16 June	Stolypin dissolves Duma and introduces a new electoral law, legalising arbitrary restrictions which had preceded the second election and also greatly increasing propertied representation.
Nov.	Election of the Third Duma.

1908

June	During public discussion of the budget, Guchkov blames the government for the military failures in the Russo–Japanese conflict.

1911

Sept.	Stolypin assassinated in a Kiev theatre.

1913 Election of Fourth Duma.

1914

Summer	General Strike in St Petersburg.
1 Aug.	Germany declares war on Russia.

Russia in Revolution, 1914–24

1914

1 Aug.	Germany declares war on Russia.
26 Aug.	Russia defeated at battle of Tannenberg.

3–12 Sept.	Russians force Austrians from Galicia.
5 Sept.	Russia suffers severe losses at battle of the Masurian Lakes.

1915

May	Austro–German offensive in Galicia defeats Russians.
July	Further Austro–German offensive leads, by the autumn, to over a million Russian casualties.
1 Aug.	Duma meets to consider the way the war is being conducted.
22 Aug.	Six parties in the Duma form the Progressive Bloc and demand a responsible ministry.
6 Sept.	Tsar assumes supreme command of the armed forces.
8 Sept.	Reform programme put before Council of Ministers by Progressive Bloc.
15 Sept.	Tsar rejects offer of resignation by his ministers to make way for a more popular administration.
16 Sept.	Tsar prorogues Duma.

1916

15 Feb.	Duma meets. Goremykin replaced as Prime Minister by Sturmer.
June–Oct.	Brusilov offensive gains territory but fails to achieve decisive victory and costs over a million casualties.
Sept.–Oct.	Wave of strikes; sporadic mutinies of soldiers at the front.
Oct.	Survey of manpower resources reveals that after February 1917 the Russian army will begin to decline in numbers.

1917

27 Feb.	Duma meets.
7 Mar.	Tsar leaves Petrograd for army GHQ; beginnings of large-scale demonstrations in the capital.
8 Mar.	Queues at bakers' shops, and crowds continue to demonstrate against the regime.
9 Mar.	Police fire on crowds.
10 Mar.	Strikes break out and soldiers join with the people; the Tsar orders suppression of the trouble.
11 Mar.	Police fire at demonstrators, but more soldiers join the protestors. Tsar prorogues Duma.
12 Mar.	Formation of Committee of State Duma to replace Tsarist government. Formation of Petrograd Soviet of Workers' and Soldiers' Deputies.
13 Mar.	Soviet news sheet *Izvestia* calls on people to take affairs into their own hands.

14 Mar.	Appointment of ministers of the provisional government. 'Army Order No. 1' issued by Petrograd Soviet puts armed forces under its authority and urges rank and file to elect representatives to the Soviet.
15 Mar.	Tsar abdicates in favour of his brother, Grand Duke Michael, at the same time confirming the new ministry and asking the country to support it. Grand Duke Michael chooses not to accept the throne unless he is bid to do so by the Assembly. The provisional government forbids the use of force against rioting peasants.
16 Mar.	Constituent assembly meets; abdication of Grand Duke Michael.
11 Apr.	All-Russian Conference of Soviets overwhelmingly votes to continue war in spite of Bolshevik opposition.
16 Apr.	Lenin arrives back in Petrograd.
3–5 May	Bolshevik-organised demonstrations by garrison in Petrograd against the Ministers Guchkov and Milyukov. Kornilov resigns command of forces in Petrograd, and Milyukov and Guchkov resign from the government.
18 May	Kerensky helps to reorganise provisional government.
18 June	Start of renewed offensive on southern front.
26 June	Soldiers at front refuse to obey orders. Kornilov insists on offensive being called off.
2 July	Start of northern offensive backed by Kerensky, Minister of War. Germans and Austrians drive Russians back after early successes.
12 July	Provisional government restores capital punishment and courts martial.
16–18 July	Bolsheviks organise demonstrations by sailors and Red Guards but the unrest is put down by loyal troops.
18 July	Fearing arrest, Lenin flees to Finland.
20 July	Lvov and Kadet ministers resign.
21 July	Formation of new government with Kerensky as Prime Minister.
1 Aug.	Kornilov appointed Commander-in-Chief.
3 Aug.	Kerensky resigns. Party leaders give him a free hand to form new government.
25–28 Aug.	Kerensky holds Moscow State Conference to settle differences with Kornilov, but fails to reach agreement.
3 Sept.	Riga falls to Germans.

8 Sept.	Troops begin to move against Petrograd, and Kerensky denounces Kornilov 'plot' against the government. Collapse of movement followed by arrest of Kornilov and fellow generals.
19 Sept.	Bolshevik majority in Moscow Soviet.
6 Oct.	Trotsky becomes Chairman of Petrograd Soviet.
23 Oct.	Decision by Bolshevik Central Committee to organise an armed rising.
25 Oct.	Formation of Military Revolutionary Committee by Bolsheviks.
1 Nov.	Provisional government tries to remove units from the Petrograd garrison, but Bolsheviks prevent this.
2 Nov.	Parliament refuses to give Kerensky powers to suppress the Bolsheviks.
6 Nov.	Bolsheviks organise headquarters in Peter and Paul fortress and move on strategic points. Lenin takes command.
7 Nov.	Bolsheviks seize power in Petrograd, taking key installations and services. The Winter Palace cut off and ministers of provisional government arrested. Kerensky flees. Lenin announces the transfer of power to the Military Revolutionary Committee and the victory of the socialist revolution.
8 Nov.	Lenin makes the Decree on Peace, an appeal for a just peace without annexations and indemnities, and the Decree on Land, affirming that all land is the property of the people. A Bolshevik government is formed.
13 Nov.	Counter-offensive by Kerensky against Petrograd fails.
15 Nov.	Bolsheviks establish power in Moscow.
1 Dec.	Left-wing social revolutionaries enter government after agreement with Bolsheviks.
2 Dec.	Escape of Kornilov and fellow generals from prison in Bykhov.
3 Dec.	Bolsheviks occupy Supreme Headquarters at Mogilev.
17 Dec.	Russia and Germany agree a ceasefire.
20 Dec.	Establishment of the *Cheka* (secret police).
22 Dec.	Russia and Germany start negotiations for a peace treaty in Brest-Litovsk.

1918

18 Jan.	Opening of Constituent Assembly.
19 Jan.	Constituent Assembly dispersed.
1–14 Feb.	Introduction of the Gregorian calendar.
9 Feb.	Central Council of the Ukraine concludes separate peace with Central Powers, having declared its independence.

10 Feb.	Brest-Litovsk negotiations broken off after German ultimatum.
18 Feb.	Germany resumes hostilities in the Ukraine.
24 Feb.	Soviet government decides to accept German peace ultimatum.
2 Mar.	Germans occupy Kiev.
3 Mar.	Russians sign Treaty of Brest-Litovsk, giving up large areas of pre-Revolutionary Russia. German troops continue to advance into central Russia and the Crimea.
12 Mar.	Soviet government moves from Petrograd to Moscow.
13 Mar.	Trotsky appointed People's Commissar of War.
5 Apr.	Allied ships and troops arrive in Murmansk.
13 Apr.	Kornilov killed fighting with anti-Bolshevik 'Volunteer army'. Bolsheviks mount drive against anarchists and other deviant elements. Germans take Odessa.
14 Apr.	Germans and Finns occupy Helsinki.
29 Apr.	Germans set up puppet Ukrainian government.
May	Georgia, Armenia and Azerbaijan declare independence.
8 May	Germans occupy Rostov.
14 May	Czech Legion (ex-prisoners recruited into service against the Central Powers) clash with Soviets at Chelyabinsk on their way to Vladivostok.
25 May	Revolt of Czech Legion who seize eastern part of Trans-Siberian railway.
29 May	Partial conscription introduced for Red Army.
23 June	Allied reinforcements arrive in Murmansk.
16 July	Execution of Imperial Family at Ekaterinburg.
2 Aug.	Establishment of anti-Bolshevik government at Archangel, followed by landing of more troops.
6 Aug.	'White' forces take Kazan.
14 Aug.	Allied forces land at Baku. British, Japanese and American forces land at Vladivostok.
10 Sept.	Bolsheviks take Kazan.
13 Sept.	Allied forces leave Baku.
23 Sept.	White forces set up Directorate as All-Russian provisional government.
9 Oct.	Directorate fixes capital at Omsk.
13 Nov.	Following armistice between Allies and Germany, the Soviet government denounces the Brest-Litovsk Treaty.
18 Nov.	Directorate suppressed at Omsk. Kolchak assumes supreme power.

14 Dec.	Collapse of Skoropadsky regime in the Ukraine.
17 Dec.	French land in Odessa.

1919

3 Jan.	Red Army takes Riga and Kharkov.
6 Feb.	Red Army occupies Kiev.
15 Feb.	Denikin assumes supreme command of White forces in south-east Russia.
2–7 Mar.	First Congress of Communist International in Moscow. Creation of Politburo and Communist International.
13 Mar.	Spring offensive by Kolchak.
21 Mar.	Allies decide to withdraw forces from Russia.
5 Apr.	British and Indian troops leave Transcaspia.
8 Apr.	French evacuate Odessa.
10 Apr.	Soviet troops enter Crimea.
19 May	Denikin begins offensive against Bolsheviks.
4 June	Kolchak defeated in centre and south, but Denikin continues advance, capturing Kharkov by end of month.
15 July	Red Army takes Chelyabinsk.
23 Aug.	Denikin takes Odessa.
31 Aug.	Denikin occupies Kiev.
19 Sept.	Allies evacuate Archangel.
28 Sept.	Yudenich reaches suburbs of Petrograd.
14–20 Oct.	Denikin takes Orel, but is forced to retreat; general retreat of White armies.
14 Nov.	Defeat of Yudenich by Red Army and occupation of Omsk.
12 Dec.	Red Army occupies Kharkov.
16 Dec.	Red Army occupies Kiev.

1920

4 Jan.	Abdication of Kolchak as Supreme Ruler.
8 Jan.	Red Army takes Rostov.
15 Jan.	Czechs hand Kolchak over to revolutionaries in control of Irkutsk.
7 Feb.	Execution of Kolchak.
19 Feb.	Northern government at Archangel collapses.
4 Apr.	Denikin succeeded by Wrangel.
24 Apr.	Outbreak of Russo–Polish War. Poles invade the Ukraine.
6 May	Polish forces take Kiev.

12 June	Red Army retakes Kiev.
11 July	Russian counter-attack takes Minsk and Vilna (14th).
20 July	Second Congress of Communist International.
17 Aug.	Russian forces almost reach Warsaw; beaten back by Polish counter-offensive.
21 Sept.	Start of Russo–Polish peace negotiations.
12 Oct.	Russo–Polish provisional peace treaty.
25 Oct.	Red Army offensive against Wrangel.
2 Nov.	Wrangel forced to retreat to the Crimea.
11–14 Nov.	Defeat and evacuation of Wrangel's forces in the Crimea.

1921

Feb.	Strikes in Petrograd. Red Army invades Georgia.
1 Mar.	Beginnings of revolt of Kronstadt sailors.
5 Mar.	Trotsky delivers ultimatum to sailors.
16–17 Mar.	Bombardment and assault on Kronstadt.
18 Mar.	Kronstadt Rising crushed. Treaty of Riga defines Russo–Polish frontier. 10th Party Congress of Russian Communists; Lenin introduces New Economic Policy (NEP), allowing peasants to keep their surplus grain for disposal on the open market.
Apr.	Beginnings of famine in the Volga regions.
Aug.	Famine relief agreements signed with America and the Red Cross.

1922

Mar.–Apr.	11th Party Congress. Stalin becomes General Secretary. Lenin forced to convalesce after operation to remove two bullets, the result of Kaplan's attempted assassination in 1918.
16 Apr.	Treaty of Rapallo with Germany establishes close economic and military co-operation.
26 May	Lenin has stroke.
2 Oct.	Lenin returns to Moscow.
Dec.	Lenin's second stroke.
23–26 Dec.	Lenin dictates the *Letter to the Congress*.
30 Dec.	Formation of Union of Soviet Socialist Republics, federating Russia, the Ukraine, White Russia and Transcaucasia.

1923

4 Jan.	Lenin adds codicil to the *Letter*, warning of Stalin's ambitions.
Mar.	Lenin's third stroke.

Apr.	12th Party Congress.
July	Constitution of USSR published.

1924

21 Jan.	Death of Lenin.

RUSSIA, 1924–53

1 Feb.	Britain recognises Soviet Union.
3 Feb.	Rykov elected Prime Minister.
23 May	13th Party Congress opens. Zinoviev demands Trotsky's recantation of belief in 'Permanent Revolution'.

1925

16 Jan.	Trotsky dismissed as War Commissar.
21 Jan.	Japan recognises Soviet Union.
Apr.	14th Party Congress adopts 'socialism in one country'.

1926

19 Oct.	Trotsky and Kamenev expelled from Politburo.

1927

26 May	Britain temporarily severs relations with Soviet Union because of continued Bolshevik propaganda.
Nov.	Trotskyists organise political demonstrations and Trotsky expelled from Party.
Dec.	15th Party Congress condemns all deviations from party line and resolves upon the collectivisation of agriculture. Stalin emerges as dominant voice.

1928

Jan.	Trotsky banished to provinces.
Spring	Serious grain procurement crisis.
Sept.	Bukharin publishes opposition articles in *Pravda* in support of peasants.
1 Oct.	Beginning of First Five-Year Plan aiming to develop heavy industries.
Nov.	Bukharin and Tomsky exiled to Turkey.

1929

Jan.	Trotsky exiled to Turkey.

Autumn	Start of forced collectivisation and dekulakisation.
17 Nov.	Bukharin and other 'rightists' expelled from Party.

1930

Jan.	Quickening of tempo of collectivisation; resistance harshly dealt with by force and deportation. Widespread disorder and destruction in rural areas.
Mar.	Stalin publishes *Dizzy with Success* calling for slowing down of collectivisation.
Nov.–Dec.	Trial of so-called 'Industrial Party' for alleged conspiracy within the State Planning Commission (Gosplan).

1931

Mar.–July	Trial of Mensheviks. Harvest failure as a result of chaos of collectivisation.

1932

Apr.	Central Committee resolves reform of literary and arts organisations. Beginnings of famine in Ukraine and other parts of Russia.
Dec.	Introduction of internal passport.

1933

Nov.	Second Five-Year Plan inaugurated. USA recognises the Soviet government.

1934

Jan.	17th Party Congress.
July	GPU (former *Cheka*) reorganised as NKVD.
Sept.	USSR joins League of Nations.
Dec.	Assassination of Kirov by Nikolayev leads Central Executive Committee to issue a directive ordering summary trial and execution of 'terrorists' without appeal.
28–29 Dec.	Nikolayev and 13 'accomplices' tried in secret and executed.

1935

Jan.	Zinoviev, Kamenev and 17 others tried in secret for 'moral responsibility' for Kirov's assassination and sentenced to imprisonment. Widespread arrests of 'oppositionists'.
Feb.	Statute regulating collective farms promulgated. Commission appointed to draw up a new constitution.
June	Draft constitution presented to Central Committee for approval.

Aug.	'Stakhanovite' programme launched to encourage industrial production.
Sept.	Reintroduction of ranks in Red Army.
Dec.	Central Committee declares that the purge is complete.

1936

Jan.	Renewed purge of party members.
19–24 Aug.	Trial and execution of Zinoviev, Kamenev and other members of the 'Trotskyite–Zinovievite Counter-Revolutionary Bloc' for alleged plotting against the leadership. Tomsky commits suicide following accusations made at their trial.
25 Sept.	Yagoda dismissed as head of NKVD and replaced by Yezhov.
5 Dec.	8th Congress of Soviets approves the new constitution.

1937

Jan.	Trial of Radek, Pyatakov and 15 others for alleged conspiracy with Trotsky and foreign powers to overthrow the Soviet system. Four are imprisoned, the rest shot.
Mar.	Bukharin, Rykov and Yagoda expelled from the Party.
June	Tukachevsky, Chief of the General Staff, and other senior officers tried in secret for plotting with Germany and executed. Widespread purge of the armed forces begins, removing over 400 senior officers.

1938

2–13 Mar.	Third Five-Year Plan inaugurated. Trial of Bukharin, Rykov, Krestinsky, Rakovsky, Yagoda, and other leading party and NKVD members for terrorism, sabotage, treason and espionage.
28 Mar.	Stalin offers support to Czechoslovakia if attacked.
9 May	Russia offers to assist Czechoslovakia if Romania and Poland will allow the passage of Russian troops across their territory; both refuse.
Dec.	Beria succeeds Yezhov as head of NKVD.

1939

Mar.	18th Party Congress.
18 Apr.	USSR proposes defence alliance with Britain and France. Offer not taken up by the Western allies.
3 May	Molotov replaces Litvinov as Commissar of Foreign Affairs in the USSR.
12 Aug.	Anglo–French mission to USSR begins talks in Moscow.

18 Aug.	Germany makes commercial agreement with USSR.
22 Aug.	Ribbentrop, German Foreign Minister, arrives in Moscow.
23 Aug.	Nazi–Soviet Pact signed. A non-aggression pact, it also contains secret clauses on the partition of Poland and allocation of Finland, Latvia, Estonia and Bessarabia to Soviet sphere of influence.
31 Aug.	Supreme Soviet ratifies German non-aggression pact.
17 Sept.	Red Army invades eastern Poland.
22 Sept.	Red Army occupies Lvov.
28 Sept.	Secret accord with Germany transfers Lithuania to Soviet sphere of influence.
29 Sept.– 10 Oct.	Estonia, Latvia and Lithuania conclude treaties with USSR, allowing Soviet military bases in their territory.
12 Oct.	Talks in Moscow between Finland and USSR. Stalin presents his territorial demands.
9 Nov.	Finns reject Soviet demands.
29 Nov.	USSR breaks off diplomatic relations with Finland.
30 Nov.	Russians bomb Helsinki and Red Army crosses Finnish frontier.
Dec.	Finnish forces inflict heavy defeats on Russia in the south and east.

1940

1–12 Feb.	Major Russian offensive on Karelian Isthmus.
12 Mar.	Treaty of Moscow concludes war. Finns cede 10 per cent of their territory including the Karelian Isthmus and territory in the north-east.
15–17 June	Soviet troops occupy Lithuania, Latvia and Estonia.
28 June	Soviet troops occupy Bessarabia and north-eastern Bukovina.
21 July	Lithuania, Latvia and Estonia 'request' incorporation into USSR.
17 Nov.	USSR demands control of Bulgaria and withdrawal of German troops from Finland before joining Tripartite Pact of Germany, Italy and Japan.
18 Dec.	Hitler issues directive for Operation Barbarossa, the invasion of Russia.

1941

13 Apr.	Non-aggression pact signed with Japan.
22 June	Germany invades USSR.

29 June	State Defence Committee formed.
3 July	Stalin broadcasts to the people.
12 July	Anglo–Soviet mutual assistance agreement signed.
15 July	Fall of Smolensk.
7 Aug.	Stalin becomes Supreme Commander of the Soviet Armed Forces.
8 Sept.	Kiev captured.
2 Oct.	German offensive against Moscow opens.
19 Oct.	Declaration of state of siege in Moscow. Stalin remains in city, though thousands are evacuated or flee in panic.
27 Nov.	German forces come within 20 miles of Moscow.
5 Dec.	Russian counter-offensive in Moscow sector. Hitler abandons Moscow offensive for winter.

1942

Mar.	Soviet winter offensive ends.
28 June	German offensive in the south.
9 Aug.	German Army Group A reaches Caucasus.
Sept.	Army Group B reaches Stalingrad.
23 Nov.	Army Group B surrounded by Russian offensive.

1943

2 Feb.	Last German forces surrender at Stalingrad.
May	Comintern dissolved as a gesture of reassurance towards Western allies.
5 July	Beginning of Operation Citadel, the German attack on the Kursk Salient. Counter-attack by Red Army (from 12 July) begins fresh Soviet advance.
23 Aug.	Kharkov captured by the Red Army. End of the battle of Kursk.
Sept.	Re-establishment of Patriarchate and Church administration in Russia. Seminaries and many churches reopened.
25 Sept.	Smolensk recaptured.
6 Nov.	Red Army recaptures Kiev.
28 Nov.–1 Dec.	Roosevelt, Churchill and Stalin meet in Tehran.

1944

27 Jan.	Siege of Leningrad lifted.
Mar.	Red Army enters Poland.
26 Mar.	Red Army enters Romania.

1 Aug.	Home Army rises in Warsaw but receives no support from Russian forces. Rising quelled by October.
24 Aug.	Romania accepts armistice terms.
8 Sept.	Russians enter Bulgaria.
26 Sept.	Estonia occupied by the Russians.
6 Oct.	Russians enter Hungary and Czechoslovakia.
15 Oct.	Russo–Bulgarian armistice.

1945

12 Jan.	Final Red Army offensive begins.
4–11 Feb.	Churchill, Roosevelt and Stalin meet at Yalta.
13 Apr.	Russian forces reach Vienna.
16 Apr.	Russians begin final drive on Berlin.
9 May	Surrender of Germany. Victory day in the Soviet Union.
17 July–1 Aug.	Potsdam meeting of Stalin, Truman and Churchill (Attlee after 27 July).

1946 Fourth Five-Year Plan inaugurated.

Aug.	Central Committee establishes Party high schools.
Sept.	Decree that all land being privately cultivated to be returned to the collectives.

1947

Sept.	Cominform established.
Dec.	Currency reform.

1948 Beginnings of collectivisation in Baltic provinces.

Jan.	Solomon Milhoels, Chairman of the Jewish State Theatre in Moscow, murdered.
June	Yugoslavia expelled from Cominform.
Autumn	Purge of Leningrad party following death of Zhdonov.
Nov.	Dissolution of Jewish Anti-Fascist Committee.

1949 Closure of Jewish State Theatre in Moscow and arrest of leading Yiddish cultural figures.

1951 Fifth Five-Year Plan inaugurated.

1953

Jan.	'Doctors' Plot' revealed, alleged to have been planned 'to wipe out the leading cadres of the USSR' by medical means.

5 Mar.	Death of Stalin: Malenkov becomes Prime Minister.
July	Arrest and execution of Beria.
Sept.	Khrushchev confirmed as First Secretary.

FASCIST ITALY

The background: 1896–1919

1896

1 Mar.	Defeat of Italian forces at battle of Adowa (Abyssinia) inflicts national humiliation.
5 Mar.	Fall of the final Crispi administration.

1898

May	Repression of widespread disturbances and food riots.

1899

	Beginning of 10-year period of economic growth symbolised by foundation of Fiat.

1900

	General elections. Resignation of Pelloux.
29 June	Assassination of Humbert I; succeeded by Victor Emmanuel III.

1901

Feb.	Start of the Giolitti era with formation of the Zanardelli–Giolitti administration.

1902

June	Beginning of the Franco–Italian entente.

1903

	Giovanni Giolitti becomes Prime Minister for first time.
Aug.	Election of Pius X as Pope following death of Leo XIII.

1904

Sept.	Failure of general strike across Italy. Followed by elections (Nov).

1906

	Foundation of *Confederazione Generale del Lavoro.*
Feb.	First Sonnino ministry (entry of Radicals and Republicans into government).

1907

Sept.	Papal encyclical attacks Modernism.

1909

Oct.   Russo–Italian accord (the Racconigi Agreement).

1910

Dec.   Italian Nationalist Association founded.

1911

Sept.   Beginning of the war in Tripolitania (the Libyan War) after declaration of war on Ottoman Empire.

1912

June   New electoral law gives near-complete manhood suffrage.

July   Mussolini rises to prominence at Reggio Emilia Conference of Socialist Party.

Oct.   Libyan War ended by Treaty of Ouchy.

Dec.   Final renewal of Triple Alliance.

1913

Oct.–Nov.   General elections.

1914

Mar.   Fall of Giolitti's fourth ministry. Antonio Salandra becomes Prime Minister.

June   General strike and widespread agitation during 'Red Week'.

3 Aug.   Italy declares itself neutral in First World War.

20 Aug.   Death of Pius X (election of Benedict on 3 Sept.).

Oct.   'Active neutrality' advocated by Mussolini. Formation of *Fascio Rivoluzionario d'Azione Internazionalista.*

25 Nov.   Mussolini founds *Il Popolo d'Italia* and is expelled from Socialist Party.

Dec.   Foundation of *Fascio d'Azione Rivoluzionaria.*

1915

26 Apr.   Italy signs Pact of London, joining the Entente powers.

24 May   War declared on Austria–Hungary.

1916

June   Paolo Boselli replaces Salandra as Prime Minister, forming a National Union Government.

28 Aug.   War declared on Germany.

1917

24 Oct.   Opening of battle of Caporetto. Retreat of Italian forces to River Piave. Vittorio Orlando becomes Prime Minister (until June 1919).

1918

Apr.   Signing of Pact of Rome of oppressed nationalities.

June   Battle of the Piave.

Oct.   Battle of Vittorio Veneto.

Nov.   Italy signs armistice.

The rise of Fascism: 1919–22

1919

Jan.   Formation of Italian Catholic Party (*Partito Popolare Italiano*)

23 Mar.   Foundation of the first *Fasci di Combattimento* by Mussolini in Milan.

Apr.   Italian delegation clashes with Woodrow Wilson over Treaty of Versailles.

25 Aug.   Italian forces evacuate Fiume.

2 Sept.   Universal suffrage and proportional representation introduced.

12 Sept.   D'Annunzio seizes Fiume.

11 Nov.   The Pope lifts the prohibition against Catholics participating in political life.

16 Nov.   Socialists (PSI) and Catholics receive strong support in the elections; Fascists gain only a fraction of the vote. PSI largest party in parliament.

1920

9 June   Giolitti takes over as Prime Minister from Nitti.

31 Aug.–Sept.   Widespread strikes and lockouts in engineering, metal and steel industries. Industrialists form *Confindustria*.

12 Nov.   Treaty of Rapallo settles disputes between Italy and Yugoslavia. Fiume to be an independent state.

21 Nov.   Fascists fire on crowd in Bologna during inauguration of mayor.

1 Dec.   D'Annunzio declares war on Italy.

24–25 Dec.   Clashes between Italian troops and Fiuman troops. *Andrea Doria* shells the royal palace.

31 Dec.   D'Annunzio makes peace with Italy.

1921

5 Jan.	D'Annunzio leaves Fiume. Foundation of Italian Communist Party (PCI).
27 Feb.	Communists and Fascists clash in Florence.
15 May	Liberals and Democrats successful at the elections. Fascist alliance with Giolitti secures them 35 seats. Mussolini elected to parliament.
26 June	Giolitti Cabinet falls, replaced by Bonomi. End of last Giolitti ministry.

1922

9 Feb.	Bonomi government resigns.
25 Feb.	Facta heads new government. Pius XI elected Pope.
May	Fascist takeover in Bologna.
3–4 Aug.	Fascist takeover in Milan. Socialist general strike fails.
24 Oct.	Mussolini calls on Facta to resign and for the formation of a Fascist Cabinet. Facta refuses.
28 Oct.	Fascist 'March on Rome'.
30 Oct.	Mussolini arrives in Rome and organises victory march.
31 Oct.	Mussolini forms Cabinet.

Italy under Mussolini

25 Nov.	Mussolini is granted temporary dictatorial powers to institute reforms.
Dec.	Creation of Fascist Grand Council.

1923

14 Jan.	King Victor Emmanuel authorises voluntary Fascist Militia.
Apr.	Popular Party (a left-wing party) leaves Mussolini's Cabinet.
21 July	Electoral law proposed, guaranteeing two-thirds of the seats in the Chamber to the majority party.
Aug.	Corfu incident.
Oct.	Francesco Giunta becomes PNF secretary.
Nov.	New electoral law passed (the Acerbo Law).
Dec.	Fusion of Nationalists with PNF. New press laws enacted. Palazzo Chigi pact between *Confindustria* and Fascist labour syndicates.

1924

27 Jan.	Treaty with Yugoslavia recognises Fiume as Italian, but cedes surrounding area to Yugoslavia.
6 Apr.	Fascists obtain almost two-thirds of votes in election amid widespread use of violence and intimidation. Fascists take 374 seats.
30 May	Matteotti launches attack on the Fascist government.
21 June	Matteotti is abducted and murdered. Non-fascists resign from Chambers and condemn violence (the Aventine secession).
July	Press censorship introduced.

1925

3 Jan.	Mussolini's speech to parliament effectively begins the dictatorship.
12 Feb.	Farinacci becomes secretary of PNF.
Apr.	Congress of Fascist Intellectuals meets.
1 May	*Dopolavoro* created (Fascist leisure time organisation).
2 Oct.	Palazzo Vidoni pact between *Confindustria* and the Fascist syndicates. Launch of 'Battle for Grain'.
24 Dec.	Mussolini's dictatorial powers increased. Press censorship tightened, secret non-fascist organisations banned, and widespread arrests. Banning of opposition parties.

1926

31 Jan.	Government decrees given the power of law.
3 Apr.	Right to strike abolished: collective contracts reserved to the Fascist syndicate. Fascist Youth Movement formed (ONB, or *Ballila*).
7 Apr.	Mussolini wounded in assassination attempt.
July	Creation of Ministry of Corporations – effective birth of the corporate state.
25 Nov.	Law for defence of the state; creation of a special tribunal for political crimes; death penalty introduced for plotting against Royal Family or head of state.

1927

21 Dec.	Exchange rate fixed at 'quota 90' (*Quota Novanta*) (92.45 lira to the pound) in a revaluation of the currency.

1929

11 Feb.	Lateran treaties with Papacy creating the Vatican City as a sovereign independent state.

1932

30 Oct.	*Decennale* celebrations – Fascists celebrate 10th year of power in Italy.

1934

17 Mar.	Mussolini signs the Rome Protocols with Austria and Hungary.
14 June	Meeting of Hitler and Mussolini in Venice.
July	Mussolini sends troops to the Austrian frontier following Hitler's attempted coup.
10 Nov.	Council of Corporations inaugurated in Rome.

1935

Mar.	Stresa Front (see p. 326).
3 Oct.	Italy begins invasion of Abyssinia (Ethiopia) following increased drive for economic autarky.

1936

5 May	Italian forces occupy Addis Ababa.
24 Oct.	Rome–Berlin Axis formed.

1938

14 July	Publication of *Manifesto della Razza* – first anti-Semitic measure.

1939

19 Jan.	Creation of the *Camera del Fascie delle Corporazioni*, replacing parliament.
7 Apr.	Italy invades Albania.
22 May	Pact of Steel signed between Hitler and Mussolini.

1940

10 June	Mussolini declares war and invades France. First air attacks on Malta.
3 Aug.	Italy invades British Somaliland.
13 Sept.	Italian forces invade Egypt.
28 Oct.	Italy invades Greece.
11–12 Nov.	Destruction of large part of Italian fleet at Taranto by British aircraft.
9 Dec.	British offensive in North Africa routs the army of Graziani.

1941

24 Mar.	Italians defeated in British Somaliland.

27–28 Mar.	Italian fleet defeated at Cape Matapan.
6 Apr.	British enter Addis Ababa.
16 May	Capitulation of Italian forces under the Duke of Aosta.
11 Dec.	Italy declares war on USA.

1942

June	Allied convoys resupply Malta.
4 Nov.	British break through Axis Line at El Alamein.

1943

May	Surrender of Axis forces in North Africa.
10 July	Allied invasion of Sicily.
25 July	Grand Council of Fascism votes Mussolini out of power. Badoglio takes over the Italian government.
17 Aug.	Sicily finally conquered by the Allies.
8 Sept.	Italian surrender announced. Nazis take over power in Italy.
9 Sept.	Salerno landing by US 5th Army.
12 Sept.	Skorzeny rescues Mussolini.
23 Sept.	Mussolini announces creation of Fascist social republic of Salo.

1944

22 Jan.	Anzio landing by US 5th Army; German counter-attack stalls advance.
15 Mar.	Allies bomb Monte Cassino.
17 Mar.	Monte Cassino falls.
4 June	Rome falls.

1945

28 Apr.	Mussolini executed by partisans at Dongo.

GERMANY: REPUBLIC, DICTATORSHIP AND DEFEAT

Weimar Germany

1919

5–11 Jan.	Spartacist revolt in Berlin put down by Ebert–Noske government using 'Free Corps' (*Freikorps*) of ex-soldiers.
15 Jan.	Rosa Luxemburg and Karl Liebknecht, leaders of the Spartacists, are arrested and murdered by the *Freikorps*.

19 Jan.	National Constituent Assembly elected on basis of proportional representation but fails to give any party an outright majority.
8 Feb.	National Constituent Assembly meets at Weimar.
11 Feb.	Ebert becomes President of Weimar Republic, following formation of coalition of Majority Socialists and the Centre and Democratic parties under Scheidemann.
13 Feb.	Scheidemann forms a Cabinet.
21 Feb.	Assassination of the premier of the Bavarian Republic, Kurt Eisner, by right-wingers.
Apr.	Socialist Bavarian Republic overthrown by Federal German forces.
29 June	Treaty of Versailles signed (see pp. 192–3).

1920

13–17 Mar.	Kapp Putsch; *Freikorps* officers attempt to make Wolfgang Kapp Chancellor of the Reich in pro-monarchist *coup d'état* in Berlin. Although troops refuse to fire on the *Freikorps*, and the government is forced to flee Berlin, a general strike frustrates the putsch.
Apr.	Hitler's German Workers' Party changes its name to the National Socialist German Workers' Party (Nazis).

1921

29 Aug.	Assassination of Matthias Erzberger, leader of Centre Party, by right-wing officers.

1922

16 Apr.	Treaty of Rapallo provides for economic and military co-operation between Germany and Russia.
24 June	Assassination of Walter Rathenau, Foreign Secretary, by right-wing nationalists.

1923

11 Jan.	Non-payment of reparations leads to French and Belgian troops occupying the Ruhr. Germany adopts passive resistance to the occupation.
12 Aug.	Stresemann becomes Chancellor.
Sept.–Nov.	Massive inflation in Germany. Interest rates raised to 90 per cent (15 Sept.) but by October German mark trading at rate of 10,000 million to the pound.
26 Sept.	Passive resistance in Ruhr ends. A state of military emergency is declared.

22 Oct.	Bavarian troops take an oath of allegiance to right-wing regime in Bavaria. Communist revolt in Hamburg is put down and left-wing governments are deposed in Saxony and Thuringia.
8–9 Nov.	Unsuccessful 'Beer Hall' Putsch in Munich led by Hitler and Ludendorff. Hitler captured.
20 Nov.	German currency stabilised by establishment of the *Rentenmark*, valued at one billion old marks.
23 Nov.	Stresemann becomes Foreign Minister.

1924

1 Apr.	Hitler sentenced to five years' imprisonment for his part in Munich Putsch (but released in Dec.).
9 Apr.	Dawes Plan provides a modified settlement of the reparations issue.
4 May	In Reichstag elections, Nationalists and Communists gain many seats from the moderate parties.
7 Dec.	In further elections, Nationalists and Communists lose seats to Socialists.
15 Dec.	Beginning of Cabinet crisis in Germany.

1925

15 Jan.	Hans Luther, an independent, succeeds Wilhelm Marx of the Centre as Chancellor with Stresemann as Foreign Minister.
28 Feb.	Death of President Ebert.
26 Apr.	Hindenburg elected President.
7 July	French troops begin to leave Rhineland.
16 Oct.	Locarno Pact guarantees Franco–German and Belgian–German frontiers and the demilitarisation of the Rhineland. (Signed 1 Dec.).

1926

17 May	Marx takes over from Luther as Chancellor.
8 Sept.	Germany admitted to the League of Nations.

1927

29 Jan.	Marx takes over from Luther as Chancellor again.
13 May	'Black Friday' with collapse of economic system.
16 Sept.	Hindenburg, while dedicating the Tannenberg memorial, repudiates Article 231 of the Versailles Treaty, the 'War Guilt' clause.

1928

20 May	Social Democrats win victory at elections, mainly at the expense of the Nationalists.
28 June	Hermann Müller, a Socialist, is appointed Chancellor, following resignation of Marx's ministry on 13 June.

1929

Feb.–June	Nazis combine with Hugenberg and German Nationalists to oppose the Young Plan.
7 June	Publication of Young Plan for rescheduling German reparation payments in the form of annuities over 59 years, amounting to a quarter of the sum demanded in 1921.
9 July	Nationalists and Nazis form a National Committee to fight the Young Plan with Hugenberg as Chairman and Hitler a leading member.
3 Oct.	Death of Stresemann.
29 Oct.	Wall Street Crash and cessation of American loans to Europe.
29 Dec.	National referendum accepts Young Plan, frustrating Nationalist hopes.

1930

Mar.	Young Plan approved by Reichstag and signed by Hindenburg.
17 Mar.	Müller's Socialist Cabinet resigns.
30 Mar.	Heinrich Brüning, of the Centre, forms a minority coalition of the Right.
17 May	Young Plan reparations come into force.
30 June	Last Allied troops leave Rhineland.
16 July	Hindenburg authorises German budget by decree on failure of Reichstag to pass it.
14 Sept.	In Reichstag elections, Hitler and the Nazi Party emerge as a major force with 107 seats, second only to the Socialists with 143 seats.
Oct.	Röhm becomes leader of SA or 'Brownshirts'.

1931

July	Worsening economic crisis in Germany. Unemployment reaches over 4.25 million. Bankruptcy of German Danatbank (13 July) leads to closure of all banks until 5 Aug.
11 Oct.	Hitler forms an alliance with the Nationalists led by Hugenberg at Hartzburg – the Hartzburg Front.

1932

7 Jan.	Brüning declares that Germany cannot and will not resume reparations' payments.
13 Mar.	In presidential elections Hindenburg receives 18 million votes against Hitler's 11 million, and the Communists' 5 million. With failure to achieve an overall majority, a new election is called for 10 Apr.
10 Apr.	Hindenburg re-elected President with an absolute majority of 19 million against Hitler's 13 million and the Communists' 3 million.
14 Apr.	Brüning attempts to disband the SA and SS.
24 Apr.	Nazis achieve successes in local elections.
30 May	At Hindenburg's withdrawal of support for disbanding the SA and SS, Brüning resigns.
1 June	Franz von Papen forms a ministry with von Schleicher as Minister of Defence and von Neurath as Foreign Minister.
16 June	Ban on SA and SS in operation since April is lifted.
31 July	In Reichstag elections Nazis win 230 seats and become largest party, producing a stalemate since neither they nor the Socialists (133 seats) will enter a coalition.
13 Aug.	Hitler refuses Hindenburg's request to serve as Vice-Chancellor under von Papen.
12 Sept.	Von Papen dissolves the Reichstag.
14 Sept.	Germany leaves disarmament conference.
6 Nov.	New elections fail to resolve the stalemate, with the Communists gaining only a few seats from the Nazis.
17 Nov.	Von Papen forced to resign by Schleicher; Hitler rejects Chancellorship.
2–4 Dec.	Schleicher becomes Chancellor and forms a ministry, attempting to conciliate the Centre and Left.

Nazi Germany, 1933–45

1933

28 Jan.	Schleicher's ministry is unable to secure a majority in the Reichstag and resigns.
30 Jan.	Hindenburg accepts a Cabinet with Hitler as Chancellor, von Papen as Vice-Chancellor and Nationalists in other posts.
27 Feb.	Reichstag fire blamed on Communists and made pretext for suspension of civil liberties and freedom of press.

5 Mar.	In elections, the Nazis make gains, winning 288 seats, but fail to secure overall majority.
13 Mar.	Goebbels becomes Minister of Propaganda and 'Enlightenment'. Pius XI praises Hitler's anti-communism.
17 Mar.	Schacht becomes President of the Reichsbank.
23 Mar.	Hitler obtains Enabling Law with the support of the Centre Party, granting him dictatorial powers for four years.
30 Mar.	German bishops withdraw opposition to Nazis.
1 Apr.	National boycott of all Jewish businesses and professions.
7 Apr.	Civil Service law permits removal of Jews and other opponents.
5 July	Centre Party disbands.
8 July	Concordat signed between Nazi Germany and Holy See.
14 July	All parties, other than the Nazis, suppressed. The Nazi Party is formally declared the only political party in Germany.
20 July	Concordat ratified.
Sept.	Ludwig Müller, leader of minority 'German Christians', becomes 'Bishop of the Reich'.

1934

21 Mar.	'Battle for Work' begins.
May	German Protestants at Barman synod express disapproval of Müller and 'German Christians' and their close complicity with Nazis.
14 June	Hitler visits Mussolini in Italy.
20 June	Hindenburg demands dissolution of SA.
30 June	'Night of the Long Knives'. Nazis liquidate thousands of opponents inside and outside the Party. Over 70 leading Nazis lose their lives, including Röhm, leader of the SA, and Gregor Strasser, leader of the Berlin Nazis. General von Schleicher is also a victim.
2 Aug.	Death of President Hindenburg. Hitler assumes Presidency, but retains title *Der Führer*. Army swears oath of allegiance. Schacht becomes Minister of Economics.
24 Oct.	German Labour Front founded, Nazi organisation to replace trade unions.

1935

13 Jan.	Saar plebiscite favours reabsorption into Germany.
16 Mar.	Germany repudiates disarmament clauses in Treaty of Versailles, restores conscription and announces expansion of the peacetime army to over half a million men.

18 June	By Anglo–German Naval Agreement, Germany agrees that her naval tonnage shall not exceed one-third of that of the Royal Navy.
15 Sept.	Nuremberg Laws prohibit marriage and sexual intercourse between Jews and German nationals.

1936

7 Mar.	German troops reoccupy the demilitarised Rhineland in violation of the Treaty of Versailles.
Aug.	Olympic Games in Berlin turned into an advertisement for Nazi Germany.
24 Aug.	Germany adopts two-year compulsory military service.
19 Oct.	Hitler announces four-year plan under Goering as Economics Minister.
1 Nov.	Rome–Berlin Axis proclaimed.
18 Nov.	Germany and Italy recognise the Franco government.

1937

Dec.	Schacht resigns as Minister of Economics. Leading members of the Protestant opposition arrested, including Pastor Niemöller.

1938

4 Feb.	Hitler appoints Joachim von Ribbentrop Foreign Minister. Fritsch is relieved of his duties as Commander-in-Chief of the army. Hitler takes over personal control of the armed forces. The War Ministry is abolished and OKW (High Command of the Armed Forces) is set up.
11 Mar.	German troops enter Austria (the *Anschluss*) which is declared part of the Reich (13 Mar.).
23 Apr.	Sudeten Germans living within boundary of Czechoslovakia demand autonomy.
12 Aug.	Germany mobilises over Czech crisis.
18 Aug.	Beck resigns as Chief of the Army General Staff.
30 Sept.	Munich Agreement gives Sudetenland to Germany.
9–10 Nov.	Anti-Jewish pogrom, the *Kristallnacht.*

1939

21 Jan.	Schacht dismissed as President of Reichsbank.
15 Mar.	German troops occupy remaining part of Czechoslovakia.
23 Aug.	Nazi–Soviet Pact signed.
1 Sept.	Germany invades Poland.

3 Sept.	Britain and France declare war on Germany.
21 Sept.	Polish Jews ordered into ghettos.
27 Sept.	Warsaw surrenders; end of Polish campaign.
7 Oct.	Himmler appointed Reich Commissioner.
8 Oct.	Western Poland incorporated in Reich.
12 Oct.	Austrian Jews deported to the East.
23 Nov.	Polish Jews ordered to wear the yellow Star of David.

1940

7 Apr.	Germany invades Norway and Denmark.
10 May	Germany invades Holland, France and Belgium.
14 May	Dutch army surrenders.
28 May	Belgium capitulates.
29 May–3 June	British and Allied forces evacuate from Dunkirk.
14 June	Germans enter Paris.
22 June	France concludes armistice with Germany.
July–Sept.	Battle of Britain fails to destroy the Royal Air Force.
23 Aug.	Beginning of 'Blitz' on Britain by *Luftwaffe*.
14 Sept.	Postponement of 'Operation Sealion', the invasion of Britain.
18 Dec.	Hitler issues secret plan for invasion of Russia – Operation Barbarossa.

1941

9 Feb.	German troops under Rommel sent to assist Italians in North Africa.
6 Apr.	German ultimatum to Greece and Yugoslavia.
18 Apr.	Yugoslav opposition collapses.
10 May	Rudolf Hess lands in Scotland on mysterious mission and is captured.
13 May	Bormann succeeds Hess as Party Chancellor.
22 June	German forces launch invasion of Russia.
16 July	Germans take Smolensk.
31 July	Goering gives Heydrich a written order to achieve a 'general solution to the Jewish problem in areas of Jewish influence in Europe'.
3 Sept.	Germans lay siege to Leningrad.
25 Oct.	German offensive against Moscow fails, followed by Russian counter-offensive (5 Dec.).
11 Dec.	Hitler declares war on USA.

1942

20 Jan.	Heydrich puts forward 'final solution' to the 'Jewish Problem'.
Feb.	Speer becomes Reich Minister of Armaments and Production.
Mar.	Sauckel made plenipotentiary general for allocation of labour.
30 May	First '1,000 bomber' raid against Cologne by RAF.
28 June	German offensive begins in southern Russia.
July	Beginning of liquidation of Jewish ghetto in Warsaw.
Aug.–Sept.	German advance in North Africa halted at El Alamein.
23 Oct.–4 Nov.	British forces defeat and pursue Axis forces at El Alamein.
8 Nov.	Anglo–American landings in North Africa – Operation Torch.

1943

27 Jan.	US Air Force makes first raid on Germany.
2 Feb.	German army at Stalingrad surrenders.
18 Feb.	Goebbels declares mobilisation for total war at mass demonstration in Berlin Sportspalast. Under direction of Speer, arms production rises threefold.
13 Mar.	Attempt to kill Hitler on a flight between Smolensk and Rastenburg fails.
5–12 July	Mass air-raids on Hamburg kill many thousands and destroy large parts of the city.
3 Sept.	Italy forced out of the war.
Oct.	American air-raids on Schweinfurt ball-bearing factories cause extensive damage but at insupportable cost to attackers.
Nov.	Series of mass air-raids on German capital known as the 'Battle of Berlin'.

1944

May	Americans begin air attacks on German synthetic oil production.
6 June	D-Day. Opening of second front with Anglo–American landings in Normandy.
23 June	Russian offensive begins on central front.
20 July	'July Plot'. Hitler wounded in bomb attack at headquarters in East Prussia. Attempted *coup d'état* is put down by loyal troops and leading conspirators and thousands of suspects are arrested and executed.
26 July	Russians reach the Vistula.
31 July	Allied break-out in Normandy.
17 Aug.	Russians reach East Prussian border.
16 Dec.	Germans begin counter-offensive in the Ardennes.

1945

12 Jan.	Red Army begins final campaign against Germany.
1 Feb.	American forces reach Siegfried Line.
13 Feb.	Allied bombing of Dresden.
22 Mar.	Allies cross Rhine.
11 Apr.	Western Allies halt on the Elbe.
16 Apr.	Russian offensive against Berlin begins.
21 Apr.	Russians reach outskirts of Berlin.
30 Apr.	Hitler commits suicide with his wife Eva Braun in the Berlin bunker, along with Goebbels and his family. Admiral Dönitz is named Hitler's successor.
2 May	Fall of Berlin to Russian forces.
7 May	General Jodl makes final capitulation of Germany to General Eisenhower.
8 May	Von Keitel surrenders to Zhukov near Berlin. Official end of the war in Europe.
5 June	Admiral Dönitz surrenders his powers to the Allied occupation forces.

FRANCE, 1918–44

1918

21 Mar.	German offensive brings them within 75 miles of Paris. Paris bombarded by long-range guns.
26 Mar.	Foch assumes united command of armies on Western Front.
27 Apr.	Renewed German offensive captures Rheims.
15 July.–4 Aug.	Second battle of the Marne halts German offensive.
22 July	Allies cross the Marne.
4 Sept.	Germans retreat to Siegfried Line.
30 Oct.	Allies sign armistice with the Ottoman Empire.
1 Nov.	Anglo–French forces occupy Constantinople.
3 Nov.	Allies sign armistice with Austria–Hungary.
11 Nov.	Allies sign armistice with Germany at Compiègne.

1919

28 June	Versailles Treaty signed.
Nov.	Victory of right-wing 'Bloc National' in elections to the Assembly.

1920

17 Jan.	Deschanel elected President of France. Resignation of Clemenceau; Millerand forms ministry.
16 May	Joan of Arc canonised.
7 Sept.	Franco–Belgian military convention.
23 Dec.	Millerand becomes French President.
29 Dec.	French socialists at Tours agree to join Moscow International; formation of French Communist Party.

1921

16 Jan.	Briand becomes Prime Minister.
24–29 Jan.	Paris Conference agrees reparations for France.
19 Feb.	Franco–Polish alliance.

1922

15 Jan.	Poincaré becomes Prime Minister and Foreign Minister.
9–11 Dec.	International conference in London considers Germany's request for a reparations moratorium.

1923

11 Jan.	Franco–Belgian occupation of the Ruhr in retaliation for non-payment of reparations; passive resistance by German workers.

1924

9 Apr.	Germany accepts Dawes Plan on reparations and agreement reached that France should withdraw from the Ruhr.
May	*Cartel des Gauches* wins victory at the elections.
10 June	Millerand resigns as President. Doumergue elected President (13th); Herriot becomes Prime Minister (15th).

1925

10 Apr.	Painlevé becomes Prime Minister.
27 July	French begin evacuation of Ruhr.
1 Dec.	Locarno Treaties guaranteeing Franco–German and Belgo–German frontiers signed.

1926

31 Jan.	First part of the Rhineland evacuated.
26 May	Rebel Abd-El-Krim submits to France.

15 July	Briand resigns over financial crisis; Poincaré becomes premier of National Union Ministry. Measures taken to stabilise the franc.

1927

11 Nov.	Treaty of friendship between France and Yugoslavia.

1928

22–29 Apr.	Left parties win victory at elections.
24 June	Devaluation of the franc. Decision to build Maginot Line; military service cut to one year.
27 Aug.	France and 64 other states sign the Kellogg–Briand Pact, outlawing war and providing for peaceful settlement of international disputes.

1929

27 July	Poincaré resigns as Prime Minister and is succeeded by Briand.
5 Sept.	Briand proposes a European federal union.

1930

17 May	Young Plan of reduced German reparations comes into force. Briand produces memorandum on united states of Europe.
30 June	Last portion of Rhineland evacuated.

1931

27 Jan.	Laval becomes French premier.
13 May	Doumer elected French President.
20 June	Hoover Plan of moratorium of one year on reparations and war debts in view of world economic crisis.

1932

21 Feb.	Tardieu ministry formed.
1 May	*Cartel des Gauches* successful in elections.
6 May	President Doumer assassinated; succeeded by Lebrun (10th).
4 June	Herriot ministry formed.
18 Dec.	Paul–Boncour ministry formed.

1933

31 Jan.	Daladier ministry formed.
Dec.	Flight of Stavisky brings about scandal of financial corruption among politicians.

1934

30 Jan.	Daladier second ministry formed.
6–7 Feb.	Rioting in Paris. Police kill 14 right-wing demonstrators.
7 Feb.	Daladier resigns and Doumergue forms National Union ministry of centre and moderate parties (8th).
12 Feb.	*Confédération Generale du Travail* (CGT) calls general strike. Demonstrations in defence of the Republic.
16 May	French complete suppression of rebel Berber tribes in Morocco.
9 Oct.	Barthou, Foreign Minister, and King Alexander of Yugoslavia assassinated at Marseilles.

1935

7 Mar.	Saar district restored to Germany following plebiscite (13 Jan.).
11–14 Apr.	Stresa Conference of Britain, France and Italy.
2 May	Franco–Russian treaty of mutual assistance.
14 July	Mass demonstrations throughout France demanding democracy and the dissolution of right-wing Leagues.
27 July	French government granted emergency financial powers.
3 Nov.	Socialist groups merge as Socialist and Republican Union under Léon Blum; later forming with Radical Socialists and Communists a Popular Front.

1936

Jan.	Popular Front agrees common programme.
3 May	Popular Front wins major success in elections with 387 seats to 231 of the Right.
4 June	Blum forms Popular Front government.
7 June	40-hour week decreed, collective labour agreements, and paid holidays.
Sept.	Widespread strike in French industry.
2 Oct.	Franc devalued.
18 Nov.	In spite of protests from the Left, Blum proposes non-intervention in the Spanish Civil War.

1937

Jan.	Blum slows down social reform programme.
27 Feb.	French Chamber passes defence plan; Schneider-Creusot factory nationalised and Maginot Line extended.
21 June	Chamber rejects Blum's programme of financial reforms. Blum resigns and is replaced by the radical Chautemps.

1938

13 Mar.	Blum forms second Popular Front government, but Senate rejects financial reforms.
10 Apr.	Blum resigns and is replaced by Daladier.
29 Sept.	France signs Munich Agreement.
9 Nov.	France recognises Italian conquest of Abyssinia.

1939

27 Feb.	France recognises Franco's government in Spain; Pétain sent as first ambassador.
17 Mar.	Daladier granted powers to speed rearmament.
31 Mar.	France and Britain guarantee support for Poland.
13 Apr.	France and Britain guarantee independence of Romania and Greece.
26–31 Aug.	Negotiations by Daladier and Chamberlain with Hitler fail.
3 Sept.	Britain and France declare war on Germany.
4 Sept.	Franco–Polish agreement.
26 Sept.	Daladier dissolves French Communist Party.
30 Sept.	British Expeditionary Force sent to France.
3 Nov.	Roosevelt allows France to purchase US arms on 'cash and carry' basis, amending Neutrality Act of May 1937.

1940

21 Mar.	Reynaud succeeds Daladier as premier.
10 May	German attack on Holland, Belgium and Luxembourg.
12 May	German panzer forces cross into France.
14 May	German forces cross the Meuse.
19 May	General Weygand takes command of the French army from General Gamelin.
20 May	German forces reach Channel, cutting off Allied armies in the north.
29 May	British begin evacuation from Dunkirk.
10 June	Italy declares war on France.
14 June	Germans enter Paris.
16 June	Reynaud resigns and replaced by Pétain.
18 June	De Gaulle, from London, calls for continued resistance.
22 June	French sign armistice with Germany at Compiègne.
23 June	British government supports London-based French National Committee, 'Free French', headed by de Gaulle and breaks off relations with Pétain government.

24 June	Armistice signed with Italy.
1 July	French government moves to Vichy.
3 July	British attack on French fleet at Oran.
5 July	Vichy regime breaks off relations with Britain.
10 July	National Assembly votes full powers to Pétain as 'Head of the French State', ending Third Republic.
22–24 Oct.	Laval, followed by Pétain, holds discussions with Hitler at Montoire.
13 Dec.	Laval dismissed. Replaced by Darlan.

1941

18 Apr.	Vichy government withdraws from League of Nations.
May	Darlan offers French air bases in Syria to the Germans.
8 June	Allied invasion of Syria.
30 June	Vichy government breaks off relations with Russia.

1942

18 Apr.	Laval returns to head government.
11 Nov.	German troops occupy Vichy France.
27 Nov.	French fleet scuttled at Toulon.

1944

6 June	Allied landings in Normandy.
25 Aug.	Paris is liberated.
23 Oct.	De Gaulle's provisional government recognised by Allies.

SPAIN, 1909–39

1909

| 26 July | *Semana Tragica*. Committee of anarchists and socialists calls a general strike in Barcelona. The strike is accompanied by the burning of ecclesiastical property, especially convents. |
| 31 July | Strike suppressed with over 10 deaths. |

1912

| 12 Dec. | Canalejas, Spanish premier, murdered by anarchists in Madrid. |

1917

| 13 Aug. | General strike in Spain, calling for Catalan independence. |

1921

8 Mar. Dato, Spanish premier, murdered by anarchists in reprisal for police actions against anarcho-syndicalists in Catalonia, following widespread campaign of terror and assassination.

1923

14 Dec. Primo de Rivera assumes Spanish dictatorship, supported by military and middle classes and with acquiescence of King Alfonso XIII.

1930

28 Dec. The King accepts the resignation of Primo de Rivera, following Spain's deteriorating economic condition and failure to achieve progress towards constitutional government.

1931

14 Apr. King Alfonso XIII abdicates. Spain becomes a constitutional republic, under a provisional government headed by Zamora. Azaña becomes Minister of War.

20 Oct. 'Protection of the Republic' Law passed in Spain.

9 Dec. Spanish Republican Constitution introduced; Zamora elected President.

1933

2–12 Jan. Rising of anarchists and syndicalists in Barcelona.

19 Nov. Spanish Right wins elections to the Cortes. Foundation of *Falango Espanola* by José Antonio Primo de Rivera (son of the dictator, Primo de Rivera).

1934

14 Jan. Catalan elections won by the Left.

4 Oct. Right forms a ministry; followed by Socialist rising in Asturias and Catalan separatist revolt in Barcelona. Moroccan troops used to suppress risings with great ferocity.

1936

16 Feb. Popular Front wins elections: Azaña becomes Premier and re-establishes 1931 constitution. Amnesty granted to rebels of 1934; growing clashes between Left and Right with assassinations and attacks on church property.

7 Apr. Cortes dismiss President Zamora.

10 May Azaña elected Spanish President, although large numbers of voters boycott the elections.

17–18 July	Outbreak of Spanish Civil War with rising of the army in Morocco under General Franco; revolt spreads to mainland led by General Mola.
19 July	Rebels reject offer of a ceasefire and the formation of an all-party national government. Republican government orders arming of revolutionary organisations.
20–31 July	Republican forces seize the Montana barracks in Madrid and secure Catalonia, the Basque country and much of the south. The rebels, or Nationalists, overrun Morocco, parts of southern Spain and much of the north.
26 July	Léon Blum declares that France cannot intervene on behalf of the Republic. Communist Comintern decides to raise international force of volunteers – the International Brigades – for service in Spain. Hitler offers aircraft and supplies to the Nationalists, as does Mussolini.
6 Aug.	France and Britain submit draft 'non-intervention' agreement to the European powers.
19 Aug.	Britain imposes embargo on arms to Spain.
21 Aug.	Italy accepts non-intervention, but makes exceptions for 'volunteers' and financial support.
23 Aug.	Germany accepts non-intervention, as does the Soviet Union, although both continue to supply advisers and other support.
4 Sept.	Formation of Largo Caballero government in Madrid, composed of republicans, socialists and communists.
27 Sept.	Nationalists capture Toledo.
1 Oct.	Nationalists appoint Franco Generalissimo and head of state.
22 Oct.	Most of Spanish gold reserves shipped to the Soviet Union. Russian advisers supervise reorganisation of Republican army and appoint political commissars.
Nov.	Nationalist forces advance on Madrid. Air-raids on Madrid and Republican forces by German Condor Legion. First International Brigades go into action and assist in repelling Nationalist advance. Republican government moves to Valencia.
18 Nov.	Germany and Italy recognise Franco government.
16 Dec.	Protocol signed in London by major powers agreeing non-intervention in Spain.

1937

8 Feb.	Malaga falls to Nationalists.
3–12 Mar.	Republican government orders disarming of workers' and anarchist militias in Catalonia following clashes between them and the Communists.

20–23 Mar.	Battle of Guadalajara. Republicans defeat Italian forces advancing on Madrid.
19 Apr.	Franco orders unification of the Nationalist movement, fusing the Falange and other political bodies into a single political body, and paramilitary groups into a militia responsible to the army.
26 Apr.	German Condor Legion destroys town of Guernica in Basque country.
30 Apr.–6 May	Street fighting in Barcelona between workers' militias and republican–communists.
15 May	Largo Caballero resigns in opposition to communist call for greater control and suppression of rival groups.
17 May	Negrin government formed with backing of Comintern to pursue victory by means of communist control of the Republican forces.
18 June	Anarchist militia (POUM) dissolved and leaders arrested; anti-Stalinist leader, Nin, executed.
19 June	Nationalists capture Basque capital of Bilbao.
5–28 July	Failure of Republican offensive at Brunete to restore position in north.
10–14 Sept.	Following attacks on shipping by Italian submarines and aircraft, Nyon Conference of nine European powers agrees to patrol the Mediterranean and sink submarines attacking non-Spanish ships. Italy and Germany do not attend, but sinkings cease.
17 Oct.	Largo Caballero denounces repressive policies of Negrin government.
20–22 Oct.	Franco's forces complete reduction of north-west with capture of Gijon and Oviedo.
31 Oct.	Republican government moves to Barcelona.
15–26 Dec.	Republican forces go over to the offensive at Teruel to avert threat to Madrid.

1938

5–22 Feb.	Nationalists launch counter-offensive at Teruel; recaptured (23rd). Nationalist offensive in Aragon.
Mar.	Nationalists begin advance from Aragon to the Mediterranean with aim of cutting Republican territory in half and achieve rapid early success.
15 Apr.	Nationalist forces reach Mediterranean at Vinaroz, cutting off Catalonia from the rest of Republican Spain.

Apr.–May	Opening of French frontier permits some resupply of Republican forces. 200,000 new conscripts called up and organised on flanks of the Nationalist corridor.
July–Aug.	Last Republican offensive on the Ebro forces Franco to suspend attack on Valencia.
Aug.	Basque and Catalan separatist ministers resign from Negrin ministry.
15 Nov.	Last Republican forces driven out of Ebro bridgehead.
Dec.	Nationalists begin offensive against Catalonia.

1939

26 Jan.	Fall of Barcelona to Nationalist forces.
7 Feb.	President Azaña goes into exile in France (resigns on 24th).
9 Feb.	End of resistance in Catalonia by Republican forces; over 200,000 cross French frontier and are disarmed. Negrin makes last attempt to obtain a negotiated peace without reprisals.
26 Feb.	Negrin tries to organise last stand of Republic at Cartagena naval base.
4 Mar.	Negrin appoints communist military leaders to key defence positions.
5–12 Mar.	Military commander in Madrid, Casado, leads rebellion against Negrin government on account of its communist domination and sets up a National Defence Council. On Comintern instructions, Communists attempt to defeat the rebellion, but are themselves defeated by non-communist elements. Negrin flees to France.
23 Mar.	Casado sends emissaries to Nationalist capital in Burgos to negotiate peace terms. Franco demands surrender of Republican Air Force by 25 March and rest of armed forces by 27 March.
25 Mar.	Franco breaks off negotiations because his terms not met.
27 Mar.	Last meeting of National Defence Council.
28 Mar.	Nationalist forces enter Madrid.
1 Apr.	General Franco announces end to the Civil War.

THE SECOND WORLD WAR

International background to the Second World War

1933

30 Jan.	Hitler becomes Chancellor of Germany.

16 Mar.	Britain's plan for disarmament fails as Germany insists on exclusion of the SA.
19 Mar.	Mussolini proposes pact between Britain, France, Italy and Germany, signed as the Rome Pact.
15 July	Rome Pact binds Britain, France, Germany and Italy to the League Covenant, the Locarno Treaties, and the Kellogg–Briand Pact.
14 Oct.	Germany leaves disarmament conference and League of Nations.

1934

14–15 June	Hitler meets Mussolini for the first time in Venice.
25 July	Austrian Chancellor Dollfuss murdered in Nazi coup.
30 July	Dr Kurt Schuschnigg becomes new Austrian Chancellor.
5 Dec.	Italian and Ethiopian troops clash at Walwal inside Ethiopia.

1935

1 Feb.	Anglo–German conference on German rearmament; Italy sends troops to East Africa.
15 Mar.	Hitler repudiates the military restrictions on Germany imposed by the Treaty of Versailles, restores conscription and announces that the peacetime army strength is to be raised to half a million men. Germany announces the existence of the *Luftwaffe*.
11–14 Apr.	Britain, France and Italy confer at Stresa to establish a common front against Germany.
2 May	France and the Soviet Union sign a treaty of mutual assistance for five years.
16 May	Czechoslovakia and Soviet Union sign mutual assistance pact.
19 May	Pro-Nazi Sudeten Party makes gains in Czechoslovak elections.
18 June	Anglo–German Naval Agreement. Germany undertakes that her navy shall not exceed one-third of the tonnage of the Royal Navy.
27 June	League of Nations Union 'Peace Ballot' in Britain shows strong support for the League.
3 Sept.	League of Nations attempts to defuse the Walwal Oasis incident by stating that neither country was to blame as possession was unclear.
2 Oct.	Italian forces invade Ethiopia.
7 Oct.	League of Nations declares Italy the aggressor in Ethiopia and votes sanctions (11th).

59

19 Oct.	League of Nations sanctions on Italy come into force.
9 Dec.	Hoare–Laval Pact, lenient to Italy, is met by hostile public reaction in Britain and France.
13 Dec.	Beneš succeeds Masaryk as President of Czechoslovakia.

1936

16 Feb.	Popular Front wins a majority in the Spanish elections.
3 Mar.	Britain increases defence expenditure, principally on the air force.
8 Mar.	German troops reoccupy the demilitarised Rhineland in violation of the Treaty of Versailles.
5 May	Italians take Addis Ababa; Emperor Haile Selassie flees. Italy annexes Ethiopia (9th).
11 July	Austro–German convention acknowledges Austrian independence.
18 July	Army revolt under Emilio Mola and Francisco Franco begins Spanish Civil War.
24 Aug.	Germany introduces compulsory conscription.
9 Sept.	Conference held in London on non-intervention in Spanish Civil War.
1 Oct.	Franco appointed 'Chief of the Spanish State' by the Nationalist rebels.
14 Oct.	Belgium renounces its military pact with France in order to ensure its liberty of action in the face of German reoccupation of Rhineland.
19 Oct.	Germany begins four-year economic plan to develop its economic base for war.
1 Nov.	Mussolini proclaims Rome–Berlin Axis.
18 Nov.	Germany and Italy recognise Franco's government.
24 Nov.	Germany and Japan sign Anti-Comintern Pact.
16 Dec.	Protocol signed in London for non-intervention in Spain.

1937

2 Jan.	Mussolini signs agreement with Britain ensuring the safety of shipping in the Mediterranean.
15 Jan.	Amnesty granted to Austrian Nazis.
27 Feb.	France extends Maginot Line.
18 Mar.	Defeat of Italian push on Madrid.
27 Apr.	Basque town of Guernica destroyed by German Condor Legion.

19 June	Spanish Nationalist forces take Bilbao.
23 June	Germany and Italy withdraw from non-intervention committee.
17 July	Naval agreements between Britain and Germany and Britain and Soviet Union.
10–14 Sept.	At Nyon Conference, nine nations adopt system of patrol in Mediterranean to protect shipping.
13 Oct.	Germany guarantees inviolability of Belgium.
17 Oct.	Riots in Sudeten area of Czechoslovakia.
21 Oct.	Franco's forces complete conquest of Basque country.
5 Nov.	Hitler informs his generals in the Hossbach memorandum that Austria and Czechoslovakia will be annexed as the first stage in *Lebensraum* for Germany.
6 Nov.	Italy joins Anti-Comintern Pact.
17–21 Nov.	Lord Halifax (Lord President of the Council) accepts unofficial invitation to visit Germany where he has inconclusive discussions with Hitler on a European settlement.
29 Nov.	Sudeten Germans secede from Czech Parliament following a ban on their meetings.
11 Dec.	Italy leaves the League of Nations.

1938

4 Feb.	Von Ribbentrop becomes German Foreign Minister.
12 Feb.	At Berchtesgaden Hitler forces the Austrian Chancellor Schuschnigg to accept a Protocol promising the release of Nazis in Austria, accepting a pro-Nazi (Seyss-Inquart) as Minister of the Interior and virtually attaching the Austrian army to that of Germany, subject to the consent of Austrian President Miklas.
16 Feb.	Amnesty for Nazis proclaimed in Austria; Seyss-Inquart becomes Minister of the Interior.
20 Feb.	In a speech to the Reichstag, Hitler proclaims the need to protect the 10 million Germans on the frontiers of the Reich.
6 Mar.	President Miklas of Austria accepts Schuschnigg's proposal of a plebiscite on the future independence of Austria. Announced on 9 Mar., voting was to take place on the 13th.
10 Mar.	Hitler mobilises for immediate invasion of Austria.
11 Mar.	Schuschnigg accepts Hitler's ultimatum demanding that the plebiscite not be held.
12 Mar.	German army marches into Austria.
13 Mar.	Austria is declared part of Hitler's Reich.
28 Mar.	Hitler encourages German minority in Czechoslovakia to make such demands as will break up the state.

16 Apr.	In Anglo–Italian pact, Britain recognises Italian sovereignty in Ethiopia in return for withdrawal of Italian troops from Spain.
24 Apr.	Germans in Sudetenland demand full autonomy.
29 Apr.	Britain reluctantly joins France in diplomatic action on behalf of the Czech government.
9 May	Russia promises to assist Czechoslovakia in the event of a German attack if Poland and Romania will permit the passage of Russian troops. Both, however, refuse.
18–21 May	German troop movements reported on Czech border; Czech government calls up reservists (20th); and partial mobilisation (21st).
22 May	Britain warns Germany of dangers of military action, but makes it clear to France that she is not in favour of military action herself.
3 Aug.	Walter Runciman visits Prague on mediation mission between Czechs and Sudeten Germans.
11 Aug.	Under British and French pressure, the Czech Prime Minister Beneš opens negotiations with the Sudeten Germans.
12 Aug.	Germany begins to mobilise.
4 Sept.	Henlein, leader of the Sudeten Germans, rejects Beneš's offer of full autonomy and breaks off relations with the Czech government (7th).
7 Sept.	France calls up reservists.
11 Sept.	Poland and Romania again refuse to allow the passage of Russian troops to assist Czechoslovakia.
12 Sept.	Hitler demands that Czechs accept German claims.
13 Sept.	Unrest in Sudetenland put down by Czech troops.
15 Sept.	Chamberlain visits Hitler at Berchtesgaden. Hitler states his determination to annex the Sudetenland on the principle of self-determination.
18 Sept.	Britain and France decide to persuade the Czechs to hand over territory in areas where over half of the population is German.
20–21 Sept.	Germany completes invasion plans. The Czech government initially rejects the Anglo–French proposals, but accepts them on the 21st.
22 Sept.	Chamberlain meets Hitler at Godesberg. Hitler demands immediate occupation of the Sudetenland and announces 28 September for the invasion. The Czech Cabinet resigns.
23 Sept.	Czechoslovakia mobilises; Russia promises to support France in the event of her aiding the Czechs.

25 Sept.	France and Britain threaten Hitler with force unless he negotiates.
26 Sept.	Partial mobilisation in France.
27 Sept.	The Royal Navy is mobilised.
28 Sept.	Hitler delays invasion for 24 hours pending a four-power conference at Munich.
29 Sept.	At the Munich conference Chamberlain, Daladier, Hitler and Mussolini agree to transfer the Sudetenland to Germany, while guaranteeing the remaining Czech frontiers.
30 Sept.	Hitler and Chamberlain sign 'peace in our time' communiqué.
1 Oct.	Czechs cede Teschen to Poland. Germany begins occupation of the Sudetenland.
5 Oct.	Beneš resigns.
6–8 Oct.	Slovakia and Ruthenia are granted autonomy.
25 Oct.	Libya is declared to be part of Italy.
1 Dec.	British prepare for conscription.
6 Dec.	Franco–German pact on inviolability of existing frontiers.
17 Dec.	Italy denounces 1935 agreement with France.
23 Dec.	Franco begins final offensive against last Republican stronghold in Catalonia.

1939

10 Jan.	Chamberlain and Halifax visit Rome for discussions with Mussolini.
26 Jan.	Franco's forces take Barcelona.
27 Feb.	Britain and France recognise Franco's government.
14 Mar.	Under Hitler's prompting, the Slovak leader Tiso proclaims a breakaway 'Slovak Free State'.
15 Mar.	German troops march into Prague and occupy Bohemia and Moravia.
28 Mar.	Hitler denounces 1934 non-aggression pact with Poland. Spanish Civil War ends with surrender of Madrid.
31 Mar.	Britain and France promise aid to Poland in the event of a threat to Polish independence.
7 Apr.	Italy invades Albania. Spain joins the Anti-Comintern Pact.
13 Apr.	Britain and France guarantee the independence of Greece and Romania.
15 Apr.	The USA requests assurances from Hitler and Mussolini that they will not attack 31 named states.

16–18 Apr.	The Soviet Union proposes a defensive alliance with Britain and France, but the offer is not accepted.
27 Apr.	Britain introduces conscription. Hitler denounces the 1935 Anglo–German naval agreement.
28 Apr.	Hitler rejects Roosevelt's peace proposals and denounces the German–Polish non-aggression pact.
22 May	Hitler and Mussolini sign a 10-year political and military alliance – the 'Pact of Steel'.
11 Aug.	Anglo–French mission to the Soviet Union begins talks in Moscow.
18 Aug.	Germany and the Soviet Union sign a commercial agreement.
23 Aug.	Germany and the Soviet Union sign non-aggression pact, with secret clauses on the partition of Poland. Chamberlain warns Hitler that Britain will stand by Poland, but accepts the need for a settlement of the Danzig question. Hitler states that Germany's interest in Danzig and the Corridor must be satisfied. The Poles refuse to enter negotiations with the Germans. Hitler brings forward his preparations to invade Poland to the 26th (from 1 Sept.).
25 Aug.	Anglo–Polish mutual assistance pact signed in London. Hitler makes a 'last offer' on Poland and postpones his attack until 1 Sept.
28–31 Aug.	Britain and France urge direct negotiations between Germans and Poles, but the Poles refuse.
31 Aug.	Hitler orders attack on Poland.
1 Sept.	German forces invade Poland and annex Danzig. Britain and France demand withdrawal of German troops.
2 Sept.	Britain decides on ultimatum to Germany. Britain introduces National Service Bill calling up men aged between 18 and 41.

The Second World War: chronology

3 Sept.	Britain and France declare war on Germany.
7 Sept.	Germans overrun western Poland.
17 Sept.	Soviet Union invades eastern Poland.
19 Sept.	Polish government leaves Warsaw.
28 Sept.	Fall of Warsaw.
30 Sept.	Germany and Soviet Union settle partition of Poland. Last of British Expeditionary Force (BEF) arrives in France.
6 Oct.	Peace moves by Hitler rejected by Britain and France.
8 Oct.	Western Poland incorporated into the Reich.

3 Nov.	USA allows Britain and France to purchase arms in US on a 'cash and carry' basis.
30 Nov.	Soviet Union invades Finland.
13 Dec.	German battleship *Graf Spee* forced to scuttle itself off Montevideo after battle of the River Plate.

1940

12 Mar.	Finland signs peace treaty with Soviet Union ceding territory on the Karelian Isthmus and in north-eastern Finland.
9 Apr.	Germany invades Norway and Denmark.
14 Apr.	British forces land in Norway.
2 May	Evacuation of British forces from Norway.
10 May	Resignation of Chamberlain as British premier, replaced by Winston Churchill.
14 May	Dutch army surrenders after bombing of Rotterdam.
28 May	Belgium capitulates.
29 May–3 June	Over 300,000 British and Allied troops evacuated from Dunkirk.
June–Sept.	Battle of Britain.
10 June	Italy declares war on Britain and France.
14 June	Germans enter Paris. French government moves to Bordeaux.
16 June	France declines offer of union with Britain. Marshal Pétain replaces Reynaud as head of French administration.
17–23 June	Russians occupy Baltic states.
22 June	France concludes armistice with Germany.
24 June	France signs armistice with Italy.
27 June	Russia invades Romania.
3 July	Britain sinks French fleet at Oran.
5 Aug.	Britain signs agreement with Polish government-in-exile in London and (on 7 Aug.) with Free French under de Gaulle.
23 Aug.	Beginning of 'Blitz' on Britain.
7 Oct.	Germany seizes Romanian oilfields.
12 Oct.	Hitler cancels Operation Sealion for the invasion of Britain.
28 Oct.	Italy invades Greece. Britain offers help.
11 Nov.	Major elements of Italian fleet sunk at Taranto, Sicily.
9–15 Dec.	Italian forces defeated at Sidi Barrani in North Africa.

1941

Jan.–Feb.	Further Italian reverses in North Africa.
6 Jan.	Roosevelt sends Lend-Lease Bill to Congress.

6 Feb.	German troops under Rommel sent to assist Italians in North Africa.
6 Apr.	German ultimatum to Greece and Yugoslavia. Britain diverts troops from North Africa to Greece.
7 Apr.	Rommel takes offensive in North Africa.
11 Apr.	Blitz on Coventry.
13 Apr.	Stalin signs neutrality pact with Japan.
17 Apr.	Yugoslavia signs capitulation after Italian and German attack.
22–28 Apr.	British forces evacuated from Greece.
10 May	Rudolf Hess flies to Scotland and is imprisoned.
27 May	*Bismarck* sunk by Royal Navy.
20–31 May	German capture of Crete.
22 June	Germans launch invasion of Russia, Operation Barbarossa, Finnish forces attack on Karelian Isthmus.
6 July	Russians abandon eastern Poland and Baltic states.
12 July	Britain and Russia sign agreement for mutual assistance in Moscow.
16 July	Germans take Smolensk.
11 Aug.	Churchill and Roosevelt sign the Atlantic Charter.
8 Sept.	Germans lay siege to Leningrad.
19 Sept.	Germans take Kiev.
30 Sept.–2 Oct.	Germans begin drive on Moscow.
16 Oct.	Russian government leaves Moscow but Stalin stays.
30 Oct.	German attacks reach within 60 miles of Moscow.
15 Nov.	Renewed German offensive takes advance elements within 20 miles of Moscow.
20–28 Nov.	German forces take, but retreat from, Rostov.
5 Dec.	Germans go on to defensive on Moscow front as Russians launch counter-offensive.
7 Dec.	Japanese bomb Pearl Harbor, Hawaii and British Malaya.
8 Dec.	Britain and the USA declare war on Japan.
11 Dec.	Germany and Italy declare war on USA.

1942

2 Jan.	Britain, the USA, Soviet Union and 23 other nations sign Washington Pact not to make separate peace treaties with their enemies.
1 Feb.	Pro-Nazi Quisling becomes premier of Norway.
6 Feb.	Roosevelt and Churchill appoint Combined Chiefs of Staff.

11 Feb.	German battleships make Channel 'dash' from Brest to Germany.
15 Feb.	Surrender of Singapore to Japanese.
10 Mar.	Rangoon falls to Japanese.
28 Mar.	RAF destroys much of Lübeck, first major demonstration of aerial bombing.
12–17 May	Russian offensive on Kharkov front defeated.
26 May	Anglo–Soviet treaty signed for closer co-operation.
29 May	Soviet Union and the USA extend Lend-Lease Agreement.
30 May	First 1,000-bomber raid on Cologne.
6 June	Germans wipe out village of Lidice in Czechoslovakia in retaliation for assassination of Gestapo leader Heydrich.
10 June	German offensive in the Ukraine.
21 June	Fall of Tobruk after Rommel's advance in North Africa. Eighth Army retreats to El Alamein.
25 June	Dwight Eisenhower appointed Commander-in-Chief of US forces in Europe.
2 July	Fall of Sevastapol.
28 July	Germans take Rostov and northern Caucasus in drive to take Baku oilfields. Zhukov takes over command of southern armies.
14 Aug.	Allied raid on Dieppe ends in failure.
23 Oct.–4 Nov.	Defeat and pursuit of Axis forces at El Alamein.
11–12 Nov.	Vichy France occupied by Germans.
19–20 Nov.	Russians begin counter-attack at Stalingrad, cutting off Von Paulus's troops.
27 Nov.	French Navy scuttled in Toulon.
29 Dec.	Final failure of effort by German forces to relieve Von Paulus.

1943

2 Jan.	German withdrawal from Caucasus begins.
14–24 Jan.	Churchill and Roosevelt meet at Casablanca Conference and declare 'Unconditional Surrender' required of Germany.
31 Jan.	Von Paulus surrenders at Stalingrad.
2 Feb.	Last German forces surrender at Stalingrad.
8 Feb.	Russian offensive takes Kursk.
14 Feb.	Russians capture Rostov.
16 Feb.	Russians take Kharkov.
15 Mar.	Russians forced out of Kharkov.
20 Apr.	Massacre of Jews in Warsaw ghetto.

26 Apr.	Discovery of the Katyn massacre and demand by Polish government in London for investigation by the Red Cross. Stalin breaks off diplomatic relations with London Poles.
12 May	Axis armies in Tunisia surrender.
17 May	RAF bombs Ruhr dams, causing widespread destruction.
4 June	French Committee of National Liberation formed under General Charles de Gaulle.
4 July	General Sikorski killed in an air crash.
5 July	Germans launch offensive on Kursk Salient, Operation Citadel.
10 July	Allied landings in Sicily.
12 July	Russian counter-offensive against Orel Salient causes Germans to halt Kursk offensive.
26 July	Mussolini forced to resign. King Victor Emmanuel asks Marshal Badoglio to form a government. Secret armistice signed with Allies.
4 Aug.	Russians take Orel.
23 Aug.	Russians retake Kharkov.
3 Sept.	Allied landings in Italy; Italy surrenders unconditionally.
25 Sept.	Russians take Smolensk.
2 Nov.	Moscow Declaration of Allied foreign ministers on international security.
6 Nov.	Russians take Kiev.
28 Nov.–1 Dec.	Churchill, Roosevelt and Stalin meet in Tehran.
20 Dec.	Britain and USA agree to support Tito's partisans.
26 Dec.	*Scharnhorst* sunk in Barents Sea by British ships.

1944

22 Jan.	Allied landing at Anzio in attempt to by-pass German forces blocking the road to Rome.
27 Jan.	Relief of Leningrad.
15 Feb.	Bombing of Monte Cassino by Allies fails to dislodge German defenders.
18 Mar.	Fall of Monte Cassino to Allied forces.
2 Apr.	Russians enter Romania.
4 June	Fall of Rome to Americans.
6 June	D-Day landings in Normandy.
13 June	V-1 Flying Bomb campaign opened on Britain.
1 July	Monetary and financial conference at Bretton Woods, New Hampshire, lays foundation for postwar economic settlement.
9 July	Fall of Caen to Allied troops.

20 July	Failure of 'July Plot' to assassinate Hitler.
26 July	Soviet Union recognises Lublin Committee of Polish Liberation in Moscow as the legitimate authority for liberated Poland.
1 Aug.	Rising of Home Army in Warsaw. American armies begin breakout from Normandy bridgehead at Avranches.
11 Aug.	Allied landings in southern France.
13–20 Aug.	German forces destroyed in Falaise Pocket in France.
25 Aug.	De Gaulle and Allied troops enter Paris.
30 Aug.	Russians enter Bucharest.
4 Sept.	Ceasefire between Soviet Union and Finland. Armistice signed on 19th.
5 Sept.	Brussels liberated by Allied troops.
8 Sept.	V-2 rockets begin landing in Britain.
17 Sept.	Arnhem airborne landings in Allied attempt to seize vital river crossings for advance into northern Germany.
3 Oct.	Final suppression of Warsaw rising by German forces.
14 Oct.	British troops liberate Athens.
20 Oct.	Belgrade liberated by Russians and Yugoslav partisans.
23 Oct.	De Gaulle's administration recognised by the Allies as provisional government of France.
3 Dec.	Rioting in Athens and British police action spark off communist insurrection.
16 Dec.	Germans begin Ardennes offensive, the 'battle of the Bulge'.
31 Dec.	Regency installed in Greece by British.

1945

3 Jan.	Allied counter-attack begins in Ardennes.
11 Jan.	Truce declared in Greek Civil War.
17 Jan.	Russians take Warsaw.
4–11 Feb.	Yalta Conference. Churchill, Roosevelt and Stalin plan for Germany's unconditional surrender, the settlement of Poland, and the United Nations Conference in San Francisco.
12 Feb.	Amnesty granted to Greek Communists.
13 Feb.	Fall of Budapest to Russians.
23 Mar.	American armies cross Rhine at Remagen.
28 Mar.	End of V-Rocket offensive against Britain.
3 Apr.	Beneš appoints a National Front government in Czechoslovakia.
20 Apr.	Russians reach Berlin.
25 Apr.	Renner becomes Chancellor of provisional Austrian government.

26 Apr.	Russian and American forces link up at Torgau.
28 Apr.	Mussolini killed by partisans.
30 Apr.	Hitler commits suicide in Berlin. Dönitz is appointed successor.
1 May	German army in Italy surrenders.
2 May	Berlin surrenders to Russians.
7 May	General Jodl makes unconditional surrender of all German forces to Eisenhower.
8 May	Victory in Europe, VE day. Von Keitel surrenders to Zhukov near Berlin.
9 May	Russians take Prague.
14 May	Democratic Republic of Austria established.
5 June	Allied Control Commission assumes control in Germany, which is divided into four occupation zones.
6–9 Aug.	Atomic bombs dropped on Hiroshima and Nagasaki.
14 Aug.	Surrender of Japan, VJ day.

Manpower and casualties of major European Powers, 1939–45

	Total mobilised	Killed or died of wounds	Civilians killed[1]
Belgium	625,000	8,000	101,000
Britain	5,896,000	265,000[2]	91,000[3]
Bulgaria	450,000	10,000	NA
Czechoslovakia	150,000	10,000	490,000
Denmark	25,000	4,000	NA
Finland	500,000	79,000	NA
France	5,000,000	202,000	108,000
Germany	10,200,000	3,250,000	500,000
Greece	414,000	73,000	400,000
Hungary	350,000	147,000	NA
Italy	3,100,000	149,000	783,000
Netherlands	410,000	7,000	242,000
Norway	75,000	2,000	2,000
Poland	1,000,000	64,000	2,000,000
Romania	1,136,000	520,000	NA
Soviet Union[4]	22,000,000	7,500,000	6–8,000,000
Yugoslavia	3,741,000	410,000	1,275,000

[1] Includes deaths of Jews in the Holocaust.
[2] Includes overseas troops serving in British forces.
[3] Includes 30,000 merchant seamen.
[4] Approximate figures.
NA Not available.

THE HOLOCAUST

German policy towards the Jews

1933

30 Jan.	Hitler becomes Chancellor.
5 Mar.	Nazi supporters go on anti-Semitic rampage following the elections which confirm the Nazis as the largest party in the Reichstag.
1 Apr.	National one-day boycott of all Jewish businesses and professions; only partially observed.
Apr.–Dec.	Legislation dismisses Jews from Civil Service, though pressure from Hindenburg allows many exemptions. Law against the 'overcrowding of German Schools and Universities' limits the proportion of Jewish pupils and students to 1.5 per cent. Jews excluded from journalism, and 'Reich entailed farm law' requires proof of Aryan identity dating back to 1800 for ownership of land.

1934

5 Mar.	Jewish actors banned from performing on stage and screen.
July–Dec.	Jewish students systematically excluded from taking examinations in law, medicine, dentistry and pharmacy.

1935

21 May	Army Law excludes Jews from military service.
May–Aug.	Increase in propaganda for the boycott of Jewish businesses.
16 July	Reich Interior Minister Frick instructs registrars not to solemnise any more 'mixed marriages'.
25 July	Jews definitively excluded from all armed forces.
15 Sep.	Nuremberg Laws, announced by Hitler at the Nuremberg party conference, defining 'Jew' and systematising and regulating discrimination and persecution: 'Reich Citizenship Law' deprives all Jews of their civil rights; 'Law for the Protection of German Blood and German Honour' makes marriages and extra-marital sexual relationships between Jews and Germans (*Deutschblütige*) crimes punishable by imprisonment.
14 Nov.	First Supplementary Decree to the 'Reich Citizenship Law'; Jews dismissed from the public service and from all other public offices.
26 Nov.	'Gypsies' and 'Negroes' included in prohibition of racially mixed marriages.

1936

24 Mar.	Benefit payments are withdrawn from large Jewish families.
26 Mar.	Jews no longer permitted to run or lease a pharmacy.
3 Apr.	Jews forbidden to practise as vets.
26 May	Reich Chamber of Fine Arts demands proof of 'Aryan' ancestry from its members.
28 May	'Whitsuntide Memorandum' of the Confessing Church condemns Nazi racial policy.
July	First Sinti and Roma (gypsies) sent to Dachau.
15 Oct.	Jewish teachers forbidden to give private tuition to 'Aryans'.
4 Nov.	Jews are forbidden to use the 'German greeting' (*Heil Hitler!*).

1937

13 Feb.	Jews forbidden to practise as notaries.
15 Apr.	Jews no longer to be awarded doctoral degrees.
12 June	Heydrich orders that after serving their prison sentences Jews guilty of 'racial disgrace' (miscegenation) are to be sent to a concentration camp, as are female Jewish partners involved in such relationships.

1938

Mar.	Anti-Jewish persecution in Austria following the *Anschluss*, including compulsory 'Aryanisation' of many Jewish firms and expulsion of Jews into neighbouring states.
26 Apr.	All Jewish assets over 5,000 RM to be registered. 'Commissioner for the Four Year Plan' (Goering) is empowered to use such assets 'in the interests of the German economy'.
9 June	Destruction of the synagogues in Munich.
15 June	Some 1,500 Jews arrested and taken to concentration camps: so-called June Operation against 'asocials'.
6 July	Conference on problem of Jewish refugees from Germany and Austria (Evian, France) fails to resolve problem.
23 July	Jews issued with separate identity cards.
25 July	Jewish doctors forbidden to practise. They are restricted to treating only other Jews.
10 Aug.	Destruction of Nuremberg synagogues.
17 Aug.	Jews must take the additional names of Sara and Israel.
27 Sep.	Jewish lawyers restricted to working for Jewish clients, and must refer to themselves as 'consultants'.

5 Oct.	Jewish passports to be stamped with 'J'.
26–28 Oct.	17,000 Jews with Polish citizenship are expelled from the German Reich, and transported to the Polish border.
7 Nov.	Herschel Grynszpan assassinates legation secretary Ernst vom Rath in the German embassy in Paris.
9 Nov.	*Reichskristallnacht*, the 'night of broken glass': a nationwide pogrom. Ninety-one murders; 191 synagogues destroyed. Almost all Jewish cemeteries desecrated. Ransacking of 7,500 Jewish businesses.
10 Nov.	Mass arrests of Jewish men.
12 Nov.	A compensation fee of a thousand million RM is imposed on German Jews. Jews are forbidden to participate in cultural events.
15 Nov.	Jewish children expelled from German schools.
3 Dec.	Start of compulsory 'Aryanisation' of Jewish businesses.
Dec.	All 'gypsies' to register with the police.

1939

24 Jan.	Goering instructs Frick to establish a Reich Central Office for Jewish Emigration; Heydrich appointed Director.
30 Jan.	In the Reichstag Hitler threatens that another war will mean the 'extermination of the Jewish race in Europe'.
21 Feb.	Jews required to surrender precious metals and jewellery.
30 Apr.	Jews evicted from their homes and forced into designated Jewish accommodation.
21 July	Adolf Eichmann appointed head of Jewish emigration office in Prague.
1 Sep.	Official date for beginning of Euthanasia Programme (authorised retroactively).
20 Sep.	Jews required to surrender radios.
21 Sep.	Decree from Heydrich initiates ghettoisation of Polish Jews; it contains references to a 'final objective' which will require 'a much greater time scale' and must be kept 'strictly secret'. Decision taken to move 30,000 'gypsies' to Poland.
Sep.–Nov.	*'Einsatzgruppen der Sicherheitspolizei'* ('Special units of the Security Police') and other Nazi formations murder large numbers of Jews. Some incidents amount to large-scale massacres. 4,000 Polish mental patients killed.
Oct.	Hitler authorises re-introduction of adult euthanasia of mental patients in Germany.

12 Oct.	Jews deported from Austria and Bohemia-Moravia to Poland.
24 Oct.	German occupation authorities in Wloclawec introduce a Jewish identification badge – first such measure in twentieth century.
23 Nov.	General introduction of the 'Yellow Star' for Jews living in the 'Government-General'.
25 Nov.	Sexual relations between foreign workers and Germans forbidden.
Dec.	87,000 Poles and Jews deported from the new *Reichsgau* Wartheland to the 'Government-General'.

1940

Jan.	First gassing of mentally handicapped ('Euthanasia Programme', or 'Operation T4').
23 Jan.	Jews are not issued with ration cards for clothing.
2–13 Feb.	First deportations of Jews from Vienna, Mährisch-Ostrau, and Teschen to Poland; first deportations from Germany (Stettin, Stralsund, Schneidemühl).
Mar.–Apr.	Ghettos 'closed' in Cracow, Lublin and Lodz.
27 Apr.	*Reichsführer* SS Heinrich Himmler orders establishment of a concentration camp at Auschwitz.
30 Apr.	First enclosed Jewish ghetto (Lodz).
Apr.–May	2,500 Sinti and Roma deported from Reich to Poland.
June–Aug.	Plans formulated for the mass deportation of European Jews to Madagascar.
29 June	Jewish telephones are disconnected.
Oct.	Jewish ghetto in Warsaw 'closed'.
22 Oct.	7,500 Jews deported from Saarland, Baden and Alsace-Lorraine to unoccupied France and interned.

1941

1 Mar.	Himmler orders building of extensions to concentration camp at Auschwitz, which is to be ready to receive about 100,000 Soviet prisoners of war.
From Mar.	Jews deployed as forced labour.
Spring	Four *Einsatzgruppen* ('special units') of Security Police and the SD created for attack on Soviet Union.
14 May	3,600 Parisian Jews arrested by French police.
31 July	Goering gives Heydrich the task of the 'comprehensive solution (*Gesamtlösung*) of the Jewish question'.

Summer	Himmler instructs commandant of Auschwitz to prepare the camp to play a central part in the 'final solution' ordered by Hitler; Heydrich orders Eichmann to prepare deportation of European Jews for the 'final solution to the Jewish question in Europe'.
	Special commission from Himmler for the SS and police leader in Lublin, Globocnik, to murder the Polish Jews ('Operation Reinhard'); the '*Führer* chancellery' provides staff from the 'Euthanasia Operation', which has been wound up, though killing continues.
1 Sep.	All Jews in the Reich from the age of six must now wear the 'Yellow Star'.
3 Sep.	First trial gassing with Zyklon B at Auschwitz; around 900 Soviet prisoners of war are victims of further experiments in September and October.
18 Sep.	Jews required to seek permission to use public transport.
Sep.–Nov.	Planning, siting and beginning of construction of death camps at Chelmno, Belzec, Majdanek and Auschwitz-Birkenau in the winter of 1941–42.
14 Oct.	Start of the mass deportation of Jews from the Reich to ghettoes in Kovno, Lodz, Minsk and Riga.
23 Oct.	All Jewish emigration from German-controlled territory is forbidden.
30 Nov.	Around 10,000 deported German and indigenous Jews shot near Riga.
12 Dec.	Jews are prohibited from using public telephones.
Dec.	Use of gas vans for murder of Jews in Chelmno.

1942

20 Jan.	Wannsee Conference in Berlin under Heydrich, for all government departments participating in 'final solution' and administration of Government-General.
Feb.	'Evacuation' of the Polish ghettos begins; continuous deportations to the death camps.
15 Feb.	Jews are prohibited from keeping pets.
Spring	Camps built at Sobibor and Treblinka for 'Operation Reinhard'.
13 Mar.	Jews are compelled to identify their homes.
24 Mar.	First deportations of south German Jews to Belzec.
26–27 Mar.	First transports of Jewish emigrants from Western Europe arrive at Auschwitz.

May–June	Introduction of 'Yellow Star' in occupied Western Europe.
12 May	Jews are prohibited from patronising 'Aryan' hairdressers.
11 June	Jews excluded from egg rations.
12 June	Jews must surrender all electrical goods, optical equipment, bicycles and typewriters.
22 June	Jews excluded from tobacco rations.
23 June	Systematic gassing of Jews begins in Auschwitz.
1 July	End of teaching for all Jewish pupils.
15–16 July	First transports of Dutch Jews to Auschwitz.
16–18 July	French police arrest 13,000 'stateless' Jews in Paris; 9,000 (including 4,000 children) deported to Auschwitz.
19 July	Himmler insists Poland must be 'free of Jews' by end of 1942.
22 July	Mass transports from Warsaw ghetto to Treblinka, where 67,000 Jews are gassed immediately after arrival.
July–Sep.	Mass deportations from Western Europe to Auschwitz.
Aug.	More than 200,000 Jews gassed at Chelmno, Treblinka and Belzec during last two weeks of the month.
26–28 Aug.	Jews arrested in Vichy France.
9 Oct.	Jews banned from 'Aryan' bookshops.
Nov.	Himmler orders all concentration camps in the Reich to become 'free of Jews'.
19 Nov.	Jews excluded from meat and milk rations.
25–26 Nov.	Beginning of deportations from Norway.

1943

Feb.	Arrest of 'gypsies' remaining in Germany.
27 Feb.	Jewish munitions workers deported form Berlin to Auschwitz.
Mar.	Himmler orders deportation of Dutch gypsies.
Apr.	Beginning of medical experiments in Auschwitz.
7 Apr.	End of mass murder in Chelmno; gas chambers destroyed by SS.
19 Apr.	Beginning of Jewish uprising in the Warsaw ghetto.
30 Apr.	Jews lose German citizenship.
16 May	*SS-Obergruppenführer* Stroop announces destruction of Jewish ghetto in Warsaw.
11 June	Himmler orders liquidation of all Polish ghettoes.
19 June	Goebbels declares Berlin 'free of Jews'.
21 June	Order to liquidate remaining ghettos on Soviet territory.

1 July	German Jews lose protection of law.
Aug.–Dec.	Liquidation of Russian ghettos; inhabitants taken to death camps.
2 Aug.	Prisoners' uprising in Treblinka; destruction of gas chambers.
16–23 Aug.	Deportation of about 8,000 Jews from Bialystok and destruction of the ghetto following resistance.
Sep.–Oct.	Around 7,000 Danish Jews smuggled to Sweden.
Oct.–Nov.	Around 8,360 Jews deported from northern Italy to Auschwitz.
14 Oct.	Prisoners' uprising in Sobibor; end of gassing.
19 Oct.	End of 'Operation Reinhard'.

1944

Mar.–Apr.	More than 6,000 Greek Jews deported to Auschwitz. 1,500 escape to Turkey.
Apr.–July	Hungarian Jews ghettoised; 437,000 deported to Auschwitz by July; 280,000 gassed.
May–Aug.	Resumption of mass gassing at Chelmno in connection with the final liquidation of the Lodz ghetto.
24 July	Soviet troops occupy Majdanek.
7 Oct.	Revolt of Jewish 'special unit' in Auschwitz.
27 Nov.	Himmler orders cessation of gassing at Auschwitz.

1945

27 Jan.	Soviet troops reach Auschwitz.
21–28 Apr.	Last gassing of mainly sick concentration camp inmates at Ravensbrück and Mauthausen.
29 Apr.	American troops occupy Dachau.
7–9 May	Unconditional surrender of armed forces of Nazi Germany.

(Source: derived from T. Kirk, *The Longman Companion to Nazi Germany*, London, 1995.)

Estimated number of Jews killed under Nazi rule

	Original Jewish population	Number killed	Percent surviving
Baltic States (Estonia, Latvia, and Lithuania)	253,000	228,000	10
Belgium	65,000	40,000	40
Bulgaria	65,000	14,000	78
Czech Protectorate (Bohemia and Moravia)	90,000	80,000	11
France	350,000	90,000	74
Germany/Austria	240,000	210,000	10
Greece	70,000	54,000	23
Hungary	650,000	450,000	30
Italy	40,000	8,000	80
Luxembourg	5,000	1,000	80
Netherlands	140,000	105,000	25
Norway	1,800	900	50
Poland	3,300,000	3,000,000	10
Romania	600,000	300,000	50
Slovakia	90,000	75,000	17
Soviet Union (areas under German control)	2,850,000	1,252,000	56
Yugoslavia	43,000	26,000	40
Total	8,851,800	5,933,900	33

Source: Lucy S. Dawidowicz, *The War Against the Jews (1933–1945)*.

THE RECONSTRUCTION OF WESTERN EUROPE

France since 1945*

1946

Jan. De Gaulle resigns as President of French provisional government after his draft constitution is rejected; he tries to rally right-wing opinion in his non-party, *Rassemblement du Peuple Français* (RPF).

Oct. Fourth Republic established in France.

* See also separate chronology of European integration, pp. 137–47.

1947

Mar.   Anglo–French Treaty of Alliance (Treaty of Dunkirk).

June   General Marshall proposes economic aid to rebuild Europe; Paris Conference (July) meets to discuss the 'Marshall Plan'.

1948

Apr.   Organisation for European Economic Co-operation (OEEC) set up to receive $17,000 million of Marshall Aid from the USA.

1950

May   Robert Schuman proposals for European Coal and Steel Community.

Oct.   René Pleven outlines proposals for European Defence Community.

1951

18 Apr.   Paris Treaty between Benelux countries (Belgium, the Netherlands and Luxembourg), France, Italy and West Germany – 'the Six' – sets up a 'Common Market' in coal and steel. A European Commission is set up as the supreme authority.

Oct.   De Gaulle retires from politics.

1953   European Court of Human Rights set up in Strasbourg.
                 De Gaulle begins to scale down RPF.

1954

May   Defeat for French forces at Dien Bien Phu.

Aug.   French parliament rejects European Defence Community.

Oct.   Creation of Western European Union.

1956

Oct.–Nov.   Anglo–French intervention at Suez (see p. 179).

1957

25 Mar.   Rome Treaties between 'the Six' set up the European Economic Community (EEC) and Euratom.

1958

May   Rioting by French settlers in Algeria leads to French army taking over (13th); De Gaulle voted into power in France after period of chronic political instability (29th) and given power to produce a new constitution.

Sept.	Referendum approves Fifth Republic.
21 Dec.	De Gaulle elected President of Fifth French Republic.
	RPF changes name to UNR (*Union pour la Nouvelle République*).

1959

Mar.	Beginning of French withdrawal from NATO's military command structure.

1960

Feb.	France explodes her first atomic device (in the Sahara).

1961

21 Apr.	French army revolt begins in Algeria against de Gaulle's plans for Algerian independence.
	Referendum supports de Gaulle's Algeria policy.

1962

	EEC agrees Common Agricultural Policy to come into operation in 1964; a system of high guaranteed prices to be paid for out of a common fund; beginning of period of agricultural prosperity in rural Europe and huge food surpluses.
Oct.	Referendum approves direct election of President.

1963

Jan.	De Gaulle vetoes British entry into EEC; Irish, Danish and Norwegian applications suspended.
	France and Germany sign treaty of friendship (Elysée Treaty).
5 Aug.	France refuses to sign Test Ban Treaty, signalling intention to build up *force de frappe.*
	French Atlantic fleet withdrawn from NATO.

1965

Dec.	Election of de Gaulle as President by universal suffrage.

1966

Mar.	France withdraws from Military Committee of NATO.
June	Visit of de Gaulle to Moscow.

1967

27 Nov.	Further British, Irish, Danish and Norwegian applications to join EEC vetoed by de Gaulle.

1968

May	Violent student unrest in Paris and mass strikes against de Gaulle's government.
	National Assembly dissolved by de Gaulle (see May Events p. 308).

1969

28 Apr.	De Gaulle resigns as President after unfavourable vote in referendum on the constitution.
June	Gaullist Georges Pompidou becomes President.
July	Pompidou withdraws French opposition to British membership of EEC.

1970

9 Nov.	Death of de Gaulle.

1971   SF10 becomes PS (*Parti Socialiste*) led by François Mitterrand.

1972   PCF and PS sign Joint Programme of Government.

1974

2 Apr.	Death of Georges Pompidou.
May	Giscard d'Estaing becomes President (narrowly defeating Mitterrand).
June	Chirac becomes Prime Minister.

1976

Aug.	Barre replaces Chirac as Prime Minister.
Sept.	Launch of the 'Barre Plan'.
Dec.	*Rassemblement pour la République* (RPR) launched with Chirac as leader. Centrist groups merge to form CDS (*Centre des démocrates sociaux*).

1977

Mar.	Chirac elected Mayor of Paris.
May	Giscard's party renamed *Parti républicain* (PR). Collapse of Socialist PCF Union of the Left.

1978

Jan.	Socialist Party abandons opposition to French nuclear force.
Feb.	The UDF created (*Union pour la démocratie française*) – a merger of PR, CDS and *Parti radical.*
Apr.	Right keeps majority in National Assembly elections.

1980
Dec.   'Freedom and Security' bill becomes law.

1981
10 May   François Mitterrand, leader of Socialists, becomes President of France in place of Giscard d'Estaing. First socialist President.

June   Mitterrand dissolves National Assembly.

Mauroy becomes Prime Minister. Communists enter Cabinet.

Unemployment rises above 1.5 million.

1982
Mar.   Approval given to nationalisation bill.

Oct.   Establishment of Franco–German Commission on Security and Defence.

1983
Mar.   Crisis economic package in France and Cabinet reshuffle.

Aug.   French troops sent to Chad.

1984
June   Large losses by Left in European elections after 'spring of discontent'. *Front national* polls 10 per cent of vote.

19 July   French Communists withdraw support from Mitterrand. Fabius replaces Mauroy as Prime Minister.

1985
July   *Rainbow Warrior* mined in Auckland Harbour.

1986
Mar.   General election in France gives Socialists largest number of seats, but neo-Gaullist Chirac forms government; beginning of period of '*cohabitation*' between socialist President Mitterrand and conservative Chirac.

July   Denationalisation and electoral reform bills passed.

Nov.–Dec. Student demonstrations against '*Loi Devaquet*'.

1987
Jan.   Campaign of public sector strikes.

1988
Apr.–May Mitterrand re-elected, defeating Chirac in French presidential elections.

5–12 June	Mitterrand calls elections for National Assembly but fails to achieve the expected overall majority. Hung parliament.
Dec.	New guaranteed minimum income introduced for the poor.

1989

June	Strong performance by Greens in European elections.
Dec.	Dreux parliamentary by-election won by *Front National.*

1990

Feb.	Re-election of Chirac as RPR leader.
May	Carpentras Jewish cemetery desecrated.

1991

Jan.–Feb.	French forces take part in Gulf War against Iraq.
May	Resignation of French premier Rocard; Edith Cresson becomes France's first woman Prime Minister.

1992

Feb.	Signing of Treaty of Maastricht on European Union.
Apr.	Pierre Bérégovoy appointed Prime Minister.

1993

Mar.	UPF formed (*Union pour la France*) from UDF–RPR and wins majority in National Assembly. Second period of *cohabitation.* Appointment of Edouard Balladur as Prime Minister.

1994

June	Resignation of French Socialist Party leader, Michel Rocard, after defeat in European elections.

1995

23 Apr.	Lionel Jospin, the socialist candidate, wins most votes in first round of presidential elections.
7 May	Chirac wins presidential election.
June	*Front National* makes inroads in municipal elections (wins Toulon, Orange, etc.) after Le Pen polls well (15 per cent) in first round of presidential elections.
July	Following end of conscription, announced in May, France announces the disbandment of a quarter of regiments to create a purely professional army by 2002.
15 Nov.	Prime Minister Alain Juppé introduces reforms to cut health and social security expenditure.

1996

8 Jan.   Death of former President François Mitterrand.

1997

Feb.   Widespread protests against new law to control illegal immigration.

May–June   General election. Centre-right heavily defeated by Socialists and Communists. Resignation of Juppé. Jospin becomes Prime Minister.

Aug.   Major boost for public sector in France aimed at reducing unemployment.

Sept.   Catholic church accepts responsibility for its part in wartime deportation of Jews.

1998

Feb.   French parliament approves reduction in working week to 35 hours by 2000.

Mar.   Advances by *Front National* in regional elections secure it the balance of power in several areas.

Apr.   France ratifies treaty banning testing of nuclear weapons.

France ratifies treaty banning testing of nuclear weapons.

French parliament votes 334 to 49 to join the single European currency.

May   Official inauguration of the single European currency.

1999

Oct. & Dec.   French government refuses to lift ban on British beef amid BSE concerns.

2000

Mar.   Changes to French government include Laurent Fabius (new Finance Minister) and Jack Lang (to Education).

Aug.   Resignation of Interior Minister over talks with Corsican separatists.

Sept.   Referendum approves reduction in length of presidential term from seven years to five (70 per cent majority on 30 per cent turnout).

Germany since 1945*

1945

5 June   Allied Control Commission set up to administer Germany.

* Prior to re-unification in October 1990 this chronology refers to the Federal Republic of Germany (i.e. West Germany).

1946

Dec. Britain and USA agree economic merger of their zones in Germany.

1947

Feb. Control Council officially dissolves State of Prussia.

June Marshall Plan announced.

1948

Feb.–Mar. London Six Power Conference proposes federal system for West Germany. OEEC established (to administer Marshall Plan).

June Total blockade of West Berlin as land communications and utilities cut off (see p. 178). Airlift for relief supplies.

Dec. Theodor Heuss elected Chairman of newly formed Free Democrats.

1949

23 May German Federal Republic comes into existence on basis of constitution drafted the previous year, with Konrad Adenauer as first Federal Chancellor. Blockade lifted.

Aug. NATO established. First Bundestag elections.

Sept. Heuss first President of Federal Republic. Adenauer first Chancellor.

Oct. Foundation of *Deutscher Gewerkschaftsbund*. West Germany joins OEEC.

1950

Mar. Rearmament of Germany taken up after Korean War begins. Rationing ends.

Aug. West German constitution adopted by West Berlin.

Oct. Theodor Blank appointed Commissioner for Security Matters (beginnings of Defence Ministry).

1951

Mar. Adenauer becomes first Foreign Minister on re-creation of *Auswärtiges Amt.*

Sept. West Germany proposes free all-German elections under UN.

1952

Feb. Bundestag votes for European Defence Community (EDC).

1955

Jan.	Germany joins NATO.
Sept.	Formulation of Hallstein Doctrine.
Oct.	New Saar Treaty (Saar to become part of West Germany on 1 Jan. 1957).

1956

July	Military service introduced.
Aug.	KPD (West German Communist Party) banned by Constitutional Court.

1957

Mar.	Germany signs Treaty of Rome.
Sept.	Diplomatic relations broken off with Yugoslavia (following its recognition of German Democratic Republic).

1958

Jan.	Walter Hallstein first President of European Commission.

1959

Jan.	West Germany rejects Soviet proposal for demilitarisation of Berlin as a 'free city'.
Mar.	German Social Democrats advocate demilitarised nuclear-free central European zone.
Nov.	'Godesberg Programme' approved by SPD at special party conference.

1960

June	SPD foreign policy switch to support European and Atlantic alliance system.

1962

Nov.	Resignation of Franz Josef Strauss following Spiegel crisis of October.

1963

Jan.	Elysée Treaty signed by Adenauer and de Gaulle.
June	US President Kennedy's *Ich bin ein Berliner* speech in West Berlin.
Oct.	Adenauer retires as Chancellor of West Germany; succeeded by Dr Ludwig Erhard.

1966

30 Nov.   Dr Kurt-Georg Kiesinger becomes Chancellor of West Germany.

1969

Oct.   German Social Democrats take power under Willy Brandt; begin policy of *Ostpolitik*, seeking friendly relations with Eastern Europe, and encourage enlargement of EEC.

1970

Mar.   Heads of East and West Germany meet for first time.

1972

Apr.   Defection from German coalition leads to early election in November.

5 Sept.   Arab terrorists kill Israeli athletes at Munich Olympics.

Nov.   Brandt's government returned to power with SPD as largest party in Bundestag.

1973

22 June   West and East Germany join the United Nations.

1974

May   Willy Brandt resigns following security scandal; Helmut Schmidt takes over as Chancellor.

1975

28 Feb.   German opposition leader, Peter Lorenz, kidnapped by terrorists.

1977

5 Sept.   German terrorists kill Dr Hans-Martin Schleyer, head of West German Employers' Federation.

1980

5 Oct.   German coalition of SPD and Free Democrats retains power in elections.

1982

Oct.   Helmut Kohl of Christian Democrats becomes Chancellor following break-up of governing coalition.

1983

6 Mar.   Kohl wins a substantial electoral victory; Green Party passes 5 per cent threshhold for seats in the Bundestag.

1984

4 Sept.   Erich Honecker, East German premier, cancels trip to West Germany because of Soviet opposition.

1987

25 Jan.   Kohl's government confirmed in office at elections.

1989

June   European elections witness rise in Green votes throughout Europe. Socialist bloc increases substantially in European Parliament.

Sept.   Hungary opens borders with Austria, allowing flight of thousands of East Germans to West.

Nov.   Collapse of East German regime; opening of Berlin Wall (9th); freedom of travel to West granted. Kohl calls for united Germany. Reformer Hans Modrow becomes East German premier.

Dec.   First Four-Power Conference since 1971 to discuss future of Berlin and East Europe. Cold War declared ended at Malta Summit. Brandenburg Gate opened and Kohl visits East Germany to wide acclaim. Preparations for free elections in East Germany.

1990

Jan.   East German elections brought forward to March.

Feb.   East German proposal for their neutrality rejected by West Germany. West German Cabinet agrees to currency union between East and West Germany.

Mar.   Pro-unification Alliance for Germany wins East German elections and prepares for economic union in July and all-German elections in December.

July   Economic unification of East and West Germany on the basis of the West German currency. West German–Soviet agreement that a united Germany will have full sovereignty, including the right to join NATO. The Soviet Union agrees to withdraw its troops from East Germany within three to four years.

3 Oct.   Political unification of East and West Germany.

Dec.   First all-German elections since 1932 result in victory for Kohl's conservative coalition.

1991

Apr.   Kohl suffers humiliating defeat in Rhineland-Palatinate local elections.

Dec.   Maastricht Summit on economic and political union.

1992

May | France's President Mitterrand and Kohl announce creation of a Franco–German 'Eurocorps'.

Aug. | Demonstrations and acts of violence against foreign workers in Germany lead to call for restrictions on asylum provisions.

23 Nov. | Neo-Nazi fire bombing in Möln kills three Turkish women.

1994

16 Oct. | Kohl's ruling Christian Democrat coalition remains in power following general election.

1996

May | Strikes in Germany against austerity measures.

1997

Mar. | Kohl declares willingness to stand for re-election as Chancellor in 1998.

1998

Mar. | Premier of Lower Saxony, Gerhard Schröder, selected as Social Democrat to run against Kohl.

Sept. | Kohl ousted in general election; Social Democrats under Schröder seek coalition with Greens.

1999

Feb. | Schröder loses majority in Upper House after gains by Christian Democrats in Hessen.

Mar. | Resignation of Oskar Lafontaine as Finance Minister (succeeded by Hans Eichel). Schröder succeeds Lafontaine as party Chairman.

Aug. | First hints of scandal involving Kohl and undisclosed financial donations to party.

Oct. | Further electoral defeat for Social Democrats in Berlin elections (SPD take only 22.4 per cent, former Communists secure 18 per cent).

Dec. | Election of Johannes Rau as President of Germany. Kohl faces increasing pressure over allegations that secret contributions had been made to the Christian Democrats.

2000

Jan. | Resignation of Kohl as Honorary Chairman of Christian Democrats.

Feb.	Resignation of Wolfgang Schäubel (leader of Christian Democrats).
	Angela Merkel is elected new Christian Democrat leader.

2001

June	Collapse of 'grand coalition' in Berlin which had ruled the city for a decade.

2002

Sept.	Schröder narrowly retains power in closest-fought postwar German elections (helped by strong showing of Greens). Stoiber's Christian Democrats poll strongly, but weak performance by their Free Democrat allies.

Italy since 1943

1943

July	Allied landings in Sicily.
	The downfall of Mussolini.
Sept.	Armistice with Allies.

1944	Creation of short-lived Salo Republic. Civil war in Italy. Togliatti returns from Soviet Union.

1945	Risings in northern Italy.
	Mussolini is executed.
Dec.	De Gasperi becomes Prime Minister of Italy as head of Christian Democrat Party.

1946	King Victor Emmanuel abdicates.
2 June	Referendum votes Italy a Republic.
	Emergence of Christian Democrats as largest single party in Constituent Assembly elections. De Gasperi of Christian Democrats becomes Prime Minister.

1947

May	Italian Communists (PCI) excluded from participation in government in de Gasperi administration.
June	Marshall Plan is announced.

1948	Christian Democrats take 48 per cent of the vote. Luigi Einaudi is elected first President of the Republic.

1949

Mar.   Italy joins NATO.

1950   Occupation of land by peasants in southern Italy.

1952   Italy joins European Coal and Steel Community.

1953   Replacement of de Gasperi by Fanfani.

1954

Aug.   Death of de Gasperi.

Oct.   Trieste is rejoined to Italy.

1955   Messina Conference.

Giovanni Gronchi is elected President of the Republic.

Italy admitted to United Nations.

1956   Reform of electoral law. Intellectuals desert Communists after Soviet invasion of Hungary is supported by PCI.

1957   Italy signs Treaty of Rome.

1958

July   Christian Democrats are largest party in elections.

Oct.   Death of Pope Pius XII; election of John XXIII.

1960   Formation of Tambroni government (with support of neo-Fascist MSI) provokes riots across Italy.

1962   Segni becomes President. First centre-left government is formed by Fanfani.

1963   Major electoral setback for Christian Democrats (down to 38 per cent of vote). Communists take 25 per cent for first time.

1964   Crisis for Aldo Moro government.

Saragat succeeds Segni as President.

1966   PSI (Socialists) and the Social Democrats (PSDI) come together briefly.

1967   Protests in universities spark era of tumult.

1968   Student riots across Italy. PSI vote declines.

1969

Dec.   Bomb kills 17, wounds 90, in Milan.

Emergence of neo-fascist violence.

Divorce law is reformed.

1970   Regional tier of government is established. *Statuto del Lavoro* is passed.

1971

Dec.   Giovanni Leone is eventually elected President (on 23rd ballot).

Ciriaco de Mita becomes Christian Democrat leader.

1972

Jan.   First Giulio Andreotti administration is formed (first of seven).

May   Neo-fascists (MSI) make gains in elections.

1973   Communists under Berlinguer consider 'historic compromise' with Christian Democrats.

1974   Referendum votes (59 per cent) to retain divorce laws. Terrorists blow up Rome–Munich express.

1975   Film director Pierpaolo Pasolini is murdered.

1976   Christian Democrats narrowly hold off strong electoral challenge by Communists (39 per cent to 34 per cent).

1977   Endemic terrorist attacks by Red Brigades.

1978

16 Mar.   Aldo Moro, former Prime Minister, is kidnapped in Rome by Italian terrorists, and found dead on 9 May.

6–26 Aug.   Death of Pope Paul VI; election of John Paul I.

28 Sept.–   Death of Pope John Paul I; election of John Paul II, former
16 Oct.   Cardinal Karol Wojtyla, first non-Italian Pope for 400 years.

1979

June   Italy joins European Monetary System (EMS).

1980

Aug.   Bologna terrorist outrage kills 76 people.

1981	Assassination attempt on Pope John Paul II.
	Beginning of P2 masonic lodge scandal. Referendum retains divorce.
1982	General Dalla Chiesa is murdered.
	Ciriaco de Mita becomes Christian Democrat leader.
1983	
June	Decline of Communist Party is revealed in elections.
Aug.	Bettino Craxi becomes Prime Minister.
1984	Death of Berlinguer during European elections campaign.
June	PCI largest party in European elections.
1985	
June	Francesco Cossiga elected President.
1986	Palermo trial of 456 *mafiosi*.
June	Fall of Craxi's government after three years in power.
1987	
June	Reverse for PCI in elections.
1989	Central Committee of PCI votes for major party reform (followed by Bologna Congress in 1990).
1991	
Jan.	Italian Communist Party changes name to Democratic Party of the Left (PDS) and adopts sweeping changes in policy at Rimini Congress.
1992	President Cossiga resigns.
Apr.	Rise of the *Lega* in elections.
	Borsellino and Falcone, two leading judges, are murdered.
June	Socialist Unity Party leader Giuliano Amato becomes Prime Minister, leading Italy's 51st administration since the war.
Sept.	Lira is forced out of EMS.
1993	Italian referendum approves modification of proportional representation system for elections to Senate.
Apr.	Carlo Ciampi forms new government after resignation of Amato.

Aug.	Italian Senate and Chamber of Deputies approve electoral reform for the Chamber.
	Corruption charges levied against Craxi and Andreotti.

1994

28 Mar.	Right-wing and nationalist Freedom Alliance coalition wins overwhelming victory in elections to reformed parliament.
Apr.	Silvio Berlusconi is appointed Prime Minister.
22 Dec.	Berlusconi resigns after Northern League abandons coalition.

1995

13 Jan.	Minister Lamberto Dini appointed Prime Minister.

1996 Olive Tree Alliance wins general election.

21 Apr.	Former Prime Minister Craxi is fined £15 million and sentenced to eight years' imprisonment for corruption.

1997

Mar.	Flood of refugees from Albania leads to state of emergency.
Oct.	Romano Prodi survives in office despite split with his Communist partners.

1998 Renewed crisis for Prodi after Communists withdraw from government. Prodi is defeated by one vote in confidence motion over tough budget.

Oct.	Massimo D'Alema forms new coalition.

1999

Mar.	Prodi is nominated to succeed Jacques Santer as EU Commission President.
May	Carlo Azeglio Ciampi, Treasury Minister, is elected President of Italy.

2000

Jan.	Death of Craxi.

2001

May	Triumph of Berlusconi in general election.

2002

Jan.	Foreign Minister Ruggiero resigns because of Cabinet colleagues' euroscepticism.

Feb.	Senate votes by overwhelming majority to allow return of male heirs of country's Royal Family, the House of Savoy.
Mar.	Two million march in Rome against terrorism and anti-labour laws.

Spain: from dictatorship to democracy

The Franco regime, 1939–75

1939

1 Apr.	Final victory of Franco in civil war (see p. 176).

1940

16 Oct.	Serrano Suñer becomes Foreign Secretary. Franco meets Hitler.

1942

3 Sept.	Suñer is dismissed.

1943

	Opening of the Cortes.

1945

	Lausanne Manifesto of Don Juan against Franco.

1946

9 Feb.	Franco regime is condemned by UN.
12 Dec.	UN urges diplomatic boycott of Spain.

1947

6 July	Referendum approves Law of Succession designating Spain a kingdom.

1950

4 Nov.	UN General Assembly approves reinstatement of ambassadors to Madrid.

1951

1 Mar.	Major strike in Barcelona.

1952

16 May	Rationing ends in Spain.

1953

27 Aug.	Concordat is signed with Vatican and bilateral treaty with USA (26 Sept.).

1954	Spain protests at visit of Elizabeth II to Gibraltar.
1955	
Dec.	Spain is admitted to UN.
1956	
Feb.	Clashes in Madrid with radical students precipitate Cabinet crisis.
Apr.	Spanish Morocco gains independence.
1957	Franco forms sixth government. Technocrats are represented.
1958	
17 May	'Fundamental Principles of the Movement' presented to the Cortes.
1959	
22 July	Economic 'Stabilisation Plan' is announced.
Dec.	US President Eisenhower visits Madrid.
	Foundation of Basque terrorist group ETA (Euskadi Ta Askatasuna – Basque Homeland and Freedom).
1960	
12 Dec.	Five-Year Development Plan is announced.
1961	First ETA attacks (on 25th anniversary of start of Civil War).
1962	Spain applies for associate status in EEC.
Feb.	Only negotiations for preferential trade agreement begin.
July	General Agustín Muñoz Grandes is appointed Deputy Head of Government (against background of workers' and students' agitation and growing opposition).
1963	Gibraltar issue is brought before UN.
1964	Franco regime celebrates 25 years in power.
1965	Demonstrations by students take place in Madrid, and professors are dismissed.
1966	
14 Dec.	Referendum approves Organic Law of the State.

1967	Admiral Carrero Blanco is appointed Deputy Head of Government. Referendum is held in Gibraltar – 12,000 people vote to stay British, 44 against.
1968	First person (a Civil Guard) is killed by ETA. Madrid University is closed from Mar. to May.

1969

Jan.–Mar.	State of emergency in Spain.
22 July	Juan Carlos is presented as Franco's successor.
	Franco closes land border with Gibraltar.

1970	Death sentence for six ETA members after Burgos trial sparks anti-Franco demonstrations.
29 June	Preferential trade agreement with EEC.

1972

Jan.–Mar.	Disturbances in Spain, with clashes at Madrid University and rioting by workers at El Ferrol.

1973

8 June	Carrero Blanco is appointed Head of Government.
20 Dec.	Blanco is assassinated by car bomb in Madrid and succeeded by Arias Navarro.

1974

Feb.	Navarro declares 'opening' of regime.
25 Apr.	Spain is rocked by revolution in Portugal.

1975	Franco suffers heart attack.
Oct.	Juan Carlos becomes Head of State.
20 Nov.	Death of Franco.
22 Nov.	Juan Carlos is crowned King.

Spain since Franco

1976

Jan.–Feb.	Spain hit by its largest ever wave of strikes.
	Formation of Democratic Co-ordination (bringing together of opposition groups).
	First legal congress of socialist UGT for 40 years.

16 Nov.	New Law of Political Reform is approved by Cortes, re-establishing democracy in Spain. Subsequently approved by referendum (15 Dec.).
1977	10 people die during 'Tragic Week' in Madrid.
9 Apr.	The Spanish Communist Party is legalised by Prime Minister Adolfo Suárez.
15 June	First democratic elections since 1936 are held.
Sept.	Re-establishment in Catalonia of the *Generalitat* (self-government).
Oct.	Josep Tarradellas is returned as new Catalan President. Pact of Moncloa between government and opposition.
Dec.	First moves begin towards autonomy in Basque country.
1978	
Feb.	Serious ministerial crisis.
Apr.	First legal Communist Congress for 40 years is held, and it rejects Leninism.
Oct.	Major ETA offensive.
31 Oct.	Congress and Senate approve Constitution. It is subsequently ratified by referendum (6 Dec.).
1980	ETA kills 118 in year of violence.
	Spain agrees to open Gibraltar border.
1981	Attempted right-wing coup fails.
1982	Socialist government is elected.
1983	Anti-terrorist Liberation Groups (GAL) begin covert war on ETA.
1986	Spain joins the EU.
12 Mar.	Referendum favours continued membership of NATO.
22 June	Gonzales and Socialists are returned to power.
1987	Barcelona supermarket bombing leaves 21 dead.
1992	Barcelona hosts Olympic Games.
	ETA central organisation is apparently crippled by police.
1993	
June	Spanish Workers' Socialist Party wins general election with reduced majority.

1995	Spaniard Javier Solana is appointed Secretary General of NATO.
	Spain imposes frontier restrictions on Gibraltar, causing major delays.

1996

3 Mar.	Conservative Popular Party, led by José María Aznar, defeats ruling Socialists in general election.

1997

Jan.	Spain refuses to recognise Gibraltar-issued passports.
July	Kidnap and murder of Basque town councillor by ETA leads to six million-strong protest.

1998

Sept.	ETA truce is followed by talks with its political wing.

1999

Aug.	Suspension of ETA talks with government; ETA demand for self-rule referendum is rejected (Oct.) followed by end of cease-fire.

2000

Mar.	José María Aznar wins overall majority in general election.

2001

June–Aug.	Wave of ETA attacks in tourist areas.

2002

Nov.	Overwhelming vote in Gibraltar referendum to stay British.

Portugal: from dictatorship to revolution

1933	The '*Estado Novo*' (New State) established in Portugal (see p. 294).

1939

3 Sept.	Portuguese neutrality in Second World War declared by Salazar.

1942	Meeting of Salazar and Franco confirms neutrality policy.

1943	Anglo-Portuguese agreement grants Allies naval and air bases. Nazi Germany protests.

1945	Increased repression by secret police (PIDE) following rigged November National Assembly elections.
1947	Attempted military coup in central Portugal is crushed.
	Newly independent India protests at continuing Portuguese colonial rule in Goa, Daman, etc.
1949	Creation of NATO. Portugal is a founding member.
1951	Revisions to constitution see overseas colonies become overseas provinces.
	Agreement with USA over military bases in Azores.
	Death of President Carmona who is succeeded by General Lopes.
1958	Flight of opposition coalition leader, General Humberto Delgado, to Brazil after losing rigged elections.
1962	
Jan.	Failed military coup.
1965	General Delgado is murdered near the Spanish border by PIDE.
1968	
Aug.	Salazar is crippled by stroke; power is handed over to Marcello Caetano who begins period of limited reforms.
1970	Death of Salazar.
1971	Minor reforms in Portuguese colonial administration.
1973	Mario Soares reforms Socialist Party.
1974	
25 Apr.	Military coup led by Armed Forces Movement overthrows Caetano.
	Provisional Government is established. Spinola is made President with promise of elections.
May	Mario Soares becomes Foreign Secretary.
May	Spinola's reforms are blocked.
Sept.	Spinola resigns over Angolan independence. General Costa Gomes becomes President.
	Revolution moves leftwards.

100

1975

Jan.   Agreement for Angolan independence under MPLA (the nationalist movement).

Mar.   Attempted conservative military coup by Spinola loyalists.

'Revolutionary Council' nationalises much of economy.

Apr.   Socialists win Constituent Assembly elections.

May   Widespread demonstrations against Costa Gomes, etc.

25 Nov.   Military coup by moderate army officers, which results in gradual move of revolution towards the right.

1976

Apr.   Establishment of new constitution. Socialists win elections.

June   General Eanes becomes President and Mario Soares Prime Minister.

1978

Aug.   Da Costa succeeds Soares as Prime Minister.

1982   Civilian control over army is established. The 1976 Constitution sees minor amendments.

1985

July   Elections produce good results for Social Democrats, who are committed to free enterprise.

Cavaco Silva becomes Prime Minister (until 1995).

1986   Portugal joins European Community.

1987   First majority government as Social Democrats, led by Silva, take 50 per cent of seats in Legislative Assembly elections.

1991

July   Social Democrat victory in legislative elections. Return to power of Mario Soares as President.

1992   Portugal holds Chairmanship of EC.

1995

12 Oct.   Socialist Party takes power in Portugal as minority government, ending 10 years of Social Democratic rule. Antonio Guterres becomes Prime Minister.

1999

Oct.   Guterres leads Socialist Party to major victory.

2001

Jan.   Jorge Sampãio is re-elected as President for second term.

Dec.   Guterres resigns as Prime Minister. José Manuel Durao Barroso becomes premier.

THE COLD WAR AND EASTERN EUROPE, 1942–85

1942

26 May   Twenty-year Anglo–Soviet treaty signed but without any territorial agreement for postwar Europe.

June–Aug.   Stalin steps up demands for opening of 'second front' to relieve pressure on Russia.

July   British suspension of convoys to Russia because of losses causes Stalin to accuse Allies of lack of genuine support.

1943

14–24 Jan.   Churchill and Roosevelt agree to insist on the 'unconditional surrender' of Germany. The decision to mount an invasion of Italy, instead of France, agreed by the Allied commanders, leads to bitter recriminations from Stalin who sees it as bad faith on the part of the Western Powers.

Aug.   Stalin objects to not being consulted about the surrender of Italy and demands a say in the Italian settlement.

Oct.   Three-power foreign ministers' conference in Moscow agrees upon an advisory council for Italy and makes broad plans for a world security organisation.

28 Nov.–1 Dec. Meeting of Big Three (Churchill, Roosevelt and Stalin) in Tehran, the first conference attended by Stalin. As well as discussing arrangements for the Allied landings in Europe and a renewed Soviet offensive against Germany, the main lines of a territorial settlement in Eastern Europe are agreed, including the Polish frontiers. No agreement is reached about the future of Germany, although there is discussion of the dismemberment of Germany.

1944

21 Aug.–9 Oct. Dumbarton Oaks Conference draws up broad framework of the United Nations.

11–17 Sept.   Churchill and Roosevelt meet in Quebec and move towards acceptance of Morgenthau Plan for the destruction of German industry and the conversion of Germany into a pastoralised state.

9–10 Oct.	Churchill and Stalin meet in Moscow and decide on 'spheres of influence'. Romania and Bulgaria are ceded predominantly to Russian influence, Greece to Britain, and Yugoslavia and Hungary equally between Russia and Great Britain.
3 Dec.	Attempted communist insurrection in Athens.

1945

11 Jan.	Communists in Greece seek truce.
4–11 Feb.	Meeting at Yalta between Churchill, Roosevelt and Stalin decides upon four occupation zones in Germany, the prosecution of war criminals, and prepares Allied Control Council to run Germany on the basis of 'complete disarmament, demilitarisation and dismemberment'. Removals of national wealth from Germany are to be permitted within two years of the end of the war and reparations are tentatively agreed. Agreement reached that the provisional government already functioning in Poland, i.e. the communist Lublin-based group, with the addition of other groups including the London Poles, act as the government. A three-power commission based in Moscow would supervise the setting up of the new regime. The provisional government was pledged to hold free and unfettered elections as soon as possible. Declaration on Liberated Europe signed by the major powers to allow European states to 'create democratic conditions of their own choice'.
12 Feb.	Greek Communists granted amnesty and lay down arms.
Apr.	Members of non-communist delegation to the three-power commission in Moscow arrested. Russians conclude a treaty of alliance with the Lublin administration of Poland.
5 July	Britain and USA recognise provisional government of National Unity in Poland.
17 July–1 Aug.	Stalin, Truman, Churchill (after 25 July Attlee) meet at Potsdam and finalise four-power agreement on administration of Germany and the territorial adjustments in Eastern Europe. The Oder–Neisse Line is to mark the new boundary between Germany and Poland. Although Germany is to be divided into zones, it is to be treated as a single economic unit. Germans living in Poland, Hungary and Czechoslovakia are to be sent to Germany.
28 Oct.	Provisional Czech National Assembly meets, representing communist and non-communist parties.
Nov.	Tito is elected President of Yugoslavia.

1946

6 Mar. Churchill makes 'Iron Curtain' speech at Fulton, Missouri: 'From Stettin in the Baltic to Trieste in the Adriatic, an Iron Curtain has descended upon the Continent.'

26 May At Czech elections Communists win 38 per cent of the vote and set up a single-party 'National Front' government.

May Fighting breaks out in northern Greece, marking renewal of civil war between monarchist forces assisted by Britain and communist guerrillas, backed by Albania, Bulgaria and Yugoslavia.

1947

21 Feb. The British inform the Americans that they cannot afford to keep troops in Greece because of their domestic economic difficulties and intend to withdraw them by the end of March.

27 Feb. Dean Acheson privately expounds the 'Truman Doctrine' of economic and military aid to nations in danger of communist takeover.

12 Mar. In message to Congress President Truman outlines the Truman Doctrine 'to support free peoples who are resisting attempted subjugation by armed minorities or by outside pressures', effectively committing the USA to intervene against communist or communist-backed movements in Europe and elsewhere.

22 Apr. Truman Doctrine passed by Congress.

24 Apr. Council of Foreign Ministers in Moscow ends without formal peace treaties for Germany and Austria.

22 May Congress passes bill for $250 million of aid for Greece and Turkey.

5 June George Marshall, American Secretary of State, calls for a European recovery programme supported by American aid.

12–15 June Non-communist nations of Europe set up Committee of European Economic Co-operation to draft European Recovery Programme.

Aug. First American aid arrives in Greece, followed by military 'advisers' to assist in the civil war against the Communists.

1948

25 Feb. Czech President Beneš accepts a communist-dominated government.

10 Mar. Czech Foreign Minister, Jan Masaryk, found dead in suspicious circumstances.

14–31 Mar.	Congress passes the Foreign Assistance Act, the Marshall Plan. $5,300 million of 'Marshall Aid' is initially allocated for European recovery.
17 Mar.	Belgium, France, Luxembourg, the Netherlands and Britain sign a treaty setting up the Brussels Treaty Organisation for mutual military assistance.
20 Mar.	Russian representative walks out of Allied Control Council.
30 Mar.	Russians impose restrictions on traffic between Western zones and Berlin.
Apr.	Paris Treaty sets up Organisation for European Economic Co-operation to receive Marshall Aid.
30 May	At Czech elections no opposition parties are allowed to stand and electors called on to vote for a single list of National Front candidates.
June	Yugoslavia is expelled from Comintern, effectively putting it outside direct Soviet control.
7 June	Beneš resigns as President of Czechoslovakia and is succeeded by Gottwald.
24 June	Russians impose a complete blockade of traffic into Berlin. Berlin airlift begins (25th).
5 Sept.	Head of Polish Communist Party, Gomulka, is forced to resign.
30 Nov.	Russians set up separate municipal government for East Berlin.

1949

Jan.	Comecon, communist economic co-operation organisation, is set up.
4 Apr.	Creation of NATO. North Atlantic Treaty signed by members of Brussels Treaty Organisation, with Canada, Denmark, Iceland, Italy, Norway, Portugal and the USA. It pledges mutual military assistance.
May	Federal Republic of Germany (West Germany) comes into existence.
4 May	Representatives of four occupation powers in Germany come to an agreement for ending Berlin blockade.
12 May	Berlin blockade lifted.
15 May	Communists take power in Hungary on the basis of a single-list election for the 'People's Front', replacing the communist-dominated coalition elected in 1947.
June	Purge of Albanian Communist Party.
30 Sept.	End of Berlin airlift.

Oct.	German Democratic Republic (East Germany) comes into existence.
16 Oct.	Greek Communists cease fighting.
Nov.	Russian Marshal takes command of Polish army.
Dec. 1949–Jan. 1950	Purge of Bulgarian Communist Party; 92,000 expelled.

1950

May–June	Last non-Communists expelled from Hungarian government.
28 May	Pro-Stalinist Hoxha confirmed in power in single-list elections in Albania.
July	Romanian Communist Party admits to expulsion of almost 200,000 members in past two years.
Sept.	USA proposes German rearmament.

1951

Sept.	First Soviet atomic bomb is exploded.

1952

18 Feb.	Greece and Turkey join NATO.
27 May	Belgium, France, Italy, Luxembourg, the Netherlands and West Germany sign mutual defence treaty for proposed creation of a European Defence Community.

1953

5 Mar.	Death of Stalin. Khrushchev confirmed as First Secretary of the Communist Party (Sept.).
June	Risings in East Germany suppressed.

1954

5 May	Italy and West Germany enter Brussels Treaty Organisation.
1954–56	Khrushchev launches 'virgin land' campaign to increase grain output in marginal land.

1955

May	Warsaw Pact formed.
9 May	West Germany admitted to NATO.

1956

Feb.	At Russian Twentieth Party Congress Khrushchev attacks abuses of Stalin era.

June	Workers' riots in Poznan, Poland, suppressed; Gomulka becomes First Secretary of Polish United Workers' Party (Oct.).
Oct.–Nov.	General strike and street demonstrations in Budapest. Russians intervene and depose Nagy and crush the rising. Kadar becomes the First Secretary of the Hungarian Communist Party and premier. Thousands of Hungarian refugees flee to the West.

1958

Feb.	Khrushchev replaces Bulganin as Prime Minister.

1961

Apr.	First manned Soviet space flight. Arrests of dissident writers.
July	Anti-clerical legislation in Russia, restricting role of the clergy in parish councils.
Aug.	Berlin Wall constructed to prevent flight from East to West Berlin.
Oct.	Twenty-Second Party Congress; new Party programme and further 'de-Stalinisation', including the removal of Stalin's body from Red Square mausoleum.

1962

Oct.	Cuban missile crisis after Soviet Union attempts to set up ballistic missile bases in Cuba. Imposition of naval 'quarantine' by the USA forces the Soviet Union to back down in the face of the threat of nuclear war.
Nov.	Publication of Solzhenitsyn's *A Day in the Life of Ivan Denisovitch* marks first public recognition of the conditions in Soviet labour camps.

1963

5 Aug.	Partial Test Ban Treaty signed in Moscow, banning nuclear weapon tests in the atmosphere, outer space, and under water (in force from Oct.).

1964

Oct.	Brezhnev replaces Khrushchev as First Secretary in Soviet Union.

1966

Feb.	Trial of leading 'dissidents', Sinyavsky and Daniel, who are given periods of imprisonment.

1967

June	Arab–Israeli 'Six-Day' War leads to acute tension between USA and Soviet Union.

1968

Jan.	Dissidents Ginsburg and Galanskov tried and imprisoned. Dubček becomes First Secretary of Czechoslovak Communist Party and process of liberalisation begins – 'Socialism with a human face' – including decentralisation of economic planning and more open contacts with the West.
1 July	Non-proliferation treaty signed in London, Moscow and Washington.
Aug.	The Soviet Union and other Warsaw Pact forces invade Czechoslovakia and end the 'Prague Spring'. The Czech leaders are forced to agree in Moscow to the reimposition of censorship, return to centralised planning, and abandon closer links with the West. Husák takes over Party Secretaryship from Dubček.

1969

Mar.	Dubček demoted and sent as ambassador to Turkey; he is eventually expelled from the Party and given menial work.
Oct.	Czechoslovakia repudiates its condemnation of the Warsaw Pact invasion and consents to the stationing of Russian troops.

1970

Dec.	Widespread rioting in Poland over food prices and economic conditions; Gierek replaces Gomulka as First Secretary of Polish United Workers' Party.

1972

26 May	Visit of President Nixon to Moscow. Strategic Arms Limitation Treaty (SALT 1) signed between USA and Soviet Union on limitation of anti-ballistic missile systems (in force from Oct.) and interim agreement on limitation of strategic offensive arms.

1974

Feb.	Solzhenitsyn deported from Soviet Union.

1975

Aug.	Helsinki agreement on European Security and Co-operation provides for 'Human Rights'.
Oct.	Soviet physicist and dissident Andre Sakharov awarded Nobel peace prize.

1976

June   Strikes and sabotage in Poland in opposition to attempted price rises which are temporarily withdrawn, although unrest is severely put down.

1977

Jan.   Dissident civil rights group 'Charter 77' formed in Prague.

June   Brezhnev replaces Podgorny as President of the Soviet Union.

1978

July   Trial of Soviet Jewish dissident and civil rights activist Shcharansky.

1979

June   Visit of Pope John Paul II to Poland helps to arouse strong national feeling.

Dec.   Soviet invasion of Afghanistan. The USA imposes a grain embargo on Russia. Large commemorative services held in Poland for those killed in the disturbances of 1970.

1980

Jan.   Sakharov sentenced to internal exile in Gorky.

Mar.–Apr.   Dissident groups in Poland advocate boycott of official parliamentary elections on 23 March and mass commemorative service for Polish officers killed at Katyn in April 1940 leads to arrests.

July   Olympic Games in Moscow boycotted by the USA.

July–Sept.   Widespread strikes among Polish workers at Gdansk (Danzig) and elsewhere as a result of rise in meat prices. In August, Gdansk workers publish demands calling for free trade unions. Soviet Union begins jamming of Western broadcasts. Resignation of Babinch as Prime Minister (24 Aug.) and of Gierek as First Secretary of the Polish United Workers' Party (6 Sept.); replaced by Pinkowski and Kania. Gierek's departure followed by the signing of the 'Gdansk agreement' with Lech Walesa, the leader of the Gdansk 'inter-factory committee'. This recognises the new Solidarity unions, grants a wage agreement and promises a 40-hour week, permits the broadcast of church services on Sunday, relaxes the censorship laws, promises to re-examine the new meat scales and review the cases of imprisoned dissidents. National Confederation of Independent Trade Unions, 'Solidarity', formed under leadership

	of Lech Walesa (8 Sept.), attracts an estimated 10 million members. 'Rural Solidarity' claims an estimated half million farmers.
Dec.	Death of Russian Prime Minister Kosygin.

1981

Jan.	Walesa visits Pope in Rome.
Feb.	General Jaruzelski replaces Pinkowski as Prime Minister.
Dec.	After visiting Moscow, Jaruzelski declares martial law in Poland. The leading members of Solidarity are arrested and the organisation is banned.

1982

Nov.	Death of Brezhnev. Andropov becomes First Secretary of the Communist Party of the Soviet Union.

1984

Feb.	Death of Andropov. Chernenko becomes First Secretary of the Communist Party of the Soviet Union.

1985

Mar.	Death of Chernenko. Gorbachev becomes First Secretary of the Communist Party of the Soviet Union in June.

THE RETREAT FROM EMPIRE: EUROPEAN DECOLONISATION

Britain

1942

Jan.	Japanese forces begin occupation of British, French, US and Dutch possessions in South-East Asia and Western Pacific.
Feb.	Singapore surrenders to Japanese.
Apr.	Indian Nationalists reject offer of self-government made by Cripps.

1946

Mar.	Transjordan becomes independent (formerly a British mandate).
Apr.	Malayan Union established.
May	Sarawak is ceded to Britain.
July	North Borneo becomes a British colony.

1947

Mar.	Netherlands recognises independence of Indonesia.
June	Partition of India is announced.
Aug.	India and Pakistan become independent.
Sept.	Britain announces withdrawal from Palestine.

1948

Jan.	Burma becomes independent and leaves the Commonwealth.
Feb.	Malayan Union becomes Federation of Malaya. Ceylon becomes independent.
May	State of Israel is established. Conflict with communist guerrillas in Malaya begins.

1949

Apr.	Eire withdraws from Commonwealth.

1951

Jan.	Gold Coast constitution becomes operative.
Dec.	Libya becomes independent.

1952

	Beginning of Mau Mau conflict in Kenya.
Jan.	Nigerian constitution becomes operative.
Sept.	Eritrea is united with Ethiopia.

1953

Feb.	Anglo–Egyptian agreement on Sudan reached.
Aug.	Southern Rhodesia, Nyasaland and Northern Rhodesia are united in the Federation of Rhodesia and Nyasaland.

1956

Jan.	Sudan becomes independent (formerly under Anglo–Egyptian rule).
Nov.	Suez Crisis: Britain and France intervene in war between Egypt and Israel. Mau Mau insurgency in Kenya suppressed.

1957

Mar.	Gold Coast becomes independent as Ghana.
Aug.	Federation of Malaya becomes independent.

1958

Jan.	Federation of West Indies is established.

1960

Feb.	Harold Macmillan makes 'Wind of change' speech.
Aug.	Cyprus becomes independent. British Somaliland gains independence, and unites with Italian Somaliland to form the Somali Republic (Somalia).
Oct.	Nigeria becomes independent.

1961

Mar.	South Africa leaves the Commonwealth.
Apr.	Sierra Leone becomes independent.
June	Northern Cameroons (British) unites with Nigeria.
Dec.	Tanganyika becomes independent.

1962

Jan.	Western Samoa gains independence.
Aug.	Federation of West Indies dissolves when Jamaica and Trinidad and Tobago become independent.
Oct.	Uganda becomes independent.

1963

Sept.	Federation of Malaysia established, including Malaya, Singapore, Sarawak, and North Borneo.
Dec.	Zanzibar and Kenya become independent. Federation of Rhodesia and Nyasaland is dissolved.

1964

July	Nyasaland becomes independent as Malawi.
Sept.	Malta becomes independent.
Oct.	Northern Rhodesia becomes independent as Zambia.

1965

Feb.	The Gambia becomes independent.
July.	The Maldive Islands gain independence.
Nov.	Southern Rhodesia unilaterally declares its independence.

1966

May	British Guiana becomes independent as Guyana.
Sept.	Bechuanaland becomes independent as Botswana.
Oct.	Basutoland becomes independent as Lesotho.
Nov.	Barbados becomes independent.

Dec.	Negotiations between Britain and Rhodesia aboard *HMS Tiger* collapse.

1967

Nov.	Aden gains independence.

1968

Jan.	Nauru becomes independent.
Mar.	Mauritius becomes independent.
Sept.	Swaziland becomes independent.
Oct.	Talks between Britain and Rhodesia aboard *HMS Fearless* reach stalemate.

1969

Mar.	British police despatched to Anguilla.

1970

Mar.	Rhodesia declares itself a republic.
June	Tonga becomes independent.
Oct.	Fiji Islands become independent.

1971

Aug.	Bahrain becomes independent.
Sept.	Qatar becomes independent.
Nov.	Oman becomes independent.
Dec.	Britain leaves Gulf States.

1973

July	Bahamas becomes independent.

1974

Feb.	Grenada becomes independent.

1975

Sept.	Papua New Guinea becomes independent.

1976

June	Seychelles becomes independent.

1977

Sept.	Anglo–American peace plan for Rhodesia receives support of 'front-line states' and provides for first elections on the basis

of universal suffrage in April 1979, though still opposed by major guerrilla armies.

1978

July   Solomon Islands become independent.

Oct.   Ellice Islands gain independence as Tuvalu.

Nov.   Dominica becomes independent.

1979

Feb.   St Lucia gains independence.

July   Kiribati becomes independent (formerly the Gilbert Islands).

Oct.   St Vincent and the Grenadines gain independence.

Dec.   Lancaster House agreement on future of Rhodesia. Ceasefire arranged and constitutional agreement reached. Commonwealth troops to supervise elections. Soviet troops invade Afghanistan. Widespread guerrilla resistance begins.

1980

Feb.   Elections in Rhodesia result in sweeping victory for Mugabe's ZANU.

Apr.   Rhodesia becomes independent republic of Zimbabwe.

July   Vanuatu becomes independent (formerly known as New Hebrides).

1981   Belize becomes independent republic.

1982

Apr.   Argentine troops invade Falkland Islands and South Georgia. Britain organises task force to recapture islands.

June   Argentine force in Falklands surrenders.

1984   Brunei becomes independent.

Sept.   Agreement with China, whereby Hong Kong reverts to Chinese sovereignty after 1 July 1997.

1994

June   South Africa rejoins Commonwealth after historic multi-racial elections (1st).

1995   Mozambique (former Portuguese colony) and Cameroon join Commonwealth.

1997

July   Return of Hong Kong to China (1st).

France

1944

Jan.   Free French hold Brazzaville Conference to discuss future of French possessions in Africa. Ho Chi Minh proclaims Vietnamese independence from France.

1946

Apr.   Forced labour in colonies abolished by Houphouët-Boigny Act. Establishment of FIDES for investment in colonial development.

May   All inhabitants of colonies declared to be citizens of the Republic.

Oct.   The constitution of the 'French Union' is confirmed by referendum.

1949

July   Laos becomes independent of France.

1953

Nov.   Cambodia becomes independent.

1954

May   French forces surrender to Vietminh at Dien Bien Phu, Vietnam.

July   French Assembly approves Indo–China settlement.

Nov.   National Liberation Front begins revolt in Algeria.

1955

June   French agreement on Tunisian home rule.

1956

Mar.   France recognises independence of Morocco and Tunisia.

1958

Jan.   French Guinea becomes independent. French Union becomes French Community.

May   Revolt of French settlers and army in Algeria.

1960

Jan.	Cameroun gains independence.
Apr.	Togo becomes independent.
June	Mali and Madagascar win independence.
Aug.	Ivory Coast, Dahomey, Upper Volta, Niger, Chad, Gabon, (French) Congo and Central African Republic gain independence.
Nov.	Mauritania and Senegal win independence.

1961

Apr.	Army revolt in Algeria collapses.
Oct.	Southern Cameroons (French) unites with Cameroun.

1962

Mar.	French and Algerians agree to ceasefire.
July	Algeria becomes independent.

1968

Aug.	French military support given to Chad to combat rebels.

1969

Mar.	French troops called into Chad again.

1975

July	Comoro Islands declare themselves independent.

1977

June	French territory of the Afars and Issas becomes independent as Djibouti.

1979

Feb.	French paratroops sent to Chad (withdrawn in May).

1983

June	French troops sent to assist Chadian troops against rebel and Libyan forces.

1987 France sends 7,000 soldiers and riot police to quell unrest in New Caledonia prior to a referendum on independence.

The Netherlands

1945

17 Aug.   Republic of Indonesia declared by Sukarno in Dutch East Indies.

Sept.   British troops despatched and use Japanese troops to restore order.

Oct.   Arrival of Dutch troops.

1946–48   Continued conflict in East Indies (see p. 186).

1949

Dec.   Formal independence granted to Indonesia by Holland.

1950   Promise of autonomy to Dutch Guiana in South America (Surinam).

1954   The Realm Statute gives large measure of self-government to Netherlands Antilles (Curaçao, Bonaire, St Maartens, St Eustatius, Seiba). Aruba separates in 1986.

1962   Agreement for Dutch New Guinea to be transferred to Indonesia. Renamed Irian Jaya on incorporation into Indonesia.

1975

25 Nov.   Dutch Guiana gains independence (as Surinam).

Belgium

1946   Ruanda-Urundi becomes trusteeship territory.

1954   First moves towards political reform in Congo by Liberal–Socialist government in Belgium.

1955   Emergence of ABAKO (*Alliance des Bakongo*) under Joseph Kasavubu as a political movement.

1957   First-ever municipal elections in Congo are won by ABAKO.

1958   Foundation of *Mouvement National Congolais* (MNC) by Patrice Lumumba coincides with economic crisis in Congo and fall of Liberal–Socialist coalition in Brussels.

1959	Rioting in Leopoldville as agitation for independence increases. Promise of independence is given (but no date announced). Proliferation of regional, tribal-based parties. Tribal conflict (Hutu versus Tutsi) in Ruanda-Urundi.
1960	
May	Conference plans independence. Fundamental Law setting up a six-province state. Indecisive result of pre-independence elections.
30 June	Kasavubu becomes President on independence, Lumumba is Prime Minister. Army mutinies are followed by anarchy. Secession of Katanga. Lumumba ousted by General Mobutu.
1961	
Jan.–Feb.	Lumumba is murdered.
Sept.	Death of UN Secretary General, Dag Hammarskjold, while attempting to mediate in continuing Congolese civil war.
1962	
July	Rwanda and Burundi (formerly trusteeships) attain independence as separate states.
1963	Secession of Katanga ended. Tshombe gains power throughout Congo.
1965	Mobutu seizes power in army coup.
1971	Country is renamed Zaïre.
1997	Mobutu dictatorship is overthrown by Laurent Kabila.

Portugal

1951	
June	Portuguese colonies are renamed 'Overseas Provinces'.
1956	Founding of independence movements in Angola (MPLA) and in Guinea (PAIGC).
1959	PAIGC strike in Guinea is followed by severe repression. Flight of PAIGC leader Cabral.

1961–2	Beginning of armed rebellion in Angola. Abolition of forced labour in minor colonial reforms by Salazar government.
Dec. 1961	Goa is occupied by Indian forces.
1962	Frelimo (Mozambique Liberation Front) is established.
1963	Armed struggle begins in Guinea.
1964	Much of Mozambique comes under Frelimo control after armed attacks.
1968	Death of Salazar in Portugal, but authoritarian regime continues.
1973	
24 Sept.	Independence unilaterally proclaimed by PAIGC in Guinea.
1974	
25 Apr.	Revolution in Portugal.
Sept.	Independence of Guinea-Bissau is recognised.
	Status of Macao is changed to 'territory under Portuguese administration'.
1975	
25 June	Mozambique becomes independent.
12 July	Independence for Cape Verde Islands, São Tomé e Principe.
11 Nov.	Independence is agreed for Angola.
Dec.	East Timor is seized by Indonesia after fighting between rival factions on the island.
1976	East Timor is declared to be an integral part of Indonesia. Prolonged civil war in East Timor.
1999	Return of Portuguese enclave of Macao to China.
2002	
May	East Timor finally achieves independence.

Note In both Angola and Mozambique prolonged civil war followed independence. A peace accord was agreed in Mozambique in 1992, but successive accords have failed to bring peace to Angola.

Spain

1956	Following independence for French Morocco, Spain withdraws from her protectorate of northern Morocco.
1957	Unsuccessful attack on Ifni by Moroccan irregulars.
1958	Spain withdraws from protectorate in South Morocco, but retains Ceuta, Melilla and Ifni.
1959	Equatorial Guinea becomes two provinces of metropolitan Spain.
1963	Autonomy for Equatorial Guinea.
1968	Independence for Spanish Equatorial Guinea (Rio Muni, Fernando Po, etc.).
1969	Ifni becomes part of Morocco.
1972	Discovery of rich phosphate deposits in Western Sahara transforms its economic importance.
1973	Polisario independence movement formed in Western Sahara.
1976	All rights over Western Sahara are abandoned by Spain.
2002	Diplomatic crisis over Spanish-held Perejil (Parsley) Island.

Note The dispute over the independent state of the Saharan Arab Democratic Republic proclaimed by Polisario in 1976 continues. Although Mauritania has renounced its claim, Morocco refuses to recognise Polisario's claims.

THE SOVIET UNION, 1953–85

Note This chronology concentrates on domestic events within the Soviet Union. For more details on international aspects (and for the Eastern Bloc) see *The Cold War and Eastern Europe* (pp. 102–10).

1953

Mar.	Death of Stalin (5th). Khrushchev is confirmed as First Secretary of the Communist Party (Sept.). Arrest of Beria confirmed.

1954	Khrushchev launches 'virgin land' campaign to increase grain output in marginal land.
	Crimea transferred to Ukraine from RSFSR (Russian Federation).
1955	
Feb.	Bulganin succeeds Malenkov as Prime Minister. Marshal Zhukov becomes Defence Minister.
May	Formation of Warsaw Pact.
Sept.	Adenauer (West German Chancellor) visits Moscow.
1956	
Feb.	At Russian Twentieth Party Congress Khrushchev attacks abuses of Stalin era.
Apr.	Dissolution of Cominform.
May	Major decentralisation of government to the republics. USSR Ministry of Justice is dissolved.
Oct.	Hungarian Rising (see pp. 178–9).
Nov.	Tito attacked in Soviet press.
1957	
Feb.	Further extension of rights of autonomous republics within USSR. Autonomous territories of some groups (Chechens, Ingushi, etc.) restored after their 1944 deportations by Stalin.
May	Decrees by USSR Supreme Soviet on decentralisation of industry and construction follows earlier decentralisation of economic decision-making.
June	Khrushchev wins internal power struggle.
July	Malenkov, Molotov and Kaganovich lose Presidium seats (Molotov is subsequently appointed Ambassador to Mongolia).
Oct.	Launch of Sputnik marks birth of space race.
1958	
Mar.	Khrushchev replaces Bulganin as Prime Minister, confirming his ascendancy in the party.
Oct.	USSR agrees to provide Egypt with financial assistance for Aswan Dam.
Nov.	New Berlin crisis begins.
1959	
Jan.	Twenty-first Extraordinary Congress. Khrushchev claims Soviet Union has now achieved full socialism.

1960

May	Shooting down of U-2 spy plane.
June	Communist Party of China attacked by Khrushchev speaking in Romania.
Aug.	Withdrawal of all Soviet Union engineers, etc. from China.
Sept.–Oct.	Histrionics by Khrushchev during visit to UN.

1961

Apr.	First manned Soviet space flight. Dissident writers are arrested.
July	Anti-clerical legislation in Russia, restricting role of the clergy in parish councils.
Aug.	Berlin Wall is constructed.
Oct.	Twenty-second Party Congress; new Party programme and further 'de-Stalinisation', including the removal of Stalin's body from Red Square mausoleum.

1962

Oct.	Cuban missile crisis.
Nov.	Publication of Solzhenitsyn's *A Day in the Life of Ivan Denisovitch* marks first public recognition of the conditions in Soviet labour camps.

1963

Mar.	Khrushchev warns Writers' Union of 'bourgeois influences'.
Apr.	Castro pays first visit to Soviet Union.
Aug.	Treaty ends atomic tests in space and under water.

1964

Khrushchev is replaced by Brezhnev as First Secretary. Kosygin becomes Prime Minister.

1965

Mar.	Central Committee of the Soviet Union makes a number of agricultural reforms.
Sept.	Central Committee approves further set of economic reforms in industry and planning.

1966

Jan.	Mediation by Kosygin in India–Pakistan conflict extends Soviet influence.
Feb.	Leading dissidents, Sinyavsky and Daniel, given terms of imprisonment after trial.

Mar.–Apr.	Removal of Khrushchev supporters at Twenty-third Party Congress.

1967

Apr.	Stalin's daughter given political asylum in USA. Partial rehabilitation of Crimean Tatars.

1968

Jan.	Dissidents Ginsburg and Galanskov jailed after trial.
July	Nuclear non-proliferation treaty is signed.
Aug.	Invasion of Czechoslovakia.

1971

Feb.	Mass Jewish demonstration at Supreme Soviet building. Jewish emigration to Israel grows.
Sept.	Four-power Berlin treaty over status of West Berlin.

1972

Jan.	Seizure of documents and leading intellectuals in the Ukraine.
May	Disturbances in Lithuania.

1973

Apr.	Andropov and Gromyko join Politburo.
May	Brezhnev visits West Germany (first visit by a Soviet leader) and signs 10-year economic co-operation agreement.

1974

Feb.	Solzhenitsyn is deported from Soviet Union.

1975

Oct.	Nobel Peace Prize is awarded to Soviet dissident Andre Sakharov.

1976

May	Helsinki Group is set up by nine Soviet dissidents to monitor implementation of Helsinki agreement.

1977

June	Brezhnev replaces Podgorny as President of the Soviet Union.
Oct.	New Soviet constitution replaces 1936 Stalin constitution.
	The CPSU is 'leading and guiding force of Soviet society'.

1978

Apr.	Demonstrations in Armenia and Georgia over language question lead to amendment of Soviet constitution.
July	Trial of Shcharansky, Soviet Jewish dissident and civil rights activist.
Aug.	Petition by Crimean Tatars to return to their homeland.

1979

Jan.	Census reveals extent of population increase in Central Asia.
June	SALT 2 signed in Vienna.
Nov.	Election of Gorbachev as candidate member of Politburo.
Dec.	Soviet invasion of Afghanistan (see p. 179). Grain embargo placed by USA on USSR (in Jan. 1980 in retaliation).

1980

Jan.	Dissident Sakharov is sentenced to internal exile in Gorky after his arrest in Moscow.
July	Olympic Games in Moscow (boycotted by USA).
Oct.	Gorbachev is elected full member of the Politburo. Kosygin resigns due to failing health and is succeeded by Tikhonov.
Dec.	Death of Kosygin.

1981

Apr.	Grain embargo on USSR is lifted by USA.

1982

May	Rise of Andropov paves way for him to succeed Brezhnev.
June	START talks begin in Geneva.
Nov.	Death of Brezhnev. Andropov becomes First Secretary of the Communist Party of the Soviet Union.

1984

Feb.	Death of Andropov. Chernenko becomes First Secretary of the Communist Party of the Soviet Union (despite obvious signs of poor health).
Dec.	Gorbachev visits Britain and meets Margaret Thatcher.

1985

Mar.	Death of Chernenko. Gorbachev becomes First Secretary of the Communist Party of the Soviet Union, inaugurating era of *glasnost* and *perestroika* (see pp. 125–9).

REVOLUTION AND RECONSTRUCTION: RUSSIA AND EASTERN EUROPE SINCE 1985

Russia since 1985

1985

June   Gorbachev becomes First Secretary of the Communist Party of the Soviet Union. Programme of *glasnost* and *perestroika* is launched.

July   Gorbachev replaces four members of Politburo with his own supporters; veteran Foreign Minister, Gromyko, is moved to Presidency and replaced by Gorbachev supporter Shevardnadze.

1986

Jan.   Gorbachev continues process of removing the personnel of the Brezhnev era from central and regional government.

26 Apr.   Chernobyl nuclear disaster tests new *glasnost*: attempted cover-up by Moscow.

1987

July   Protests by Crimean Tatars in Moscow permitted to take place.

Aug.   Protests in the Baltic states demanding greater autonomy and an end to 'Russification'.

Nov.   Boris Yeltsin is dismissed as head of Moscow Party for outspoken criticisms of conservatives.

Dec.   Reagan and Gorbachev sign Intermediate Nuclear Forces Treaty in Washington, a major breakthrough in East–West arms negotiations.

1988

Jan.   Gorbachev calls for acceleration of drive to democratisation; calls special Party Congress in the summer. Major reform of Soviet Constitution sets up a Supreme Soviet consisting of two chambers to meet in almost continuous session, the members selected by a Congress of People's Deputies representing national areas, social organisations and constituencies.

Feb.   Serious ethnic riots in Naborno-Karabakh region of Azerbaijan.

May   Russia agrees to withdraw all troops from Afghanistan by Feb. 1989.

Dec.   Gorbachev announces unilateral force reductions of 500,000 troops and 10,000 tanks.

1989

Dec. Malta Summit between Bush and Gorbachev; declares the Cold War 'at an end' (4th).

1990

Feb. Unanimous vote of the Central Committee of the Communist Party of the Soviet Union to end the leading role of the Party. Lithuanian Communist Party secedes from the CPSU to fight elections in March.

Mar. Soviet Congress of People's Deputies votes to abolish Articles 6 and 7 of the Soviet Constitution and end the leading role of the Communist Party. Congress approves the election of Gorbachev to the new post of Executive President with sweeping powers; subsequent elections to be by popular vote. Nationalist movements win victories in multi-party elections in Baltic Republics. Sweeping victory for Lithuanian *Sajudis* movement is followed by declaration of independence and election of non-communist Vytautas Landsbergis as the Republic's first President. Soviet government begins economic blockade of Lithuania.

July Gorbachev obtains mandate from Communist Party Congress for further reform, but breakaway group declares it will form a separate party.

Aug. Yeltsin asserts the sovereignty of the Russian Republic and offers economic assistance to Lithuania.

Dec. Gorbachev is granted sweeping new powers.

20 Dec. Soviet Foreign Minister Shevardnadze resigns because of 'reactionary elements'.

1991

13 Jan. Soviet special forces kill 14 Lithuanian demonstrators in Vilnius.

20 Jan. Special forces assault on key buildings in Latvian capital, Riga, kills five.

Mar. Huge majorities in Latvia and Estonia for independence. Anti-Gorbachev rally in Moscow; pro-Union majority for his referendum on maintaining the Union, but many abstentions.

Apr. Soviet Georgia declares independence. Miners' strikes in the Soviet coalfields.

Aug. Gorbachev prepares new all-Union treaty to preserve the Soviet Union. Attempted hard-line coup in Moscow while Gorbachev is on holiday in the Crimea. Russian premier Boris

Yeltsin defies coup and prepares to defend Russian parliament building with aid of loyal troops and populace. Coup collapses in face of popular resistance and declarations of independence by Republics. The leading plotters are arrested. Gorbachev returns to Moscow. Under pressure from Yeltsin, he adopts sweeping reforms. Baltic states become independent states of Latvia, Estonia and Lithuania; Communist Party of Soviet Union is dissolved, ending 74-year rule; Gorbachev resigns as General Secretary, retaining office of Executive President of rapidly dissolving Soviet Union. Negotiates an association with 10 Republics for a looser union with a common foreign and defence policy.

Sept.	Armenia becomes 12th Soviet Republic to declare independence.
1 Dec.	Ukraine votes overwhelmingly for independence.
8 Dec.	Leaders of Belorussia, Russian Federation and Ukraine declare that the Soviet Union is dead; in the Declaration of Minsk they proclaim new 'Commonwealth of Independent States' (CIS) with headquarters at Minsk in Belorussia.
10 Dec.	Ukrainian Parliament ratifies new Commonwealth.
12 Dec.	Russian Parliament votes 188 to six to approve new Commonwealth. Gorbachev declares 'My life's work is done'.
13 Dec.	Five Central Asian Republics, meeting in Ashkhabad, vote to join new Commonwealth as founding members: Gorbachev accepts existence and legitimacy of Commonwealth.
22 Dec.	Leaders of 11 former Soviet Republics sign Treaty of Alma Ata, establishing new Commonwealth of Independent States. The 11 Republics comprise: Armenia, Azerbaijan, Belarus (formerly Belorussia), Kazakhstan, Kyrgyzstan (formerly Kirghizia), Moldova (formerly Moldavia), the Russian Federation, Tajikistan, Turkmenistan (formerly Turkmenia), Uzbekistan and Ukraine. Only Georgia (where bitter fighting erupts in Tbilisi) does not join new CIS.
25 Dec.	Formal resignation of Mikhail Gorbachev as President of the now defunct Soviet Union; the Russian flag replaces the Hammer and Sickle above the Kremlin; key European states (and the USA) recognise independence of Russian Federation.
30 Dec.	Minsk Summit of Commonwealth of Independent States agrees future of strategic nuclear forces; no agreement on conventional forces (Ukraine, Azerbaijan and Moldova insist on separate armies) or economic policy.

1992

June	Yegor Gaidar becomes premier of Russia.

Sept.	Lithuania signs agreement with Russia for withdrawal of former Soviet troops.
Oct.	In Georgia, Shevardnadze, Chairman of State Council, is elected parliamentary Speaker and *de facto* head of state.
Nov.	Lithuanian ex-communist Democratic Labour Party defeats nationalist Sajudis Party in first post-Soviet parliamentary elections.
Dec.	Russian Congress blocks President Yeltsin's plans for a referendum on the powers of the President; also removes Yegor Gaidar as premier and replaces him with Viktor Chernomyrdin (14th).

1993

21 Mar.	Yeltsin announces rule by decree and plan to hold a national referendum on 25 Apr.
28 Mar.	Move by Congress to impeach the President is defeated.
25 Apr.	Russian referendum gives vote of confidence to Yeltsin and his socio-economic policy.
July	Guntis Alamanis of Farmers' Union is elected President of Latvia.
Aug.	Last Russian troops leave Lithuania.
21 Sept.	Yeltsin suspends parliament and calls for elections.
3–4 Oct.	Suppression of rising against Yeltsin's suspension of parliament.

1994

Jan.	Reformers Gaidar and Fedorov leave Yeltsin government.
July	New constitution adopted in Moldova, establishing a presidential parliamentary republic.
1 Dec.	Russia gives ultimatum to breakaway Chechen Republic to disband army and free all prisoners; failure to reach agreement leads to major military assault on Chechen Republic (27th).

1995

June	Russia and Ukraine finally settle dispute over Black Sea fleet.
Nov.	Shevardnadze wins new term as President of Georgia.
3 Nov.	Yeltsin forced to relinquish control of four key ministries after second heart attack.
26 Dec.	Yeltsin resumes powers.

1996

5 Jan.	Liberal Russian Foreign Minister Andrei Kozrev resigns.
15 Feb.	Yeltsin announces intention of seeking second term.
Apr.	Presidents of Belarus and Russia sign a treaty providing for political, economic and military integration.
July	Prime Minister of Ukraine survives an assassination attempt.
4 July	Yeltsin wins presidential election in second round run-off.
Nov.	Constitutional referendum in Belarus gives greater powers to President.

1997

Jan.	Russian withdrawal of troops from Chechnya is completed.
Mar.	Reorganisation of government favours reformists.
Nov.	Agreement with Japan aims to end dispute over Kurile Islands and formally end Second World War.

1998

Mar.	Chernomyrdin is dismissed by Yeltsin.
Apr.	Sergei Kiriyenko is confirmed as Prime Minister.
Aug.	Kiriyenko is dismissed; Yeltsin reappoints Chernomyrdin.
Sept.	Yevgenii Primakov approved by Duma as compromise candidate after Duma continues to reject the reappointment of Chernomyrdin.
Nov.	Constitutional Court confirms Yeltsin cannot stand for a further term in presidency.

1999

31 Dec.	Resignation of Yeltsin.

2000

May	Putin inaugurated as President of Russian Federation.

2001

July	Russia and China sign Treaty of Friendship, cementing the post-Soviet relations of their countries.
	Pact with USA on missile talks.
	Land Bill passes Duma (257–130), reversing nationalisation of land carried out in Soviet era.

129

Eastern Europe since 1985

1986

Sept. Solidarity announces intention of working within the existing system in Poland.

1987

June Karoly Grosz, an economic liberal, becomes Prime Minister in Hungary.

Nov. Polish government holds referendum for programme of radical reform; Solidarity calls for boycott and the proposals are rejected.

17 Dec. Gustav Husák resigns party leadership in Czechoslovakia, and is succeeded by another conservative, Milos Jakes.

1988

Jan. Hungarian government announces end of price controls.

Mar.–Aug. Wave of strikes and unrest in Poland; Solidarity demands talks with government.

May In Hungary, Kadar is relegated to post of Party President; Grosz becomes Party Secretary and Prime Minister; purge of conservatives in Central Committee and Politburo.

Dec. Polish government accepts 'round table' talks with Solidarity.

1989

Jan. Law on Association in Hungary allows political parties to be formed; new draft constitution (Mar.) drops reference to leading role for Communist Party.

6 Feb. Solidarity and Polish government open talks on Poland's future.

Mar.–Apr. Solidarity accepts terms for participation in elections; government agrees to admit opposition to the lower house of parliament (*Sejm*), a freely elected Senate, and create office of President. Solidarity legalised.

June First free parliamentary elections in Poland since Second World War; Solidarity obtains landslide victory in seats it is allowed to contest. Hungarian government recognises Imre Nagy, leader of 1956 rising, and permits his reburial with full honours.

July General Jaruzelski elected President of Poland by one-vote margin. General Kiszczak appointed Prime Minister but fails to form a government and resigns; Solidarity activist, Tadeuz Mazowiecki, becomes Prime Minister, heading first non-communist government.

Sept.	Hungary opens border with Austria allowing flight of thousands of East Germans to the West.
Oct.	Erich Honecker is replaced as President by Egon Krenz in East Germany (18th) following flight of East Germans to the West and mass demonstrations in East German cities organised by New Forum opposition group. Krenz meets opposition group (26th); travel restrictions are discussed.
Nov.	East German Council of Ministers resigns *en masse* following huge demonstrations in East Berlin and other cities. New Forum opposition legalised and Politburo resigns (7th–8th). Berlin Wall opened and travel restrictions lifted on East German citizens (9th). Reformer, Hans Modrow, becomes President (13th). President Todor Zhivkov of Bulgaria resigns (10th). Entire Czech Politburo resigns (24th) following mass demonstrations in Prague by Civic Forum opposition group.
Dec.	Resignation of Czech Prime Minister, Adamec, is forced by further mass demonstrations and general strike. Communist monopoly of power is ended and joint interim government formed with members of Civic Forum (7th–9th). Resignation of Egon Krenz as communist leader in East Germany (8th). Preparations for free elections begin. Hundreds are reported killed in anti-Ceausescu demonstrations in Romanian city of Timisoara (17th). Bulgaria declares it will hold free elections (19th). Brandenburg Gate is opened between East and West Berlin as symbolic act of reconciliation between the two Germanies (22nd). Mass demonstrations in Bucharest and other Romanian cities. After initial attempts to disperse them, the army joins the crowds and Ceausescu and his wife flee (22nd). Heavy fighting between pro-Ceausescu forces and the army leaves several hundred killed and wounded in Bucharest and other Romanian cities; Ceausescu and his wife are arrested and executed by Military Tribunal (25th). Free elections are announced for April 1990; Ion Iliescu becomes President (26th). Václav Havel, former dissident and political prisoner, is unanimously elected President of Czechoslovakia (29th); Alexander Dubček is earlier elected Chairman (Speaker) of Czech parliament (28th).

1990

Mar.	East German elections lead to victory (18th) of pro-unification Alliance for Germany, consisting of the Christian Democratic Union and allies, with over 48 per cent of the vote; coalition government under CDU leader Lothar de Mazière prepares for economic unification in July and all-German elections in December. Hungarian elections result in victory for

Democratic Forum with 43 per cent of the vote; coalition government is formed with Christian Democrat and Small-holder parties, seeking access to the EEC and rapid adoption of Western economic models.

May   Romanian elections lead to overwhelming victory of National Salvation Front under former communist minister, Ion Iliescu. The Bulgarian Socialist Party, formerly the Communist Party, obtains a clear majority in the first free elections since the overthrow of the communist regime.

June   Protests in Bucharest at domination of former communists in government lead to serious rioting; police attack demonstrators and National Salvation Front calls on miners to restore order. Czech elections lead to victory for Civic Forum/Public Against Violence with 169 of 300 seats, with backing of President Havel.

July   East and West German economic unification on the basis of the West German currency. German–Soviet agreement between Chancellor Kohl and President Gorbachev (16th) that a united Germany will have full sovereignty, including the right to join NATO; Soviet Union agrees to withdraw its 350,000 troops from East Germany within three to four years. Paris meeting (17th) of 'Two plus Four' talks, consisting of representatives from East and West Germany and the four former Allied powers, the USA, the United Kingdom, the Soviet Union and France, with participants from the Polish government, agrees to guarantee the existing Polish–German border along the Oder–Neisse River with a definitive treaty to be signed following German unification. Agreement to negotiate a second treaty on Polish–German relations, including reparations and protection for the rights of German minorities living in Poland. Ukraine declares its intention to become a sovereign state with its own army and foreign policy.

Aug.   Lech Walesa declares he will be a candidate for President in forthcoming elections. Growing evidence of splits within Solidarity ranks.

Sept.   Treaty signed (12th) after 'Two plus Four' talks, agreeing to end special powers by the wartime Allies over Germany and for the unification with full sovereignty of East and West Germany.

3 Oct.   Reunification of Germany.

Dec.   Widespread anti-communist riots in Albania after first legal opposition party formed. First all-German elections elect conservative Kohl's CDU/CSU government; ex-communist PDS is reduced to 17 seats (2nd).

9 Dec.   Walesa is elected President of Poland.

1991

Mar.	Albania opens diplomatic relations with the West.
Oct.	First completely free election in Poland produces inconclusive result, proliferation of parties and turnout below 50 per cent.
4 Nov.	Formation of independent National Guard in the Ukraine.

1992

3 Apr.	The leader of Albanian Democratic Party, Sali Berisha, is elected President by People's Assembly.
June	Vote of no confidence in Polish government of Prime Minister Jan Olszewski. Czechoslovakian general elections held, dominated by issue of dissolution of the state. Klaus becomes Czech premier, Meciar becomes premier of Slovakia; talks on split proceed in earnest.
July	Slovak National Council approves declaration of sovereignty; resignation of Václav Havel as Federal President.
Aug.	Agreement is reached on split of Czechoslovakia into two independent states on 1 Jan. 1993.
Oct.	President Iliescu wins further four-year term in Romania.
Nov.	Czechoslovak federal parliament approves split into Czech and Slovak states.

1993

Jan.	Formal separation of Czech and Slovak states; Havel re-appointed as President of Czech Republic.
26 Oct.	Coalition government is formed under Polish Peasant Party leader Waldemar Pawlak.

1994

29 May	Former communists, now Hungarian Socialist Party, come to power after two rounds of voting.
June–July	Lukashenka wins presidential elections in Belarus.
Dec.	Former communists win outright majority in Bulgaria.

1995

1 Mar.	In Poland, former communist Jozef Oleksy is elected Prime Minister following resignation of Pawlak.
Nov.	Walesa is defeated by former communist Aleksander Kwaśniewski in Polish presidential election.

1996

Jan.	Resignation of Polish Prime Minister Oleksy over allegations that he once spied for Russia.
May	Ruling Albanian Democratic Party claims to have won 100 of 140 seats in general election; widespread protests by the opposition.
June	Ruling Civic Democratic Party wins Czech elections.
Nov.	Lukashenka is given authoritarian powers in Belarus referendum.

1997

Jan.	Massive street demonstrations take place in Bulgaria against Socialist (ex-communist) government. Serious rioting in major towns in Albania.
June	Internationally supervised elections are held in Albania.
8 July	Hungary, Poland and the Czech Republic are invited to join NATO.

1998

Jan.	Havel is re-elected President in Czech Republic. National Assembly in Poland ratifies Concordat with Roman Catholic Church.
June	Viktor Orban becomes Prime Minister in Hungary.
July	Zeman becomes Prime Minister in Czech Republic.

1999

Mar.	Czech Republic, Hungary and Poland become full members of NATO.
Dec.	Solidarity announces its withdrawal from politics to become an 'organisation of employees'.

2000

Feb.	Moldova becomes first former Soviet republic to vote Communist Party back into power.
June	Ferenc Mádl is elected President of Hungary.
Oct.	Kwaśniewski is re-elected President of Poland.
Dec.	Ion Iliescu is re-elected President in Romania.

2001

5 Apr.	Moldovan parliament elects Communist Party leader Vladimir Voronin as President – first ex-Soviet republic to elect a communist to be head of state.

26 Apr.	Ukraine's pro-Western and reformist Prime Minister, Viktor Yushchenko, is dismissed.
17 June	National Movement for Simeon II wins Bulgarian election (with 120 seats and 43 per cent of the vote), defeating ruling UDF (Union of Democratic Forces). Bulgaria becomes first East European country where a former monarch has made a political comeback.
July	Former King Simeon II (Simeon Saxe-Coburgotski) formally returns to power as Prime Minister in Bulgaria.
Sept.	Polish general election gives electoral humiliation to Solidarity.
Nov.	Bulgarian presidential election is won by former communist Georgi Parvanov (now Socialist Party leader).

2002

Dec.	Copenhagen Summit admits former Eastern bloc states to EU (see p. 204). This follows major NATO expansion eastwards.

The disintegration of Yugoslavia

1987

May	Milosevic secures control of Serbian Communist Party.

1989

May	Milosevic becomes Serbian Prime Minister. Removal of autonomy for Kosovo.

1990

Apr.	First multi-party elections in Yugoslavian Republics lead to victories for anti-communist parties in Slovenia and Croatia, increasing pressure of independence movements and the effective dissolution of the Yugoslav Communist Party.

1991

May	First serious casualties in fighting between Serbs and Croats in Yugoslavia.
25 June	Croatia declares independence from Yugoslavia. Widespread fighting begins as Yugoslav army seizes Slovenian border posts. Fighting between Croatian militias and Serbian irregulars and Federal army.
18 Nov.	European Community imposes sanctions on Yugoslavia.

1992

Jan.	European Union recognises Croatia and Slovenia.
21 Feb.	UN Security Council agrees to send a 14,000-strong force to Bosnia. Bosnia–Herzegovina declares independence; Bosnian Serbs proclaim separate state.
6 Apr.	Bosnia is recognised as independent by EU and USA; Serbs begin campaign of 'ethnic cleansing' in north and east Bosnia, expelling Muslim population to create a pure Serb corridor linking Serb areas of western Bosnia with Serbia. Serbian forces begin artillery bombardment of Sarajevo.
May	'Cleansing' of Muslims and Croats from Brcko begins and systematic killing at Banja Luka and elsewhere, resulting in some 3,000 dead. UN trade embargo is placed on Serbia.
July	Airlift of relief supplies into Sarajevo begins.
Aug.	Existence of Serb-run concentration camps is disclosed. President Franco Tudjman and Croatian Democratic Union win victory in first Croatian elections. London Conference sets up Geneva peace talks for former Yugoslavia.
15 Sept.	Federal Republic of Yugoslavia is excluded from UN General Assembly.
Nov.	UN enforces naval blockade on Serbia and Montenegro.
Dec.	Ex-communist President Milan Kučan and ruling Liberal Democrat Party win elections in Slovenia; UN peacekeeping forces are deployed in Macedonia to prevent spread of unrest.
21 Dec.	Milosevic wins presidential elections in Serbia.

1993

Jan.	Geneva peace conference on Bosnia opens; Bosnian Serbs provisionally agree to end the war, but fighting continues.
Feb.	UN Security Council votes to create war crimes tribunal for Yugoslavia. Bosnian town of Cerska falls to Serbs.
1 Apr.	Athens peace talks on former Yugoslavia open.
3 Apr.	Serbs reject UN peace plan; Bosnian Serbs also reject UN peace plan (25th). Former Yugoslav Republic of Macedonia is admitted to UN.
May	War crimes tribunal for former Yugoslavia is established at The Hague.
6 May	UN Security Council declares Sarajevo and other Muslim enclaves UN-monitored safe areas.
June	Provisional agreement at Geneva on three-way partition of Bosnia–Herzegovina into Muslim, Serb and Croat areas.

1994

9 Feb.	Serb mortar attack on Sarajevo market, killing over 60 people, leads to UN ultimatum on removal of Serb artillery from 20km exclusion zone.
28 Feb.	NATO fighters shoot down Serbian aircraft.
Apr.	UN safe area of Gorazde comes under Serb attack; NATO aircraft bomb Serb positions; Serbs retaliate by taking UN observers hostage.
July	Contact Group of diplomats from Russia, USA, France, Britain and Germany proposes division of Bosnia, but rejected by Serbs.
Aug.	Serbian government imposes sanctions on the Bosnian Serbs.
Nov.	USA announces unilateral suspension of international arms embargo following renewal of fighting in Bosnia.
Dec.	Four-month truce agreed in Bosnia.

1995

May	Croatian forces open fighting against Serbs. NATO planes attack Serb positions and Bosnian Serbs again take UN hostages.
June	Western nations send 'rapid reaction' force to Bosnia.
July	Serb forces overrun UN safe areas of Srebrenica and Zepa; by the end of the month photographic evidence of mass graves leads to the indictment of Bosnian Serb leader, Radovan Karadzic, and military chief, Ratko Mladic, for crimes against humanity.
Aug.	Further Serb mortar attacks on Sarajevo lead to NATO air strikes against Bosnian Serb military positions.
12 Oct.	New ceasefire comes into effect in Bosnia.
Nov.	Yugoslav peace talks open in Dayton, Ohio (1st); peace plan agreed (21st).
14 Dec.	Yugoslav peace agreement is signed in Paris.

1996

29 Feb.	Siege of Sarajevo officially ends.
Sept.	First elections in Bosnia.
Dec.	Street demonstrations in Serbia against government's refusal to accept opposition successes in municipal elections.

1997

Jan.	Serbian government concedes opposition victories after international inspection.

	Growing attacks on Serbian leaders in Kosovo by separatist Kosovo Liberation Army (KLA) which had first begun attacks in 1996.
July	Federal Parliament elects Milosevic Yugoslav President.

1998

Feb.–Mar.	Serbian police kill dozens of ethnic Albanians in operations against separatists. Massive anti-Serb demonstrations in Pristina, capital of Kosovo.
Apr.	Serbs vote 95 per cent against international intervention in a referendum.
May	Shuttle diplomacy by US envoy Richard Holbrooke.
July–Aug.	KLA expands control to 40–50 per cent of Kosovo. Massive Serbian offensive weakens KLA. Continued heavy fighting.
Sept.	USA demands ceasefire in Kosovo. UN Security Council endorses call.
Oct.	NATO allies authorise air strikes; Milosevic agrees to withdraw troops (27th). Observers from Organisation for Security and Co-operation in Europe (OSCE) to enter Kosovo.
Dec.	Renewed clashes of KLA with Serb border guards. Mediation attempts by US envoy Christopher Hill.

1999

15 Jan.	Discovery of 45 bodies (presumed to be ethnic Albanians) in village of Racak. Expulsion of OSCE chief (18th).
6–23 Feb.	Peace talks at Rambouillet fail to achieve breakthrough.
18–19 Mar.	Peace deal is signed by Kosovo Albanians in Paris, but rejected by Yugoslavia. Massing of Yugoslav troops around Kosovo.
20 Mar.	Yugoslav armed units begin ethnic cleansing of Kosovo.
24 Mar.	NATO aircraft begin air strikes against Yugoslav targets. Start of the NATO war on Yugoslavia over Kosovo (see p. 181).
27 Mar.	Refugees pour into Macedonia and Albania.
Apr.	NATO missiles hit Ministry of Interior in Belgrade and Socialist Party of Serbia HQ. Yeltsin warns NATO. Serb Deputy Prime Minister Vuk Draskovic is sacked.
27 May	UN War Crimes Tribunal confirms that Milosevic has been indicted as a war criminal. NATO war missions continue.
10 June	Suspension of NATO bombing campaign after withdrawal of Serbian troops from Kosovo. NATO troops (KFOR) are based in Kosovo which becomes an international protectorate.

2000

Sept.	Election called for 24 Sept. (after amendment to Yugoslav Constitution allows Milosevic to serve two more terms). Bitterly disputed and rigged election. Federal Elections Commission calls for second round of voting. Growing discontent and protests.
3 Oct.	Milosevic threatens to crack down on growing number of protestors.
4 Oct.	Protests gather momentum in southern Serbian town of Nis. Thousands of riot police are sent to fight striking miners south of Belgrade.
5 Oct.	Storming of Serbian parliament in Belgrade. Workers and sympathisers break through barriers, setting fire to parliament building.
6 Oct.	Milosevic (now ousted from power) has meeting with Russian Foreign Minister Igor Ivanov.
7 Oct.	Arrival of Kostunica at Belgrade's Sava centre to be sworn in as President.
9 Oct.	Resignation of Momir Bulatovich; end of some EU sanctions.
10 Oct.	Belgrade renews diplomatic ties with UK and other NATO countries.

2001

Mar.	Arrest of Milosevic (30th) after long police surveillance.
July	Milosevic is taken to The Hague to face War Crimes Tribunal. President Kostunica appoints Dragisa Pesic (of Montenegrin Socialist People's Party) as Prime Minister (17th).
Aug.	Peace deal is agreed in Macedonia (13th).
Sept.	Arms embargo on Yugoslavia (imposed in Mar. 1998) is lifted by UN Security Council, marking end of last international sanctions against Belgrade.

2002

Feb.	Trial of Milosevic for war crimes begins at The Hague.

THE ROAD TO EUROPEAN UNION

Note This chronology refers to the abbreviations current at the time (e.g. EEC after 1957, EU after Maastricht Treaty takes effect).

1946

19 Sept.	Winston Churchill, in a speech at Zurich, urges Franco–German reconciliation with 'a kind of United States of Europe'.

1947

5 June General Marshall proposes US aid to stimulate recovery in Europe.

29 Oct. Creation of Benelux – economic union of Belgium, Luxembourg and the Netherlands.

1948

16 Apr. Convention for European Economic Co-operation is signed – the birth of OEEC. OEEC is established to receive Marshall Aid from the USA (see p. 308).

1949

5 May Statute of the Council of Europe signed by Belgium, Denmark, France, Ireland, Italy, Luxembourg, the Netherlands, Norway, Sweden and Britain.

1950

9 May Robert Schuman makes his historic proposal to place French and German coal and steel under a common authority.

1951

18 Apr. Treaty setting up the European Coal and Steel Community (ECSC) is signed in Paris by Belgium, France, Germany (Federal Republic), Luxembourg, Italy and the Netherlands.

1952

27 May European Defence Community (EDC) established by the Six. French National Assembly rejected the EDC Treaty in Aug. 1954. EDC collapsed.

European Political Community proposed by the Six to incorporate EDC and ECSC. Collapses.

10 Aug. ECSC High Authority begins functioning, with Jean Monnet as President.

Nordic Council established by Denmark, Iceland, Norway and Sweden; Finland joins in 1955.

Greece and Turkey join NATO.

1953

10 Feb. ECSC common market for coal, iron ore, and scrap is opened.

1 May ECSC common market for steel is opened.

1955

1–3 June Messina Conference: the Foreign Ministers of the ECSC's six member states propose further steps towards full integration in Europe.

1957

25 Mar. Signing of the Rome Treaties setting up the European Economic Community (EEC) and the European Atomic Energy Community (Euratom). The Treaty of Rome is signed by Belgium, France, Germany (Federal Republic), Luxembourg, Italy and the Netherlands.

1958

1 Jan. Rome Treaties come into force: the EEC and Euratom are established.

19–21 Mar. First session of the European Parliament – Robert Schuman is elected President.

1959

1 Jan. First tariff reductions and quota enlargements in the EEC. Establishment of common market for nuclear materials.

20 Nov. European Free Trade Association (EFTA) convention is signed between Austria, Denmark, Norway, Portugal, Sweden, Switzerland and Britain.

1961

9 July Greece signs association agreement with EEC (comes into force 1 Nov. 1962).

1 Aug. Republic of Ireland applies for membership of EEC.

10 Aug. UK and Denmark request negotiations aimed at membership of EEC.

8 Nov. Negotiations with the UK open in Brussels.

15 Dec. The three neutral countries (outside the NATO alliance) – Austria, Sweden and Switzerland – apply for association with EEC.

1962

30 Apr. Norway requests negotiations for membership of EEC.

 Common Agricultural Policy (CAP) is agreed between EEC members to come into operation in 1964; a system of high guaranteed prices for European farmers paid for out of a common agricultural fund with protective tariffs against imports.

1963

14 Jan. President de Gaulle declares that the UK is not ready for membership of EEC.

29 Jan. UK negotiations with the EEC broken off.

1 July Yaoundé Convention is signed, associating 18 independent states in Africa and Madagascar with the EEC for five years from 1 June 1964.

12 Sept. Turkey signs association agreement with EEC (comes into force 1 Dec. 1964).

1964

15 Dec. Council adopts the Mansholt Plan for common prices for grains.

1965

31 Mar. European Commission proposes that, as from 1 July 1967, all EEC countries' import duties and levies be paid into Community budget and that powers of European Parliament be increased.

8 Apr. Six sign treaty merging the Community Executives.

31 May European Commission publishes first memorandum proposing lines of Community policy for regional development.

1 July Council fails to reach agreement by deadline on financing common farm policy; French boycott of Community institutions begins seven-month-long crisis.

26 July Council meets and conducts business without French representative present.

1966

17 Jan. Six Foreign Ministers meet in Luxembourg without Commission present and agree to resume full Community activity.

10 Nov. UK Prime Minister Harold Wilson announces plans for 'a high-level approach' to the Six with intention of entering EEC.

1967

11 May Britain lodges formal application for membership of the European Economic Community (along with Ireland, Denmark and Norway).

1968

16 May Second de Gaulle veto on British application.

1969

25 Apr.   De Gaulle resigns as President of France.

2 Dec.   At a Summit conference at The Hague the Community formally agrees to open membership negotiations with the UK, Norway, Denmark and the Republic of Ireland on their applications of 1967.

1970

29 June   Talks begin in Luxembourg between the Six and the UK, Norway, Denmark and the Republic of Ireland.

27 Oct.   Davignon Report (on political co-operation) approved.

Oct.   Presentation of Werner Report on full Economic and Monetary Union (EMU).

1971

23 June   The Council of Ministers of the Community announces that agreement has been reached with Britain for the basis of the accession of the UK to the Communities.

11–13 July At a ministerial-level negotiating session, agreement is reached on major outstanding issues: the transitional period for the UK, Commonwealth Sugar, Capital Movements, and the common commercial policy.

28 Oct.   Vote in the House of Commons on the motion 'That this House approves Her Majesty's Government's decision of principle to join the European Communities on the basis of the arrangements which have been negotiated'. The voting figures in the House of Commons were 356 for, 244 against, a majority of 112; in the House of Lords 451 for, 58 against, a majority of 393.

1972

22 Jan.   Treaty of Accession is signed in Brussels between the European Communities (France, Belgium, Germany, Italy, Luxembourg and the Netherlands) on the one side and Britain, Denmark, Norway and the Republic of Ireland on the other.

22 July   EEC signs free trade agreements with Austria, Iceland, Portugal, Sweden and Switzerland.

26 Sept.   Rejection by Norway of full membership of EEC following a referendum.

31 Dec.   UK and Denmark withdraw from EFTA.

1973

1 Jan.   UK, Republic of Ireland and Denmark join the EEC.

1974	Agreement that heads of government should meet three times a year under the title of the European Council.
1975	Britain confirms membership of the EEC by referendum. Greece applies for membership.
June	European Regional Development Fund is set up.
1977	Portugal and Spain apply for membership of the EEC. Roy Jenkins is appointed President of the Commission.
1979	
May	European Monetary System is introduced with a common European Currency Unit (ECU) linking the exchange rates of individual countries.
June	First direct elections held to the European Parliament, when 410 members (MEPs) are elected.
1980	'Crocodile Group' established by MEPs wishing to see radical reform of the Community.
1981	
Jan.	Greece becomes 10th member of the EEC: entry to be phased over five years.
1983	
June	Agreement at Stuttgart Summit on principle of budgetary reform and reform of Common Agricultural Policy (CAP); Common Fisheries Policy is established.
1984	
June	Fontainebleau Summit agrees principles of budgetary discipline and UK budget rebate.
1985	Spain and Portugal sign accession treaty to join the EC from 1 Jan. 1986. At summit meeting in Luxembourg heads of state draw up main principles of a 'single Europe', defining 1992 as date for completion of frontierless internal market within the EC with open frontiers, harmonisation of regulations, free movement of labour and capital. These principles were contained in the Single European Act which also extended majority voting in the Council of Ministers.
1986	
Feb.	Single European Act is signed by member states and ratified by their parliaments. European flag is adopted.

1988

Feb. Delors reforms of the European budget agreed, putting controls on farm spending and expanding structural funds. Committee is set up under Delors to prepare plans for European Monetary Union (EMU).

Sept. Mrs Thatcher makes Bruges speech attacking attempts to create a European 'superstate'.

1989

Apr. Agreement is reached that first stage of EMU will begin on 1 July 1990 with all 12 members beginning to adhere to the EMS. Austria applies to join Community.

June Third direct elections to European Parliament. Madrid Summit receives Delors Plan for three-stage European Monetary Union.

1990

Oct. Britain joins EMS.

Dec. Inter-government Conference on EMU plans further development of EMU.

1991

Oct. Luxembourg plan for inter-government conference at Maastricht turned down.

Dec. Maastricht Summit gives Britain opt-out clauses over monetary union and Social Charter.

1992

June Danes reject Maastricht in referendum.

Mitterrand announces French referendum for 20 Sept.

Irish ratify Maastricht.

Britain and Italy forced out of Exchange Rate Mechanism (ERM), following huge speculation.

France, Belgium, Britain, Spain, Germany and the Netherlands vote to ratify Maastricht.

Nov. Norway applies for membership.

1993

Jan. Irish punt devalued. Spanish and Portuguese currencies follow. Single market comes into force. Austria agrees to seek EC membership.

May Danes finally approve Maastricht Treaty.

Aug.	ERM bands widened to 15 per cent, virtually destroying the existing system.
Nov.	Maastricht Treaty on European Union takes effect; European Community (EC) now becomes European Union (EU).

1994

Feb.	EU agrees basis for discussing membership applications of Finland, Austria, Norway and Sweden.
Mar.	Britain opposes dilution of veto rules consequent on EU enlargement.
Apr.	Hungary and Poland apply for EU membership.
May	European Parliament votes to approve accession treaties of Austria, Finland, Norway and Sweden.
July	Jacques Santer of Luxembourg is chosen to succeed Jacques Delors as President of European Commission. Austrian, Finnish and Swedish referendums approve EU membership. Norway votes against.

1995

July	Schengen Group, seven out of 15 EU states, remove all border controls.
	Czech Republic, Latvia and Estonia apply for EU membership. EU Summit in Madrid confirms timetable for a single European currency by 1999, to be named the 'euro'.
Nov.	Italy rejoins ERM.

1996

Dec.	Plans for 'euro' currency and timetable for single currency confirmed at Dublin Summit.

1997

Jan.	John Major effectively rules out Britain joining single currency in 1999 (now 'extremely unlikely').
May	Labour victory in British general election followed by outline acceptance of Social Chapter.
June	Amsterdam Treaty signed on European border controls.
	European Union accepts principle of negotiated entry for Cyprus, Slovenia, Estonia, Hungary, Poland and the Czech Republic.

1998

Mar. Start of entry negotiations for 11 former communist bloc states (plus Cyprus) under British presidency. Brussels Summit gives formal go-ahead for monetary union for 11 states.

1999

1 Jan. Eleven countries of the European Union enter the third phase of EMU and adopt the euro.

1 May Amsterdam Treaty comes into force.

8–13 June Fifth direct elections to European Parliament.

15 Sept. Romano Prodi invested as President of European Commission.

2000

Sept. Referendum in Denmark narrowly (53.2 per cent) rejects adoption of euro.

Nice Summit agrees framework for enlargement in Treaty of Nice.

2001

1 Jan. Greece becomes 12th country to join up to euro.

Ireland votes against enlargement in referendum.

Mar. Referendum in Switzerland rejects talks with EU on membership.

2002

1 Jan. Successful launch of euro in 12 participating countries signals final end for mark, franc, lira, etc.

19 Oct. Second referendum in Republic of Ireland approves Treaty of Nice, paving way for expansion of EU.

Dec. Copenhagen Summit agrees on admission of 10 new members from May 2004. These are the Czech Republic, Poland, Hungary, Slovenia, Slovakia, Latvia, Lithuania, Estonia, Cyprus and Malta.

NATIONS, RULERS AND MINISTERS

Albania

Albania achieved independence from Ottoman rule in 1912, but Italian forces occupied the country from 1914 to 1920. Albania became a republic in 1925 and a monarchy in 1928. The ruler from 1928 to 1939 was King Zog I (Ahmed Zogu). During the Second World War Albania was under Italian and German rule. A republic was proclaimed on 12 Jan. 1946. The effective ruler until 1985 was Enver Hoxha.

Presidents

O. Nishani   1946–53
H. Lleshi   1953–82
R. Alia   1982–92

Following the collapse of communism, Sali Berisha was President from 1992 to 1997. He was succeeded by R. Mejdani in July 1997.

Austria

Emperors

Francis Joseph   1848–1916 (after 1867 Emperor of Austria–Hungary)
Charles   1916–18 (abdicated)

Principal ministers

The following individuals wielded effective power in the last days of the Empire.

M. W. von Beck   1906–08
Count R. von Biernerth   1908–11
Count C. von Sturgkh   1912–16

Presidents (after the proclamation of the Republic on 12 Nov. 1918)

Dr X. Seits   1918–20 (stood in for head of state)
Dr M. Hainisch   1920–28
Dr W. Miklas   1928–38

From 1938 to 1945, Austria was part of the German Reich.

Presidents after 1945

K. Renner   1945–50
T. Körner   1951–57
A. Schárf   1957–65
F. Jonas   1965–74
B. Kreisky   1974 (Apr.–July)
R. Kirchschläger   1974–86

| K. Waldheim | 1986–92 |
| T. Klestil | 1992– |

Belarus

Belarus adopted a declaration of independence from the Soviet Union on 25 Aug. 1991. It adopted the name Republic of Belarus in Sept. A new constitution was only adopted in 1994.

Presidents

S. Shuskevich	1991–94
M. Hryb	1994 (Jan.–July)
A. Lukashenka	1994–*

* Re-elected 2001.

Belgium

Kings

Leopold II	1865–1909
Albert I	1909–34
Leopold III	1934–51*
Prince Charles (Regent)	1944–50
Leopold III	1950 (20 July–10 Aug.)
Baudouin, Prince Royal	(after 11 Aug. 1950)
Baudouin I	1951–93
Albert II	1993–

* Leopold III was a prisoner of war, May 1940–45. There was a Regency (1944–50) after which Leopold briefly resumed his duties (1950), Baudouin then took over, and Leopold formally abdicated in July 1951.

Bosnia–Herzegovina

Formerly part of the Ottoman Empire, it became a protectorate of the Austro–Hungarian Empire in 1878 (and was annexed to Austria–Hungary in 1908). Became a part of newly-formed Yugoslavia after the First World War. Following the disintegration of Yugoslavia, and after a referendum within Bosnia–Herzegovina, a declaration of independence was promulgated in Mar. 1992.

Presidents

A. Izetbegovič	1990–98
Z. Radisič	1998–99
A. Jelavič	1999–

Bulgaria

Bulgaria remained under Turkish rule until 1878. It gained full independence (as the Kingdom of Bulgaria) in 1908. An ally of Germany, it was occupied by the Soviet Union in 1944 and a Socialist People's Republic was founded in 1946. A new constitution was adopted in 1991.

Kings

Ferdinand I	1908–18
Boris III	1918–43
Simeon II	1943–46

On 8 Sept. 1946 a plebiscite ended the monarchy and established a republic, but there was no head of state until the new constitution came into force in Dec. 1947. During communist rule after 1946 the head of state was the Chairman of the Praesidium. The most important figure was T. Zhivkov who was in power from 1971 to 1989.

Heads of State (since fall of communism)

Z. Zhelev	1990–97
P. Stoyanov	1997–02
G. Parvanov	2002–

Croatia

Before 1918 Croatia was part of the Austro–Hungarian Empire. It subsequently formed part of Yugoslavia. An independent Fascist puppet state existed in the Second World War. Following a declaration of disassociation from Yugoslavia in June 1991, a formal declaration of independence was promulgated on 8 Oct. 1991.

Presidents

F. Tudjman*	1990–99
S. Mesic	2000–

* Elected by the *Sabor*, May 1990; re-elected by popular vote, Aug. 1992. Died in office, 1999.

Czechoslovakia

Founded as an independent state on 14 Nov. 1918. The state was dissolved and the Czech Republic and Slovakia became independent states on 1 Jan. 1993.

Presidents

T. Masaryk	1918–35
E. Beneš*	1935–38
E. Hácha	1938–45

* Beneš was President of the Czech government-in-exile after the proclamation of a German Protectorate in Mar. 1939. Beneš returned to Czechoslovakia in 1945.

E. Beneš	1945–48
K. Gottwald	1948–53
A. Zápotechý	1953–57
A. Novotný	1957–68
L. Svoboda	1968–75
G. Husák	1975–89
V. Havel*	1989–92

* Havel became President of the new Czech Republic.

Czech Republic

The Czech Republic was formed on 1 Jan. 1993 when Czechoslovakia ceased to exist, having split into the separate Czech and Slovak Republics.

President

V. Havel	1993–2003
V. Klaus	2003–

Denmark

Sovereigns

Christian IX	1863–1906
Frederick VIII	1906–12
Christian X	1912–47
Frederick IX	1947–72
Margaret II	1972–

Estonia

Before 1918, part of Tsarist Russia. An independent republic, 1918–40. Forcibly incorporated into Soviet Union, 1940. Following the collapse of communism, Estonia declared independence on 20 Aug. 1991.

Presidents

L. Meri	1992–2001
A. Ruutel	2001–

Finland

Finland proclaimed independence on 6 Dec. 1917 (having previously been part of Tsarist Russia).

Presidents

Prof. K. J. Ståhlberg	1919–25
Dr L. Relander	1925–31
Dr P. E. Svinhufvud	1931–37
K. Kallio	1937–40
Dr R. Ryti	1940–44
Field-Marshal C. Mannerheim	1944–45
J. Paasikivi	1945–56
Dr U. Kekkonen	1956–81
Dr M. Koivisto	1981–94
M. Ahtisaari	1994–2000
T. Halonen	2000–

France

Third Republic

Presidents

E. Loubet	1899–1906
A. Fallières	1906–13
R. Poincaré	1913–20
P. Deschanel	1920 (Jan.–Sept.)
A. Millerand	1920–24
G. Doumergue	1924–31
P. Doumer	1931–32
A. Lebrun	1932–40

On 11 July 1940 Marshal Pétain took over the powers of President and added them to his own as Prime Minister. He then appointed a chief of state.

Chief of State

Adm. Darlan	1941–42
P. Laval	1942–44

The provisional government of de Gaulle was recognised in Oct. 1944. A new constitution came into force on 24 Dec. 1946 (Fourth Republic).

Prime Ministers: Interwar France

G. Clemenceau	1917–20
A. Millerand	1920 (Jan.–Oct.)
M. Leygues	1920–21

A. Briand	1921–22
R. Poincaré	1922–24
F. Marsal	1924 (June only)
E. Herriot	1924–25
M. Painlevé	1925 (May–Nov.)
A. Briand	1925–26
R. Poincaré	1926–29
A. Briand	1929 (July–Nov.)
A. Tardieu	1929–30
M. Steeg	1930–31
P. Laval	1931–32
A. Tardieu	1932 (Feb.–June)
E. Herriot	1932 (June–Dec.)
J. Paul-Boncour	1932–33
E. Daladier	1933 (Jan.–Oct.)
A. Sarraut	1933 (Oct.–Nov.)
C. Chautemps	1933–34
E. Daladier	1934 (Jan.–Feb.)
G. Doumergue	1934 (Feb.–Nov.)
P.-E. Flandin	1934–35
F. Bouisson	1935 (June only)
P. Laval	1935–36
A. Sarrault	1936 (Jan.–June)
L. Blum	1936–37 (June–June)
C. Chautemps	1937–38 (June–Mar.)
L. Blum	1938 (Mar.–Apr.)
E. Daladier	1938–40
P. Reynaud	1940 (Mar.–June)
Marshal P. Pétain	1940–42

Fourth Republic

Presidents of the Republic

V. Auriol	1947–53
R. Coty	1953–58

A new constitution came into force on 5 Oct. 1958 (Fifth Republic).

Fifth Republic

Presidents of the Republic

Gen. C. de Gaulle	1958–69
G. Pompidou	1969–74
A. Poher	1974 (Apr.–May, interim)

V. Giscard d'Estaing	1974–81
F. Mitterrand	1981–95
J. Chirac*	1995–

* Re-elected, May 2002.

Prime Ministers (after 1946)

F. Gouin	1946 (Jan.–June)
G. Bidault	1946 (June–Dec.)
L. Blum	1946–47 (Jan.)
P. Ramadier	1947 (Jan.–Nov.)
R. Schuman	1947–48 (July)
A. Marie	1948 (July–Sept.)
R. Schuman	1948 (Sept.)
H. Queuille	1948–49
G. Bidault	1949–50
H. Queuille	1950 (July)
R. Pleven	1950–51
H. Queuille	1951 (Mar.–Aug.)
R. Pleven	1951–52
E. Fauré	1952 (Jan.–Mar.)
A. Pinay	1952–53
R. Mayer	1953 (Jan.–June)
J. Laniel	1953–54
P. Mendès-France	1954–55
E. Fauré	1955–56
G. Mollet	1956–57
F. Gaillard	1957–59
M. Debré	1959–62
G. Pompidou	1962–68
M. Couve de Murville	1968–69
J. Chaban-Delmas	1969–72
P. Messmer	1972–74
J. Chirac	1974–76
R. Barre	1976–81
P. Mauroy	1981–84
L. Fabius	1984–86
J. Chirac	1986–88
M. Rocard	1988–91
Mme E. Cresson	1991–92
P. Bérégovoy	1992–93
E. Balladur	1993–95
A. Juppé	1995–97
L. Jospin	1997–2002
J.-P. Raffarin	2002–

Germany

The German Empire was established on 18 Jan. 1871. Henceforth, until 1918, the Kings of Prussia were Emperors of Germany.

Emperors

William (Wilhelm) II   1888–1918 (abdicated)

Chancellors

Baron von Bülow	1900–09
T. Bethmann-Hollweg	1909–17
G. Michaelis	1917
G. von Herling	1917–18
Prince Max of Baden	1918
Friedrich Ebert	1918

The Republic was proclaimed on the abdication of Kaiser William II, on 9 Nov. 1918.

Presidents

Friedrich Ebert	Feb. 1919–Feb. 1925
P. von Hindenburg	Apr. 1925–Aug. 1934

Reich Chancellors, 1919–33

P. Scheidemann	1919 (Feb.–June)
G. Bauer	1919–20
H. Müller	1920 (Mar.–June)
C. Fehrenbach	1920–21
J. Wirth	1921–22
W. Cuno	1922–23
G. Stresemann	1923 (Aug.–Nov.)
W. Marx	1923–24
H. Luther	1925–26
W. Marx	1926–28
H. Müller	1928–30
H. Brüning	1930–32
F. von Papen	1932 (May–Nov.)
K. von Schleicher	1932–33 (Jan.)

Chancellors and Führer

Adolf Hitler	Aug. 1934–Apr. 1945
Adm. C. Dönitz	Apr. 1945–June 1945

After the Allied administration of Germany since 1945, the Federal Republic of Germany (i.e. West Germany) came into being in Sept. 1949. In Oct. 1990, the two halves of Germany were reunited and Kohl became first Chancellor of a reunited Germany.

(1) Heads of State (Presidents)

T. Heuss	1949–59
H. Lübke	1959–69
G. Heinemann	1969–74
W. Scheel	1974–79
K. Carstens	1979–84
R. von Weizsächer	1984–94
R. Herzog	1994–99
J. Rau	1999–

(2) Chancellors

K. Adenauer	1949–63
L. Erhard	1963–66
K. Kiesinger	1966–69
W. Brandt	1969–74
H. Schmidt	1974–82
H. Kohl	1982–98
G. Schröder*	1998–

* Re-elected 2002.

In the German Democratic Republic (East Germany), the position was:

Heads of State (President until 1960, Chairman of the Council of State thereafter)

W. Pieck	1949–60
W. Ulbricht	1960–73
W. Stoph	1973–76
E. Honecker	1976–89*

* After the collapse of communist rule, Manfred Gerlach became interim Head of State. East Germany was united with West Germany in Oct. 1990.

Great Britain

Sovereigns

Victoria	1837–1901
Edward VII	1901–10
George V	1910–36
Edward VIII	1936 (abdicated, never crowned)
George VI	1936–52
Elizabeth II	1952–

Prime Ministers

Marquess of Salisbury	1895–1902
A. J. Balfour	1902–05
Sir Henry Campbell-Bannerman	1905–08

H. H. Asquith	1908–16
David Lloyd George	1916–22
A. Bonar Law	1922–23
Stanley Baldwin	1923–24 (Jan.)
J. Ramsay MacDonald	1924 (Jan.–Nov.)
Stanley Baldwin	1924–29
J. Ramsay MacDonald	1929–35
Stanley Baldwin	1935–37
Neville Chamberlain	1937–40
Winston Churchill	1940–45
Clement Attlee	1945–51
Winston Churchill	1951–55
Anthony Eden	1955–57
Harold Macmillan	1957–63
Sir Alec Douglas-Home	1963–64
Harold Wilson	1964–70
Edward Heath	1970–74
Harold Wilson	1974–76
James Callaghan	1976–79
Margaret Thatcher	1979–90
John Major	1990–97
Tony Blair*	1997–

* Re-elected 2001.

Greece

Kings

George I	1863–1913
Constantine I	1913–17
Alexander	1917–20
Constantine I (again)	1920–22
George II	1922–23
A Republic was in existence, 1924–35	
George II (again)	1935–44
Regency	1944–46
George II (again)	1946–47
Paul I	1947–64
Constantine II	1964–74*

* When the monarchy was formally voted out.

Presidents (after 1973)

G. Papadopoulos	1973 (June–Nov., Provisional President)
P. Ghizikis	1973–74
M. Stassinopoulos	1974–75

K. Tsatsos	1975–80
K. Karamanlis	1980–85
C. Sartzetakis	1985–90
K. Karamanlis	1990–95
C. Stepanopoulos*	1995–

* Re-elected Feb. 2000.

Hungary

Hungary became an independent republic on 16 Nov. 1918.

Count Karolyi   Nov. 1918–Mar. 1919 (Provisional President)

In Jan. 1920, Hungary was proclaimed a monarchy, but Admiral M. von Horthy was Regent, 1920–45. The absent Charles (*see* Austria) never assumed the throne. A republic was proclaimed in 1945 and a republican constitution came into effect in 1946.

Presidents (Chairman of Praesidium after 1952, Chairman of the Presiding Council after 1967)

Z. Tildy	1946–48
A. Szakasits	1948–50
S. Rónai	1950–52
I. M. Dobi	1952–67
P. Losonczi	1967–88
B. F. Straub	1988–89
I. Pozsgay	1989 (Jun.–Oct.)

The People's Republic was abolished on 23 Oct. 1989. Presidents since the fall of communism have been:

| A. Göncz | 1990–2000* |
| F. Mádl | 2000– |

* Re-elected 1995.

Ireland

Heads of State

After 1922, although Ireland was a self-governing Dominion, the British sovereign was still recognised as Head of State. After Dec. 1937, when the constitution of the Irish Free State as an independent sovereign state came into force, the following have been presidents:

Presidents

| Douglas Hyde | 1938–45 |
| Sean T. O'Kelly | 1945–59 |

161

Eamon de Valera   1959–73
Erskine Childers   1973–74
Cearbhall O. Dalaigh   1974–76
Patrick Hillery   1976–90
Mary Robinson   1990–97
Mary McAleese   1997–

Prime Ministers (Taoiseachs) (after 1922)

Michael Collins   1922
(Finance and General Minister in the Provisional Government)
W. Cosgrave   1922–32
E. de Valera   1932–48
J. A. Costello   1948–51
E. de Valera   1951–54
J. A. Costello   1954–57
E. de Valera   1957–59
S. Lemass   1959–66
J. Lynch   1966–73
L. Cosgrave   1973–77
J. Lynch   1977–79
C. Haughey   1979–81
G. FitzGerald   1981–82
C. Haughey   1982 (Mar.–Dec.)
G. FitzGerald   1982–87
C. Haughey   1987–92
A. Reynolds   1992–94
J. Bruton   1994–97
B. Aherne   1997–

Italy

Kings

Umberto I   1878–1900
Victor Emmanuel III   1900–46 (abdicated)
Umberto II   1946 (abdicated)

A republic was proclaimed on 18 June 1946.

Presidents

L. Einaudi   1948–55
G. Gronchi   1955–62
A. Segni   1962–64
G. Saragat   1964–71
G. Leone   1971–78
A. Fanfani   1978 (June–July)
A. Pertini   1979–85

F. Cossiga   1985–92
O. Scalfaro   1992–99
C. A. Ciampi   1999–

Latvia

Before 1918, Latvia was part of Tsarist Russia. It was an independent republic from 1918 to 1940 when it was forcibly incorporated into the Soviet Union. Independence was restored in 1991.

Presidents

G. Ulmanis   1993–99
V. Vike-Freiberga   1999–

Lithuania

Before the 1917 Revolution, Lithuania was part of Tsarist Russia. It was an independent republic from Feb. 1918 to June 1940. It regained its full independence in 1991.

Heads of State

V. Landsbergis (Chairman of the Supreme Council)   1990–93
A. Brazauskas* (President)   1993–98
V. Adamkus   1998–2003
R. Paksas   2003–

* Elected by popular vote, 14 Feb. 1993.

Macedonia

Before 1992, Macedonia was part of former Yugoslavia. It declared independence on 20 Nov. 1992 and was admitted to the United Nations as the 'Former Yugoslav Republic of Macedonia' in deference to Greek unease.

Presidents

K. Gligorov   1991–99
B. Trajkovski   1999–

Moldova

With the collapse of the Soviet Union, Moldova declared its independence in Aug. 1991.

Presidents

M. Snegur   1991–96
P. Lucinschi   1996–2001
V. Voronin   2001–

The Netherlands

Sovereigns

Wilhelmina	1890–1948 (abdicated)
Juliana	1948–80 (abdicated)
Beatrix	1980–

Norway

Kings (of independent Norway after 1905)

Haakon VII	1905–57
Olaf V	1957–91
Harald V	1991–

Ottoman Empire   *See* Turkey

The Papacy

Popes

Pope	*Family name*	
Leo XIII	Gioacchino Vincenzo Rafaele Luigi Pecci	1878–1903
Pius X	Giuseppe Sarto	1903–14
Benedict XV	Giacomo della Chiesa	1914–22
Pius XI	Achille Ratti	1922–39
Pius XII	Eugenio Pacelli	1939–58
John XXIII	Angelo Giuseppe Roncalli	1958–63
Paul VI	Giovanni Battista Montini	1963–78
John Paul I	Albino Luciani	1978
John Paul II	Karol Wojtyla	1978–

Poland

The Congress of Vienna created a Kingdom of Poland (under the Russian Crown). After the 1830 Rising this was suppressed. Not until 1918 did Poland regain independence, when an independent state was proclaimed on 5 Nov. 1918.

Presidents

J. Pilsudski	1918–22
G. Narutowicz	1922 (assassinated)
S. Wojciechowski	1922–26
I. Mościcki	1926–39

On 29 Sept. 1939 the German occupation of Poland began. The Polish government was in exile until the end of the war.

Prime Ministers of the Government-in-Exile

General Wladyslaw Sikorski   1939–43
Stanislaw Mikolajczyk   1943–45

In July 1945 a Provisional Government of National Unity was set up, composed of the London government-in-exile and the Russian-backed Committee of National Liberation. Its task was to run Poland until free elections could take place. The elections were held in 1947, resulting in an overwhelming victory for the Communist–Socialist candidates.

President

Boleslaw Bierut   1945–52

On 22 July 1952 a new constitution replaced the office of President with a Council of State.

President of the Council of State

A. Zawadski   1952–64
E. Ochab   1964–68
Marshal M. Spychalski   1968–70
J. Cyrankiewicz   1970–72
H. Jabloński   1972–85
W. Jaruzelski   1985–89*

From 1956 to 1970, Gomulka was the most powerful figure in Poland, when he was succeeded by Gierek. From 1981 until the collapse of communist rule, General Jaruzelski was Poland's strong-man.

* President 1989–90.

President (by popular election)

L. Walesa   1990–95
A. Kwaśniewski   1995*–

* Re-elected Oct. 2000.

Portugal

Monarchs (Braganza dynasty) (to 1910)

Carlos I   1889–1908
Manuel II   1908–10

A republic was proclaimed in 1910.

Presidents

A. Carmona   1926–51
A. Salazar[1]   1951 (Apr.–July)

Marshal F. Lopes	1951–58
A. Tomás	1958–74
A. de Spinola	1974 (Apr.–Sept.)[2]
F. Gomes	1974–76
A. Eanes	1976–86
M. Soares	1986–96
J. Sampãio	1996[3]–

[1] Salazar ruled Portugal as a dictator.
[2] A military junta seized power on 25 Apr., ending the dictatorship.
[3] Re-elected Jan. 2001.

Prussia

Kings

William II   1888–1918 (abdicated)

Note   The creation of the German Empire was in 1871, after which the Kings of Prussia became German Emperors.

Romania

Kings

Carol I	1881–1914
Ferdinand	1914–27
Michael I	1927–30
Carol II	1930–40 (abdicated)
Michael I*	1940–47 (abdicated)

* Michael I resumed the throne in 1940. However, in 1947, as a result of a plebiscite, a republic was established and the King abdicated.

Presidents

C. Parhon	1948–52
P. Groza	1952–58
I. Maurer	1958–61
G. Gheorghiu-Dej	1961–65
C. Stoica	1965–67
N. Ceausescu	1967–89
I. Iliescu	1989–96*
E. Constantinescu	1997–2000
I. Iliescu	2000–

* A new constitution was adopted by referendum on 8 Dec. 1991. Iliescu was elected President in May 1990 and re-elected 11 Oct. 1992.

Russia (USSR, 1922–91)

Tsars

Nicholas II   1894–1917 (abdicated)

Prime Ministers

J. N. Durnovo	1895–1903
S. J. Witte	1900–06
I. L. Goremykin	1906 (May–July)
P. A. Stolypin	1906–11
W. N. Kokovtsov	1911–14
I. L. Goremykin	1914–16
B. W. Stürmer	1916 (Feb.–Nov.)
A. F. Trepov	1916 (Nov.)–1917 (Jan.)
N. D. Golitsin	1917 (Jan.–Mar.)

Under the provisional government

G. J. Lvov	1917 (Mar.–July)
A. F. Kerensky	1917 (July–Nov.)

A constitution for the Federal Republic was adopted on 10 July 1918, by a government which had taken office on 8 Nov. 1917.

President of the Council of People's Commissars

V. I. Lenin   1917–22

A new constitution of 30 Dec. 1922 replaced this office by a Central Executive Committee with four chairmen. A new constitution came into force on 5 Dec. 1936 establishing the office of Chairman of the Praesidium of the Supreme Soviet of the USSR, as Head of State.

Chairmen

M. I. Kalinin	1936–46
N. M. Shvernik	1946–53
Marshal K. E. Voroshilov	1953–60
L. I. Brezhnev	1960–64
A. I. Mikoyan	1964–65
N. V. Podgorny	1965–77
L. I. Brezhnev	1977–82
Y. V. Andropov	1983–84
K. V. Chernenko	1984–85
M. Gorbachev*	1985–91

Effective rulers (1917–91)

V. I. Lenin	1917–22
J. Stalin	1927–53

N. Khrushchev   1953–64 (deposed)
L. I. Brezhnev   1964–82
Y. V. Andropov   1982–84
K. V. Chernenko   1984–85
M. Gorbachev*   1985–91

* Gorbachev became President of the USSR in 1988 then (1990) Executive President until the collapse of the USSR. He resigned on 25 Dec. 1991. Following the collapse of the Soviet Union that month, the Russian Federation became a founder member of the Commonwealth of Independent States (see pp. 202–3). Boris Yeltsin was directly elected President of the Russian Federation in 1991.

President

B. Yeltsin   1991 (June)–99*
V. Putin   1999**–

* Re-elected in 1996, resigned 31 Dec. 1999.
** At first, acting President.

Prime Ministers

The first Prime Minister of the Russian Federation after the fall of the USSR was Yeltsin, who was succeeded by Gaidar (June–Dec. 1992). Apart from Chernomyrdin (1992–98), the 1990s saw a succession of short-lived appointments. In May 2000, Kasyanov became Prime Minister under Putin.

Serbia

An independent kingdom after 1878.

Kings

Alexander Obrenovitch   1889–1903
Peter   1903–21*

* See also reference to Yugoslavia in this section.

Slovakia

Part of Czechoslovakia from 1918 to 14 Mar. 1939 when it was declared an independent country with Dr J. Tiso as President (Oct. 1939–Apr. 1945). Slovakia, which had been a Nazi-puppet state, was reincorporated into Czechoslovakia in Apr. 1945. Slovakia split from Czechoslovakia to become an independent republic on 1 Jan. 1993 (the so-called 'Velvet Divorce').

Presidents

M. Kovac   1993–98
R. Schuster   1999–

Slovenia

Slovenia declared its independence from former Yugoslavia on 8 Oct. 1991, the culmination of a series of moves towards separation which began in Oct. 1989.

President

M. Kučan   1992*–2003
J. Drnovsk   2003–

* Re-elected Nov. 1997.

Spain

Kings

Alfonso XIII   1886–1931 (abdicated)

A republic was proclaimed on 14 Apr. 1931.

Presidents

N. A. Zamora y Torres   1931–36
M. Azaña   1936–39

Chief of the State

Gen. Francisco Franco   1939–75

King

Juan Carlos I   1975–

Prime Ministers

Gen. Francisco Franco   1939–73
L. Carrero Blanco   1973 (June–Dec.)
T. Fernández Miranda (acting) 1973–74
C. Arias Navarro   1974–76
A. Suarez Gonzalez   1976–81
L. Calvo-Sotelo Bustelo   1981–82
F. González Márquez   1982–96
J. M. Aznar Lopez   1996–

Sweden

Kings

Oscar II   1872–1907 (renounced Norwegian throne, 1905)
Gustavus V   1907–50
Gustavus VI, Adolphus   1950–73
Charles XVI, Gustavus   1973–

Turkey

Sultans

Abdul Hamid II	1876–1909
Mohammed V	1909–18
Mohammed VI	1918–22

The office of Sultan was abolished in Nov. 1922. Prince Abdul Mejid was Caliph from 1922 to 1924. A republic was proclaimed on 29 Oct. 1923.

Presidents

M. Kemal Atatürk	1923–38
I. Inönü	1938–50
C. Bayar	1950–60
C. Gursel	1961–66
C. Sunay	1966–73
F. Korutürk	1973–80
I. S. Caglayangil	1980 (Apr.–Sept.)
K. Evren	1980–89
T. Özal	1989–93
S. Demirel	1993–2000
A. N. Sezer	2000–

Ukraine

Ukraine, formerly part of the Russian Empire, was independent between 1919 and 1922, when it became a constituent republic of the Soviet Union. The independence of Ukraine was declared on 5 Dec. 1991.

Presidents

L. Kravchuk	1991–94
L. Kuchma	1994–

United Kingdom   *See* Great Britain

USSR   *See* Russia

Yugoslavia

The independent Serb, Croat and Slovene State was formed in Dec. 1918. The name was changed in Oct. 1929 to Yugoslavia.

Kings

Peter I	1903–21 (formerly King of Serbia)
Alexander I	1921–34
Peter II	1934–45 (abdicated)

A republic was proclaimed in 1945.

President of the Praesidium

Dr I. Ribar   1945–53

President of the Republic

Marshal J. Broz Tito   1953–80

After 1980, a 'Collective Presidency' was established, with the Presidency rotating on an annual basis. After a civil war in 1991, Yugoslavia officially ceased to exist in Jan. 1992. Slovenia and Croatia were recognised as independent states by the international community in Jan. 1992. The independence of Bosnia–Herzegovina (declared in 1992) was delayed by the civil war (see p. 180). Meanwhile, a reconstituted 'rump' Yugoslavia (consisting of Serbia and Montenegro) was declared in Apr. 1992.

The effective ruler of this rump Yugoslavia was Slobodan Milosevic from 1992 to 2000. After the revolution of Oct. 2000 the President was Vojislav Kostunica.

WAR, DIPLOMACY AND INTERNATIONAL ORGANISATIONS

PRINCIPAL EUROPEAN WARS AND CAMPAIGNS

Russo–Japanese War, 1904–05

The conflict began without declaration of war when Japan attacked the Russian fleet at Port Arthur (Feb.). Japanese forces eventually took Port Arthur, Korea and much of Manchuria. Russia was severely defeated at the battle of Mukden (21 Feb.–10 Mar. 1904). The Japanese scored a naval triumph at the battle of Tsushima (27 May 1905). After US mediation, peace was secured by the Treaty of Portsmouth (New Hampshire). Russian humiliation in the war was a major factor in provoking the 1905 revolution in Russia.

The Italo–Turkish War, 1911–12

On 29 Sept. 1911 Italy declared war on the Ottoman Empire, with the aim of seizing Cyrenaica and Tripoli (modern Libya) to which they had long advanced claims. By Nov. they had defeated the Turks in North Africa and in May 1912 occupied the Dodecanese islands in the Aegean. Italian finances suffered severely in the war, but the Ottoman Empire recognised their gains by the Treaty of Ouchy in Oct.

The Balkan Wars, 1912–13

Encouraged by Italy's success the Balkan states of Serbia, Bulgaria, Greece and Montenegro went to war with the Ottoman Empire in Oct. 1912 and soon overran most of the Ottoman Empire in Europe. The Ottoman Empire acknowledged her losses in London in May 1913 but in June war broke out between Bulgaria, who felt cheated by the peace, and her Serb and Greek allies, supported by the Ottoman Empire and Romania. The Bulgarians were defeated and forced to surrender territory.

The First World War, 1914–18

On 28 July 1914 Austria–Hungary declared war on Serbia whom she blamed for the assassination of the Austrian heir to the throne a month earlier. Austria was supported by her ally Germany, but they were faced by the 'Entente' powers, Russia, France and Britain. In late 1914 the Germans failed to capture Paris, despite the boldness of their invasion plan (the Schlieffen plan), and the war settled into the deadlock of trench warfare. In 1915 the Entente tried to break the deadlock by expeditions to the Dardanelles and Salonika in southeast Europe, and by inducing Italy to attack Austria, but to no avail. In 1916 both sides launched grand offensives on the Western Front, the Germans against Verdun and the Allies on the Somme, but despite enormous casualties the deadlock continued. At sea the British and Germans fought the drawn battle of Jutland. In 1917 both sides were given hope – the Germans by the Russian Revolution (which eventually removed Russia from the war) and the Allies by the USA's entry into the war. The next year proved decisive. The Germans launched a last great offensive in spring 1918 but this was halted, and American support tipped the scales the Allied way. Germany agreed to an armistice in Nov. Her allies, Austria and the Ottoman Empire, had already given up the fight – the Austrians defeated at Vittorio Veneto in Italy and the Turks defeated by the British in Palestine and Mesopotamia.

The Russian Civil War, 1917–20

In Nov. 1917 the Communists seized power in Russia but were opposed by the Tsarists and others. In 1918 the victorious Allied powers intervened to help the Tsarists, but the divisions between the 'White' generals, and the strong central position of the Bolsheviks, ensured that the intervention ended in failure. The Poles, who invaded Russia in April 1919, were able to make gains, following their unexpected victory over the Russians in 1920, and Estonia, Latvia and Lithuania gained their independence, but the communist government survived.

The Hungarian–Romanian War, 1919

In 1919 a communist government under Béla Kun took power in Hungary. Resentful of the armistice terms proposed by the Allies after the war, the Hungarians invaded Slovakia and the Romanians, fearing that they too would be attacked, attacked Hungary to forestall any further communist advances. In Aug. the Romanians captured Budapest and Béla Kun fled. The Romanians left in Nov. In 1920 Hungary's territorial losses were confirmed by the Treaty of the Trianon.

The Greek–Turkish War, 1920–23

By the Treaty of Sèvres, 1920, the Allies handed territory in Asia Minor to Greek control, but the Turks refused to accept this change, and General Mustapha Kemal resisted the Greek occupation. In 1922 he drove the Greeks from their last stronghold at Smyrna, secured control of the area around Constantinople, and overthrew the Ottoman Sultan. In 1923 the Allies renegotiated the peace treaty with Turkey at Lausanne.

The Italo–Abyssinian War, 1935–36

In Oct. 1935 Mussolini invaded Abyssinia (Ethiopia) and caused an international outcry. An Anglo–French plan to partition Abyssinia between its ruler, Haile Selassie, and Italy failed, as did economic sanctions against Italy to force her to end her aggression. In May 1936 the Italian conquest was complete.

The Spanish Civil War, 1936–39

In July 1936 Spanish generals, led by Franco, rose against the Republican government and plunged Spain into civil war. Despite international declarations against foreign involvement, Italy, Germany and Portugal aided the generals and Russia and France helped the Republicans. In addition, International Brigades were formed by volunteers from many states to fight for the Republicans, and helped to defeat the Nationalists in the battle of Guadalajara, 1937. But by early 1939 the Nationalists held most of Spain. Madrid fell on 28 Mar.

The Second World War, 1939–45

Britain and France declared war on Germany on 3 Sept. 1939, following Hitler's invasion of Poland. Poland soon fell and in 1940 Germany overran Denmark, Norway, the Low Countries and, finally, France. Italy joined the Germans, and for a year Britain and her Empire stood alone against the 'Axis' Powers. In 1941, however, the war was vastly extended, Japan joining the Axis, and Russia, China and the USA joining Britain. The Japanese rapidly overran many of the European colonies in South-East Asia, but Hitler's invasion of Russia (June 1941) eventually proved a decisive mistake. In 1942 the Germans were defeated in North Africa and Russia, in 1943 the Allies invaded Italy, and in 1944 Britain and the USA opened the 'Second Front' in France. The Third Reich finally collapsed on 8 May 1945 and in Aug. the Japanese were defeated by the use of atomic bombs.

The Russo–Finnish War (The Winter War), 1939–40

War broke out on 30 Nov. over Russian border claims, but Finnish resistance along the Mannerheim Line ensured that Russia's victory was hard-fought. The war ended in Mar. and peace was made in Moscow. In June 1941 the Finns joined the German invasion of Russia but were again defeated.

Cold War

Protracted state of tension between countries falling short of actual war. The term was first used in a US Congress debate on 12 Mar. 1947 on the doctrine, expounded by Harry S. Truman (1894–1972), promising aid to 'free peoples who are resisting attempted subjugation by armed minorities or by outside pressures'. A direct product of the civil war in Greece (1946–49), the doctrine bore the wider implication that the USA would actively respond anywhere in the world to what it saw as direct encroachment by the USSR. The practical division of Europe occurred as a result of the Eastern European states' rejection of US Marshall Aid, often under pressure from the Soviet Union, and their subsequent membership of Comecon. This division into two hostile camps was completed by the creation of NATO (1949–50) and the Warsaw Pact (1955). The Cold War between the Soviet Union and the USA continued into the 1970s before being superseded by a period of *détente*. The main crises within the Cold War period were the Russian invasion of Hungary in 1956; of Czechoslovakia in 1968; the Berlin Blockade of 1948 and the Cuban Missile Crisis of 1962. Western outrage at these supposed manifestations of Soviet expansion was tempered by the British and French involvement in Suez in 1956 and the US involvement in Vietnam during the 1960s and early 1970s. With the advent of Gorbachev in the USSR, and the fall of communist regimes in Eastern Europe after 1989, it was effectively over. It was formally ended by the signing of the Conference on Security and Co-operation in Europe (CSCE) on 19 Nov. 1990 and reinforced by the signing of the Founding Act in 1997 (on NATO–Russian co-operation).

The Greek Civil War, 1944–49

The Greek Civil War developed out of the rivalry between communist and monarchist partisans for control of Greece as the Axis forces retreated at the end of the Second World War. British troops were sent to aid the pro-monarchist forces in 1944, while the Soviet Union took the side of the communist insurgents. After 1945 American aid enabled British troops to remain in Greece and assist the return of the monarchy. Communist resistance was seriously weakened by the break between Yugoslavia and Russia in 1948, resulting in the closure of much of Greece's northern border to infiltration and aid. The communists announced an end to open conflict in Oct. 1949.

Berlin Blockade, 1948–49

With Berlin under four-power administration, the USSR, alleging the West had broken postwar agreements on German status, and hoping to force out the USA, Britain and France, imposed obstacles to road and river traffic entering the western sector of Berlin in June 1948. The West responded with a round-the-clock airlift of fuel and food to relieve the beleaguered city. The blockade ended in May 1949.

Korean War, 1950–53

North Korean troops invaded the South on 25 June 1950. The United Nations decided to intervene following an emergency session of the Security Council, which was being boycotted by the Soviet Union. The first American troops landed at Pusan airport on 1 July 1950. General MacArthur mounted an amphibious landing at Inchon on 15 Sept. 1950, and Seoul was recaptured on 26 Sept. The advance of the UN forces into North Korea on 1 Oct. 1950 led to the entry of China into the war on 25 Nov. Seoul fell to the Chinese on 4 Jan. 1951, but was retaken by UN forces on 14 Mar. General MacArthur was relieved of his command on 11 Apr. after expressing his desire to expand the war into China. Truce talks began on 10 July 1951, and an armistice was finally signed at Panmunjon on 27 July 1953.

East German Workers' Uprising, 1953

Demonstrations by building workers in East Berlin on 16 June 1953 spread to a number of factories the following day. More than 300 places in East Germany were affected, including major towns such as Magdeburg, Jena, Gorlitz and Brandenburg. The disorders were suppressed by security police, and curfew and martial law restrictions remained in force until 12 July 1953.

Polish Workers' Uprising, 1956

A revolt of workers seeking better conditions broke out in Poznan on 28 June 1956. It was suppressed by the security forces.

Hungarian Uprising, 1956

Student demonstrations in Budapest on 23 Oct. 1956 led to a general uprising against the government of Erno Gero. The Stalin statue was torn down and the radio headquarters were seized by the crowds. The insurgents fought against the troops of the State Defence Authority (ÁVH) and the intervening Soviet troops. On 25 Oct., the ÁVH troops, hiding on rooftops around Kossuth Square, shot into the peaceful demonstrators, thus causing more people to join the insurgents. At dawn on 24 Oct., Imre Nagy became the Prime Minister and gradually a supporter of the revolution. On 26 Oct., he invited non-communist politicians into the government. On the 27th Soviet troops were withdrawn from Budapest. On 1 Nov. Imre Nagy announced Hungary's withdrawal from the Warsaw Pact and asked the United Nations to recognise its neutrality. Soviet reinforcements surrounded Budapest and entered the city early on 4 Nov. Resistance ended on 14 Nov. 1956.

Suez Invasion, 1956

Egypt nationalised the Suez Canal on 26 July 1956. After secret talks with Britain and France, Israel invaded Sinai on 29 Oct. When Egypt rejected a ceasefire ultimatum by France and Britain, their air forces began to attack Egyptian air bases on 31 Oct. On 5 Nov. British and French forces invaded the Canal Zone. Pressure from the United Nations and world opinion forced a ceasefire at midnight on 6–7 Nov. 1956.

Soviet Invasion of Czechoslovakia, 1968

During the night of 20–21 Aug. 1968 some 250,000 Soviet troops, accompanied by token contingents from Warsaw Pact allies Poland, Hungary and Bulgaria, crossed the Czech frontier and occupied Prague and other leading cities to reverse the liberalising reforms of Alexander Dubček's government, the so-called 'Prague Spring'. The Czech army was ordered to offer no resistance, but there were extensive civilian demonstrations against the occupying forces. The Soviet invasion led to the installation of a new Soviet-backed government and the end of the 'Prague Spring'.

The Partition of Cyprus, 1974

In July 1974 a coup in Cyprus brought to power a government favouring 'enosis' (union) with Greece, but Turkey quickly responded by invading the island to safeguard the Turkish half of the population. An armistice was agreed on 16 Aug., which left Turkish rule over one third of the island.

Soviet Invasion of Afghanistan, 1979–89

The instability of the Soviet-backed regime and growing resistance to reforms led to a full-scale Soviet invasion of Afghanistan on 27 Dec. 1979. A new government was installed under Babrak Karmal, but a considerable Soviet military presence had to be maintained in the country to combat the Mujaheddin guerrillas. Following Babrak Karmal's resignation on 4 May 1986, his successor, Major General Najibullah, announced a six-month ceasefire on 15 Jan. 1987, but this was rejected by the Mujaheddin. Russian troops began to withdraw in 1988 and completed their withdrawal in early 1989, having lost 15,000 dead.

The Collapse of the Soviet Union, 1988–91

During the final days of the Soviet Union, ethnic clashes were already developing. Rioting between Armenians and Azerbaijanis, sparked by a dispute over control of the Nagorno-Karabakh region, began on 20 Feb. 1988. In Uzbekistan, fighting between Uzbeks and Meskhetian Turks began on 4 June 1989. The armed forces also moved against nationalist movements in Georgia, Moldova, Azerbaijan and the Baltic Republics. After the collapse of the Soviet Union, serious conflicts developed in the following areas: Azerbaijan-Armenia; the Abkhazia region of Georgia; Moldova and Tajikistan. By far the most serious conflict within Russia was in Chechnya (see below).

Romanian Revolution and Civil War, 1989

On 16–17 Dec. 1989 security forces fired on protestors in the Romanian city of Timisoara. On 18 Dec. Romania closed its frontiers. On the 20th troops surrendered in Timisoara. Fighting spread to Bucharest and other major cities. The army switched sides, joining the popular uprising against the Ceausescu dictatorship and the hated security police (the *Securitate*). By 24 Dec. all strategic points were controlled by the revolutionary National Salvation Front. Ceausescu and his wife were executed by firing squad on 25 Dec. 1989.

Yugoslavian Civil War (Serbo–Croat War), 1991–95

Declarations of independence by the former Yugoslav Republics of Slovenia and Croatia led to clashes on Slovenia's borders from July, followed by heavy fighting on Croatian territory between Croatian militia and Serbian irregulars (chetniks) backed by the Yugoslav Federal Army. Main centres of fighting were eastern and central Croatia and the Adriatic coast around Dubrovnik. Yugoslavia officially ceased to exist in Jan. 1992 and Slovenia and Croatia were recognised as independent states. On 29 Feb. 1992, Muslim leaders in Bosnia–Herzegovina declared independence. Bosnian Serbs and the Serbian leadership in Belgrade rejected this, and war began on 6 Apr. with the opening of the siege of the capital, Sarajevo. Serbs were accused of 'ethnic cleansing' to secure territorial domination, and a UN trade embargo was imposed on Serbia on 31 May. Peace talks in Geneva, mediated by Lord Owen and Cyrus Vance, began on 26 Aug. On 16 Nov. a UN naval blockade was mounted against Serbia and Montenegro. Fighting continued as a further peace conference was held in Geneva on 22–23 Jan. 1993, with Serbs attacking Muslim enclaves at Srebenica and Goradze. Numerous peace talks collapsed. In 1995 Croatia launched major offensives and an uneasy peace accord was signed at Dayton, Ohio.

Russia–Chechnya War, 1994–96, 1999–

Russian troops were ordered into Chechnya in Dec. 1994 to end the rebel republic's bid for independence. Fighting ensued for 21 months as Russian troops failed to subdue the population. The fighting was the worst on Russian soil since the Second World War, with Grozny, the Chechnyan capital, razed to the ground. The Russian army suffered a major loss of face. On 31 Aug. 1996 Russia and Chechnya signed a peace deal, freezing the issue of independence for five years. In Jan. 1997 the withdrawal of all Russian troops from Chechnya was completed.

However, partly provoked by Chechen support for guerrillas in the adjacent Caucasus region of Dagestan, and partly because of terrorist bomb outrages in Russia itself, a renewed Russian offensive was launched against Chechnya in Sept. 1999. Massive Russian aerial bombardment was followed by a major ground offensive against Grozny launched on 25 Dec. 1999.

The Balkan War, 1999

Conflict in Kosovo, until 1989 an autonomous province in 'rump' Yugoslavia mainly inhabited by Kosovar Albanians, gradually intensified as Serbian forces embarked on a policy of ethnic cleansing. Yugoslav President Slobodan Milosevic ignored a series of NATO warnings during 1998. On 24 Mar. 1999 NATO forces (including British aircraft) launched air strikes against Yugoslavia. Cruise missile attacks followed. Milosevic intensified his ethnic cleansing policy, producing a human tide of refugees into Macedonia and Albania. NATO air strikes were marked by a series of calamitous errors (including the missile attack on the Chinese embassy in Belgrade on 8 May) and a serious worsening of relations with Russia. Eventually air power (backed by a threat of a land offensive) caused Milosevic to sue for peace and a mainly NATO peacekeeping force (KFOR, with some Russian troops) was stationed in Kosovo.

NUCLEAR RIVALRY AND ARMS CONTROL IN EUROPE SINCE 1945

1946

June	Baruch Plan (by which USA would surrender its atomic weapons and reveal the secrets of controlling atomic energy to an International Control Agency) rejected by the Soviet Union.

1949

29 Aug.	Soviet Union explodes an atomic bomb, ending the American monopoly of nuclear weapons.

1950

Jan.	Soviet Union withdraws from the Atomic Energy Commission.

1952

3 Oct.	Britain tests its first atomic bomb.

1953

12 Aug.	Soviet Union tests its first hydrogen bomb in Siberia.

1954

27 June   First atomic power station is opened at Obninsk, USSR.

1955

July   At the Geneva Summit, President Eisenhower puts forward his 'open skies' proposal for mutual aerial photography of each other's territory by the Soviet Union and USA as a step towards disarmament.

1956

23 Oct.   Britain opens first large-scale commercial nuclear power station at Calder Hall, Cumbria, but mainly used for defence purposes.

1957

15 Aug.   First British hydrogen bomb is exploded near Christmas Island.

26 Aug.   Soviet Union announces the successful launch of an intercontinental ballistic missile.

2 Oct.   Adam Rapacki, Foreign Minister of Poland, proposes in a speech to the UN General Assembly the creation of a nuclear-free zone in central Europe. Plan rejected by NATO on the grounds that nuclear weapons are essential to offset Soviet superiority in conventional forces.

1958

17 Feb.   First meeting of Britain's Campaign for Nuclear Disarmament (CND) held in London.

1959

7 Sept.   Establishment of the Ten-Power Committee on Disarmament, comprising representatives from Britain, Canada, France, Italy, the USA, Bulgaria, Czechoslovakia, Poland, Romania and Soviet Union.

1960

13 Feb.   France explodes its first atomic device in the Sahara.

Dec.   USA offers five submarines with 80 Polaris missiles to create a NATO Multilateral Nuclear Force at the NATO ministerial meeting in Paris.

1962

14 Mar.   First meeting in Geneva of the Eighteen-Nation Disarmament Committee, the former Ten-Power Committee with the

addition of Brazil, Burma, Egypt, Ethiopia, India, Mexico, Nigeria and Sweden.

Dec.   President Kennedy meets British Prime Minister, Harold Macmillan, at Nassau in the Bahamas and agrees to make US Polaris missiles available to Britain for use with British warheads.

1963

5 Apr.   'Hot-line' agreement between the USA and the Soviet Union.

5 Aug.   Partial Test-Ban Treaty, outlawing nuclear tests in the atmosphere and outer space and under water.

1966

14 Dec.   NATO establishes the Nuclear Defence Affairs Committee (all members except France, Iceland and Luxembourg) and the Nuclear Planning Group (all except France and Iceland).

1967

28 Jan.   Treaty banning all nuclear weapons in outer space opened for signature in London, Moscow and Washington.

1968

1 July   Non-Proliferation Treaty is opened for signature in London, Moscow and Washington.

25 Aug.   France explodes its first hydrogen bomb.

17 Nov.   Preparatory negotiations on Strategic Arms Limitation Talks (SALT) between the USA and the Soviet Union begin in Helsinki.

1970

16 Apr.   Strategic Arms Limitation Talks open in Vienna.

1971

11 Feb.   Sea-bed Treaty prohibiting the emplacement of nuclear weapons on the sea-bed opened for signature in London, Moscow and Washington.

1972

26 May   SALT I anti-ballistic missile (ABM) agreement and five-year interim agreement on the limitation of strategic arms signed by the USA and the Soviet Union.

1973

30 Oct.   Mutual and Balanced Force Reduction talks between NATO and the Warsaw Pact begin in Vienna.

1974

3 July   Protocol to the US–Soviet SALT ABM agreement, limiting ABM deployment to a single area.

3 July   US–Soviet Threshhold Test Ban Treaty is signed, limiting underground nuclear tests.

24 Nov.   Vladivostok Accord between the USA and the Soviet Union, setting out the framework for future negotiations on controlling the strategic arms race.

1976

28 May   US–Soviet Treaty restricting nuclear explosions for peaceful purposes.

1979

18 June   SALT II Agreement signed by the USA and Soviet Union, restricting numbers of strategic offensive weapons. USA withholds ratification of the treaty following the Soviet invasion of Afghanistan in Dec. 1979.

12 Dec.   NATO announces its intention to modernise its long-range theatre nuclear systems by the deployment of 464 ground-launched Cruise missiles and 108 Pershing II medium-range ballistic missiles in Europe.

1980

June   Agreement to site Cruise missiles in Europe.

1981

30 Nov.   US–Soviet negotiations on intermediate-range nuclear forces open in Geneva.

1982

29 June   Strategic Arms Reduction Talks (START) between the USA and Soviet Union begin in Geneva.

1983

Nov.   Intermediate-range Cruise missiles deployed in Britain, Holland and Germany.

1986

26 Apr.   Major nuclear accident in the Soviet Union at the Chernobyl site, north of Kiev, involving explosions, fire and release of radioactivity from No. 4 Reactor.

11–12 Oct.	Summit meeting on arms control between Presidents Reagan and Gorbachev at Reykjavik, Iceland, founders on the issue of the US Strategic Defense Initiative.

1987

8 Dec.	Intermediate Nuclear Forces Treaty is signed in Washington. See p. 201.

1990	Conference on Security and Co-operation in Europe (CSCE) signs agreement in Paris marking formal end of the Cold War.

1991	Gorbachev and Bush agree START I Treaty after nearly 10 years of discussions.

1993	Yeltsin and Bush sign START II Treaty (designed to halve stockpiles of nuclear warheads held by each country). Never ratified by US Congress.

1997	Russia–NATO agreement concluded.

2001

Nov.	Failure of Putin–George Bush Jnr. talks on US National Missile Defence.
Dec.	Bush signifies intention to withdraw from 1972 ABM Treaty.

2002

12 May	Major agreement to cut operational nuclear warheads by two-thirds over 10 years is signed by Putin and Bush in Moscow.

Nuclear warhead stockpiles						
	1945	**1955**	**1965**	**1975**	**1985**	**1995**	**2002**
USA	6	3,057	31,265	26,675	22,941	14,776	12,000
USSR/Russia	0	200	6,129	19,443	39,197	27,000	22,500

Totals are estimates and include strategic (long-range) and non-strategic warheads, as well as warheads awaiting dismantling.
Source: US National Resources Defense Council

WARS OF DECOLONISATION SINCE 1945

Note There have been numerous struggles linked to the process of decolonisation since 1945. Two of the worst defeats were suffered by the French in the Indo–China War, 1946–54, and Algeria, 1956–62. The Dutch were forced to recognise Indonesian independence in 1949, the British were forced to abandon Palestine in 1948, and in 1956 the British and French were forced to give up an attempt to reassert control of the Suez Canal.

Indonesian War of Independence, 1945–49

The independence of the Republic of Indonesia (formerly Netherlands East Indies) was proclaimed by the nationalist leaders, Sukarno and Hatta, on 17 Aug. 1945. British, Indian and Dutch troops began to arrive on 29 Sept. British troops captured the rebel capital of Surabaya on 29 Nov. The Dutch recognised the Indonesian Republic (comprising Java, Sumatra and Madura) on 13 Nov. 1946. The withdrawal of British troops was completed on 30 Nov. 1946. A nationalist uprising on West Java on 4 May 1947 led to Dutch military action on Java on 20 July. A truce arranged under UN auspices on 17 Jan. 1948 broke down, and the Dutch occupied the rebel capital, Jogjakarta, on 19 Dec. 1948. International opposition and guerrilla warfare led to the Dutch decision to withdraw, and to the independence of Indonesia on 27 Dec. 1949.

First Indochina War, 1946–54

Following the surrender of Japan, Ho Chi Minh proclaimed the Democratic Republic of Vietnam at Hanoi on 2 Sept. 1945. French and British forces regained control in Saigon, and after negotiations, French troops entered Hanoi on 16 Mar. 1946. After French naval forces shelled the Vietnamese quarter of Haiphong on 23 Nov., an abortive Viet Minh uprising took place in Hanoi on 19 Dec. Guerrilla warfare grew into full-scale conflict between the French and the Viet Minh forces under General Giap. On 20 Nov. 1953 the French established a forward base at Dien Bien Phu to lure the Viet Minh into a set-piece battle, but the garrison of 15,000 men was overwhelmed on 7 May 1954. An agreement for a ceasefire and the division of the country at latitude 17°N was signed at the Geneva Conference on 27 July 1954.

Malayan Emergency, 1948–60

The Federation of Malaya was proclaimed on 1 Feb. 1948. Communist guerrilla activity began, and on 16 June a state of emergency was declared. In Apr. 1950 General Sir Harold Briggs was appointed to co-ordinate anti-communist operations by Commonwealth forces. He inaugurated the Briggs Plan for resettling Chinese squatters in new villages to cut them off from the guerrillas. After the murder of the British High Commissioner Sir Henry Gurney on 6 Oct. 1951, General Sir Gerald Templer was appointed High Commissioner and director of military operations on 15 Jan. 1952, and on 7 Feb. a new offensive was launched. On 8 Feb. 1954. British authorities announced that the Communist Party's high command in Malaya had withdrawn to Sumatra. The emergency was officially ended on 31 July 1960.

Tunisian War of Independence, 1952–56

In Feb. 1952 Habib Bourguiba and other leaders of the New Constitution Party were arrested, and the ensuing disorders led to the introduction of martial law. In the countryside the Tunisian nationalists waged a guerrilla campaign, while in the towns there were terrorist outrages by nationalists and by the 'Red Hand', a secret settler organisation. Preoccupied with the Algerian revolt, France granted Tunisia independence on 20 Mar. 1956.

Mau Mau Revolt, 1952–60

Violence by the Mau Mau, an African secret society in Kenya, led to a British declaration of a state of emergency on 20 Oct. 1952. Leading Kikuyu nationalists were arrested and Jomo Kenyatta was given a seven-year prison sentence in Oct. 1953. A separate East African command consisting of Kenya, Uganda and Tanganyika was set up under General Sir George Erskine. In campaigns in the first half of 1955 some 4,000 terrorists in the Mount Kenya and Aberdare regions were dispersed. Britain began to reduce her forces in Sept. 1955; the state of emergency in Kenya ended on 12 Jan. 1960.

Moroccan War of Independence, 1953–56

Nationalist agitation grew when Sultan Muhammad V was forced into exile on 20 Aug. 1953 after refusing to co-operate with the French authorities. The Army of National Liberation, composed of Berber tribesmen who had seen service with the French army during the Second World War and the First Indochina War, began a large-scale guerrilla campaign in 1955. The Sultan returned on 5 Nov. 1955, and a Franco–Moroccan declaration on 2 Mar. 1956 ended the French protectorate and established the independence of Morocco.

Algerian War of Independence, 1954–62

Algerian nationalists staged attacks on French military and civilian targets on 1 Nov. 1954. In Aug. 1956 the guerrilla groups formed the *Armée de Libération Nationale*. The French army conducted a brutal counter-insurgency campaign, which, while effective, alienated its supporters. On 13 May 1956 criticism of army methods led the commander-in-chief in Algeria, General Massu, to refuse to recognise the government of France. General de Gaulle, returned to power on 1 June 1958, set a course for Algerian self-determination. A mutiny by the French army in Algeria, led by generals Challe and Salan, began on 22 Apr. 1961, but was suppressed. Despite terrorism by French settlers of the OAS, peace talks began at Evian-les-Bains in May 1961, and a ceasefire was agreed on 18 Mar. 1962. Algeria was declared independent on 3 July 1962.

Cyprus Emergency, 1955–59

Agitation for union with Greece (*Enosis*) led in Apr. 1955 to the start of a campaign of terrorism and guerrilla warfare by EOKA, the militant wing of

187

the *Enosis* movement. A state of emergency was declared on 27 Nov. 1955. Archbishop Makarios of Cyprus was deported to the Seychelles on 9 Mar. 1956. A ceasefire came into effect on 13 Mar. 1959, and the state of emergency was lifted on 4 Dec. 1959. Cyprus became an independent republic on 16 Aug. 1960.

Ifni Incident (Morocco), 1957

On 23 Nov. 1957, some 1,200 Moroccan irregulars attacked the Spanish territory of Ifni. The Spanish garrison was strengthened and Madrid announced that order had been restored on 8 Dec. 1957.

Tunisian conflict with France, 1958–61

On 8 Feb. 1958 the French Air Force bombed the Tunisian town of Sakiet, killing 79 people, in retaliation for Tunisian assistance to the Algerian rebels. Clashes took place as Tunisia demanded the evacuation of French bases. On 17 June 1958 the French agreed to withdraw from all bases except Bizerte. On 5 July 1961 Tunisia made a formal claim to the French Bizerte base and imposed a blockade on 17 July. France sent reinforcements, who occupied the town of Bizerte in heavy fighting on 19–22 July. An agreement for the withdrawal of French troops from the town was signed on 29 Sept. 1961, and the French base was evacuated by 15 Oct. 1963.

Congolese Civil War, 1960–67

Belgium granted independence to its Congo colony on 30 June 1960. Widespread disorder soon followed. The army mutinied, and on 11 July 1960 Moise Tshombe declared the rich mining province of Katanga an independent state. The Prime Minister of the Congo, Patrice Lumumba, appealed to the United Nations and the establishment of a peace-keeping force was approved by the Security Council on 14 July 1960. On 14 Sept. 1960 the army chief of staff, Colonel Mobutu, seized power. Lumumba was seized by Mobutu's troops, handed over to the Katangese and murdered on 9 Feb. 1961. For the next two years, periods of armed conflict and negotiation (during which Dag Hammarskjöld, UN Secretary-General, was killed in a plane crash on 18 Sept. 1961) failed to solve the Congo's problems. Katanga's secession eventually ended when a UN offensive in Dec. 1962 forced Tshombe into exile (15 Jan. 1963). The last UN forces left the Congo on 30 June 1964. Violence continued until Nov. 1967, when a revolt by mercenaries in the eastern provinces, which had begun on 5 July, was finally suppressed.

Angolan War of Independence, 1961–75

The liberation struggle commenced in Portuguese Angola on 3 Feb. 1961, when insurgents attempted to free political prisoners in Luanda. The risings were suppressed with great bloodshed, but a guerrilla campaign developed, and by 1974 Portugal was maintaining an army in Angola of 25,000 white and 38,000 locally enlisted troops. After the coup in Portugal on 25 Apr. 1974, negotiations began, and on 15 Jan. 1975 the Portuguese agreed to Angolan independence. As rival liberation groups fought for control of the country, the independence of Angola was proclaimed on 11 Nov. 1975.

Guinea-Bissau War of Independence, 1963-74

Armed resistance to Portuguese rule was launched by PAIGC in 1963. PAIGC proclaimed the independence of the republic on 24 Sept. 1973. Following the coup d'état in Lisbon on 25 Apr. 1974, led by General Antonio de Spinola (who had been governor and commander-in-chief in Guinea), the Portuguese recognised the independence of Guinea on 10 Sept. 1974.

Mozambique War of Independence, 1964-74

FRELIMO launched its first attacks in Sept. 1964, and gradually took control of large areas of the countryside. By 1974 Portugal was forced to maintain an army in Mozambique of 24,000 white and 20,000 locally enlisted troops. After the coup in Portugal of 24 Apr. 1974, negotiations were opened with FRELIMO. Despite a violent revolt by white settlers in Lourenco Marques (now Maputo) on 3 Sept. 1974, a ceasefire agreement was signed on 7 Sept. and Mozambique officially became independent on 25 June 1975.

Aden, 1964-67

On 18 Jan. 1963 Aden acceded to the South Arabian Federation. British troops were involved in frontier fighting with the Yemen, and in suppressing internal disorders in Aden. A large-scale security operation was launched in Jan. 1964 in the Radfan region, north of Aden. On 26 Nov. 1967 the People's Republic of South Yemen was proclaimed, and the British military withdrawal from Aden was completed on 29 Nov. In the period 1964–67, British security forces lost 57 killed and 651 wounded in Aden.

Falkland Islands, 1982

Argentina has sustained a long-standing claim to the sovereignty of the Falkland Islands and on 2 Apr. 1982 the Argentine dictatorship under General Galtieri launched a successful invasion of the islands, forcing its garrison of 18 Royal Marines to surrender. Argentine forces also seized the island of South Georgia. On 5 Apr. a British task force set sail to recapture the islands and on 7 Apr. an exclusion zone of 200 miles was declared. On 25 Apr. South Georgia was recaptured and on 1 May air attacks began on the Argentine garrison on the Falklands. The next day the Argentine cruiser *Belgrano* was sunk by a British submarine and on 4 May HMS *Sheffield* was hit by an Exocet missile. On 21 May British troops went ashore at San Carlos. Two British frigates, *Ardent* and *Antelope*, were sunk and others damaged by air attack, but British troops took Darwin and Goose Green by the end of May and on 11–14 June an attack on Port Stanley led to the surrender of the Argentine forces. During the conflict 255 British and 720 Argentine troops were killed. A large permanent garrison and modern airstrip were placed on the island for their future security.

KEY EUROPEAN TREATIES AND ALLIANCES

The Alliance system before 1914

1879

7 Oct.   The Dual Alliance, between Germany and Austria–Hungary, is signed in Vienna. Mutual aid in the event of war with Russia; neutrality in the event of war with other powers.

1881

18 June   Formal agreements are made under the League of the Three Emperors, between Germany, Austria–Hungary and Russia, including a commitment to consultation in the event of problems in the Balkans.

28 June   Alliance between Austria–Hungary and Serbia is made in Belgrade.

1882

20 May   Triple Alliance between Germany, Austria–Hungary and Italy is formed in Vienna, extending the Dual Alliance of 1879. Renewed in 1887, 1891, 1902 and 1912.

30 Oct.   Alliance between Austria–Hungary and Romania. Later extended to Germany and Italy. Renewed 1892, 1896, 1902 and 1913.

1884

27 Mar.   The League of the Three Emperors is renewed in Berlin.

1885

26 Feb.   Act of the Conference of Berlin, between Austria–Hungary, Belgium, Denmark, France, Germany, Holland, Italy, Portugal, Russia, Spain, Sweden and the Ottoman Empire settles claims with regard to colonisation in Africa.

1886

3 Mar.   Treaty of Bucharest ends war between Serbia and Bulgaria.

1887

24 Mar. and   Mediterranean Agreements between Britain, Austria–Hungary
16 Dec.   and Italy, to preserve stability in the Balkans and Mediterranean, are made in London. Lapses in 1896.

18 June   The Reinsurance Treaty between Germany and Russia is made in Berlin following the end of the League of the Three Emperors. Neutrality in war with another power. Lapses in 1890.

1890

1 July   Berlin agreement between Britain and Germany on colonies.

1893

27 Dec.   'Dual Entente' is formed between France and Russia in St Petersburg. Mutual aid in the event of war with Germany. Ratified in 1894.

1897

17 May   Vienna agreement between Austria–Hungary and Russia on policy in the Balkans.

4 Dec.   Treaty of Constantinople establishes peace between the Ottoman Empire and Greece.

1900

20 Mar.   Exchange of letters between Britain, France, Germany, Italy, Russia, the USA and Japan accepts an open door for trade with China.

1902

Nov.   Secret treaty between France and Italy. Italy to be neutral in any war involving France.

1904

31 Mar.   Treaty of Sofia establishes an alliance between Serbia and Bulgaria.

8 Apr.   The 'Entente Cordiale' between Britain and France settles colonial disputes and promises friendship.

1906

7 Apr.   Act of the Conference of Algeçiras between Austria–Hungary, Belgium, Britain, France, Germany, Holland, Italy, Morocco, Portugal, Russia, Spain, Sweden and the USA regarding the future of Morocco.

1907

31 Aug.   'Triple Entente' of Britain, France and Russia comes into being with an agreement between Britain and Russia in St Petersburg on areas of influence in Asia.

1911

4 Nov.   Berlin Convention between France and Germany gives France predominance in Morocco in return for German gains elsewhere in Africa.

1912

Feb.–Sept.   The 'Balkan League' of Bulgaria, Serbia, Greece and Montenegro is formed against the Ottoman Empire by a series of agreements.

15 Oct.   Treaty of Ouchy between Italy and the Ottoman Empire. The Ottoman Empire cedes Tripoli and Cyrenaica to Italy.

1913

13 May   Treaty of London establishes peace between the Ottoman Empire and the Balkan League. The Ottoman Empire in Europe is reduced to the area around Constantinople; Albania established.

10 Aug.   Treaty of Bucharest establishes peace between Bulgaria, Serbia, Greece, Romania and Montenegro. Bulgaria is reduced in size.

1914

15 June   London agreement between Britain and Germany concerning the Baghdad Railway.

5 Sept.   London Declaration by Britain, France and Russia not to make a separate peace with the Central Powers.

1915

25 Apr.   Treaty of London between Britain, France and Italy promises Italy territorial gains in return for entering the First World War.

Peace treaties after the First World War

The Treaty of Versailles, 28 June 1919

1. Germany surrenders territory:
   (a) Alsace-Lorraine to France.
   (b) Eupen-Malmédy to Belgium (following plebiscite in 1920).
   (c) Northern Schleswig to Denmark (following plebiscite in 1920).
   (d) Pozania and West Prussia to Poland, Upper Silesia to Poland (following plebiscite in 1921).
   (e) Saar is put under League of Nations control for 15 years and mining interests under French control (returned to Germany following 1935 plebiscite).
   (f) Danzig (Gdansk) put under League of Nations control.
   (g) Memel is placed under Allied control, then transferred to Lithuania.
   (h) German colonies become mandated territories of the League of Nations: German East Africa (to Britain); German South-West Africa

(to South Africa); Cameroons and Togoland (to Britain and France); German Samoa (to New Zealand); German New Guinea (to Australia); Marshall Islands and Pacific Islands north of the Equator (to Japan).

2. Germany loses concessions and trading rights in China, Egypt and Middle East.
3. Demilitarisation of the Rhineland and Heligoland.
4. German army is limited to 100,000 men, denied U-boats and air force.
5. Army of occupation on west bank of the Rhine and bridgeheads at Cologne, Coblenz and Mainz from Jan. 1920.
6. Germany accepts 'war guilt' clause.
7. Germany agrees to pay reparations and accepts responsibility for war damage.
8. The Treaty of Brest-Litovsk is declared void; Germany is required to evacuate Baltic States and other occupied territory.
9. The Covenant of the League of Nations is written into the Treaty.

The Treaty of Saint-Germain, 10 Sept. 1919

1. The Austro–Hungarian Empire is effectively dissolved:
    (a) Austria and Hungary to become separate states with total loss of control over other former parts of the Austro–Hungarian Empire.
    (b) New state of Czechoslovakia is created.
    (c) New state of Yugoslavia is set up.
    (d) Galicia is ceded to Poland.
    (e) Transylvania is ceded to Romania.
    (f) South Tyrol, Trentino and Istria are ceded to Italy.
    (g) Plebiscite to define boundary with Austria in southern Carinthia.
2. Austria is forbidden to unite with Germany without League of Nations approval.
3. Austrian army is limited to 30,000 men.
4. Reparations are required for war damage.
5. Covenant of League of Nations is written into the Treaty.

The Treaty of the Trianon, 4 June 1920

1. Hungary accepts break-up of Austro–Hungarian Empire and surrender of territory to Romania, Czechoslovakia, Yugoslavia, Poland, Italy and the new Austrian Republic.
2. Hungarian army is limited to 35,000 men.
3. Hungary is required to pay reparations.
4. Covenant of the League of Nations is written into the Treaty.

The Treaty of Sèvres, 10 Aug. 1920 (*never ratified by Turkey*)

1. Turkish Empire loses territory:
    (a) Cyprus to Britain.
    (b) Rhodes, the Dodecanese, and Adalia are ceded to Italy.

    (c) Part of European Turkey to Bulgaria.

    (d) Eastern Thrace to Greece; Greek claim to Chios and other islands is recognised; Greece is allowed to occupy Smyrna for five years until a plebiscite is held.

    (e) Hejaz and Arabia become independent.

    (f) League of Nations mandates over Syria (to France); Palestine, Iraq and Transjordan (to Britain).

2. The Straits are placed under international control.
3. Turkey is occupied by British, French and Italian troops.
4. The Covenant of the League of Nations is written into the Treaty.

The Treaty of Neuilly, 27 Nov. 1919

1. Bulgaria loses territory:
    (a) Territory along Bulgaria's western boundary is ceded to Yugoslavia.
    (b) Part of western Thrace is ceded to Greece.
2. Bulgaria gains territory from European Turkey.
3. Bulgarian army is limited to 20,000 men.
4. Bulgaria is made liable for reparations.
5. The Covenant of the League of Nations is written into the Treaty.

Treaty of Lausanne, 24 July 1923

1. Turkey surrenders its claims to territories of the Ottoman Empire occupied by non-Turks, effectively surrendering the Arab lands.
2. The Turks retain Constantinople and Eastern Thrace in Europe; both sides of Greek–Turkish border demilitarised.
3. Turkey takes Smyrna from Greece but surrenders all the Aegean Islands except Imbros and Tenedos which return to Turkey.
4. Turkey recognises the annexation of Cyprus by Britain and of the Dodecanese by Italy.
5. Turkey is left free of foreign troops.
6. The Straits are declared to be demilitarised (in July 1936 by the Montreux Convention Turkey is allowed to refortify the Straits).
7. No restrictions are placed on Turkey's armed forces and no reparations are required.

Diplomatic agreements and alliances of the Cold War era

1945

11 Feb.   Yalta Agreement between Britain, USSR and the USA on the future of Germany, Europe and world security.

11 Apr.   Treaty of friendship, co-operation and mutual assistance between USSR and Yugoslavia (abrogated by Soviet Union on 28 Sept. 1949).

21 Apr. Treaty of friendship, co-operation and mutual assistance between USSR and Poland.

26 June United Nations charter establishes new world security system, with Britain, USSR, France, the USA and China as leading powers.

2 Aug. Potsdam Agreement between Britain, USSR and the USA expands on the Yalta Agreement.

1946

27 Feb. Soviet treaty of friendship and mutual assistance with Mongolia.

15 Nov. Linggadjati Agreement between Dutch and Indonesians on creation of Indonesian Republic.

1947

10 Feb. Peace treaties of Allies with Italy, Finland, Hungary, Bulgaria and Romania.

4 Mar. Treaty of Dunkirk between Britain and France promises mutual aid against German aggression.

10 Mar. Czech–Polish Pact.

14 Mar. Benelux customs union created between Belgium, Holland and Luxembourg.

5 June Marshall Plan aid for reconstruction accepted by 16 European countries through European Recovery Programme.

20 June Military assistance agreement between Greece and the USA.

27 Nov. Bulgarian 20-year treaty of friendship and co-operation with Yugoslavia (abrogated by Bulgaria on 1 Oct. 1949).

8 Dec. Hungary signs 20-year treaty of friendship and co-operation with Yugoslavia (abrogated by Hungary on 30 Sept. 1949).

16 Dec. Bulgaria signs 20-year treaty of friendship and co-operation with Albania.

19 Dec. Twenty-year treaty of friendship and co-operation between Romania and Yugoslavia (abrogated by Romania on 2 Oct. 1949).

1948

16 Jan. Bulgarian–Romanian Pact.

24 Jan. Hungarian–Romanian Pact.

4 Feb. Soviet–Romanian Pact.

18 Feb. Soviet–Hungarian Pact.

16 Mar.	Soviet–Bulgarian Pact.
17 Mar.	Brussels Treaty between Britain, France, Belgium, Holland and Luxembourg provides for mutual aid against aggression, and for economic and social co-operation.
6 Apr.	Soviet mutual assistance pact with Finland (extended 19 Sept. 1955, 20 July 1970 and 6 June 1983).
16 Apr.	Organisation for European Economic Co-operation (OEEC) is formed by 16 West European nations.
9 June	Polish–Hungarian Pact.
18 June	Bulgarian–Hungarian Pact.
21 July	Romanian–Czech Pact.

1949

21 Jan.	Romanian–Polish Pact.
25 Jan.	Comecon (Council for Mutual Economic Assistance) is set up by the USSR and communist East European states for economic co-ordination and development.
21 Feb.	Greek agreement with the USA on use of certain Greek islands for future training exercises by US Mediterranean fleet.
4 Apr.	North Atlantic Treaty between the USA, Canada, Britain, France, Belgium, Holland, Luxembourg, Norway, Denmark, Portugal and Iceland. Later joined by Greece, Turkey and West Germany. Mutual aid against aggression.
16 Apr.	Hungarian–Czechoslovakian Pact.
5 May	Statute of the Council of Europe signed in London by 10 West European states.

1950

| 14 Feb. | Soviet treaty of friendship, alliance and mutual assistance with China. |
| 7 June | East German agreement with Poland on the Oder–Neisse frontier. |

1952

18 Feb.	Greece joins North Atlantic Treaty.
26 May	West German agreement on relations with Britain, France and USA (amended by Paris agreements of 23 Oct. 1954).
27 May	Treaty is signed in Paris between France, West Germany, Italy, Belgium, Holland and Luxembourg to create a European Defence Community and common army. Later rejected by France and common army fails to develop.

9 Sept.	West German agreement with Britain on bases in Germany (further agreements Oct. 1954 and May 1957).

1953

26 Sept.	Mutual defence agreement between USA and Spain, allowing US bases.
12 Oct.	Agreement between Greece and USA on military facilities.

1954

21 July	Geneva Agreement on future of Indochina.
9 Aug.	Balkan Pact. A treaty of alliance, political co-operation and mutual assistance is signed by Greece, Turkey and Yugoslavia, valid for 20 years.
3 Oct.	London Agreement to extend the Brussels Pact to West Germany and Italy, forming the West European Union.
12 Oct.	Soviet Agreement on political co-operation with China.

1955

24 Feb.	Baghdad Pact is signed, a mutual assistance treaty signed by Turkey and Iraq. Britain joins the Pact on 5 May.
5 May	London and Paris agreements. The occupation regime in West Germany is ended, and the German Federal Republic attains full sovereignty and independence. The Federal Republic becomes a member of NATO, and of the Western European Union, the expanded Brussels Treaty Organisation which comes into being on 5 May.
13 May	Warsaw Pact between USSR, East Germany, Poland, Czechoslovakia, Hungary, Bulgaria, Romania and Albania. Mutual assistance in the event of war.
15 May	Austrian State Treaty between Britain, the USA, USSR and France establishes a neutral but sovereign Austria.
30 June	West German mutual defence agreement with the USA.
20 Sept.	Treaty by which Soviet Union recognises East Germany as a sovereign state.
18 Dec.	Soviet Union 10-year extension of 1931 treaty of neutrality and non-aggression with Afghanistan (further extension 6 Aug. 1965 and 10 Dec. 1975).
25 Dec.	East German 10-year treaty of friendship with China.

1956

27 Oct.	Franco–German agreement on the incorporation of the Saar into West Germany.

1957

22 Mar.   Treaty of Rome between France, West Germany, Italy, Belgium, Holland and Luxembourg establishes the European Economic Community (EEC). Extended to Britain, Denmark and Eire, 1973.

1959

19 Feb.   Agreement on future of Cyprus between Britain, Greece, Turkey and Cypriot communities.

6 May   Russo–Chinese Treaty of Friendship.

7 Sept.   Ten-Power Committee on Disarmament is set up representing Britain, Canada, France, Italy, the USA, Bulgaria, Czechoslovakia, Poland, Romania and the Soviet Union.

1960

3 May   Stockholm Convention between Britain, Denmark, Norway, Portugal, Austria, Sweden and Switzerland establishes the European Free Trade Association. Later joined by Finland and Iceland. Britain and Denmark leave in 1972 to join the EEC.

1961

30 Sept.   Organisation for Economic Co-operation and Development (OECD) replaces the OEEC and includes the USA and Canada.

1963

22 Jan.   Treaty of co-operation between France and West Germany.

5 Aug.   Partial nuclear test ban treaty between Britain, the USA and USSR limits nuclear tests.

27 Nov.   Soviet–Czech Pact.

1964

12 June   Soviet Pact with East Germany.

1966   France withdraws from military commitments to NATO.

9 Nov.   Soviet agreement with France on establishment of a 'Hot Line'.

1967

27 Jan.   Treaty banning nuclear weapons in space is opened for signature in London, Moscow and Washington.

25 Aug.   Anglo–Soviet agreement on establishment of a 'Hot Line'.

1968

1 July   Nuclear Non-Proliferation Treaty is agreed and opened for signature.

1969

26 Aug.   Disarmament Committee is renamed Conference of the Committee on Disarmament with 24 members.

1970

12 Aug.   Soviet–West German Treaty signed in which the two countries renounce the use of force.

18 Nov.   Polish–West German Treaty, an agreement that the existing boundary line on the Oder and the West Neisse constitutes the western frontier of Poland, and renouncing the use of force for the settlement of disputes.

1971

3 Sept.   USSR, USA, Britain and France reach agreement on Berlin.

21 Dec.   Agreement between West Germany and East Germany on transit to West Berlin.

1972

27 Jan.   Treaty of Accession is signed, bringing Britain, Ireland and Denmark into the EEC with effect from 1 Jan. 1973.

26 May   Soviet SALT anti-ballistic missile agreement with the USA and interim agreement on limitation of strategic arms.

5 Nov.   Agreement of the USA, Britain, Soviet Union and France on the maintenance of four-power rights and responsibilities in Germany.

21 Dec.   Agreement between West Germany and East Germany on the basis of relations between their two countries.

1973

11 Dec.   West German Treaty with Czechoslovakia for the normalisation of relations.

1974

19 Sept.   West German declaration on normalisation of relations with Finland.

24 Nov.   Vladivostok Accord between the USA and Soviet Union establishes framework for future negotiations controlling strategic arms race.

1975

1 Aug.   Act of the Helsinki Conference, between 35 nations regarding European security, including a reaffirmation of human rights and proposals for economic collaboration between Eastern and Western blocs.

10 Nov.   Treaty of Osimo is signed, an agreement between Italy and Yugoslavia in which the two countries accept border changes around Trieste slightly in favour of Italy, and that national minorities are to be protected and there is to be greater economic co-operation.

1977

18 Oct.   West German agreement with Britain to end payments to off-set British foreign exchange costs of stationing troops in West Germany.

1978

5 Dec.   Soviet Treaty of friendship, good-neighbourliness and co-operation with Afghanistan.

1979

28 May   Greece signs Treaty of Accession to the EEC with effect from 1 Jan. 1981.

18 June   SALT II agreement between Soviet Union and the USA on limitation of strategic offensive arms (unratified by USA).

1982

30 May   Spain joins NATO; decision to remain part of NATO is confirmed by referendum, 12 Mar. 1984.

1985

12 June   Portugal and Spain sign Treaties of Accession to the EEC with effect from 1 Jan. 1986.

15 Nov.   Anglo–Irish Agreement (Hillsborough Agreement) confirms that any change to the status of Northern Ireland must only be with the consent of the majority of its people, but gives the Irish Republic a consultative role in Northern Irish affairs through Intergovernmental Conferences.

1986

1 Feb.   Single European Act is signed between heads of EEC governments, coming into force on 1 July 1987 to create a single European market by 31 Dec. 1992 and to promote greater harmonisation of monetary and economic policy.

1987

8 Dec.   Intermediate Nuclear Forces Treaty is signed in Washington between the USA and the Soviet Union, providing for the withdrawal and destruction of all land-based nuclear missiles in Europe with ranges of between 500 and 5,500kms, including American Cruise and Pershing II missiles and Soviet SS-20s. Verification procedures provide for on-site inspection of compliance.

1988

14 Apr.   Geneva Accord on removal of Soviet troops from Afghanistan by mid-Feb. 1989.

1989

2 Dec.   Agreement in principle between Pope John Paul II and President Gorbachev in Rome to re-establish diplomatic relations between the Vatican and the Soviet Union and for lifting of ban on the Catholic (Uniate) Church in the Ukraine dating from 1946.

1990

Feb.   Hungary and Vatican to resume diplomatic relations.

27 Feb.   Soviet Agreement with Czechoslovakia for withdrawal of forces by July 1991.

10 Mar.   Soviet Agreement with Hungary for withdrawal of forces by July 1991.

16 July   East and West Germany agree and adopt economic unification on the basis of West German currency. West German–Soviet Agreement, that united Germany will have full sovereignty, including freedom to join NATO, and on Soviet withdrawal of 350,000 troops from East Germany within three to four years.

17 July   Paris Agreement in 'Two-Plus-Four' talks guarantees existing Polish–German border to be secured in treaty after German unification to define German–Polish relations. London Declaration of NATO leaders accepts need to remodel NATO as a political rather than a military alliance and agrees to invite Warsaw Pact representatives and President Gorbachev to future meetings.

12 Sept.   Treaty concluding 'Two-Plus-Four' talks ends special Allied Powers over Germany and agrees to unification with full sovereignty of East and West Germany.

19 Nov.   Conference on Security and Co-operation in Europe (CSCE) signs agreement in Paris, marking formal end of the Cold War.

	Signature of Conventional Forces in Europe (CFE) Treaty by 22 NATO and Warsaw Pact countries formalising largest cuts in weapons and manpower since 1945.
1991	Massive reductions in armaments agreed between Presidents Bush and Gorbachev with signature of START Treaty. Signing of Treaty of Maastricht on European Union.
1992	Russian agreements with Baltic states on withdrawal of troops and with Ukraine on fleet.
1996	
May	Russian peace accord is signed with Chechnyan rebels.
Dec.	Agreement between Russia and China on troop reductions along their common frontier.
	Hungary and Romania sign treaty to respect mutual borders and protect rights of Hungarian minority in Transylvania.
1997	
May	Founding Act is signed (agreement between Russia and NATO).
	Treaty of Amsterdam is signed (the successor to the Treaty of Maastricht). Only limited progress towards further European integration.
1998	
Dec.	Agreement on future EU defence policy concluded at St Malo between Britain and France.
1999	
Dec.	Anglo–Irish Treaty to implement the Good Friday Agreement.
2002	
May	Establishment of NATO–Russia Council (NRC).
Nov.	Prague Summit sees extension of NATO.

PRINCIPAL INTERNATIONAL ORGANISATIONS AND GROUPINGS

Commonwealth of Independent States (CIS)

A voluntary association of 11 (formerly 12) states formed when the Soviet Union disintegrated. Its history to date suggests it is little more than a forum to keep alive some vague form of co-operation after the demise of the old USSR. Early 'agreements' were made at Minsk (14 Feb. 1992, on strategic forces), Kiev (20 Mar. 1992, on state frontiers) and Tashkent (15 May 1992, on collective security).

Council for Mutual Economic Assistance (COMECON)

Organisation established in Moscow in Jan. 1959 to improve trade between the Soviet Union and other East European states. Regarded by Stalin as an instrument to enforce an economic boycott on Yugoslavia, and also used as a Soviet response to growing West European economic interdependence. Apart from the East European countries, Mongolia joined in 1962, Cuba in 1972 and Vietnam in 1978. Changes in Europe since 1989 left its future role uncertain and it was formally dissolved in Jan. 1991.

Secretaries

Nikolai Faddeyev (USSR)	1949–83
Vyacheslav Sychev (USSR)	1983–91

Council of Europe

Organisation established in 1949 to achieve greater European unity based on the common heritage of its member states. Matters of national defence are excluded. The original states were Belgium, Britain, Denmark, France, Ireland, Italy, the Netherlands, Norway and Sweden. They were soon joined by Greece, Iceland and Turkey later in 1949, West Germany in 1951, Austria in 1956, Cyprus in 1961, Switzerland in 1963 and Malta in 1965. With the fall of communism, and the new political order in Central and Eastern Europe, membership has grown rapidly (to 43 by 2002). It is quite separate from the European Union.

Secretaries-General

Jacques Camille-Paris (France)	1949–53
Leon Marchal (France)	1953–57
Ludovico Benvenuti (Italy)	1957–64
Peter Smithers (UK)	1964–69
Lujo Toncic-Sorinj (Austria)	1969–74
Georg Kahn-Ackermann (Federal Republic of Germany)	1974–79
Franz Karasek (Austria)	1979–84
Marcelino Oreja Aguirre (Spain)	1984–89
Catherine Lalumière (France)	1989–94
Daniel Tarschys (Sweden)	1994–99
Walter Schwimmer (Austria)	1999–

European Union (EU) (formerly European Community)

Formerly also referred to as the Common Market. The European Community came into being on 1 Jan. 1958, following the signing by the original six states (Belgium, France, Italy, Luxembourg, the Netherlands and West Germany) of the Treaty of Rome on 25 Mar. 1957. The original six states, who bound themselves to work together for economic and political union, have been enlarged with the entry of Denmark, Ireland and the UK on 1 Jan. 1973, Greece on 1 Jan. 1981, Spain and Portugal on 1 Jan. 1986 and Austria, Finland and Sweden on 1 Jan. 1995. The Copenhagen Summit of December 2002 agreed to admit 10 new members from 2004. These were the Czech Republic, Hungary, Poland, Estonia, Latvia, Lithuania, Slovakia, Slovenia, Cyprus and Malta.

Presidents of the European Commission

Walter Hallstein (Federal Republic of Germany)	1958–66
Jean Rey (Belgium)	1966–70
Franco Malfatti (Italy)	1970–72
Sicco Mansholt (Netherlands)	1972–73
François-Xavier Ortoli (France)	1973–77
Roy Jenkins (UK)	1977–81
Gaston Thorn (Luxembourg)	1981–85
Jacques Delors (France)	1985–95
Jacques Santer (Luxembourg)	1995–99
Romano Prodi (Italy)	1999–

Membership of the European Union, Jan. 2003

Country	Date of Joining	Country	Date of Joining
Austria	Jan. 1995	Italy	1957
Belgium	1957	Luxembourg	1957
Denmark	Jan. 1973	Netherlands	1957
Finland	Jan. 1995	Portugal	Jan. 1986
France	1957	Spain	Jan. 1986
Germany*	1957	Sweden	Jan. 1995
Greece	Jan. 1981	United Kingdom	Jan. 1973
Ireland	Jan. 1973		

* As the Federal Republic of Germany (i.e. West Germany).

European Parliament

The European Parliament consists of 626 members elected by all member states. The division of the seats (2003) was as follows:

Austria	21	Italy	87
Belgium	25	Luxembourg	6
Denmark	16	Netherlands	31
Finland	16	Portugal	25
France	87	Spain	64
Germany	99	Sweden	22
Greece	25	United Kingdom	87
Ireland	15		

Presidents of the European Parliament

Robert Schuman (France)	1958–60
Hans Furler (Federal Republic of Germany)	1960–62
Gaetano Martino (Italy)	1962–64
Jean Duvieusart (Belgium)	1964–65
Victor Leemans (Belgium)	1965–66
Alain Poher (France)	1966–69
Mario Scelba (Italy)	1969–71
Walter Behrendt (Federal Republic of Germany)	1971–73
Cornelius Berkhouwer (Netherlands)	1973–75
Georges Spénale (France)	1975–77
Emilio Colombo (Italy)	1977–79
Simone Veil (France)	1979–82
Pieter Dankert (Netherlands)	1982–84
Pierre Pflimlin (France)	1984–87
Lord Plumb (UK)	1987–89
Enrico Barón Crespo (Spain)	1989–91
Egon Klepsch (Germany)	1992–94
Klaus Hänsch (Germany)	1994–97
Jose Maria Gil-Robles (Spain)	1997–02
Pat Cox (Ireland)	2002–

European Free Trade Association (EFTA)

Grouping of European countries whose aims are to achieve a free trade in industrial goods between members, to help achieve the creation of a general West European market and to expand world trade in general. Six members have left to join the European Economic Community (Denmark and the UK in 1972, Portugal in 1985, Austria, Finland and Sweden in 1994). Indeed, EFTA had arisen partly as a response to the original veto by France on Britain joining the European Community.

Secretaries-General

Frank Figgures (UK)	1960–65
John Coulson (UK)	1965–72
Bengt Rabaeus (Sweden)	1972–75
Charles Muller (Switzerland)	1976–81
Magnus Vahlquist (Sweden) (Acting)	1981 (Oct.–Nov.)
Per Kleppe (Norway)	1981–88
Georg Reisch (Austria)	1988–94
Kjartan Jóhannsson (Iceland)	1994–

League of Nations

International organisation set up as an integral part of the Versailles Settlement in 1920 to preserve the peace and settle disputes by negotiation. Although the USA refused to participate, it comprised 53 members by 1923. Based in Geneva, the League relied upon non-military means to coerce states, such as 'sanctions', but found itself virtually powerless in the face of the Japanese invasion of Manchuria and the Italian invasion of Abyssinia. The League was discredited by 1939 and was dissolved in Apr. 1946 with the formation of the United Nations.

Secretaries-General

Sir Eric Drummond (Earl of Perth) (UK)	1919–32
Joseph Avenol (France)	1933–40
Sean Lester (Ireland) (Acting)	1940–46

The following European states joined the League on the dates given below:

Albania	16 Dec. 1920
Belgium	10 Jan. 1920
Bulgaria	16 Dec. 1920
Czechoslovakia	10 Jan. 1920
Denmark	8 Mar. 1920
Estonia	22 Sep. 1921
Finland	16 Dec. 1920
France	10 Jan. 1920
Germany	8 Sep. 1926
Greece	30 Mar. 1920
Hungary	18 Sep. 1922
Irish Free State	10 Sep. 1923
Italy	10 Jan. 1920
Latvia	22 Sep. 1921
Lithuania	22 Sep. 1921
Luxembourg	16 Dec. 1920
Netherlands	9 Mar. 1920
Norway	5 Mar. 1920
Poland	10 Jan. 1920
Portugal	8 Apr. 1920
Romania	8 Apr. 1920
Spain	10 Jan. 1920
Sweden	9 Mar. 1920
Switzerland	8 Mar. 1920
Turkey	18 July 1932
USSR	18 Sep. 1934
UK	10 Jan. 1920
Yugoslavia	10 Feb. 1920

North Atlantic Treaty Organisation (NATO)

Created by the North Atlantic Treaty of 4 Apr. 1949. The organisation represented the first US commitment to European defence in peacetime. NATO came in response to Western fears about the power of the Soviet Union and the failure of the UN Security Council to operate in the face of the Soviet veto. The treaty states are obliged to take such action as they deem necessary to assist a fellow signatory subjected to aggression, although there is no obligation to fight. The treaty states are Belgium, Luxembourg, the Netherlands, Britain, the USA, Canada, Italy, Norway, Denmark, Iceland and Portugal, who were original signatories, plus Greece and Turkey (1952) and West Germany (1955). The reunited Germany acceded in Oct. 1990. Spain joined in 1982. With the fall of communism, the role of NATO is changing and its membership is reaching out to Central and Eastern Europe. The 2002 Prague Summit expanded its membership to 26 nations. NATO has provided support for peacekeeping operations in Bosnia. France was an original signatory, but withdrew from the organisation in 1966.

Secretaries-General

Lord Ismay (UK)	1952–57
Paul-Henri Spaak (Belgium)	1957–61
Alberico Casardi (Acting)	1961 (Mar.–Apr.)
Dirk Stikker (Holland)	1961–64
Manlio Brosio (Italy)	1964–71
Joseph Luns (Holland)	1971–84
Lord Carrington (UK)	1984–88
Manfred Wörner (Federal Republic of Germany)	1988–95
Javier Solana (Spain)	1995–99
Lord Robertson (UK)	1999–2003

Supreme Allied Commanders, Europe

Dwight D. Eisenhower (US)	1950–52
Matthew Ridgway (US)	1952–53
Alfred M. Gruenther (US)	1953–56
Lauris Norstad (US)	1956–63
Lyman L. Lemnitzer (US)	1963–69
Andrew J. Goodpaster (US)	1969–74
Alexander Haig (US)	1974–79
Bernard Rogers (US)	1979–87
John R. Galvin (US)	1987–92
John Shalikashvili (US)	1992–93
George Joulvan (US)	1993–97
Wesley Clark (US)	1997–00
Joseph W. Ralston (US)	2000–02
James L. Jones (US)	2002–

Organisation for Economic Co-operation and Development (OECD)

The organisation consists of over 20 countries, mostly the richer nations. Its aims are to encourage and co-ordinate the economic policies of members, to contribute to the expansion of developing countries and to promote the development of world trade on a multi-lateral basis. It publishes economic statistics and compiles reports on specific aspects of world economics. It is the successor to the Organisation for European Economic Co-operation (OEEC).

Secretaries-General

Thorkil Kristensen (Denmark)	1961–69
Emile van Lennep (Netherlands)	1969–84
Jean-Claude Paye (France)	1984–96
Donald Johnston (Canada)	1996–

United Nations, the

International peace-keeping organisation set up in 1945 to replace the League of Nations. From the 50 states who signed the Charter of the UN in 1945, numbers had more than doubled by 1970 with the rise of independent ex-colonial states. All states have one vote in the General Assembly, and its executive, the Security Council, can call on member states to supply armed forces. UN troops have been involved in peace-keeping duties in many parts of the world since 1945, notably in the Middle East, Africa and Cyprus.

Secretaries-General

Trygve Lie (Norway)	1946–53
Dag Hammarskjöld (Sweden)	1953–61
U Thant (Burma)	1961–71
Kurt Waldheim (Austria)	1972–81
Javier Pérez de Cuellar (Peru)	1982–91
Boutros-Boutros Ghali (Egypt)	1992–96
Kofi Annan (Ghana)	1997–

Warsaw Pact, the

Military grouping of the USSR and East European states, with a political consultative committee intended to meet twice a year with rotating venue and chairmanship. In fact it met every alternate year, with delegations led by first secretaries of the party. Committee of defence ministers also met annually. Committee of foreign ministers met annually from 1976. Military Council of national chiefs of staff met twice a year. Following the collapse of communism in Eastern Europe, by late 1990 the Warsaw Pact had effectively ceased to exist as a military alliance.

Commanders-in-Chief

Marshal I.S. Konev (USSR)	1955–60
Marshal A.A. Grechko (USSR)	1960–67
Marshal I.I. Yakubovsky (USSR)	1967–76
Marshal Viktor G. Kulikov (USSR)	1977–91

Members

Albania (ceased to participate in 1961 because of Stalinist and pro-Chinese attitudes. Withdrew in 1968)

Bulgaria

Czechoslovakia

German Democratic Republic (formally withdrew on 24 Sept. 1990)

Hungary

Poland

Romania

USSR

SOCIAL AND ECONOMIC HISTORY

COMPARATIVE POPULATION OF MAJOR EUROPEAN COUNTRIES

(millions, rounded up to the nearest 100,000)

	1850	1900	1950	2000
Austria	17.5	26.2	6.9	8.1
Belgium	4.3	6.7	8.5	10.2
Bulgaria	—	3.8	7.0	7.7
Czech Republic	—	—	—	10.3
Czechoslovakia	—	—	12.3	—
Denmark	1.4	2.5	4.3	5.4
Finland	1.6	2.7	4.0	5.2
France	35.8	38.5	42.8	59.5
Germany	33.4	56.4	69.1[1]	82.1[1]
Great Britain	20.8	37.0	49.0	58.8
Greece	1.0	2.4	7.6	10.7
Hungary	13.2	19.3	9.2	10.0
Ireland	6.6	4.5	3.0	3.8
Italy	24.4	32.5	46.7	57.7
Netherlands	3.1	5.1	9.6	15.9
Norway	1.4	2.2	3.3	4.5
Poland	—	25.1	25.0	38.6
Portugal	3.8	5.4	8.4	10.0
Romania	3.9	6.0	15.9	22.4
Russia	68.5	126.4	208.8[2]	145.5[3]
Slovakia	—	—	—	5.4
Spain	15.5	18.6	28.0	39.5
Sweden	3.5	5.1	7.0	8.9
Switzerland	2.4	2.3	4.7	7.1
Ukraine	—	—	—	48.8
Yugoslavia	—	—	15.7	—

* Figures are given for the nearest year where not otherwise available.

[1] East and West Germany; unified Germany in 1997.

[2] USSR.

[3] Russia only.

(Sources: B. R. Mitchell, *European Historical Statistics, 1750–1975* (2nd edn), Macmillan, 1980; C. M. Cipolla (ed.), *The Fontana Economic History of Europe*, vol. VI, Collins/Fontana, 1975; J. Paxton (ed.), *The Statesman's Year-Book 1989–90*, Macmillan, 1989).

Readers should note that for more comprehensive figures the authoritative work is the third edition of B. R. Mitchell's *European Historical Statistics, 1750–1988* (Macmillan, 1992).

POPULATION OF MAJOR EUROPEAN CITIES

(thousands)

	1800	1850	1900	1950	1981*	1991
Amsterdam	201	224	511	804	965	694
Athens	12	31	111	565	886	3,016[1]
Barcelona	115	175	533	1,280	1,754	1,707
Belgrade	30	—	69	368	1,400	936[2]
Berlin	172	419	1,889	3,337	3,083[3]	3,124
Birmingham	71	233	523	1,113	1,050	934
Brussels	66	251	599	956	1,029	970
Budapest	54	178	732	1,571	2,093	2,016
Cologne	50	97	373	595	1,014	946
Copenhagen	101	127	401	1,168[4]	1,214[4]	1,353[4]
Dresden	60	97	396	494	509	521
Edinburgh	83	194	394	467	464	434
Genoa	100	120	235	648	804	667
Glasgow	77	345	776	1,090	832	689
Hamburg	130	132	706	1,606	1,717	1,600
Leipzig	30	63	456	618	567	549
Lisbon	180	240	356	790	1,708[4]	2,048[4]
Liverpool	80	376	704	789	537	448
London	1,117	2,685	6,586	8,348	6,970[5]	6,378
Lyons	110	177	459	650	1,153[4]	1,262[4]
Madrid	160	281	540	1,618	3,146	3,120
Manchester	75	303	645	703	491	397
Marseilles	111	195	491	661	1,005[4]	1,230[4]
Milan	170	242	493	1,260	1,723	1,400
Moscow	250	365	989	5,046	7,734	8,408
Munich	40	110	500	832	1,315	1,315
Naples	350	449	564	1,011	1,221	1,220
Palermo	140	150	228	491	666	696
Paris	547	1,053	2,714	2,850	2,317	2,152
Prague	75	118	202	922	1,889	1,889
Rome	153	175	463	1,652	2,884	2,830
St Petersburg/Leningrad	220	485	1,267	3,321	4,372	5,000
Stockholm	76	93	301	744	1,375[4]	1,577[4]
Turin	78	135	336	711	1,199	962
Vienna	247	444	1,675	1,766	1,581	1,524
Warsaw	60	114	423	279	1,463	1,649

Note: As totals are based on varying definitions of the conurbations concerned, they are not exactly but only generally comparable between countries.

* Where no figure for 1981 is available, figure given to the nearest census.

[1] City area only.

[2] Metropolitan area.

[3] East and West Berlin totals combined.

[4] Conurbation totals.

[5] Based on a more restricted boundary of the area controlled by the Greater London Council after 1966.

(Sources: B. R. Mitchell, *European Historical Statistics, 1750–1975* (2nd edn), Macmillan, 1980; C. M. Cipolla (ed.), *The Fontana Economic History of Europe,* vol. IV, Collins/Fontana, 1975; A. F. Weber, *The Growth of Cities in the Nineteenth Century,* Macmillan, New York, 1899; B. Hunter (ed.), *The Statesman's Year-Book, 1996–97,* Macmillan, 1996.)

EMIGRATION FROM EUROPE: SELECTED COUNTRIES

(in thousands)

	1881–90	1891–1900	1901–10	1911–20	1921–30	1931–40	1941–50	1951–60
Austria–Hungary*	248	440	1,111	418	61	11	—	53
Belgium	21	16	30	21	33	20	29	109
Denmark	82	51	73	52	64	100	38	68
Finland	16	59	159	67	73	3	7	32
France	119	51	53	32	4	5	—	155
Germany[1]	1,342	527	274	91	564	121	618	872
Italy	992	1,580	3,615	2,194	1,370	235	467	858
Netherlands[2]	52	24	28	22	32	4[2]	75[2]	341[2]
Norway	187	95	191	62	87	6	10	25
Poland	—	—	—	—	634	164	—	—
Portugal	185	266	324	402	995	108	69	346
Russia	911	420	—	—	—	—	—	—
Spain	572	791	1,091	1,306	560	132	166	543
Sweden	327	205	324	86	107	8	23	43
UK and Ireland[3]	3,259	2,149	3,150	2,587	2,151	262	755	1,454

* Austria only after 1921.
[1] West Germany only after 1941.
[2] Excludes emigration to Dutch colonies.
[3] Excludes direct emigration from Irish ports.
(Source: B. R. Mitchell, *European Historical Statistics, 1750–1970*, Macmillan, 1975, p. 135.)

OUTPUT OF WHEAT: SELECTED COUNTRIES

(thousands of metric tons)

	1913	1924	1938	1950	1962	1972	1986	1993
Bulgaria	1,184	672	2,149	1,757	2,086	3,582	3,600[4]	3,681
France	8,690	7,650	9,800	7,700	14,050	17,850	27,504	29,252[5]
Germany*	5,094	3,053	6,250	2,614	4,592	7,134	10,068	15,766
Greece	357[1]	210	980	850	1,722	1,768	2,131	2,344[5]
Hungary	4,119	1,403	2,688	2,040	1,973	4,095	4,800[4]	4,874
Italy	5,690	4,479	8,184	7,774	9,497	9,421	8,974	8,938
Poland	—	884	2,172	1,888	2,700	5,147	5,165[4]	8,243
Romania	2,291	1,917	4,821	2,219	4,054	6,041	5,000[4]	5,355
Spain	3,059	3,314	4,300	3,374	4,812	4,562	5,163	4,989
USSR	28,000[2]	13,000	40,800	31,100	70,800	85,993	84,565	99,100[6]
UK	1,566	1,435	1,990	2,646	3,968	4,780	12,634	12,870
Yugoslavia	417[3]	1,662	3,030	1,833	3,514	4,844	5,519[4]	—

* West Germany after 1938; united Germany in 1993.
[1] 1914.
[2] Includes Baltic states.
[3] Serbia only.
[4] 1983.
[5] 1992.
[6] Russia only; all grains.

(Sources: B. R. Mitchell, *European Historical Statistics, 1750–1970*, Macmillan, 1975, pp. 249–75; J. Paxton (ed.), *The Statesman's Year-Book 1989–90*, Macmillan, 1989; B. Hunter (ed.), *The Statesman's Year-Book 1996–97*, Macmillan, 1996.)

OUTPUT OF COAL AND LIGNITE: SELECTED COUNTRIES

(Annual total in million metric tons)

	1900	1925	1935	1955	1975	1993
Austria	33[1]	3	3	4	3	2
Belgium	23	23	26	27	7	—
Bulgaria	—	1	1	6	24	29
Czechoslovakia	—	31	26	45	107	—
France	33	48	47	53	27	10
Germany	150	273	290	188	214	259
(E. Germany)	—	—	—	140	245	—
Hungary	6	6	7	13	26	13
Italy	—	1	1	2	2	—
Netherlands	—	7	12	12	—	—
Poland	—	29	28	83	211	200
Romania	—	3	2	4	29	42
Russia/USSR	16	16	110	261	701	306
Spain	2	6	7	12	14	27
UK	229	247	248	220	124	68
Yugoslavia	—	4	4	13	23	—

[1] Austria–Hungary, including Czechoslovakia.
(Sources: B. R. Mitchell, *European Historical Statistics, 1750–1970*, Macmillan, 1975, pp. 365–8;
J. Paxton (ed.) *The Statesman's Year-Book 1989–90*, Macmillan, 1989; B. Hunter (ed.),
The Statesman's Year-Book 1996–97, Macmillan, 1996.)

RAW COTTON CONSUMPTION: SELECTED COUNTRIES

(thousands of metric tons)

	1880	1910	1930	1950	1970
Austria*	64	173	22	20	23
Hungary	—	—	15	30	67
Belgium	23	63	100	87	63
Czechoslovakia	—	—	113	60	108
Bulgaria	—	1	3	22[†]	72
Finland	3	7	7	11	16
France	89	158	361	252	244
Germany	137	383	346	189 (W)	255
				43[†] (E)	89
Great Britain	617	740	577	461	176
Greece	—	—	—	21	46
Italy	—	175	205	203	221
Netherlands	14	20	52	61	62
Poland	—	—	61	87	141
Portugal	3	16	18	36	85
Romania	—	—	3	17	80
Russia	94	362	257	953	1,713
Spain	45	73	99	59	108
Sweden	9	21	23	28	15
Switzerland	22	24	31	30	41
Yugoslavia	—	—	88	35	91

* Figures for Austro–Hungarian Empire to 1910.
[†] 1951.
(Source: B. R. Mitchell, *European Historical Statistics, 1750–1970*, Macmillan, 1975, pp. 428–32.)

OUTPUT OF STEEL: SELECTED COUNTRIES

(Annual production in million metric tons)

	UK	France	Belgium	Germany		Italy	Russia*
1880	1.3	0.4	0.1	0.7		—	0.3
1890	3.6	0.7	0.2	2.2		0.1	0.4
1900	5.0	1.6	0.7	6.6		0.1	2.2
1910	6.5	3.4	1.9	13.7		0.7	3.5
1930	7.4	9.4	3.4	11.5		0.5	5.8
1940	13.4	4.4	1.9	19.0		1.0	18.0
				W	E		
1950	16.6	8.7	3.8	12.1	1.0	2.4	27.3
1960	24.7	17.3	7.1	34.1	3.8	8.2	65.3
1975	20.2	27.0	11.6	40.4	6.5	21.8	141.3
1986	14.8	17.7	9.7	37.1	7.2[†]	22.9	160.5
1993	14.4	17.1	9.4	40.8		24.8	58.3

* USSR for 1930–86.
[†] 1983.
(Sources: B. R. Mitchell, *European Historical Statistics, 1750–1970*, Macmillan, 1975, pp. 399–402; B. Hunter (ed.), *The Statesman's Year-Book, 1996–97*, Macmillan, 1996.)

OUTPUT OF CRUDE OIL: SELECTED COUNTRIES

(thousand metric tons)

	1900	1920	1930	1950	1960	1970	1987	1994
Austria	349	—	—	1,700	2,440	2,798	1,000	1,100
Germany*	50	35	174	1,119	5,560	7,536	3,727	2,930
Denmark	—	—	—	—	—	—	4,602	9,100
Netherlands	—	—	—	705	1,920	1,919	4,663	3,437
UK	—	—	—	40	90	84	119,244	126,900
France	—	55	76	128	2,260	2,308	3,236	2,900
Italy	2	5	8	8	1,990	1,408	3,908	4,468
Spain	—	—	—	—	—	156	1,639	816
Norway	—	—	—	—	—	—	56,000	126,000
Russia	10,684	3,851	18,451	37,878	147,859	352,667	625,000[1]	354,000
Romania	247	1,109	5,792	5,047	11,500	14,637	12,000[2]	6,700[3]
Yugoslavia	—	—	—	110	1,040	2,854	4,000[2]	—
Hungary	2	—	—	512	1,215	1,937	2,000[2]	1,361
Poland	—	765	663	162	195	424	250[2]	158

* West Germany from 1950 to 1987.
[1] Estimated output, 1986.
[2] 1984.
[3] 1993.
(Sources: B. R. Mitchell, *European Historical Statistics, 1750–1970*, Macmillan, 1975, p. 371; J. Paxton (ed.) *The Statesman's Year-Book 1989–90*, Macmillan, 1989; B. Hunter (ed.), *The Statesman's Year-Book, 1996–97*, Macmillan, 1996.)

MOTOR VEHICLES PRODUCED: SELECTED COUNTRIES

(in thousands, commercial and private)

	1910	1925	1930	1938	1950	1965	1975	1985	1993
France	38	177	142	227	357	1,616	1,694	3,536	2,836
Germany	10	49	96	338	301 (W) 13 (E)	3,063 (W) 118 (E)	3,172 (W) NA	4,566 (W) 118[1] (E)	3,497[2]
Great Britain	34	198	136	445	784	2,180	1,647	1,245	1,621
Italy	—	49	47	71	129	1,186	1,459	1,842	1,684
Spain	—	—	—	—	—	234	967	1,533	1,505
Sweden	—	—	2	7	17	207	NA	487	—
USSR	—	—	4	231	259	814	763*	2,229	—

* Commercial vehicles only.

[1] 1983.

[2] Unified Germany total.

(Sources: B. R. Mitchell, *European Historical Statistics, 1750–1970*, Macmillan, 1975, pp. 467–9; J. Paxton (ed.), *The Statesman's Year-Book 1989–90*, Macmillan, 1989; B. Hunter (ed.), *The Statesman's Year-Book, 1996–97*, Macmillan, 1996.)

OUTPUT OF ELECTRICITY

(in million kWhr)

	1920	1935	1955	1975	1987	1993
Austria	1.8	2.6	10.6	35.2	49.0	53.3
Belgium	1.2	4.3	10.9	39.0	60.0	68.4
Bulgaria	—	0.1	2.1	25.2	40.5[1]	37.9
Czechoslovakia	1.4	2.6	15.0	56.0	74.8[1]	—
Denmark	0.3	0.9	3.9	17.4	27.5	35.3
Finland	—	2.1	6.8	25.1	50.9	62.2
France	5.8	17.5	49.6	180.0	360.7	454.1
Germany	15.0	35.7	78.9 (W)	301.8 (W)	392.7 (W)	452.7
			28.7 (E)	84.5 (E)	104.9 (E)[2]	
Great Britain	8.5	26.0	89.0	272.1	282.5	302.1
Greece	0.1	0.4	1.4	8.9[3]	27.9	33.5
Hungary	—	0.9	5.4	20.5	25.8[2]	33.5
Ireland	—	0.2	1.6	7.3	12.2	—
Italy	4.0	12.6	25.6	140.8	190.9	226.0
Netherlands	0.7	2.8	11.2	54.3	66.1	79.5
Norway	5.3	7.8	22.6	76.7	103.3	120.0
Poland	—	2.8	17.8	97.2	118.0[1]	134.8
Portugal	0.1	0.4	1.9	10.7	19.3	21.1
Romania	—	0.9	4.3	53.7	70.3[1]	55.5
Russia[4]	0.5	26.2	170.2	1,039.0	1,665.0	956.0
Spain	1.0	3.3	11.9	76.3	126.8	165.0
Sweden	2.6	6.9	24.7	80.6	142.3	137.7
Switzerland	2.8	5.7	15.5	42.9	58.2	54.1[5]
Yugoslavia	—	0.6	4.3	40.0	64.6[2]	—

[1] 1982.
[2] 1983.
[3] 1970.
[4] USSR apart from 1993.
[5] 1990.
(Sources: B. R. Mitchell, *European Historical Statistics, 1750–1970*, Macmillan, 1975, pp. 479–82;
J. Paxton (ed.), *The Statesman's Year-Book 1989–90*, Macmillan, 1989; B. Hunter (ed.),
The Statesman's Year-Book 1996–97, Macmillan, 1996.)

RAILWAY MILEAGE OPEN

(kilometres)

	1920	1950	1975	1988
Austria	6,639	6,734	5,858	5,772
Belgium	4,938	5,046	3,998	3,554
Bulgaria	2,205	3,967	4,045	4,294[‡]
Czechoslovakia	13,430	13,124	13,241	13,103
Denmark	4,328	4,815	2,493	2,344
Finland	3,988	4,726	5,963	5,863
France	38,200	41,300	34,787	34,570
Germany	57,545	36,924 (W)	32,072 (W)	27,278
		12,895 (E)	14,298 (E)	13,750
Great Britain	32,707	31,353	17,093	17,038[†]
Greece	2,396	2,553	2,572	2,479
Hungary	8,141	8,756	8,392	7,770
Ireland	5,542	2,440	1,361	1,244
Italy	20,385	21,550	20,176	19,538
Netherlands	3,606	3,204	2,825	2,929
Norway	3,286	4,469	4,241	4,168
Poland	13,763	26,312*	23,773	24,309
Portugal	3,268	3,597	3,618	3,607[‡]
Romania	4,968	10,853	10,403	11,275
Russia	71,600	116,900	138,300	146,700
Spain	15,886	18,098	13,497	12,721
Sweden	14,869	16,516	12,065	11,194
Switzerland	5,078	5,152	NA	5,034[†]
Yugoslavia	9,321	11,541	10,068	9,270

* Figure reflects major boundary changes in 1945.
[†] 1986.
[‡] 1987.
(Source: B. R. Mitchell, *European Historical Statistics, 1750–1970*, Macmillan, 1975, pp. 585–7.)

TOTAL VALUE OF EXTERNAL TRADE: SELECTED COUNTRIES

	Germany (million marks)	France (million francs)	Russia (million roubles; million $ for 1993)	Italy (million lira)	Great Britain (million pounds)
1913	20,848	15,301	2,894	6,143	1,404
1925	27,713	99,850	1,020[4]	44,370	2,248
1938	10,713	76,655	475[4]	21,750	1,453
1955	50,089[1]	3,409,973	5,839[4]	2,855[2]	6,854
1965	142,099[1]	100,661[3]	14,610[4]	9,111[2]	10,652
1975	—	458,854[3]	50,699[4]	47,846[2]	43,790
1985	—	1,495,001[3]	127,476[4]	232,539[2]	163,168
1993	1,194,882	2,301,939[3]	61,104	499,269[2]	268,338

* New roubles.
[1] West Germany.
[2] Thousand million lira.
[3] New francs.
[4] USSR; Russia only after 1985.
(Sources: B. R. Mitchell, *European Historical Statistics, 1750–1970*, Macmillan, 1975, pp. 494–500; J. Paxton (ed.), *The Statesman's Year-Book 1989–90*, Macmillan, 1989; B. Hunter (ed.), *The Statesman's Year-Book, 1996–97*, Macmillan, 1996.)

MAJOR EVENTS IN RELIGIOUS HISTORY

1901 *France* Law allows associations to be formed, but congregations have to be licensed.

1903 *Denmark* Congregational councils of clergy and laity set up in each parish to manage church fabric and funds and elect clergy and bishops.

1904 *France* Law suppressing teaching orders. Quarrel over choice of bishops between French government and Papacy.

1905 *France* Separation of Church and State. Napoleon's concordat and organic articles repealed. Churches remain property of State but at the disposal of the ministers and orders.

Russia Fr Gapon leads ill-fated 'Bloody Sunday' procession. Group of 32 formed by St Petersburg priests and petition for Church reform. Their leader Fr Petrov elected to the second Duma, but sentenced by the Synod to three months confinement and unfrocked. Group of 32 produce a declaration, approved by Metropolitan Antoni, calling for freedom from State control, the restoration of the patriarchate abolished in 1700, and local religious councils. Religious tolerance law passed. Now legal to leave State Church. Evangelical sects form league of freedom whose platform includes schooling, equal rights for denominations, constitutional monarchy and equal suffrage. Nonetheless persecution of evangelicals, Old Believers, Jews and Roman Catholics (especially in Poland) continues.

	Italy	Bishops allowed to decide if Catholics of diocese can participate in political life.
1906	*Papacy*	Pius X refuses to recognise the separation of Church and State in France.
	Netherlands	Catholic Social Weeks start.
	Russia	Fr Gapon assassinated.
1907	*Russia*	Holy Synod declares it incompatible with priestly office to belong to parties opposed to the State and the Tsar.
	Britain	Three Methodist churches unite as United Methodist Church.
1908	*Portugal*	New Portuguese republic expels religious congregations, parish administration is taken over by lay committees, and financed solely from contributions. Religious teaching in schools abolished and religious oaths for university and other courses.
	Russia	Holy Synod tells bishops to encourage the participation of the Orthodox clergy in the right-wing League of the Russian People and other conservative societies. Russian Evangelical League founded, calling for moral regeneration to replace class struggle.
1909	*Papacy*	Pope condemns modernism in encyclical *Pascendi gregis*.
	Spain	During '*Semana Tragica*' in Barcelona over 50 religious buildings destroyed by the populace during socialist uprising.
1910	*General*	World Missionary Conference in Edinburgh sees beginning of modern ecumenical movement.
	Portugal	Prelates publish a pastoral censuring government. Minister of Justice orders its suspension. When defied, the Bishop of Oporto is deposed.
	Russia	Protestant conferences to be vetted by Minister of Interior. They are not allowed to educate their children in their faith.
1911	*Portugal*	Law of separation. Church disestablished. Clergy forbidden to criticise the government or laws of the republic. Boards of laymen to take charge of Catholic worship. Ministers permitted to marry.

	Russia	Rasputin, whose influence at court is great, causes increasing embarrassment to ecclesiastical and political authorities and is forced to make pilgrimage to Holy Land, but returns and causes fresh scandals.
1912	*Russia*	40 conservative clergy elected to the fourth Duma.
1914	*France*	Clemenceau condemns Pope Benedict XV as 'the Bosche Pope'.
1916	*Russia*	Duma condemns Rasputin.
1917	*Russia*	Synod refuses to condemn February revolution. Provisional government puts church schools under Ministry of Education. All-Russian Council of the Church convened and rejects separation of Church and State. Patriarch Tikhon (elected Nov.) and Council oppose Soviet revolution. Liberal clergy support it.
1918	*Russia*	Separation of Church and State (Jan.). Abolition of religious teaching and publications, censorship of sermons, and ban on church youth groups. Clergy deprived of vote, have to pay higher taxes, and children debarred from higher education. Churches may be used for secular purposes.
	Portugal	Conservative regime of Sidonia Pais revokes anti-clerical measures and reopens diplomatic relations with the Papacy. Cult of Our Lady of Fatima becomes increasingly popular after three children claim to have seen the Virgin on a hillside in Estremadura.
1919	*Italy*	Catholic *Partito Popolare* formed (Jan.). Pope lifts ban on Catholic participation in political life and in following elections (Nov.) Catholics strongly represented.
	Sweden	Religious instruction in schools made non-denominational.
	Germany	United Evangelical Protestant National Church reorganised.
1920	*France*	Moves towards reconciliation with Papacy. Canonisation of Joan of Arc.
	Germany	Cardinal Pacelli, later Pius XII, becomes papal nuncio in Berlin.
1921	*Russia*	Anti-Soviet clergy call a *Sobor* (Church council) at Karlovtsy in Yugoslavia, endorsing anti-Bolshevik cause and calling for return of the monarchy.
1922	*Russia*	Trial and execution of Metropolitan Veniamin for resistance to seizure of church treasure decreed by State for famine relief in Volga region. Patriarch Tikhon put under house arrest.

1923	*Russia*	Reformist clergy of so-called 'Living Church' hold *Sobor*, strip Patriarch Tikhon of titles and clerical status, pass resolutions in favour of socialist reconstruction of society; also give more influence to clergy in church administration and make married priests eligible to become bishops. Produces split among faithful and eventually among the 'Living Church'. Patriarch Tikhon offers muted support for Soviet State and is released from house arrest.
1927	*Russia*	After period of uneasy compromise, Metropolitan Sergei proclaims full support for Soviet State. Beginnings of widespread persecution of Islam and Islamic customs; mosques closed, mullahs displaced, veils banned, and Islamic courts and schools closed. Polygamy, bride-money and Ramadan stopped or discouraged.
	General	World Conference on Faith and Order at Lausanne.
1928	*General*	Ecumenical Missionary Conference in Jerusalem stresses partnership of churches.
1929	*Russia*	Legislation on 'religious associations'. Religious activity only permitted to registered congregations each of which has to consist of at least 20 people over eighteen, who can hire church buildings and engage a priest. All outside religious activity prohibited. Evangelism banned.
	Italy	Lateran treaties with Papacy recognising the Vatican as a State and the Pontiff as its head. The Church assumes privileged status in Italy and formal reconciliation between the Papacy and Kingdom of Italy takes place.
	Scotland	Presbyterian Churches of Scotland unite in the Church of Scotland.
	General	World Conference of Lutherans in Copenhagen.
1931	*Spain*	Constitution of Republic separates Church and State; reduces clerical salaries; forbids Orders to teach and suppresses the Jesuits.
	Papacy	Pius XI publishes encyclical *Quadragesimo Anno* on his ideas of the corporate state.
1932	*Spain*	Widespread attacks on Church property in Madrid, Barcelona and southern Spain. Over 55 churches or convents destroyed.
	Germany	Protestant group founds pro-Nazi 'German Christians'.
1933	*Papacy*	Pope protests in encyclical *Dilectissima nobis* about anti-clerical measures in Spain.
	Germany	Pope Pius XI publicly praises Hitler for his stand against communism and German bishops withdraw their

opposition. Hitler and chairman of German Catholic Centre Party hold discussions and Centre Party supports Enabling Act (Mar.). Centre Party dissolves itself (July). Concordat signed between Nazi Germany and Holy See (July); ratified in Sept.; Ludwig Müller of German Christians becomes Bishop of the Reich. Protestant Churches amalgamate as German Evangelical Church.

1934 *Spain* Priests and religious in Oviedo murdered during Asturias rising.

Germany The Protestant Barman Synod accuses German Christians of departing from the Gospels and abandoning the legal basis of the Protestant Churches.

1935 *Germany* Nuremberg Laws deprive Jews of citizen rights and forbid sexual relations and inter-marriage. Hitler sets up ministry of Church affairs.

Russia Soviet Muslims prohibited from visiting Mecca.

Spain Widespread attacks on Church property in the areas where anarchism and communism are strong.

1936 *Russia* Widespread purge of clergy and bishops. Of 163 bishops active in 1930 only 12 still at liberty in 1939.

Spain Attacks on Church property following election of Popular Front; 160 churches or convents destroyed and 269 clergy killed. Renewed attacks and atrocities following the outbreak of war. 12 bishops and over 7,000 religious and clergy killed. Pius XI denounces 'the satanic enterprise' and blesses Franco's cause. Franco declares 'Spain shall be an empire turned towards God'.

1937 *Germany* Protestant Church deprived of control of its finances. Protestant opposition forbidden. Pastor Niemöller and other Protestant pastors arrested and sent to concentration camps.

Papacy Papal encyclical on atheistic communism.

1938 *Spain* Diplomatic relations renewed between Papacy and Nationalists. The Pope calls for the re-establishment of a Catholic Spain.

Germany Anti-Jewish pogrom on 9–10 Nov., the *Kristallnacht*, arouses protests from some Church groups.

1939 *Papacy* Cardinal Pacelli becomes Pius XII.

1940 *Britain* In letter to *The Times*, leading churchmen urge creation of a more egalitarian and just society as a postwar objective.

1941 *Jewry* Germans begin extermination of Jews in occupied territories of Poland and Russia. By 1942 an estimated

		1,400,000 Jews massacred by *Einsatzgruppen* murder squads. Beginning of construction of camps primarily for the systematic murder of Jews. Mass deportations of Jews from Germany to camps in the east begin.
	Russia	Russian Orthodox Church pledges support for war with Germany.
	Germany	Cardinal Galen of Munster condemns Nazi euthanasia programme.
1942	*Jewry*	Heydrich chairs 'Wannsee Conference' of Nazi officials in Berlin which adopts the 'final solution' of deportation and extermination of European Jewry. Extermination camps opened at Sobibor, Treblinka, Birkenau and elsewhere. Widespread deportations of French, Dutch, Polish and Slovak Jews to the camps for forced labour and gassing. Continued massacres of Russian, Baltic and Yugoslav Jews.
	Britain	Archbishop William Temple's *Christianity and the Social Order* outlines advances in social welfare as necessary to a Christian society.
	Papacy	Hitler closes diplomatic channels with the Vatican.
	Holland	Dutch bishops issue a public protest against the deportation of Jews to Germany.
1943	*Russia*	Patriarchate and ecclesiastical administration re-established. Seminaries and theological academies opened, and churches permitted to reopen. Government appoints special Council for Church Affairs to supervise.
	France	Archbishop Suchard of Paris founds worker-priest movement.
	Jewry	Continuation of mass extermination programme by the Nazis. Belsen concentration camp opened. Destruction of Jewish Ghetto in Warsaw.
1945	*Jewry*	Mass extermination of European Jews continues until the last days of the war. Between 5 and 6 million Jews estimated to have been murdered or died of ill-treatment out of a European total of over 8.5 million in 1941.
1946	*Russia*	'Living Church' abolished.
	General	Committee of World Council of Churches drafts plan for a reconstructed World International Assembly. International Christian Conference at Cambridge aims at closer relations between Protestant and Orthodox Churches.
1948	*General*	Representatives of 147 churches from 44 countries meet in Amsterdam to inaugurate World Council of Churches.

	Jewry	End of British mandate in Palestine. Jews proclaim new State of Israel.
1950	*Papacy*	Papal decree *Humani Generis* against Existentialism and erroneous scientific theories. Pius XII pronounces dogma on bodily Assumption of the Virgin Mary.
1959	*Papacy*	Pope John XXIII announces the calling of the first Vatican Council since 1870. Vatican orders French worker-priest movement to discontinue.
1960	*Britain*	Archbishop of Canterbury visits Rome and meets the Pope. First to do so since the Reformation.
1961	*Russia*	Synod of bishops removes priests' function as legal administrators of parishes and explicitly confines them to spiritual function. In next three years over half of existing parishes are disbanded, 10,000 churches and most monasteries closed. Closure of Jewish synagogues in Moscow.
	Papacy	Papal encyclicals on Catholic social doctrine and for Christian reconciliation under Rome's Primacy.
	General	Meeting of World Council of Churches at Delhi is joined by members of the Russian Orthodox Church and by Roman Catholic observers. The International Missionary Council is integrated with the World Council of Churches.
1962	*Papacy*	John XXIII insists on retention of Latin as the language of the Roman Catholic Church. Vatican Council opens with observer delegates from other Christian Churches.
1963	*Britain*	Anglican–Methodist 'Conversations' about unification.
	Papacy	Vatican Council approves use of vernacular liturgies. Encyclical *Pacem in Terris* deals with peaceful settlement of disputes and with relations with non-Catholics and communists.
1964	*Papacy*	Paul VI makes pilgrimage to Holy Land.
1965	*Papacy*	Vatican Council promulgates documents exonerating the Jews from the death of Christ. The Catholic Church and the Eastern Orthodox Church agree to retract the excommunications put on each other in 1054. Worker-priests allowed to resume work.
1968	*Papacy*	Papal encyclical *Humanae Vitae* reaffirms Catholic doctrine of opposition to artificial birth control.
1970	*Papacy*	Pope reaffirms celibacy of clergy as a law of the Church.
1972	*Britain*	Presbyterian and Congregationalist Churches merge to form the United Reform Church.

1973	*Papacy*	Sacred Congregation for the Doctrine of the Faith reaffirms Papal Infallibility and the Church's unique claim to be the authentic Church of Christ.
1978	*Papacy*	Cardinal Karol Wojtyla of Cracow becomes first non-Italian Pope for 450 years as Pope John Paul II.
1979	*Poland*	Papal visit to Poland marks first visit of a Pope to a communist country since the Second World War.
	Ireland	First papal visit to Ireland; Pope calls on young people to turn away from violence.
1980	*Poland*	Gdansk agreement with striking shipyard workers includes permission for religious broadcasts (Aug.); Roman Catholic hierarchy pledge their support for newly formed Solidarity organisation (Oct.).
1981	*Papacy*	Pope John Paul II is seriously wounded by a Turkish gunman in Rome (13 May).
	Yugoslavia	Appearance of the Virgin Mary (24 June) to six young people in Croatian village of Medjugorje.
	Britain	Anglican General Synod votes overwhelmingly to admit women to Holy Orders as deacons.
	Poland	Archbishop Glemp criticises introduction of martial law (Dec.), but urges Poles to refrain from violence.
1982	*Papacy*	Pope attempts to mediate in dispute between Argentina and Britain after Argentina invades the Falkland Islands; first papal visit to Britain since 1531 is followed by papal visit to Argentina.
1983	*Poland*	Pope meets Lech Walesa during visit to Poland (June) and defends right to join free trade unions.
1984	*Spain*	Spanish socialist government introduces law requiring private schools in receipt of State funds to accept pupils without regard for religious views of the parents; mass demonstrations by Catholics who fear loss of control over church schools.
	Poland	Pro-Solidarity priest Fr Jerzy Popieluszko kidnapped and killed by policemen. Major outcry leads to arrest, trial and imprisonment of the perpetrators.
1986	*Ireland*	Irish referendum votes against changes in the law on divorce following clerical opposition to the measure.
	Papacy	First ever visit by a Pope to a Jewish Synagogue.
1987	*USSR*	President Gorbachev indicates a major relaxation towards the Russian Orthodox Church, the training of priests, and opening of places of worship.

1988	*USSR*	Russian Orthodox Church openly allowed to celebrate its millennium and three seminaries opened.
1989	*USSR*	Soviet Muslims demonstrate in Tashkent demanding the dismissal of the head of the 'spiritual directorate' of Central Asia and Kazakhstan and obtain his replacement by a religious leader; many mosques and religious training centres opened; new edition of the Koran prepared. President Gorbachev promises to allow Jewish 'refuseniks' the right to emigrate; confirmed in Dec. at summit with President Bush in Malta. President Gorbachev meets the Pope in Rome and reaches agreement in principle on the opening of diplomatic relations with the Vatican and the ending of the ban on the Catholic Church (Uniate) of the Ukraine in force since 1946.
	Britain	Salman Rushdie's novel, *The Satanic Verses*, is condemned by the Ayatollah Khomeini, whose *fatwa* pronounces a death sentence on the author; widespread protests in Britain by Muslims against the book and its author, who is forced to go into hiding.
1990	*Papacy*	Diplomatic relations re-established with many former East European communist states.
	USSR	Catholics in Latvia and Lithuania in forefront of nationalist protests.
1991	*Britain*	Salman Rushdie apologises for offence caused to Muslims and partial pardon offered by Iran.
1992	*Russia*	Kremlin cathedrals returned to Orthodox Church by State.
	Britain	Vote for ordination of women in Anglican Church passed; many Anglicans defect to Rome.
1995	*Ireland*	Scandals over pay-offs of ex-mistresses of priests rock Catholic Church.
	Scandinavia	Porvoo conference brings together Lutherans and Anglicans.
1996	*Scotland*	Desertion of Roman Catholic bishop to live with his mistress raises question of celibacy.
	Britain	Question of gay clergy in Anglican orders continues to cause dissension in Church of England.
1997	*Bosnia*	Pope visits Bosnia, preaching reconciliation of religious and ethnic groups.
	Poland	Pope visits Poland.
2002	*Poland*	Pope visits Poland again to revisit scenes of his early life.
	Papacy	Pope canonises founder of Opus Dei, Mgr Josemaria Escriva de Balaguer, who died in 1975.

ANTI-SEMITISM AND THE ZIONIST MOVEMENT

1886	Publication of anti-Semitic tract *La France Juive* by Edouard Drumont (1844–1917).
1894	Start of the Dreyfus affair. Alfred Dreyfus, a Jewish officer, is accused of spying and removed from the army.
1895	Vienna elects anti-Semitic Karl Lueger (leader of Christian Socialist Party) as Mayor.
1897	Theodor Herzl organises a congress of Zionist organisations at Basle 'to secure for the Jewish people a home in Palestine guaranteed by public law'. Herzl becomes first President.
	Emile Zola writes article '*J'accuse*' condemning the treatment of Dreyfus.
1899	After a retrial which does not completely exonerate him, Dreyfus is pardoned by Presidential decree.
1902	Beginning of new wave of anti-Jewish pogroms in Russia.
1905	Right-wing Union of the Russian People calls for the extermination of all Jews. Over 1,000 Jews killed and 5,000 injured in massacres in Odessa.
1913	Britain passes Aliens Act, partly aimed at halting the flow of poor East European and Russian Jews to Britain.
1917	Balfour Declaration. A communication made by the British Foreign Secretary Arthur Balfour, to Lord Rothschild, a prominent Zionist, declaring British support for the establishment of a Jewish 'national home' in Palestine.
1918	Mass killings of Jews in western Ukraine, extensive attacks on Jews in Poland in Vilna, Lvov and Galicia.
1919	Jews killed following collapse of Béla Kun regime in Hungary.
1920	San Remo Conference confirms the assignment of the League of Nations Mandate for Palestine to Britain on the basis of the Balfour Declaration and the safeguarding of the rights of the indigenous people.
1922	Jewish population of Palestine is c. 84,000, compared with 590,000 Arabs. Murder of German Foreign Minister, Walter Rathenau, in anti-Semitic attack. Romanian Jews begin to come under persecution with restrictions of numbers allowed to attend Cluj University, and attacks on Jewish schools and cemeteries.
1923	Publication of anti-Semitic *Der Sturmer* in Germany.
1925	Publication of first part of Hitler's virulently anti-Semitic *Mein Kampf* (July); second part published in Dec. 1926.

1927	Growing anti-Semitic violence in Weimar Germany reflected in desecration of Jewish cemeteries, destruction of synagogues in Osnabruck and Krefeld.
1929	Arab rioting in Palestine at continued Jewish immigration.
1931	Anti-Jewish attacks on eve of Jewish New Year in Berlin.
1933	Hitler becomes Chancellor of Germany (see pp. 71–8 for subsequent German policy towards the Jews, and the Holocaust).
	British attempt to restrict Jewish immigration to Palestine leads to Jewish rioting. Jewish population estimated at 180,000 in 1932.
1937	Renewed emigration of Jews from Europe and the USA swells Jewish population in Palestine to c. 400,000.
1939	Last pre-war Zionist Congress meets in Geneva.
1946	British government seeks to ban Jewish immigration to Palestine but widely evaded.
	Nuremberg Trials condemn leading Nazis for 'crimes against humanity'.
1947	British request the United Nations to take over responsibility for Palestine.
	UN Commission suggests partition into Jewish and Arab sectors.
1948	State of Israel declared (May) amid widespread fighting between Arabs and Jews.
	Stalin launches new purge – the alleged 'Doctors' plot' with strong anti-Semitic overtones. Many leading Jews fall victim to persecution.
1949	Closure of Jewish State Theatre in Moscow and arrest of leading Jewish cultural figures.
	Borders of the state of Israel secured after first Arab–Israeli war; Jewish population of Israel, many of them European refugees, estimated at 720,000.

THE EMANCIPATION OF WOMEN

1900

General	Women participate in Olympic Games for the first time.
Germany	German women petition the Reichstag to be allowed to sit state examinations and enter university.

1901

Norway	Women in Norway gain vote in local elections.

1902

Germany	Prussian government prohibits women from forming political associations.

1903

General	Marie Curie wins the Nobel Prize.
Britain	Women's Social and Political Union is formed by Mrs Pankhurst to campaign for women's rights.

1905

General	Austrian Bertha von Suttner wins Nobel Peace Prize.
Britain	Suffragettes jailed after demonstrations.

1906

Britain	Suffragettes go on hunger strike in prison.

1907

Austria	Women in Austria obtain equal employment rights in universities and hospitals.

1908

France	New divorce law grants automatic divorce after three years' legal separation.
Britain	London 'Women's Parliament' meets to discuss women's issues.
Denmark	Women taxpayers over 25 obtain the vote.

1910

Spain	Women admitted to Spanish universities.

1911

France	French Academy of Sciences refuses to admit Madame Curie.
Norway	Women admitted as MPs.
Portugal	Portuguese Constitutional Court acknowledges women's right to the vote.
Britain	Mass demonstration by 60,000 women in London demanding voting rights.

1912

Austria	First woman admitted to Austrian parliament.
Britain	Suffragettes launch campaign of terror after Women's suffrage bill is defeated. Women on hunger strike are force-fed.

1913

Russia   Russian government bars women lawyers.

Britain   'Cat and Mouse Act' passed allowing release and rearrest of women on hunger strike. Suffragette Emily Davison kills herself by throwing herself under the King's horse at the Derby.

1914

Britain   Leading suffragettes declare support for the war.

1916

Britain   Government figures reveal that over two million extra women have been recruited for war work since 1914 and announce recruitment of up to 400,000 women for a 'land army'

Norway   Women win right to vote in Norway.

1917

Russia   Women's battalion is formed by Provisional Government.

1918

Britain   Women over 30 given the vote and allowed to become MPs. *Married Love* by Marie Stopes calls for sexual fulfilment for women in marriage.

Soviet Union   Marriage Law Book of Apr. 1918 institutes civil marriage and permits divorce; women given equal rights in relation to children.

1919

General   Women's International League for Peace and Freedom founded, an international, non-violent disarmament organisation.

Germany   Weimar constitution gives women the vote for the first time.

Britain   Nancy Astor becomes first woman MP to take her seat. Sex Disqualification Removal Act opens professions to women.

1920

Soviet Union   The first country to allow women to obtain abortion on demand.

France   Pope canonises Joan of Arc.

1921

Britain   First birth control clinic in Europe is opened.

1922

General   Pius XI attacks new women's fashions as 'immodest'.

First Congress of the International Federation of Feminine Athletes takes place in Geneva.

Hungary   New Hungarian constitution grants limited women's suffrage.

1923

France   First woman admitted to *Academie Française.*

Italy   Women given vote in Italian local elections.

1925

Greece   New Greek constitution provides for women to vote.

Italy   Launch of 'women into the home' campaign. Organisation set up to supervise children's and mothers' welfare.

1926

Italy   Mussolini bars women from holding public office.

1927

Soviet Union   Marriage Law Book confirms right to divorce.

1929

General   World Congress on women's work meets in Berlin.

Britain   Women under 30 vote for the first time following act of 1928 admitting them to the franchise.

Italy   Law provides maternity leave and maternity grants for working mothers.

1930

General   Papal encyclical *Casti Connubi* urges women to return to home and family and find true equality as wives and mothers.

Britain   Women civil servants vote in favour of compulsory retirement of women at marriage in return for opening up more positions to women.

1931

Britain   First woman cabinet minister, Margaret Bondfield, appointed by the Labour government.

1932

France   French government of Laval resigns after French Senate rejects votes for women.

1933

Germany   Nazis declare in favour of abolishing voting rights for women.

Italy   Extra allowances, loans and prizes offered to large families.

1934

Poland   Poland extends conscription to women.

1936

Soviet Union   New family law attempts to strengthen families; divorce made more difficult and abortion banned.

1937

Italy   Fascists set up organisation for domestic women workers, enrolling 1.65 million by 1940.

1940

France   Vichy regime bans married women from public service occupations.

1941

Britain   Unmarried women between 20 and 30 conscripted for war work.

1944

Soviet Union   Monetary awards made to large families and single persons taxed.

1946

France   Constitution of Fourth Republic gives women the vote.

1948

Germany   Basic Law of the Federal Republic of Germany established on the basis of equal suffrage for men and women.

Italy   Italian Republic establishes full female suffrage.

1949

General   Simone de Beauvoir publishes *The Second Sex*.

1951–55

General   Research biologist Gregory Pincus develops oral contraceptive pill in the USA.

1955

Soviet Union   Abortion again made legal.

1961

General   Contraceptive pill goes widely on sale in Western Europe.

1967

Britain   Abortion Act legalises abortion.

1968

General   Papal encyclical *Humanae Vitae* reaffirms Catholic doctrine of opposition to artificial birth control.

Italy   Italian women demonstrate for women's rights and the legalisation of abortion.

1969

Britain   Divorce law liberalised to allow 'no fault' divorce.

1970

General   Germaine Greer's *The Female Eunuch* popularises feminist cause.

Britain   Equal Pay Act gives women equal pay for work of equal value.

Italy   Divorce law liberalised, giving women greater access to easy divorce.

1971

Switzerland   Women obtain the vote.

1972

General   International Women's Year.

Italy   Birth control legalised.

1975

Britain   Sex Discrimination Act forbids discrimination in employment, education, training and the supply of goods and services.

France   Abortion legalised.

Italy   Major demonstrations by women for right to abortion.

1977

General   Northern Ireland peace women win Nobel Peace prize.

Italy   Abortion legalised.

1978

France   Monique Pelletier appointed France's first minister for women.

1979

Britain   Mrs Thatcher becomes first woman Prime Minister of Britain.

1980

Iceland   First woman becomes Prime Minister.

1981

Norway   First Norwegian woman Prime Minister.

1982

General   Women play leading role in opposition to siting of NATO Cruise missiles in Britain, Holland and Germany.

1986

Austria   Austrian Green Party candidate, Frieda Meisser-Blau campaigns unsuccessfully for the Presidency.

Ireland   Irish referendum votes against change in divorce law.

1990

Ireland   Mary Robinson becomes first woman President of Ireland.

1990–91

General   Collapse of East European regimes removes system of guaranteed employment, childcare, and access to free healthcare for women.

1991

France   Edith Cresson becomes first woman Prime Minister.

1994

Britain   First women priests ordained in the Anglican communion.

1997

Britain   Labour Party adopts 'women only' shortlists in some constituencies for the 1997 General Election, producing the largest ever number of women MPs.

Note   The above table of events and legislation is intended as an indicative rather than a fully comprehensive list of all key dates affecting women in this period.

SOCIAL WELFARE

1902	German Garden City Association is formed.
1908	Old Age Pension is introduced in Britain.
1911	National Insurance is introduced in Britain.
1917	Family Endowment Society founded in Britain to campaign for family allowances.
1919	40-hour week introduced in Sweden.
	British government introduces subsidies for local authorities to build 'council houses' under the Addison Acts.
1924–28	Era of Weimar welfare state. Extensive expenditure on housing, public works and leisure facilities. 1927 Act on Labour Exchanges and Unemployment Insurance extends statutory unemployment insurance to c. 17 million workers not covered by existing schemes.
1929	Italy provides maternity grants and maternity leave to working mothers.
1929–33	Economic crisis in Germany forces cuts of up to one third in war pensions and the need to raise insurance contributions.
1931	Financial crisis forces British government to cut unemployment pay by 10 per cent and introduce 'Means Test' for many on unemployment insurance.
1932	Accession to power of Swedish Social Democratic Party begins establishment of Swedish welfare state.
1933	Italian government offers incentives to large families.
	Nazi government inaugurates major public works programme to reduce unemployment.
1935	Unemployment insurance is introduced in Sweden.
1936	Election of Popular Front government in France leads to introduction of 40-hour week, collective labour agreements, and paid holidays.
1937	Family allowances introduced in Sweden. French forced to slow down social welfare schemes due to financial crisis.
1938	Eight-hour day is introduced for Swedish agricultural workers and paid holidays. Holidays With Pay Act is passed in Britain.
1942	Beveridge Report in Britain proposes system of comprehensive social insurance, including free health care, family allowances and full employment.
1944	British Government White Papers on National Insurance and Employment Policy make commitments to a postwar welfare state. Butler Education Act gives free secondary education to

all on basis of tripartite division of type of schools according to the ability of children as tested at age eleven.

1945 Family Allowances Act is passed in Britain.

1946 Comprehensive National Insurance Act is passed in Britain.

1947 Non-means tested family allowances are introduced in Sweden.

1948 National Health Service is introduced in Britain, offering free health care 'at the point of delivery'.

1949 Sweden introduces comprehensive schooling.

1950 British Conservatives win election on pledge to build 300,000 houses per year.

1953 Three weeks' paid holidays introduced in Sweden.

Fall of Stalin leads gradually to introduction of more consumer and welfare-orientated policies in Eastern Europe and the Soviet Union, concentrating on housing and childcare facilities.

1954 Swedish National Health Service is introduced.

1959 Index-linked pensions are introduced in Sweden.

1964 Labour government in Britain pledges itself to comprehensive school system and launches major housing drive.

1993 Maastricht Act of the European Union contains Social Chapter, pledging member states to minimum social provisions and employee rights.

BIOGRAPHIES

Adenauer, Konrad (1876–1967): German statesman. Mayor of Cologne, 1917–33. Removed by Nazis. Prominent member of Catholic Centre Party in Weimar Republic. President of Prussian State Council, 1920–33. Twice imprisoned by Nazis. Founded Christian Democratic Union, 1945. Elected first Chancellor of Federal Republic, 1949; re-elected 1953, 1957. Also Foreign Minister, 1951–55. Negotiated German entry into NATO, EEC. Established diplomatic relations with USSR, 1955. Resigned 1963.

Alexander I Karageorgevic (1888–1934): First ruler of the new 'South Slav' state created by the Paris Peace Conference. King of the Kingdom of the Serbs, Croats and Slovenes, 1921–29; King of renamed Yugoslavia, 1929–34. Son of Peter I of Serbia and Commander-in-Chief of the Serbian army in the First World War. Pro-Serbian, he attempted to create a centralised state based on Belgrade. Growing instability and conflicts between Serbs and Croats led him in Jan. 1929 to suspend parliament and the constitution, ruling with the support of the army. Supported by the Little Entente (Czechoslovakia, Romania and Yugoslavia, with French support), he was assassinated while on a visit to Marseilles by a Croatian terrorist.

Azaña, Manuel (1881–1940): Spanish President. Founded Republican Party, 1924. Subsequently imprisoned. War Minister, 1931. First Prime Minister of Second Republic, 1931–33, again 1936. Imprisoned for advocacy of Catalan self-rule, 1934. President, 1936–39. Fled to France, Feb. 1939.

Badoglio, Pietro (1871–1956): Italian soldier and politician. Distinguished military career in the First World War, becoming Chief of Staff, 1919–21 and Field Marshal in 1925. As Governor-General of Libya, 1928–33, put down a major uprising; put in charge of and concluded Ethiopian campaign, 1935–36. Appointed Chief of Staff in June 1940, he resigned following military failures in Greece. Viewed as a potential successor to Mussolini, on the latter's arrest he was appointed Chief of Government in July 1943 and concluded an armistice with the Allies. In Apr. 1944 he headed a broad coalition government, but was forced to stand down because of his fascist background. He retired to private life.

Beneš, Eduard (1884–1948): Czech statesman. Worked with Masaryk in Paris during First World War, seeking Czech independence. Principal Czech representative at Paris Peace Conference. Prime Minister, 1921–22. Foreign Minister, 1918–35. Active diplomat, chief proponent of Little Entente. President of League of Nations Assembly, 1935. Succeeded Masaryk as President, 1935. Resigned, 1938, following Munich Agreement. President of Czech government-in-exile in London, 1941–45. Re-elected President, 1946. Resigned shortly after communist coup, 1948.

Beria, Lavrenti Pavlovich (1899–1953): Chief of Soviet secret police under Stalin. A native Georgian, he became Soviet Commissar for Internal Affairs in 1938 and responsible for the latter phase of the purges. As Vice-President for the State Committee for Defence in the Second World War, he continued the terror during and after the war. After Stalin's death in 1953 he was briefly part of the collective leadership, but was accused of conspiracy and summarily executed.

Berlusconi, Silvio (1936–): Media tycoon and politician. Created his own party, *Forza Italia*, which gained support amid the break-up of the postwar Italian system in the 1990s. Formed his first government in 1994, but forced out of office in Dec. as a result of accusations of corruption. Returned as leader of a coalition government in May 2001, supported by the right-wing Northern League and *Alleanza Nazionale*, pursuing pro-enterprise and anti-immigration policies.

Blum, Léon (1872–1950): French socialist statesman. Elected to Chamber of Deputies, 1919. By 1925, established as a leader of Socialist Party. First socialist Prime Minister, 1936, leading 'Popular Front'. Introduced important reforms, including 40-hour working week. Formed second Popular Front, 1938. Imprisoned by Vichy regime, 1940. Accused of being responsible for French military weakness and tried, 1942. Interned in Germany during Second World War. Briefly Prime Minister of caretaker government, 1946.

Bormann, Martin (1900–45): Nazi politician. Joined the Party in 1925 and rose as aide to Hess. Developed a powerful role for himself through control of the Party's central office and regular access to Hitler. After Hess's flight to Britain in 1941, became head of the Party Chancellery and the main channel of communication with Hitler. Appointed Hitler's Secretary in Apr. 1943; used his position to undermine rivals hoping to succeed Hitler. Disappeared in May 1945; condemned to death at Nuremberg *in absentia* in Oct. 1946; officially pronounced dead by a West German court in Apr. 1973.

Brandt, Willy (1913–92): West German Social Democratic statesman. Active in opposition to Hitler. Member of Bundestag, 1949–57. President of Bundesrat, 1955–57. Mayor of West Berlin, 1957–66. Chairman of Social Democratic Party, 1964–89. Joined coalition with Christian Democrats under Chancellor Kiesinger, 1966. Chancellor in SPD–Free Democrat coalition, 1969. Awarded Nobel Peace Prize, 1971. Resigned following spy scandal, 1974, remaining Chairman of SPD until 1987. Consistent advocate of improved relations with Eastern Europe (*Ostpolitik*).

Brezhnev, Leonid Ilyich (1906–82): Soviet politician. Communist Party official in Ukraine and Moldavia. Held military posts; 1933–34. Member of Praesidium of Supreme Soviet, 1952–57. President of Praesidium, 1960–64, succeeding Marshal Voroshilov. Succeeded Khrushchev as First Secretary of Central Committee, 1964. General Secretary of Central Committee, 1966. His period in power epitomised the ailing old-guard leadership of the Soviet Union.

Briand, Aristide (1862–1932): French statesman. Allied with Socialists, 1894–1906. Elected deputy, 1902. Expelled by Socialists for accepting office as Minister of Public Instruction and Worship in Radical coalition, 1906–09. Drafted and implemented separation of Church and State. Prime Minister 11 times between 1909 and 1929. Used force to end railway strike, 1910. Foreign Minister, 1925–32. Major diplomatic role, worked for European unity. Sought *rapprochement* between France and Germany. Successes included Locarno Treaty, 1925, and Kellogg–Briand Pact, 1928. Awarded Nobel Peace Prize with Stresemann, 1926. Defeated in presidential elections, 1931.

Caballero, Francisco Largo (1869–1964): Spanish socialist politician. Elected to parliament, 1918. Became leader of UGT, 1925. Minister of Labour in several governments, 1931–33. Proponent of genuinely socialist policy, helping to provoke military reaction against government, 1936. Prime Minister, 1936–37. During Civil War, failed to achieve cohesion among parties of the left. Went into exile in France, 1939. Interned by Germans, 1942–45. Minister of Interior of Republican government-in-exile, 1946.

Ceausescu, Nicolae (1918–89): Romanian dictator. Member of underground Communist Party, 1936. Party Secretariat member, 1954. Deputy leader, 1957–65. General Secretary, 1965. Head of State, 1967. Combined independent foreign policy, notably criticism of the 1968 Warsaw Pact invasion of Czechoslovakia, with authoritarian regime, massive repression and personality cult. Repressed demonstrations prompted by economic crisis, 1967. Showed little sympathy for the Soviet line instituted by Gorbachev. His corrupt regime and bankrupt economy provoked riots in 1989. Their savage repression led to the Dec. 1989 'Winter Revolution'. Executed with his wife Elena by firing squad after secret trial, 25 Dec. 1989.

Chamberlain, Neville (1869–1940): British Conservative politician. Son of Joseph Chamberlain. Lord Mayor of Birmingham, 1915–16. Director General of National Service, 1916–17. Member of Parliament, 1918–40. Postmaster General, 1922–23. Paymaster General, 1923. Minister of Health, 1923, 1924–29. Chancellor of the Exchequer, 1923–24, 1931–37. Prime Minister, 1937–40. Resigned, May 1940, becoming Lord President of the Council in wartime coalition, following rebellion by Conservative MPs in favour of Churchill. Much criticised for attempts to appease Germany and Italy, especially in Munich Agreement, 1938. Retired from politics due to illness, 1940.

Chirac, Jacques (1932–): French Gaullist politician; elected to the National Assembly in 1967. Served as Prime Minister, 1974–76, 1986–88. Maintained power base as Mayor of Paris from 1977. Unsuccessful candidate in the 1981 and 1988 Presidential elections, he was elected in May 1995 and re-elected overwhelmingly in 2002 against the far-right candidate Le Pen.

Churchill, Sir Winston (1874–1965): British statesman. Conservative MP, 1900–04. Became a Liberal in protest at Tariff Reform policies. Liberal MP, 1906–08, 1908–22. Constitutionalist, later Conservative MP, 1924–45. Conservative MP for Woodford, 1945–64. Under-secretary at Colonial Office, 1906–08. President of the Board of Trade, 1908–10. Home Secretary, 1910–11. First Lord of the Admiralty, 1911–15. Chancellor of the Duchy of Lancaster, 1915. Minister of Munitions, 1917–19. Secretary for War and Air, 1919–21. Secretary for Air and Colonies, 1921. Colonial Secretary, 1921–22. Chancellor of the Exchequer, 1924–29. First Lord of the Admiralty, 1939–40. Prime Minister and Minister of Defence, 1940–45. Leader of the Opposition, 1945–51. Prime Minister, 1951–55. Minister of Defence, 1951–52. Made Knight of the Order of the Garter, 1953. Resigned, 1955. Chequered career; during First World War involved in disputes over Admiralty policy and Gallipoli campaign. Opposed Conservative policies over India and rearmament during 1930s. Advocated prevention of German expansion. Wartime leadership earned him legendary status, though not returned to power in 1945. Negotiated wartime alliance with USA and USSR. After Second World War, favoured alliance with USA against USSR.

Ciano, Count Galeazzo (1903–44): Italian politician. Son-in-law of Mussolini. Prominent fascist Minister of Propaganda, 1935. Minister of Foreign Affairs, 1936–43. Negotiated 'Axis' agreements with Germany. Supported expansionist policy, e.g. annexation of Albania, 1939 and entry into the Balkans, 1940–41, but suspicious of German dominance. Increasingly opposed to Mussolini's policy as its failures became clear after 1943, with defeats in North Africa and the threat of invasion. Dismissed as Foreign Minister in Feb. 1943, he was appointed Ambassador to the Vatican. He voted against Mussolini in the Grand Council in July 1943. He fled to Germany after Mussolini's arrest but was returned to be executed by the Italian fascists in 1944. His *Diaries* are an important source for Italian foreign policy in the period.

Clemenceau, Georges (1841–1929): French Radical statesman. Mayor of Montmartre, 1870–71. Entered National Assembly, 1871. Elected deputy, 1876, becoming leader of extreme left, 1876–93. Founded radical newspaper, *La Justice*, 1880. Critical of government. Contributed to downfall of several ministries. Instrumental in securing resignation of President Grévy after honours scandal, 1887. Lost seat in Chamber, 1893. Returned after supporting Dreyfus. Senator, 1902–20. Minister of Interior, 1906. Prime Minister, 1906–09. Completed Church–State separation. Strike-breaking measures aroused Socialist opposition. Attacked military mismanagement during First World War. Appointed Prime Minister and Minister of War, 1917–20. Semi-dictatorial rule. Secured appointment of Foch as Chief of Allied forces, Mar. 1918. Presided at Paris Peace Conference, 1919, pressing for harsh penalties on Germany. Lost presidential election, 1920.

Cohn-Bendit, Daniel (1948–): German student leader known as 'Danny the Red' who played a significant part in the 1968 student demonstrations in Paris. During the 1980s he was active in the German Green movement and has latterly supported free markets, European integration and decriminalisation of illegal immigration.

Couve de Murville, Maurice (1907–2001): French diplomat and politician, De Gaulle's last premier. Served in the Vichy government but joined the resistance in 1943. Served in various ambassadorial posts, 1945–58, before becoming Foreign Minister. Helped to block British entry to the EEC in 1962. Succeeded Pompidou as premier after the protests of May 1968; resigned in

Oct. 1969 after a narrow general election defeat. Returned to the Assembly in 1973 to chair its Foreign Affairs Committee.

Craxi, Bettino (1934–2000): Italian socialist politician and first socialist Prime Minister of Italy. Member of central committee of Italian Socialist Party (PSI) after 1957. General Secretary from 1976. Revived the fortunes of the Party by adopting more centrist policies and entering coalitions with the Christian Democrats. Became first socialist premier in 1983. Survived until 1987 and remained influential until corruption charges forced his resignation as leader of the PSI in 1994. Fled to Tunisia, sentenced to 26 years' imprisonment but remained in exile until his death.

Cresson, Edith (1936–): French socialist and first female Prime Minister. Appointed by Mitterrand to succeed Michel Rocard in May 1991, but failed to improve the Party's electoral performance and was replaced in Apr. 1992. Her subsequent period as European Commissioner for Education and Research was criticised for nepotism and incompetence, leading to a mass, but temporary, resignation of Commissioners in 1999.

D'Annunzio, Gabriele (1863–1938): Italian nationalist, writer, and adventurer, seen as a forerunner of fascism. As a prominent literary figure supported Italian entry to the First World War; served in Italian Air Force with distinction. Highly critical of Italy's treatment at the Paris Peace Conference, in Sept. 1919 he and some followers seized the port of Fiume in dispute between Italy and Yugoslavia. Ejected by an Italian naval force in Jan. 1921, his actions stimulated nationalist sentiment against the Liberal government of Giolitti. He welcomed Mussolini's accession to power but played no active part in his regime.

De Gaulle, Charles (1890–1970): French soldier and statesman. Member of French military mission to Poland, 1919–20. Lectured at Staff College. Sought to modernise army. Published *The Army of the Future*, 1932–34. Ideas subsequently employed by German Army. Briefly a member of Reynaud's government, 1940. Fled to Britain after fall of France. Became head of Committee of National Liberation ('Free French'), 1943. Claimed status of head of government. Led unsuccessful attempt to recapture Dakar. Entered Paris, Aug. 1944. President of provisional government, 1945. Suspected of authoritarian ambitions. Resigned, 1946. Founded political party (Rally of the French People), retiring from its leadership, 1953. During Algerian Crisis, 1958, invited by President Coty to form temporary government with wide executive powers. Won overwhelming victory in referendum on new constitution. Elected first President of Fifth Republic, 1959. Granted independence to former French colonies in Africa, 1959–60. Granted Algeria independence, 1962. Developed independent nuclear deterrent. Encouraged closer ties with West Germany. Twice vetoed British entry to EEC, 1962–63, 1967. Re-elected on second ballot, 1965. Re-elected after May 1968 'Events', but resigned, 1969, following opposition to his plans to reform constitution.

Delcassé, Théophile (1852–1923): French politician. Elected deputy, 1889. Minister of Colonies, 1893–95, favouring territorial expansion. Foreign

Minister, 1898–1905, 1914–15. Encouraged *Entente Cordiale* with Britain, 1904. Active in Moroccan Crisis, 1905. Forced to resign. Naval Minister, 1911–13. Ambassador to St Petersburg. Involved in negotiations for Treaty of London, 1915.

Delors, Jacques (1925–): French socialist politician. Leading advocate of European federalism as embodied in the Delors Plan. President of the European Commission, 1985–95.

De Valera, Eamon (1882–1975): Irish statesman. Led group of Irish Volunteers in Easter Rising, 1916. Imprisoned, released 1917. Elected MP, 1917. Leader of Sinn Fein, 1917–26. Elected President of Dáil Eireann. Opposed 1921 treaty with Britain. Led extreme nationalists during Civil War, 1922–23. Leader of Fianna Fail, winning 1932 elections. Between 1932 and 1938 reduced links with Britain. After 1937, Prime Minister under revised constitution. Maintained Irish neutrality during Second World War. Lost power, 1948. Re-elected, 1951–54, 1957–59. President, 1959–73.

Dollfuss, Engelbert (1892–1934): Austrian politician. Leader of Christian Socialist Party. Chancellor, 1932–34. Opposed by Nazis and Socialists. Used political violence as pretext for dictatorial government. Suspended parliamentary rule, 1933. Provoked and suppressed socialist revolt. Granted authority by parliament to implement new fascist-style constitution. Murdered during attempted Nazi coup.

Dreyfus, Alfred (1859–1935): French soldier. Artillery captain appointed to General Staff. Wrongly accused of espionage and imprisoned. Case revealed depth of anti-Semitism within French establishment (Dreyfus was himself Jewish), and provoked bitter division between 'Dreyfusards' (the left, intellectuals, anti-clericals) and 'anti-Dreyfusards' (especially army and Church). Retried and pardoned. Verdict finally overturned, 1906.

Dubček, Alexander (1921–92): Czech politician. First Secretary of the Czechoslovak Communist Party and key figure in the 'Prague Spring' reform movement, which culminated in the Soviet invasion of Czechoslovakia in Aug. 1968. Dismissed from his post, he was first President of the New Federal Assembly (Aug. 1968–Sept. 1969) then Ambassador to Turkey (Dec. 1969–June 1970) before being expelled from the Communist Party. This attempt to build a national socialism with a 'human face' posed a threat to Soviet control of Eastern Europe. By 1989, however, circumstances had changed. In Dec. 1989 Dubček was elected Chairman (speaker) of the Czech parliament.

Eichmann, Adolf (1906–62): Nazi SS officer engaged in the implementation of the 'Final Solution'. Joined the Nazi security service in 1935; from 1939 organised the deportation of East European Jews to Poland and engaged in planning the settlement of Jews overseas. From late 1941 carried out mass executions of Jews in Russia and summoned the Wannsee Conference in Jan. 1942 at the behest of his superior Heydrich which sanctioned the extermination of the Jews. Directly responsible for the deportation of Jews from occupied

Europe to the extermination camps, Eichmann played a central role in the Holocaust. He escaped to Argentina in 1946, but was kidnapped by Israeli agents in 1960, brought to Israel, tried, and hanged in 1962.

Erhard, Ludwig (1897–1977): Architect of postwar West German 'economic miracle'. Finance Minister, 1949–63 and subsequently Chancellor, 1963–66. Resigned when his party refused to support his planned tax increases.

Foch, Ferdinand (1851–1929): French soldier, Marshal of France. Served as military instructor, 1894–99. Director of *École de Guerre*, 1907–11. Wrote *Principles and Conduct of War*, 1899. Appointed Chief of Staff, 1917. Created Generalissimo of Allied forces from Mar. 1918. Field Marshal, 1919. Supervised implementation of military provisions of Treaty of Versailles.

Francis Ferdinand (1863–1914): Archduke of Austria. Nephew of Emperor Francis Joseph. Became heir to throne, 1896. Hoped to give autonomy to subject Slav peoples. Assassination by Bosnian Serb at Sarajevo, 28 June 1914, immediate cause of First World War.

Francis Joseph (1830–1916): Emperor of Austria, 1848–1916. Succeeded during Revolution. King of Hungary from 1867. Quickly restored order after 1848 in Hungary and Lombardy. Abolished constitution, 1851. Ruled personally until 1867. Favoured government by strong central bureaucracy. Hostile to party politics. Allied monarchy with Catholic Church. Accepted *Ausgleich*, 1867. Sought to maintain balance of power in Europe, but by annexing Bosnia–Herzegovina, 1908, provoked ill-feeling. Precipitated First World War by attacking Serbia, 1914.

Franco, Francisco (1892–1975): Spanish soldier and military dictator. Held command of Foreign Legion in Morocco. Chief of Staff, 1935. Governor of Canaries, 1936. On outbreak of Civil War, integrated Foreign Legion and Moorish troops into rebel army. Became leader of Nationalist forces, 1936. Defeated Republican government, 1939. Established corporatist, authoritarian state, acting as '*Caudillo*' ('Leader'), and permitting only one political party, the Falange. Maintained Spanish neutrality during Second World War. Presided over Spain's rapid postwar economic development. Faced growing problem of regional separatism in last years. Ensured his own succession by King Juan Carlos I.

Frank, Anne (1929–45): Jewish girl of German parents who had fled to Holland in 1933. The family went into hiding in a friend's house in Amsterdam to evade capture by the occupying Germans. The family was betrayed and she, her sister, and mother died in a German concentration camp. Anne's *Diary*, the record of the period in hiding, published by her father in 1947, remains one of the most moving of Holocaust memoirs. The house in Amsterdam where she lived has become a museum.

Giolitti, Giovanni (1842–1928): Italian statesman. Entered parliament as a liberal, 1882. Became Minister of Finance, 1889. Prime Minister five times between 1892 and 1921. First ministry, 1892–93, was ended by 'Tanlongo Scandal', involving irregularities at Bank of Rome. Prime Minister again, 1903–05, 1906–09. Sought reconciliation with Church. Fourth ministry, 1911–14, saw annexation of Tripoli, war with the Ottoman Empire, acquisition of Libya, Rhodes and Dodecanese. Ministry fell after general strike in protest at heavy taxation. Fifth ministry, 1920, saw Italy convulsed by civil strife and disputes over Fiume. Resigned 1921. Had introduced universal suffrage, attempted to maintain Italian neutrality during First World War. Introduced wide-ranging social reforms after war. Critical of Mussolini after 1924.

Goebbels, Joseph (1897–1945): German Nazi propagandist. Early recruit to Nazi Party. Party chief in Berlin, 1926–30. Became Party's propaganda chief, 1929. Elected to Reichstag, 1930. Minister of Propaganda, 1933–45. Held powerful position in Nazi leadership. Made skilful use of oratory, parades, demonstrations and radio. Attracted to 'radical' aspect of Nazi ideology. Death by suicide.

Goering, Hermann (1893–1946): German Nazi military and political leader. First World War ace pilot. Joined Nazi Party, 1922. Given command of Storm Troopers, 1923. Elected to Reichstag, 1928. President of Reichstag, 1932–33. Entered government, 1933, as Reich Commissioner for Air, Minister President of Prussia and Prussian Minister of the Interior (hence controlled Prussian police). Created Gestapo, 1933. Head of *Luftwaffe*. Responsible for preparing Germany's war economy. Created General, 1933, Field Marshal, 1938 and Reich Marshal, 1940. Became Hitler's deputy during Second World War. Influence declined after Battle of Britain, 1940. Disgraced after plotting to oust Hitler, 1945. Condemned to death at Nuremberg. Death by suicide.

Gorbachev, Mikhail (1931–): Soviet statesman who succeeded Chernenko as General Secretary of the Communist Party in 1985. His advent to power, after a succession of ailing old-guard leaders, marked a major departure in the Soviet leadership. Succeeded Gromyko as President, 1988. His reforming policies, especially *perestroika* and *glasnost*, were soon threatened by nationalism in such areas as Azerbaijan and the Baltic. His policy of non-interference was vital in the 1989 revolutions in Eastern Europe which overthrew the old communist regimes. He survived the Aug. 1991 coup attempt, but his power base was fatally eroded as the old Soviet Union disintegrated. Resigned as President, 25 Dec. 1991, after formation of Commonwealth of Independent States. Although Gorbachev has enjoyed popularity outside Russia, since 1991 his influence within Russia has been negligible.

Gramsci, Antonio (1891–1937): Italian communist and influential theoretician. A founder member of the Italian Communist Party in 1921; leader of the Party Jan. 1926, arrested Nov. 1926 and sentenced to 20 years' imprisonment. Produced his *Prison Notebooks*, published after his death, notable for dropping insistence on violent proletarian revolution and the need to work through society as a whole. Died in prison in 1937. His ideas influenced what later came to be known as 'socialism with a human face'.

250

Grey, 1st Viscount, Sir Edward Grey (1862–1933): Liberal MP for Berwick-on-Tweed, 1885–1916. Foreign Secretary, 1905–16. His support of Britain's obligation to help Belgium in 1914 took Britain into the First World War. He believed in international arbitration, which was used successfully in the Balkan Wars. Later a champion of the League of Nations.

Griffiths, Arthur (1871–1922): Irish political leader; founded Sinn Fein newspaper. Supported the Irish Volunteers and arranged importation of arms in July 1914. Opposed Irish participation in the First World War, but not involved in 1916 Easter Rising. Elected Vice-President of the Republic in 1918, acting as effective Head of State to the proto-Irish state, 1919–20, setting up a shadow government under the official British administration. Imprisoned Nov. 1920 to July 1921, he led the Irish side of the negotiations which produced the Anglo-Irish Treaty of Dec. 1921. Supported the Treaty through the Dail and elected President of the Irish Free State. Died suddenly in June 1922.

Gromyko, Andrei Andreevich (1909–89): Soviet statesman. Attached to Soviet embassy in Washington, 1939. Ambassador in Washington, 1943. Attended Tehran, Yalta and Potsdam conferences. Elected deputy of Supreme Soviet, 1946. Became Deputy Foreign Minister, and permanent delegate to United Nations Security Council, using veto frequently. Ambassador to Britain, 1952–53. Foreign Minister, 1957–85. Signed nuclear test ban agreement, 1963. President, USSR, 1985–88.

Havel, Václav (1936–): President of Czechoslovakia since unanimous election, 29 Dec. 1989, until its demise on 31 Dec. 1992. Subsequently, first President of the Czech Republic, 1993–2003. Former dissident and political prisoner. Born Prague. Playwright. Co-founder of Charter 77. Jailed for four months. Victim of smear campaign. Jailed again, 1979, for four and a half years for subversion. Co-founder of Civic Forum, Nov. 1989. Reluctantly accepted popular draft as presidential candidate, Dec. 1989. He presided over the 'Velvet Divorce' of the Czech and Slovak parts of Czechoslovakia, leading to the independence of the Czech Republic, 1 Jan. 1993.

Heath, Sir Edward (1916–): British Conservative politician. Entered parliament, 1950. Party Whip, 1951–55. Chief Whip, 1955–59. Minister of Labour, 1959–60. Lord Privy Seal, 1960–63. Secretary for Trade and Industry, 1963–64. First leader of Conservative Party to be elected by ballot, 1965. Prime Minister, 1970–74. Proponent of European integration. Achieved British entry into EEC, Jan. 1973. Failed to solve problems of inflation and industrial relations. Improved British relations with China. Following electoral defeats of 1974, replaced as leader of Party by Margaret Thatcher, 1975. He has been a consistent critic of many aspects of Thatcherism.

Herzl, Theodor (1860–1904): Zionist leader, born in Hungary. Influenced by the anti-Semitism of the Dreyfus Affair. In pamphlet, *Judenstaat*, 1896, proposed creation of a Jewish State. Called first Zionist Congress at Basel, 1897. First President of World Zionist Organisation. Later years spent in unsuccessful negotiations with Kaiser, Ottoman Sultan, Russian Prime Minister etc. with aim of securing land for new state.

Himmler, Heinrich (1900–45): German Nazi leader and Chief of Police. Early member of Nazi Party. Involved in Munich Putsch, 1923. Head of *Schutzstaffel* (SS), 1929. Head of Gestapo, 1934, subsequently of all police forces, 1936. Head of Reich administration, 1939. Minister of the Interior, 1943. Commander-in-Chief of Home Forces, 1944. Used elaborate system of terror, espionage, detention and murder to reinforce totalitarian state. Bore major responsibility for racial extermination policies. Made attempts to negotiate unconditional surrender before end of war. Tried at Nuremberg. Death by suicide.

Hindenburg, Paul von (1847–1934): German soldier and President. Fought at Königgratz, 1866, and in Franco–Prussian War, 1870–71. Became General, 1903. Retired, 1911. Recalled to duty on outbreak of First World War. Victories won with Ludendorff at Tannenberg, 1914, and Masurian Lakes, 1915, made him a national hero. Became Chief of General Staff, 1916. Organised withdrawal from Western Front, 1918 (giving rise to myth of undefeated German Army). Advised Kaiser to abdicate and arranged Armistice. Retired, 1919. Elected President of Weimar Republic, 1925–34. Defeated Hitler in presidential election, 1932, but appointed him Chancellor, Jan. 1933.

Hitler, Adolf (1889–1945): Dictator of Germany. Born in Austria. Served in Bavarian Army during First World War, becoming lance corporal, twice decorated with Iron Cross. Joined German Workers' Party in Munich, 1919, transforming it into National Socialist German Workers' Party (NSDAP/Nazi Party), based on extreme nationalism and anti-Semitism. Attempted putsch in Munich, 1923, which proved abortive, though making him a national figure. While in prison, wrote political testament, *Mein Kampf.* Began to reorganise Nazi Party, 1925. Established unrivalled position as leader of Party. Created efficient propaganda machine and organised elite guard, *Schutzstaffel* (SS). Helped to power by Great Depression. Nazi Party won 107 seats in 1930 Reichstag elections, becoming second-largest party. In elections, July 1932, won 230 seats (highest they ever achieved). Appointed Chancellor by Hindenburg, Jan. 1933, though Nazis still a minority in Reichstag. Following Reichstag fire and Enabling Act, assumed dictatorial powers. Other political parties dissolved. Nazi Party purged of rivals by 1934. On death of Hindenburg, 1934, became President, uniting position with that of Chancellor or *Führer* ('Leader'). Internal opposition ruthlessly suppressed. Rearmament programme expanded, 1935, aiding economic recovery. Occupied Rhineland, 1936. Rome–Berlin 'Axis' negotiated, 1936. Annexed Austria, 1938 (*Anschluss*). Gained Sudetenland after Munich Agreement, 1938. Seized remainder of Czechoslovakia, 1939. After Non-Aggression Pact with USSR (Molotov–Ribbentrop Pact, Aug. 1939), invaded Poland, 1 Sept. 1939, precipitating Second World War. Achieved swift military successes through *Blitzkrieg* campaigns, but fatal error was in attacking Russia, June 1941. Faced combined opposition of USSR, USA and Britain. Survived assassination attempt, July 1944. Committed suicide during closing stage of war.

Honecker, Erich (1912–94): Head of State, German Democratic Republic (East Germany) 1976–89. Having held various offices in the East German Communist Party from 1958, he succeeded Ulbricht as First Secretary in 1971, and in 1976 became Chairman of the Council of State (Head of State) and undisputed leader of East Germany. Ousted from power when communism collapsed in 1989. Faced numerous accusations of abuse of power. Given sanctuary in Soviet Union.

Horthy de Nagybánya, Miklós (1886–1957): Hungarian Admiral and Regent. Commander-in-Chief of Austro–Hungarian Navy, 1917. Minister of War in 'White' government, 1919. With Romanian help, crushed communist regime of Béla Kun, 1920. Chosen to be Regent, acting as Head of State, on behalf of absent King Charles. Refused to give up office in favour of King Charles, 1921. Ruled virtually as a dictator. Formed alliance with Germany, 1941, but withdrew 1944. Imprisoned by Germans but freed by Allies. Retired to Portugal.

Husak, Gustav (1913–91): President of Czechoslovakia, 1975–89. Became First Secretary of the Communist Party when Dubček was ousted from office in 1969, following Soviet invasion. Retained this position when he became President in 1975, thus strengthening his ascendancy in the leadership. Fell from power after the 'Velvet Revolution' of 1989. Expelled from the Communist Party, Feb. 1990.

Ibarruri, Dolores (1895–1989): Spanish communist leader from the Basque country. Adopted as a journalist the *nom de plume* 'La Pasionara'. Joined Spanish Communist Party in 1930 and imprisoned several times. Elected Deputy for the Asturias in 1936. After the nationalist rising, her radio broadcasts became well known, including her famous phrase '*No pasaran*' ('They shall not pass'). Went into exile in Russia in Mar. 1939. Secretary-General to the Communist Party from 1942 to 1960. Returned to Spain in 1976 and elected to the Cortes in 1977 for the Asturias, though played little active role in post-Francoist politics.

Izvolski, Alexander (1856–1919): Russian statesman. Entered diplomatic service, 1875. Held important post in Tokyo, 1899. Transferred to Copenhagen, 1903. Unexpectedly appointed Foreign Minister, 1905, holding post for five years. Worked for better relations with Britain and Japan. Successes marred by Bosnian Crisis, 1908–09. Aggrieved by Austria's seizure of Bosnia–Herzegovina before Russia had secured 'compensation' through fresh solution to Straits Question. As Ambassador in Paris, 1910–16, strengthened military alliance between Russia and France.

Jaruzelski, General Wojciech (1923–): Polish soldier and politician. Long and distinguished army career. Became Chief of General Staff, 1965, Minister of Defence, 1968, and member of Politburo, 1971. Became Prime Minister after resignation of Pinkowski, 1981. Declared martial law in effort to tackle economic crisis and to counter growth of Solidarity movement. Solidarity banned and its leaders detained and tried. Lifted martial law, July 1983. Became President in 1989, but succeeded in 1990 by Lech Walesa, elected by a nationwide vote.

Jaurès, Jean (1859–1914): French socialist leader and writer. Elected deputy, 1885, again 1889, 1893. Founded socialist newspaper, *L'Humanité*, 1904, giving support to Dreyfus. By 1905 had become leader of united Socialist Party. Never held office, in accordance with decision of Congress of Socialist International, 1905. Not a Marxist, but in French revolutionary tradition. Hoped to mobilise French and German workers to prevent outbreak of war. Assassinated by French nationalist fanatic.

John Paul II, Pope (1920–): Born Karol Wojtyla at Wadowice, near Cracow. Ordained 1945. Became Archbishop in Jan. 1964 and Cardinal in 1967. Elected Pope in Oct. 1978, following the sudden death of John Paul I. First non-Italian Pope since 1522. Seriously wounded in assassination attempt in 1981. Gave tacit support to the Solidarity movement in Poland with two visits in 1982 and 1987 and personal audience with Lech Walesa. Widely travelled, he has maintained a conservative line on most of the Church's teachings on contraception, abortion, the celibacy of the clergy, homosexuality, and so-called 'liberation theology'.

John XXIII, Pope (1881–1963): Born Angelo Giuseppi Roncalli, son of a Lombard peasant farmer; ordained in 1904. Served in Papal diplomatic service and as papal nuncio to France after the Liberation. Made a Cardinal in 1953. Aged 77 when elected Pope in Oct. 1958. Seen by many as a caretaker figure, but called the Second Vatican Council in 1959. Meeting in 1962, the first for 94 years, the Council instituted far-reaching changes in Catholic relations with other churches, to the liturgy, including the adoption of the vernacular for services, and relations with the Eastern Bloc, seeking peaceful co-existence with communist regimes.

Juan Carlos I (1938–): King of Spain. Succeeded to the throne, 22 Nov. 1975. Married Princess Sophia of Greece, 1962. After the long years of the Franco dictatorship, his accession marked the entry of Spain into a more modern, liberal era. Acted decisively to frustrate right-wing coup in 1981.

Kádár, János (1912–89): First Secretary of the Hungarian Communist Party, 1956–65, and Prime Minister, 1956–58 and 1961–65. Minister of Interior, 1948–50; arrested and imprisoned, 1951–54. First Secretary in 1956, Kádár initially favoured reform, but later supported Soviet intervention, which crushed the Hungarian rising. Remained Prime Minister until 1958 and First Secretary thereafter. Greater freedom of expression was allowed from 1959 and when Kádár held the premiership for a second term, 1961–65, he took positive measures of reconciliation and cautious liberalisation.

Kapp, Wolfgang (1868–1922): German civil servant. Collaborated with group of ex-soldiers in attempt to overthrow Weimar Republic, 1920. Thwarted by general strike. Fled to Sweden. Returned to Germany, 1922. Died awaiting trial.

Károlyi, Count Mihály (1875–1955): Hungarian statesman. Entered parliament, 1905. Politically liberal, became increasingly radical. Led Independent Party during First World War. Became Prime Minister, 1918 and sought armistice. Provisional President of Hungarian Republic, aimed to introduce reforms. Overthrown by communist coup, 1919 and went into exile. Returned, 1946, after downfall of Horthy. Served as a diplomat, 1946–49, before resuming exile.

Kautsky, Karl (1854–1938): German socialist of Czech descent. Colleague of Marx. Collaborated with Engels in London, 1881–82. Founded socialist newspaper, *Die Neue Zeit*, 1883. Criticised 'revisionism' of German Social Democrats. Disagreed with Lenin over interpretation of Marxism. Condemned Russian Revolution and refused to join German Communist Party. Remained a pacifist during First World War. Joined Austrian Social Democrats after war. Fled to Holland after *Anschluss*.

Kemal Atatürk (Mustafa Kemal) (1881–1938): Creator of modern Turkish nation. Joined Young Turk reform movement. Entered army, winning quick promotion. Fought Italians in Tripoli, 1911, and in Balkan Wars. Involved in Gallipoli campaign during First World War. Led national resistance after Greek invasion following the Ottoman Empire's defeat. Renounced loyalty to Sultan and formed provisional government in Ankara, 1920. Led Turks in War of Independence until 1922, expelling Greeks, deposing Sultan and establishing Republic. Became first President of Republic, 1923–38. Architect of modern, secularised state. Emancipated women. Sought to build strong nation from homelands of Anatolia and residue of European Turkey. Did not attempt to regain former Arab possessions. Territorial settlement with Greece achieved at Treaty of Lausanne, 1923.

Kerensky, Alexander (1881–1970): Russian politician. Entered Duma, 1912, as critic of Tsarist government. Led Social Revolutionary Party. Leading role in Revolution, Mar. 1917. Became Minister of Justice, then Minister of War. Prime Minister of provisional government, July 1917. Continued war with Germany and attempted major offensive which reduced his popularity. Defeated Kornilov's military rising, Sept. 1917. Overthrown by Bolsheviks in Nov. Revolution, 1917. Spent rest of life in exile in France, Australia and the USA.

Keynes, John Maynard, 1st Baron Keynes (1883–1946): British economist. Worked at Treasury during First World War. Chief representative at negotiations prior to Treaty of Versailles. Criticised reparations plans in *The Economic Consequences of the Peace*, 1919. Made radical proposals for dealing with unemployment by provision of public works. Ideas influenced Liberal Party's election manifesto, 1929. Full proposals on economic controls in interests of maintaining full employment appeared in *The General Theory of Employment, Interest and Money*, 1936. Inspired 'Keynesian Revolution' during and after Second World War. Rejected classical belief in self-regulating economy. Argued need for government expenditure to be adjusted to control level of public demand. Advised Chancellor of the Exchequer during Second World War. Chief British delegate at Bretton Woods Conference, 1944. Involved in discussions leading to creation of International Monetary Fund and World Bank.

Khrushchev, Nikita Sergeyevich (1894–1971): Soviet politician. Joined Communist Party, 1918. Fought in Civil War. Member of Central Committee of Party, 1934. Full member of Politburo and of Praesidium of Supreme Soviet, 1939. Organised guerrilla warfare against Germans during Second World War. Premier of Ukraine, 1944–47. Undertook major restructuring of agriculture, 1949. Became First Secretary of All Union Party on death of Stalin, 1953. Denounced Stalinism, 1956. Relegated Molotov, Kaganovich and Malenkov (potential rivals), 1957. Succeeded Bulganin as Prime Minister, 1958–64. Official visits to USA, 1959, India and China, 1960. Deposed, 1964, following economic failures, especially Virgin Lands Campaign (see p. 331).

Kohl, Helmut (1930–): Chancellor of the Federal Republic of Germany, 1982–98. Christian Democrat Minister-President of Rhineland Palatinate, 1969–76; leader of the opposition in the Bundestag, 1976–82. Presided over the reunification of Germany in 1990 and became first Chancellor of a reunited Germany following victory in the 1990 election. By Nov. 1996 Kohl had become the longest-serving Chancellor in German history (except for Bismarck), but in 1998 was the first German Chancellor to lose an election. A strong advocate of European Monetary Union, the single currency and expansion of the European Union in the East. In 2000 he was forced to resign as honorary Chair of the CDU because of accusations of illegal funding.

Kolchak, Alexander Vasilyevich (1874–1920): Russian sailor. After Russo–Japanese War, 1904–05, reorganised navy. Commanded Black Sea Fleet from 1916. After 1917 Revolution, led counter-revolutionary government in Siberia. Captured by Bolsheviks and executed.

Kornilov, Lavr Georgyevich (1870–1918): Russian soldier. Fought in Russo–Japanese War, 1904–05. Divisional commander in Galicia during First World War. Appointed Commander-in-Chief after Revolution, Mar. 1917. Accused of planning military coup. Arrested, but managed to join anti-Bolshevik forces on Don. Killed in action.

Kruger, (Stephanus Johannes) Paulus (1825–1904): Afrikaner politician. One of leaders of revolt against British, 1880, which restored independence of Transvaal. Elected President of Transvaal, 1883; re-elected 1888, 1893, 1898. Refused to grant political rights to incoming (non-Afrikaner) miners following discovery of gold on Rand. Resulting tensions contributed to Boer War, 1899–1902. Canvassed European support for Afrikaner cause, 1900.

Kun, Béla (1886–1937): Hungarian communist leader. Following capture by Russians during First World War, established brief Soviet Republic in Hungary, Mar.–Aug. 1919. Escaped to Vienna after counter-revolution, settled in USSR. Died in Stalinist purge.

Landsbergis, Vytautas (1932–): President of Lithuania, 1990–92, when his harsh nationalist position and failures of economic policy produced defeat. The symbol of modern Lithuanian nationalism.

Laval, Pierre (1883–1945): French politician. Member of Chamber of Deputies, 1914–19, and from 1924 onwards. Originally a socialist, became an independent after 1927, on elevation to Senate. Minister of Public Works, 1925. Minister of Justice, 1926. Prime Minister, 1931–32, 1935–36. Foreign Minister, 1934–36. Negotiated Hoare–Laval Pact with Britain, 1935. Proponent of closer ties with Germany and Italy. After fall of France, 1940, played major role in creation of Pétain's Vichy regime. Prime Minister, 1942–44. Collaborated with Germany, e.g. in supply of forced labour. Fled to Germany, then Spain, after liberation of France. Repatriated, tried and executed for treason.

Le Pen, Jean-Marie (1928–): French right-wing politician. Served in the Foreign Legion and youngest member of the National Assemby in 1956. From 1972 built up the *Front National* (FN) on an anti-immigrant platform, establishing a strong base in the area around Marseilles. Secured 35 seats in the 1986 elections and entered the presidential race in 1988, winning 14 per cent of the vote, but eliminated on the first round. The Party lost all but one of its seats in June 1988 and illness and scandals reduced Le Pen's influence. In 2002, however, he secured second place in the first round of the presidential elections, but was heavily defeated by Chirac in the next round.

Lenin, Vladimir Ilyich (V. I. Ulyanov) (1870–1924): Russian revolutionary leader and architect of Soviet State. After expulsion from Kazan University for political activity, absorbed writings of Marx. In St Petersburg, organised League for the Liberation of the Working Class. Exiled to Siberia, 1897. In London, 1903, when Russian Social Democratic Labour Party divided into Mensheviks and Bolsheviks. Led Bolshevik wing and published newspaper, *Iskra* ('The Spark'). Involved in abortive Russian Revolution, 1905. Controlled revolutionary movement from exile in Switzerland. Smuggled into Russia by Germans, 1917. Overthrew Kerensky's provisional government and became head of Council of People's Commissars. Ended war with Germany and concluded Treaty of Brest-Litovsk, Mar. 1918. Civil War with 'White' armies continued until 1921. As Chairman of Communist Party, established virtual dictatorship and dissolved Constituent Assembly. Created Communist International, 1919, to encourage world revolution. Introduced New Economic Policy, 1921, in diversion from planned communist transformation of economy. Recognised dangers implicit in rise of Stalin. Important both as theoretical writer on Marxism and as practical revolutionary organiser. Marxist-Leninist era in Soviet Union officially ended after 1991 coup attempt.

Litvinov, Maxim Maximovich (1876–1951): Soviet diplomat. Early recruit to Bolshevik Party. Diplomatic representative in Britain after Nov. Revolution, 1917. Deported, 1918. Deputy Foreign Commissar, 1921–30, 1939–46. Foreign Commissar, 1930–39. Sought to improve USSR's foreign relations. Took USSR into League of Nations, 1934. Advocate of collective security, supporting Franco–Russian Pact, 1935. Dismissed in favour of Molotov when Stalin required agreement with Hitler, 1939. Ambassador to Washington, 1941–42.

Lloyd George, David, 1st Earl Lloyd George of Dwyfor (1863–1945): British Liberal statesman. Member of Parliament, 1890–1945. President of the Board of Trade, 1905–08. Chancellor of the Exchequer, 1908–15. Introduced controversial People's Budget, 1909, proposing increased taxation to fund social reform and naval rearmament. Budget rejected by House of Lords, causing constitutional crisis leading to Parliament Act, 1911. Minister of Munitions, 1915–16. Secretary for War, 1916. Prime Minister, 1916–22. Leader of the Liberal Party, 1926–31. Created Earl Lloyd George, 1945. Dynamic and efficient wartime leader. Attended Paris Peace Conference, 1919. Opposed calls at Versailles for draconian penalties on Germany. Faced economic problems at home in postwar period. Continuing violence in Ireland led to creation of Irish Free State, 1921, weakening Lloyd George's position, as did revelations of his sale of honours. Forced to resign, 1922, when Conservatives left coalition. Never held office again.

Ludendorff, Erich (1865–1937): German soldier. Entered army, 1882. Major-General by 1914. Planned deployment of German armies at outbreak of First World War. With Hindenburg, won victory at Tannenberg, 1914. Transferred to Western Front, 1916. Shared increasing control of government with Hindenburg after 1916. Conceived spring offensive, 1918. Involved in abortive Kapp Putsch, 1920. Took part in Hitler's Munich Putsch, 1923. Founded extreme nationalist party, 1925. Unsuccessful candidate for Reich presidency, 1925.

Luxemburg, Rosa (1870–1919): Polish-born German revolutionary leader. Major theoretician of Marxism. Imprisoned for opposition to First World War, 1915–18. Founded German Communist Party in 1918 with Karl Liebknecht, based on earlier Spartacist group. Opposed the nationalism of existing socialist groups, as shown by their participation in the war. Critical of German Social Democrats in government. Sought to restrain more violent colleagues, but unable to prevent Spartacist uprising, Jan. 1919. Brutally murdered by counter-revolutionary troops.

Mannerheim, Baron Carl Gustaf Emil (1867–1948): Finnish soldier and statesman. Served in Russian Imperial Army, 1889–1917. Became General during Russo–Japanese War, 1904–05. Commanded 'White' Guards, 1918, retaking Helsinki from communists. Regent of Finland, 1918–19. Head of State, 1919–20. Led Finnish armies against Russia. Gained independence of Finland from USSR. Created Field Marshal, 1933. President of Defence Council, 1931–39. Active in defence of Finland following Russian attack, 1939. Made pact with Germany against Russia, 1941. Marshal of Finland, 1942. President, 1944–46. Declared war on Germany, Mar. 1945.

Masaryk, Tómaš (1850–1937): Czech philosopher and statesman. Became Professor of Philosophy at Prague, 1882. Represented Young Czech Party in Austrian parliament, 1891–93. Led 'Czech Realists', 1907–14. Critical of Austrian policies. Became Chairman of Czech National Council in London, 1914. Described views on nationality question in *The New Europe* (periodical), from

1916 onwards. Organised Czech Legion in Russia, 1917. Won support of President Wilson. Accepted by USA as head of an allied government, 1918. Returned to Czechoslovakia as president-elect, 1918. Re-elected twice. Resigned, 1935.

Matteotti, Giacomo (1885–1924): Italian socialist politician. Elected deputy, 1919. Became General Secretary of Socialist Party, 1924. Denounced fascist violence in *The Fascisti Exposed*. Murdered by Fascists as a result. Death produced political crisis. Non-fascist deputies blocked normal operation of parliament. Party meetings banned by Mussolini, censorship introduced. Incident cost Fascists foreign sympathy.

Mihailovíc, Draža (1893–1946): Yugoslavian resistance leader. A pro-royalist Serbian army colonel at the time of the German occupation in 1941, he led the first guerrilla movement, the Chetniks, with support from the Yugoslav government in exile and Churchill. Rivalry with Tito's (*q.v*) partisans and other ethnic groups and collaboration with the Germans and Italians led to him being dropped by Churchill in favour of Tito. He was executed in 1946 by the Tito government.

Milosevic, Slobodan (1941–): Serbian politician, former communist who manipulated nationalist forces to maintain his hold on power. President of Serbia from 1990, he played a key role in the wars against Croatia and Bosnia and was widely held responsible for policies of terror and 'ethnic cleansing'. Subject to UN economic sanctions from 1992 to 1995, he faced mass protests in 1996–97 for refusing to accept opposition victories in municipal elections and in Montenegro. Became President of the Federal Republic of Yugoslavia (Serbia and Montenegro) in July 1997. Following his involvement in the Kosovo crisis from 1997 and the bombing campaign against Serbia, he was removed from government and arraigned on war crime charges by international bodies. He was brought to trial in 2001 (the first head of state to be so charged).

Mitterrand, François Maurice (1916–95): French politician. Socialist deputy, 1946. Ministerial office in 11 governments under the Fourth Republic. Unsuccessful Left candidate against de Gaulle in presidential election, 1965. Socialist Party Secretary, 1971. Defeated in presidential election, 1974. Elected President, defeating Giscard d'Estaing, 1981. Backed by a National Assembly socialist majority, attempted radical economic policy, 1981–86. After 1986 Assembly elections, shared power with Gaullist majority led by Chirac and moderated policy. Re-elected President, 1988, defeating Chirac. Failed to win socialist majority in ensuing Assembly elections. Longest-serving President of the Fifth Republic.

Molotov, Vyacheslav Mikhailovich (1890–1986): Soviet politician. Emerged as prominent Bolshevik during Nov. Revolution, 1917. Loyal colleague of Stalin, 1921 onwards. Member of Politburo, 1926–57. Helped implement Five-Year Plan, 1928. Premier, 1930–41. Foreign Minister, 1939–49. Negotiated pact with Ribbentrop, Aug. 1939. Deputy premier, 1941–57. Negotiated treaties with Eastern Bloc countries, 1945–49. Became member of ruling triumvirate following death of Stalin, 1953. Negotiated Austrian State Treaty, 1955. Minister of State Control, 1956–57. Became Foreign Minister again, 1957. Influence declined with rise of Khrushchev. Ambassador to Mongolia, 1957–60. Retired, 1961–62.

Monnet, Jean (1888–1979): French politician, economist and diplomat. Member of Inter-Allied Maritime Commission, 1915–17. First deputy Secretary-General of League of Nations, 1919–23. Chairman, Franco–British Economic Co-ordination Committee, 1939–40. Became Minister of Commerce, 1944. Fostered establishment of National Planning Council, becoming head of Council, 1945–47. Architect of European Community. Chairman, Action Committee for United States of Europe, 1955–75. Instrumental in foundation of European Coal and Steel Community. President of ECSC, 1952–55.

Montgomery, 1st Viscount, Sir Bernard Law Montgomery (1887–1976): British soldier. Lieutenant-Colonel and battalion commander by end of First World War. Evacuated from Dunkirk with 3rd Division under his command, 1940. By Dec. 1941, head of South-Eastern Command as Lieutenant-General. Chosen to command 8th Army in North Africa, 1942. Halted Rommel's advance, defeating him at El Alamein. Led invasion of Sicily and Italy. Appointed land commander of Operation Overlord (Normandy landings), 1944. Uneasy relationship with American allies. Commander of occupation forces in Germany. After war, became Chief of Imperial General Staff. Deputy commander of NATO, 1951–58.

Mussolini, Benito (1883–1945): Dictator of Italy. Originally a socialist. Imprisoned for political activities, 1908. Editor of socialist national newspaper, *Avanti*, 1912–14. Resigned from Party having been criticised for supporting war with Austria. Founded newspaper, *Il Popolo d'Italia*, Milan, 1914. Organised groups (*fasci*) of workers to campaign for social improvements. Amalgamated into Fascist Party, 1919. Elected to Chamber of Deputies, 1921. During period of civil unrest, led 'March on Rome', 1922. Appointed Prime Minister by King Victor Emmanuel III, 1922. Headed Fascist–Nationalist coalition, as *Duce*. Acquired dictatorial powers, 1922. Dictatorship established, 1925. Single party, corporatist state instituted 1928–29. Large-scale public works introduced. Lateran Treaty settled Church–State relations, 1929. Expansionist foreign policy: Corfu incident, 1924; invasion of Abyssinia, 1935. Created 'Axis' with Hitler, 1936. Left League of Nations, 1937. Annexed Albania, 1939. Declared war on France and Britain, 1940. Invaded Greece, 1940. Military setbacks in East Africa and Libya. Heavily dependent on Germany by 1941. Forced to resign following coup by Victor Emmanuel III and Marshal Badoglio, 1943. Detained, but freed by Germans. Established Republican Fascist government in German-controlled North Italy. Captured and executed by Italian partisans, Apr. 1945.

Nicholas II (1868–1918): Tsar of Russia, 1894–1917. Son of Alexander III. Reluctant to introduce political reforms. Influential in achievement of International Peace Conference in The Hague, 1898. Encouraged building of Trans-Siberian Railway. Forced by revolutionary mood of 1905 (stemming from industrial unrest, poor harvests and disastrous Russo–Japanese War) to summon elected Duma. Made gestures of reform under Prime Minister Stolypin. Fell under influence of Rasputin after 1906. Undertook Supreme Command of Russian Armies, 1915. Accused of maintaining communications with Germany during First World War. Abdicated after Revolution, Mar. 1917. Murdered by local Bolsheviks at Ekaterinburg, 1918, together with family.

Orlando, Vittorio Emmanuele (1860–1952): Italian statesman. Professor of Constitutional Law at Palermo. Elected to parliament, 1897. Minister of Justice, 1916. Prime Minister, 1917–19, in aftermath of military defeat at Caporetto. President of Chamber of Deputies, 1919. Led Italian delegation at Paris Peace Conference, 1919–20. Disagreed with President Wilson over Italy's territorial aspirations. Influence declined thereafter. Resigned presidency of Chamber of Deputies in protest at fascist electoral malpractice, 1925. President, Constituent Assembly, 1946–47.

Papandreou, Andreas (1919–96): Greek politician. One of the leading political figures of postwar Greece. Prime Minister from 1981–89 and again 1993–96. His father, George Papandreou, was a centrist Prime Minister in 1964. Andreas Papandreou founded PASOK in 1974 after the collapse of the rule of the military junta. Although in the late 1980s his image became tarnished with political scandals (and revelations of his own private life), the 30 years during which he dominated Greek politics helped define modern democratic Greece as a part of the West.

Pasic, Nikola (1845–1926): Serbian/Yugoslavian politician. One of founders of Radical Party, 1881. Became member of legislature, 1878. Exiled, 1883–89. Chief Minister of Serbia, 1891–92. Ambassador to Russia, 1893–94. Exiled, 1899–1903. Helped engineer establishment of Karageorgvic dynasty in Serbia, 1903. Chief Minister, 1904–08. Minister of Foreign Affairs, 1904. Chief Minister, 1910–18. Faced opposition from militant Serbian 'Black Hand' organisation, which he suppressed in 1917. Led joint delegation of Serbs, Croats and Slovenes at Paris Peace Conference, 1919. Chief Minister of Yugoslavia, 1921–26, giving priority to Serbian interests.

Pétain, Henri Philippe (1856–1951): French soldier and politician. Entered army, 1876. Lectured at *École de Guerre*, 1906 onwards. Became colonel, 1912. Commanded an army corps, 1914. National renown followed defence of Verdun, 1916. Commander-in-Chief of French armies in the field, 1917. Created Marshal of France, 1918. Vice-President, Higher Council of War, 1920–30. Led joint French–Spanish campaign against insurgents in Morocco, 1925–26. Inspector-General of Army, 1929. Became Minister of War, 1934. Ambassador to Spain, 1939. Became Prime Minister, June 1940. Secured Armistice with Germany. Given powers by National Assembly to rule by authoritarian means, July 1940. Became Head of State in unoccupied ('Vichy') France, 1942. Obliged to flee France with retreating Germans, 1944. Sentenced to death for treason, 1945, but sentence commuted to life imprisonment by de Gaulle.

Pilsudski, Josef (1867–1935): Polish soldier and statesman. Exiled to Siberia for political activities, 1887–92. Founded Polish Socialist Party, 1892. Became editor of Polish underground socialist newspaper, *Robotnik.* Increasingly nationalist in outlook. Sought Japanese support for Polish rising during Russo–Japanese War, 1904. Recruited by Austria to lead Polish legion against Russia, 1914. Interned by Germans, 1917. On release, became commander of all Polish armies. Elected Chief of State, 1918. Remained dictator until constitution established, 1922. Led Polish campaign against Bolsheviks, 1919–20. Created Field Marshal, 1920. Commanded army until retirement, 1923. Executed military coup, 1926. Served as Prime Minister, 1926–28, 1930. Retained dictatorial powers until death, 1935. Unable to convince France of threat from Nazi Germany. Concluded Non-Aggression Pact with Germany, 1934.

Pius XII (Eugenio Pacelli) (1876–1958): Elected Pope 1939. Prior to this, he had been papal nuncio in Germany and papal Secretary of State. Much controversy surrounds his conduct during the Second World War, in particular his failure to condemn the Nazi regime.

Poincaré, Raymond (1860–1934): French statesman. Elected deputy, 1887. Education Minister, 1893–94. Finance Minister, 1894–95. Senator and Finance Minister, 1906. Became Prime Minister, 1912. Strengthened Dual Alliance with Russia. Supported *Entente* with Britain. President, 1913–20, influential on legislation. Prime Minister, 1924–26, simultaneously Foreign Minister. Pursued nationalistic policy, disagreeing with Britain over reparations question. Authorised French occupation of Ruhr, 1923. Prime Minister and Finance Minister of Government of National Union, 1926–29, imposing rigorous economies and achieving currency stabilisation.

Pompidou, Georges (1911–74): French politician. Member of Resistance during Second World War. Aide to General de Gaulle, 1944–46. Member of Council of State, 1946–54. Deputy Director-General of Tourism, 1946–49. Director-General of Rothschild's (banking house), 1954–58. Chief of de Gaulle's personal staff, 1958–59. Involved in drafting of Constitution of Fifth Republic. Negotiated ceasefire agreement with Algerian Nationalists, 1961. Prime Minister, 1962–68. President, 1969–74. Pursued policies similar to those of de Gaulle.

Primo de Rivera, Miguel (1870–1930): Spanish dictator, 1923–30. Entered Spanish army, 1888. Served in Morocco, Cuba and Philippines. Became Major-General, 1910. Military Governor of Cadiz, 1915–19, Valencia, 1919–22, Barcelona, 1922–23. Assumed power with support of King Alfonso XIII, 1923. Dissolved Spanish parliament, suspended trial by jury, imposed censorship of press. Political opponents imprisoned. Intended to establish fascist regime. Faced growing opposition, e.g. over failure to implement agricultural reforms. Ended Moroccan War, 1927. Continued in office as Prime Minister, but obliged to resign when he lost support of army, 1930. Actions and policies contributed to collapse of monarchy.

Putin, Vladimir (1952–): Russian President since Jan. 2000. Former KGB officer, entered politics with the collapse of the Soviet Union and became head of the Federal Security Service in 1998 and secretary to the presidential Security Council in 1999. Appointed premier by President Yeltsin in Aug. 1999 and on Yeltsin's resignation at the end of the year succeeded him and was then confirmed as President in the Mar. 2000 elections. Presided over attempts to conclude the Chechnya war and signed a major nuclear arms reduction treaty with President Bush in May 2002.

Quisling, Vidkun (1887–1945): Norwegian soldier, politician and traitor. Military attaché in Petrograd, 1918–19, Helsinki, 1919–21. Minister of War, 1931–33. Expanded right-wing National Unity Party. Visited Germany, 1939. Advised Hitler on creation of sympathetic regime in Norway. Headed puppet regime following German occupation, 1940. Tried and executed, 1945.

Rasputin, Gregori (1869–1916): Russian mystic. Used hypnotic talents over ailing Tsarevich Alexei (1904–18) to gain influence at court. Interference in politics damaged position of monarchy and provoked opposition among court. Suspected of working on behalf of Germany during First World War. Murdered by aristocrats.

Rathenau, Walther (1867–1922): German statesman. Director of giant AEG electrical combine. Made responsible for organising war economy, 1916. Founded (liberal) Democratic Party, 1918. Became Minister of Reconstruction, 1921, and Minister of Foreign Affairs, 1922. Represented Germany at Cannes Conference, 1922. Engineered reduction of Germany's reparations commitment for 1922. Played leading role in achieving Treaty of Rapallo with Russia, 1922. Assassinated by anti-Semitic nationalists.

Ribbentrop, Joachim von (1893–1946): German Nazi diplomat. Involved in negotiations between Hitler and German government. Helped organise Nazi government, 1933. Ambassador at large, 1935. Concluded Anglo–German Naval Treaty, 1935, and Anti-Comintern Pact, 1936. Ambassador in London, 1936–38. Foreign Minister, 1938–45. Responsible for giving German foreign policy a distinctly 'Nazi' character. Negotiated Molotov–Ribbentrop Pact, 1939, and Pact with Italy and Japan, 1940. Tried as war criminal at Nuremberg. Hanged, 1946.

Robinson, Mary (1944–): Irish politician, first woman President of the Irish Republic. Trained as a lawyer, Professor in Law at Trinity College, Dublin, from 1969. Member of the Irish Senate, 1969–89. Noted for her support of progressive social and feminist causes. Became President in the Nov. 1990 elections as the nominee of the minority Labour Party and re-elected in 1997, but retired early from her post to take up a position in the UN.

Rommel, Erwin (1891–1944): German soldier. Served on Romanian and Italian fronts during First World War. Lectured at War Academy. Joined Nazi Party, 1933. Commanded 7th Panzer Division, Penetrated Ardennes, May 1940. Became commander of 'Afrika Corps', 1941, earning nickname 'The Desert

Fox'. Defeated by campaigns of Alexander and Montgomery, 1942–43. Given task of strengthening defences in France, 1944. Active in resistance to Allied landings in Normandy, June 1944. Implicated in plot to assassinate Hitler. Apparently forced to commit suicide, Oct. 1944.

Sakharov, Andrei (1921–89): Russian physicist and dissident. Major figure in Soviet nuclear physics, developing the Soviet hydrogen bomb. Became involved in the dissident movement with his wife Elena Bonner in the 1960s, urging co-operation between the USA and the Soviet Union which led to him being removed from top-secret work. Became involved in human rights issues and awarded the Nobel Peace Prize in 1975. Exiled to the closed city of Gorky in 1980 where he and his family were harassed by the Soviet authorities. Invited to Moscow by Gorbachev as part of *glasnost* in Dec. 1986. Elected to the Congress of People's Deputies where he called for an end to the war in Afghanistan and radical democratic reforms.

Salazar, Antonio de Oliveira (1889–1970): Portuguese dictator. Professor of Economics at Coimbra University, 1916. Minister of Finance, 1926, 1928–32. Prime Minister, 1932–68. Also Minister of War, 1936–44, Foreign Minister, 1936–37. Principal architect of authoritarian constitution introduced in 1933. Implemented fascist-type government on virtually dictatorial lines, stifling political opposition. Restored public finances and modernised transport system. Organised public works schemes. Maintained Portuguese neutrality during Second World War.

Schlieffen, Alfred, Count von (1833–1913): German soldier. Chief of German General Staff, 1891–1905. Prepared strategic planning for war with France ('Schlieffen Plan'). In modified form, plan was used in German attack on France, 1914. Believed rapid defeat of France was essential to German success. Plan provided for violation of neutrality of Holland, Belgium and Luxembourg, by-passing France's defences.

Seeckt, Hans von (1866–1936): German soldier. Chief of Staff to Mackensen on Eastern Front during First World War. Won victory at Gorlice, 1915. Served in Balkans and the Ottoman Empire. Appointed Head of *Truppenamt*, 1919. Supervised Germany's secret rearmament, 1919–26, especially through co-operation with Russia. Head of *Reichswehr*, 1920–26. Resigned in response to President Hindenburg's hostility, 1926. Member of Reichstag, 1930–32. Created an army capable of rapid expansion after 1933.

Shevardnadze, Eduard (1928–): Soviet Foreign Minister from 1985 until his shock resignation in Dec. 1990 over fears of right-wing coup. As Gorbachev's key lieutenant, presided over the ending of the Cold War and the freeing of the Eastern Bloc from Soviet control. Born in Georgia, he established his earlier reputation for rooting out corruption and nepotism in Georgia. His prophetic resignation increased very considerably the pressures on Gorbachev. Briefly reappointed Foreign Minister, Nov. to Dec. 1991. Subsequently became Head of State in Georgia, 1992, and first elected President, 1995.

Sikorsky, Wladyslaw (1881–1943): Polish general and politician. Retired from the armed forces in 1926 and out of favour with Pilsudski and ruling groups in Poland. From Paris, organised a government-in-exile and a Polish army after Poland's defeat. As Prime Minister and Commander-in-Chief of the Free Polish Forces, he commanded about 100,000 men who had made their way to Britain. Following the German invasion of Russia, he concluded an agreement with the Soviet Union, repudiating the partition of Poland, re-establishing its frontiers, and permitting the recruitment of Polish prisoners in Russian hands, a force eventually transferred to the West via Iran and Italy. Relations with the Soviets, however, were shattered by the discovery in 1943 of the massacre of Polish officers by the Soviets at Katyn in 1939. Sikorsky was killed in an air accident in July 1943, removing a figure who might have been able to overcome Soviet and Western disagreement about the future of Poland.

Solzhenitsyn, Alexander (1918–): Leading Russian writer and dissident. Educated at Rostov University. Served and decorated in Second World War, but imprisoned in 1945 for criticism of the regime. Used his experiences as basis for his novels. Rehabilitated in 1957, his novel of the camps, *A Day in the Life of Ivan Denisovitch*, was published in the prestigious *Novy Mir* in 1962 with Khrushchev's permission as an anti-Stalinist work. After Khrushchev's fall, persecution resumed and he was deported to the West in 1974 following publication in the West of his history of the labour camps, *The Gulag Archipelago* (1971–73). Living first in Switzerland then the USA, he was a spokesperson for anti-communism and Russian nationalism and orthodoxy. His works were published under Gorbachev and he returned to Russia.

Sorel, Georges (1847–1922): French syndicalist philosopher. Studied Marxism after engineering career. Saw need for violent revolution under trade union control. Had little influence on French trade unions. Criticised both Socialist and Radical parties. Lent support to monarchist movement, 1909, and to Bolsheviks, 1917. Ideas on manipulating popular opinion impressed Hitler and Mussolini.

Speer, Albert (1905–81): German architect and Minister for Armaments and War Production in Nazi Germany. Trained as an architect. Joined the Nazi Party in 1931. Stage-managed mass rallies and designed buildings for the Party and drew up plans for the rebuilding of Berlin. On the death of Todt in Feb. 1942, appointed Minister of Armaments and Munitions, seeking full mobilisation of the economy. He achieved dramatic increases in production in 1943–44 and was a central figure in the Nazi regime's ability to sustain the war effort against superior odds. Opposed Hitler's 'scorched earth' policy in the final months. Sentenced to 20 years' imprisonment at Nuremberg. His memoirs, *Inside the Third Reich* (1970) were the first by a leading Nazi.

Stalin, Josef Visarionovitch (J. V. Djugashvili) (1879–1953): Soviet leader. Expelled from seminary for political activities, 1899. Exiled to Siberia twice. Attended conferences of Russian Social Democrats in Stockholm, 1906, and London, 1907. Expert on racial minorities in Bolshevik Central Committee,

1912. Became editor of *Pravda*, 1917. Worked with Lenin in Petrograd during Revolution, 1917. Member of Revolutionary Military Council, 1920–23. People's Commissar for Nationalities, 1921–23. General Secretary of Central Committee of Communist Party, 1922–53. During Civil War, supervised defence of Petrograd. Co-operated with Kamenev and Zinoviev to exclude Trotsky from office, 1923. (Secured Trotsky's exile, 1929.) Gained control of Party at Fifteenth Congress, 1927. Embarked on policy of 'Socialism in One Country' through Five Year Plans, 1928. Achieved rapid economic development. Eliminated political opponents in series of 'show trials', 1936–38. Chairman of Council of Ministers, 1941–53. During Second World War, as Commissar of Defence and Marshal of the Soviet Union, took over direction of war effort. Present at Tehran, Yalta and Potsdam conferences. Established firm control of Eastern European communist 'satellites', with exception of Yugoslavia, during postwar period. 'Personality cult' of Stalin officially condemned by Khrushchev at Party Congress, 1956.

Stambolisky, Alexander (1879–1923): Bulgarian politician. Involved in peasant agitation, 1897. As member of Agrarian Union, won fame as popular orator, 1908–15. Imprisoned for opposing entry into First World War. Instrumental in forcing King Ferdinand to abdicate, 1918. Proclaimed Republic, 1918. Prime Minister, 1919–23. Wielded almost dictatorial power. Concluded Treaty of Neuilly, 1919. Introduced land reforms and revised taxation in favour of peasants. Deposed and murdered in coup, 1923, having sought to help Yugoslav government crush Macedonian revolutionaries.

Stavisky, Serge (d. 1934): Central figure in 'Stavisky Case', 1934. Russian–Jewish financier, living in France. Sold valueless bonds. Took own life before charges could be made. Revelations of his involvement in other questionable activities and protection by public figures caused outcry. Murder of member of Public Prosecutor's staff attributed to attempted cover-up. Case had political repercussions, providing ammunition for extremes of right and left against corruption in Third Republic. Rioting and general strike, Feb. 1934, led to formation of broad coalition government.

Stolypin, Peter (1862–1911): Russian statesman. Governor of Saratov Province. Subdued agrarian disturbances, 1905. Became Minister of Interior, 1906. Prime Minister, 1906–11. Advocated moderate political reforms. Sought to create class of independent middle-sized farmers (*Kulaks*) as counterweight to liberals in Duma. Introduced property qualification for candidates for Duma. Took repressive line with rioters. Renewed anti-Semitic policies. Planned improvements in education, local government and system of social insurance. Assassinated, 1911.

Stresemann, Gustav (1878–1929): German statesman. Elected to Reichstag, 1907–12, 1914–29. Leader of National Liberals, 1917. Took nationalistic position during First World War, supporting High Command. Became more moderate after war. Founded People's Party (DVP), 1919. Advocated meeting Germany's commitments under Treaty of Versailles, thereby gaining confidence of Allies. Became Chancellor during crisis year, 1923. Foreign Minister, 1923–29. Restored Germany's diplomatic position. Concluded Locarno Pact, 1925. Achieved German entry into League of Nations, 1926. Secured reduction of reparations demands. Negotiated terms for Allied evacuation of Rhineland. Supported Dawes Plan, 1924, and Young Plan, 1929. Awarded Nobel Peace Prize, 1926.

Thatcher, Baroness, Margaret Hilda Thatcher (*née* Roberts) (1925–): Conservative MP for Finchley, 1959–92. Parliamentary Secretary to the Ministry of Pensions and National Insurance, 1961–64, and Secretary of State for Education and Science, 1970–74. In 1975 she was elected leader of the Conservative Party. Between 1975 and 1979 she led the Party away from the centrist policies of Heath and adopted a monetarist stance on economic problems and a tough line on law and order, defence and immigration. In May 1979 she became Britain's first woman Prime Minister, following her election victory. In spite of considerable unpopularity and very high unemployment, Mrs Thatcher's conduct of the Falklands War and Labour's disarray led to a landslide victory at the polls in 1983. Second term marked by growing emphasis on liberalising the economy, especially the privatisation of major public concerns. In 1987 she achieved a record third term of office with a majority of over 100. Third term marked by economic problems, differences over Europe and major personality clashes over her style of government. She resigned in Nov. 1990 after a leadership challenge undermined her position. Since losing office she has been a leading Eurosceptic. Created Baroness Thatcher of Kesteven, 1992.

Tirpitz, Alfred von (1849–1930): German Grand Admiral. Entered Prussian Navy, 1865. Won support of Kaiser after stressing importance of battle fleet, 1891. Minister of Marine, 1897–1916. Expanded High Seas Fleet. Proponent of unrestricted submarine warfare. Resigned when suggestions not acted upon.

Tisza, István (1861–1918): Son of Kálmán Tisza. Prime Minister, 1904–05, 1913–17. Took strong line in quelling political disputes. Linked Hungary's policy closely with that of Austria during crisis, 1914. Engineered succession of Charles after abdication of Francis Joseph. Murdered during violence in Hungary in last stage of war.

Tito, Josip Broz (1892–1980): Yugoslav statesman. Member of Yugoslav Communist Party since early 1920s, becoming its Secretary-General, 1937. Led Yugoslav partisan forces during Second World War. Became Marshal 1943. After war, secured independence from USSR, 1948. First President of Yugoslav Republic, 1953–80. Pursued independent foreign policy, encouraging co-operation among non-aligned nations.

Togliatti, Palmiro (1893–1964): Italian politician, one of the founders of the Italian Communist Party (PCI) in 1921. Forced into exile by Mussolini; based in Moscow from 1926 to 1944. Organised Communist agents in the Spanish Civil War. Returned to Italy and participated in government until 1947 when the Communists were expelled. Took a flexible view of communist theory and built the Italian Communist Party up to the largest in Western Europe, promoting ideas of Eurocommunism.

Trotsky, Lev Davidovich (L. D. Bronstein) (1879–1940): Russian revolutionary of Ukrainian–Jewish descent. Exiled to Siberia, 1898. Joined Lenin in London, 1902. Became an independent socialist, 1902. Hoped to achieve reconciliation between Bolsheviks and Mensheviks. Returned to Russia, 1905, and organised first soviet in St Petersburg. Exiled to Siberia again. Returned to St Petersburg from New York, May 1917. Chairman of Petrograd Soviet, Nov. 1917. First Commissar for Foreign Affairs. Delayed conclusion of Treaty of Brest-Litovsk, 1918. Commissar for War during Civil War, creating Red Army. After death of Lenin, and disagreements with Stalin, excluded from office. Theory of 'Permanent Revolution' condemned by Communist Party. Lost influence over Party policy, 1925. Expelled from Communist Party, 1927. Deported, 1929. Wrote *History of the Revolution* while in France. Murdered by Stalinist agent in Mexico, 1940.

Tudjman, Franco (1922–2002): Architect of independent Croatia. Fought with Tito's partisans and became a Yugoslav general. Left the army in 1961 and became a Professor at Zagreb University, taking up the cause of Croatian nationalism. Twice imprisoned as a nationalist dissident during the Tito era. He seized the opportunity on the break-up of the former Yugoslavia to declare independence in 1990. He led his Croatian Democratic Union (HDZ) to landslide victory in the first free elections, becoming President. After military reverses in 1991, he built up a strong army, intervening in Bosnia in 1995 and seizing Krajina. Signed the Dayton Accords, dividing Bosnia, and later securing eastern Slavonia as Croat territory. Although criticised for his corrupt and dictatorial control of Croatia, he was re-elected President in June 1997, though already terminally ill.

Venizelos, Eleutherios (1864–1936): Greek statesman. Involved in rising against the Ottoman Empire, 1896. President of Cretan Assembly. Declared union of Crete with Greece, 1905. Became Prime Minister of Greece, 1910. Introduced financial, military and constitutional reforms. Took Greece into Balkan War. Gained Macedonia from peace settlement. Attempted to enter First World War on Allied side, 1915. Removed from office by King Constantine. Formed rebel government in Crete, 1916, later moved to Salonika. Declared war on Germany and Bulgaria. Secured abdication of Constantine and became legitimate Prime Minister in Athens, 1917. Attended Paris Peace Conference. In seeking to gain Anatolia for Greece, provoked war with the Ottoman Empire which produced electoral defeat, 1920. Briefly in office, 1924. Prime Minister, 1928–32, again, 1933. Supporters staged uprising, 1935, leading to short civil war. Fled to France.

Walesa, Lech (1943–): Polish trade unionist. Former Gdansk shipyard worker. Emerged as leader of independent 'Solidarity' trade union. Solidarity comprised some 40 per cent of Polish workers by late 1980. Mounted outspoken opposition to economic and social policies of government. Detained following imposition of martial law, Dec. 1981. Released 11 months later. During his detention, Solidarity was banned. Continued to hold prominent position. Granted audience with Pope John Paul II, 1983. Awarded Nobel Peace Prize, 1983. Guided Solidarity throughout 1980s, but declined to hold office when, in Sept. 1989, Solidarity became part of Poland's first non-communist government for 40 years. However, in 1990 elected by direct vote as President of Poland. He was defeated in the 1995 presidential elections by a former communist.

Weizmann, Chaim (1874–1952): Zionist leader. Headed British Zionist movement before First World War. Advised Foreign Office during planning of Balfour Declaration, 1917. Head of World Zionist Movement after 1920. Became head of Jewish Agency for Palestine, 1929. Elected first President of Israel, 1948.

William II (1859–1941): German Emperor, King of Prussia, 1888–1918. Son of Emperor Frederick III. Dismissed Bismarck from chancellorship, 1890. Implemented 'New Course' in policy, aiming to assert German claims to world leadership. Increasingly under control of German High Command. Obliged by them to abdicate following Germany's military defeat, 1918. Went into exile in Holland.

Witte, Serge (1849–1915): Russian statesman. Minister of Communications during 1880s. Minister of Finance, 1892–1903, with supervisory role over commerce, industry and labour relations. Principal achievement was construction of Trans-Siberian Railway. Able to stimulate industry with loans from France. Dismissed as result of military opposition, 1903. Returned to office to negotiate peace following Russo–Japanese War. Became Prime Minister after 1905 Revolution. Substantial loans from Britain and France allowed him to by-pass Duma. Dismissed after six-month term of office. Strong critic of First World War.

Yeltsin, Boris Nikolayevich (1931–): Russian politician. Former Communist Party leader in Sverdlovsk, 1975. Promoted by Mikhail Gorbachev to be Party leader in Moscow, 1985. At that time, seen as Gorbachev's chief radical ally. In 1987, after increasingly bitter disagreements with Gorbachev, forced to resign. In 1989, elected for Moscow constituency with 90 per cent of the vote. In May 1990, elected President of the Russian Federation, the largest republic within the former Soviet Union. A popular politician with his calls for more radical reform, his defence of democracy during the Aug. 1991 coup attempt made him the undisputed leader of the Russian Federation. Created the Commonwealth of Independent States and this brought to an end the Soviet Union, Dec. 1991. Became President of Russia in direct elections that month. Although he successfully overcame the 1993 communist rising in Moscow, he faced grave economic problems, a resurgence of nationalism and the war in Chechnya. Re-elected 1996 despite serious health problems which necessitated heart surgery; his increasingly erratic policies witnessed the appointment of five premiers in 17 months. In Aug. 1999 he appointed Putin, who succeeded him when Yeltsin finally resigned at the end of that year.

Zhdanov, Andrei (1896–1948): Soviet politician. First Secretary to the Leningrad Party, 1934–44 and Secretary to the Central Committee. Best known for his ideological control over the arts, enforcing socialist realism, enunciated in 1934 at First Congress of the USSR Union of Writers. Later put in charge of incorporating Estonia into the Soviet Union and led the defence of Stalingrad in 1941–44. After the war resumed with greater intensity anti-Western cultural xenophobia, including anti-Semitism, in the phase known as the Zhdanovshchina. A founder of Cominform, he died suddenly in 1948.

Zhivkov, Todor (1911–98): Bulgarian communist. As president of Bulgaria from 1954 to 1989, was Eastern Europe's longest-serving political leader. Resigned office as the revolutions in Eastern Europe spread to the streets of Sofia, the capital. He was jailed for embezzlement in Sept. 1992. Released from house arrest in 1997.

Zhukov, Georgi (1896–1974): Soviet Marshal and the most prominent and successful Soviet general in the Second World War. Former Tsarist officer; fought for the Red Army in the Russian Civil War. Led the successful campaign against the Japanese in Manchuria in July–Aug. 1939. Appointed Chief of Staff of the Red Army in Jan. 1941. Defended Leningrad and then Moscow, involved thereafter in all of Russia's major military operations, including the battle of Stalingrad, the relief of Leningrad, the battle of Kursk, and the advance on and capture of Berlin. Demoted by Stalin in 1946, he went into semi-retirement, but was reinstated as First Deputy Minister of Defence on Stalin's death and Minister of Defence in 1955. Siding with Khrushchev, he became a member of the Praesidium in 1957, but was demoted, when seen as a potential rival. After Khrushchev's fall he was partially rehabilitated and awarded the Order of Lenin in 1966.

Zimmermann, Arthur (1864–1940): German Foreign Minister. Sent telegram to German diplomat in Mexico, 1917, proposing alliance between Germany and Mexico, on understanding that Mexico would invade USA if USA entered war against Germany. In return, Mexico would receive lost territory in Texas, Arizona and New Mexico. Telegram intercepted by Britain and contents revealed to Washington. Instrumental in winning approval of Congress for US entry into war, 1917.

Zinoviev, Gregori (1883–1936): Russian Bolshevik leader. Returned to Russia from exile with Lenin, Apr. 1917. Held prominent office in Third International, 1920–26. Alleged to have written to British communists calling on them to cultivate revolution ('Red Letter Scare', 1924). Disagreed with Stalin, 1926. Discredited as ally of Trotsky and deposed from Politburo. Tried and sentenced to imprisonment for treason, 1935. Executed after second trial, 1936.

GLOSSARY OF TERMS

Abwehr The espionage, counter-espionage, and sabotage service of the German High Command in the Second World War.

Action Directe French anarchist group formed in 1979 by libertarians, Maoists, Trotskyists and left-wing fascists, connected with international terrorist movements and responsible for a number of assassinations and bombings in the 1980s. The group claimed the murder of Georges Besse, Managing Director of Renault, in 1986.

Action Française French right-wing political movement founded by Charles Maurras in 1899 based on a royalist, nationalist and anti-Semitic programme. Although nominally supporting the Roman Catholic Church, the movement's other policies led to a papal ban in 1926. During the Second World War, the movement actively supported the Vichy regime, which resulted in its being banned after the war.

Agadir crisis Diplomatic and military crisis in 1911 caused by arrival of German warship *Panther* in Moroccan port of Agadir. Although supposedly sent to protect German residents, the main aim was to gain colonial concessions from the French elsewhere in Africa in exchange for recognition of the French interest in Morocco.

Agitprop Agitation Propaganda, a theatrical device employed by the left-wing in Europe and the USA during the 1950s; in the 1960s it developed into what is now termed 'street theatre'. Its purpose was to convey a political message, or political education, by seeking to interest and entertain. It was a feature of the former USSR.

Algérie Française The rallying cry (French Algeria) of the right in France and in Algeria who opposed independence for Algeria. It was the call to arms of the *Organisation de l'Armée Secrète* (OAS).

Anglo–French Entente *See* **Entente Cordiale**.

Anschluss The idea of union between Austria and Germany, current after the collapse of the Habsburg Monarchy in 1918 and given further impetus after Hitler became German Chancellor in 1933. The deliberate destabilisation of the Austrian government by the Nazis in 1938 led to the resignation of Chancellor Schuschnigg and his replacement by Arthur Seyss-Inquart, a Nazi nominee who invited the Germans to occupy Austria. The union of Austria with Germany was proclaimed on 13 Mar. 1938.

Anti-Clericalism Term applied to the opposition to organised religion, and largely directed against the power of the Roman Catholic Church. Anti-clericalism was prevalent during the revolutionary period in France and throughout the nineteenth century. Also apparent in Spain, especially during the Second Republic, 1931–39, in Germany as a result of the *Kulturkampf* and sporadically in Italy.

Anti-Comintern Pact The agreement between Germany and Japan signed on 25 Nov. 1936 which stated both countries' hostility to international communism.

The pact was also signed by Italy in 1937 and, in addition to being a commitment to oppose the Soviet Union, it recognised the Japanese regime which had ruled Manchuria since 1931.

Anti-Party Group   The term given in July 1957 to those who opposed Khrushchev's policies of de-Stalinisation, reconciliation with Tito's Yugoslavia and administrative reform. The major figures in the group, such as Bulganin and Molotov, were effectively removed from positions of influence.

Anti-Semitism   Term used to describe animosity towards the Jews, either on a religious or a racial basis. Originally coined by racial theorists of the late nineteenth century, anti-Semitism can take a number of different political, economic or racial forms. A number of political parties in Germany and Austria were based on anti-Semitism, and it also appears in France via *Action Française.* Economic and political anti-Semitism was a feature of Tsarist Russia with frequent pogroms against Jewish communities, a form of activity which seems to have recurred in the Soviet Union in 1958–59 and 1962–63. Anti-Semitism was one of the central planks of Nazi ideology and the major theme in Hitler's thinking, in which the Jews epitomised all that was wrong with German society. The idea of making Germany 'Jew-free' was given practical form in anti-Semitic legislation and the 'final solution' put into operation during the Second World War.

Apparatchik   Full-time paid official working in the Soviet Communist Party *apparat* (party machine), particularly in the Central Party Secretariat and its various sections.

Apparentement   An electoral alliance between two or more parties in France.

April Revolution   Bloodless military coup, led by junior officers who constituted the Armed Forces Movement, which took place in Portugal on 25 Apr. 1974, overthrowing the Caetano dictatorship, and opening the way to democracy and to independence for Portugal's African colonies. The coup was also known as the Carnation Revolution.

April Theses   Programme for power announced by the Bolshevik leader Lenin on his return to Petrograd in Apr. 1917. Lenin – in effect challenging the Provisional Government – called for an end to the war, the handing of political and economic power to the Soviets, abolition of the police, bureaucracy and armed forces, and the confiscation of private land. The Social Democratic Party was to be renamed the Communist Party and the Socialist International reconstructed as the Third International. Despite significant internal party opposition, and criticism from the Moscow and Petrograd Soviets, the theses became Bolshevik policy.

Armed Forces Movement   *See* **April Revolution**.

Armenian massacres   The systematic destruction of the monophysite Christian Armenian people in the Ottoman Empire by Muslim Turks in 1894–95. This action signalled the end of British support for the Empire and was followed by the extermination or deportation of the entire Armenian people by the Turkish government in 1914 and 1915.

Arrondissement In France, a subdivision of the larger political and administrative unit, the *département*. The *arrondissements* are electoral districts for elections to the National Assembly.

Arrow Cross Hungarian fascist movement led by Ferenc Szalasi who became Prime Minister following a German-supported coup in 1944. Arrow Cross participated in deportation of the Jews as part of Nazi Germany's anti-Semitic programme.

Article 82 An article of the Belgian constitution which allows for a temporary relinquishment of responsibility by the monarch as, for example, on 3 Apr. 1990 when King Badouin felt unable to sign an abortion law for religious reasons but did not wish to directly oppose the government.

Aryanisation Nazi racial policy based on Hitler's view that 'A State which in the epoch of race poisoning, dedicates itself to the cherishing of its best elements, must some day be master of the world.' The Nuremberg Laws for the 'Protection of German Blood and German Honour', 15 Sept. 1935, forbade marriage or sexual relations between Jews and non-Jews, punishable by imprisonment and later by death. Later regulations excluded Jews from the professions and the civil service.

Asylanten People seeking asylum in Germany who are not ethnic Germans. *See also* **Aussiedler**.

Atlantic Charter A statement of principles agreed by Churchill and Roosevelt on behalf of Britain and the USA in Aug. 1941, on the conduct of international policy in the postwar world. These included no territorial or other expansion; no wish for territorial changes other than those agreed by the peoples concerned; respect for the rights of all peoples to choose their form of government; desire for general economic development and collaboration; the need to disarm aggressor nations and the wish to construct a general system of international security. Although mainly a propaganda exercise, the USA refused to acknowledge any future international obligations in spite of British pressure. The charter was endorsed by the Soviet Union and 14 other states at war with the Axis Powers in Sept. 1941.

August coup Attempt on 19–21 Aug. 1991 by a section of the Communist Party of the Soviet Union to overthrow President Mikhail Gorbachev and prevent conclusion of a treaty giving sovereignty to the 15 Soviet republics. Gorbachev was placed under house arrest but, following resistance led by Boris Yeltsin and the reluctance of the KGB and the military to support them, the rebels fled.

Ausgleich (Ger. 'compromise') Agreement reached between the Austrian government and moderate Hungarian politicians in 1867 which transformed the Austrian Empire into the Dual Monarchy of Austria–Hungary. The system remained in operation until 1918, despite tensions resulting from commercial union and the resentment of other nationalities within the Empire at the privileged position of the Hungarians.

Aussiedler   Immigrants from Eastern Europe into Germany who are ethnic Germans. Prior to the 1990 reunification, the term was not used in West Germany to describe East Germans. *See also* **Asylanten**.

Austrian State Treaty   The treaty signed in Vienna on 15 May 1955 by which the USA, USSR, Britain and France ended their joint occupation of Austria and withdrew all troops by 25 Oct. 1955. Austria was restored to its frontiers of 1937, and union with Germany was prohibited. The willingness of the ascendant Khrushchev regime to signal an end to Stalinist foreign policy ensured the first unconditional and voluntary Soviet withdrawal from occupied territory since 1945.

Austro-fascism   The right-wing authoritarianism of Engelbert Dollfuss (1892–1934) in the interwar Austrian Republic. Appointed Chancellor as leader of the Christian Socialist Party in 1932, Dollfuss suspended parliamentary government in 1933, pushing working-class supporters of the Socialists to rise in defence of the constitution. Following the brutal crushing of the rising, parliament gave Dollfuss authority to remodel the state. But local Nazis attempted to overthrow him on 25 July 1934, expecting support from Germany. Support was not forthcoming but Dollfuss was murdered. Germany occupied Austria with no resistance in Mar. 1938.

Austro-Marxism   Revisionist Marxist trend which emerged in Austria in 1907. Its main figures were Max Adler, Otto Bauer and Rudolf Hilferding. Adler emphasised Marxism's scientific rather than ethical basis, Bauer wrote on the national question and imperialism, and Hilferding provided an economic analysis of imperialism which strongly influenced Lenin.

Autarky (deriv. Gk. *autarkeia*, self-sufficient).   In economic terms, a policy aimed at total home-production to the exclusion of imported goods. Pre-Second World War Germany's search for a blockade-proof economy provides a good example of economic autarky. Mussolini made efforts to achieve this in Italy after 1934–35.

Axis   A term first used by Mussolini on 1 Nov. 1936 to describe fascist Italy's relationship with Nazi Germany established by the Oct. protocols of 1936. He referred to the Rome–Berlin Axis, a term which was reinforced by a formal treaty in May 1939, the Pact of Steel. In Sept. 1940, Germany, Italy and Japan signed a tripartite agreement which led to the term 'Axis Powers' being used to describe all three, as well as their Eastern European allies.

Baader–Meinhof Group   Urban guerrillas in West Germany who emerged from the radical student movement of 1968. Led by Andreas Baader and Ulrike Meinhof, they were responsible for six killings, 50 attempted killings, bombings of American military installations, etc. Their aim was to expose the reactionary forces in West Germany and to oppose the US military presence in Europe. Their leaders were eventually captured and imprisoned in high-security jails where they soon died in suspicious circumstances. The West German authorities maintained they committed suicide.

Bad Godesberg Declaration   Statement adopted by the West German Social Democratic Party (SPD) at a congress held in Bad Godesberg in 1959. The SPD abandoned its historic (though largely notional) Marxism, described itself as a democratic socialist party, and accepted the market economy. The declaration opened the way for the SPD's electoral success.

Balance of power   A theory of international relations which aimed to secure peace by preventing any one state or group of states from attaining political or military strength sufficient to threaten the independence and liberty of others. The policy was based on the maintenance of a counterforce equal to that of the potential adversaries, and was the central theme of British policy in Europe against the French, and from 1904 to 1914, the Germans. This was epitomised by the creation of the *Entente Cordiale* with France to counter the threat from Germany, and later the Triple Entente of Britain, France and Russia to balance the Triple Alliance of Germany, Austria–Hungary and Italy. In the interwar period, Britain again attempted to create a balance against French power by encouraging the rapid recovery of Germany. The policy was abandoned in the 1930s as Germany and Japan began to pursue more aggressive foreign policies which could not be countered by the League of Nations' security system, nor by further alliances.

Baltic States   Term used for Estonia, Latvia and Lithuania, part of the Soviet Union from 1940 to 1991. The Soviet Union had seized them in 1940 as part of the 1939 Nazi-Soviet Pact. Growing agitation for independence in the late 1980s came to a head with the abortive 19 Aug. 1991 coup in Moscow. Declarations of independence resulted in international diplomatic recognition, membership of the United Nations and phased withdrawal of Russian troops.

Barre Plan   Austerity programme introduced in Sept. 1976 by French Prime Minister Raymond Barre to combat inflation. A further stage was introduced in Apr. 1977. Ultimately unsuccessful, Barre's programme aroused the opposition of the trade unions, which responded with a general strike.

Basic Law   (1) In Germany, *see* **Grundgesetz**.

(2) In Russia, the new constitution approved by the referendum of 12 Dec. 1993 which replaced the 1978 constitution passed under Brezhnev. The new constitution greatly strengthened the powers of the President, who is elected for four years and can serve no more than two terms. The new powers as Head of State include the right to pass decrees without reference to parliament (although they can be vetoed by a two-thirds majority); the right to declare a state of emergency (with parliamentary consent); the appointment of the Prime Minister, the approval of ministerial appointments, etc. Under the 1993 Basic Law, Parliament consists of two chambers. The lower house, the State Duma,

has 450 deputies, half elected by 'first past the post' and the remainder by proportional representation from party lists. The upper house, the Federation Council, has 178 representatives, two from each member state of the Federation. The constitution's provisions marked a decisive break with the communist past.

Battle of Britain   Period of aerial warfare over Britain between 10 July and 31 Oct. 1940. The German air force, numbering 1,400 bombers and 1,020 fighters at the outset, sought to achieve decisive air superiority over southern England as a prerequisite to the success of Operation Sealion, the planned cross-channel invasion of England. England's air defences consisted largely of 700 Hurricane and Spitfire fighters, although fighter production was running at 100 a month by the peak of the battle, to replenish losses. German air attacks began with attempts to disrupt shipping, then transferred first to fighter air bases and then to towns and cities. After suffering heavy losses in Aug. (on 15 Aug., 75 German planes were lost to only 34 British), Germany seemed to have regained the tactical initiative in the first week of Sept. But in two separate engagements on 15 Sept. 1940 they lost 56 planes, and on 17 Sept. Operation Sealion was indefinitely postponed.

Beer Hall Putsch   Hitler's attempt to seize Bavaria on 9–10 Nov. 1923 as a preliminary to overthrowing the Weimar Republic. The coup, the headquarters of which were in a beer cellar, collapsed when police fired on 2,000 Nazis, killing 14. Hitler was sentenced to five years in prison.

Belgrade Declaration   Joint Yugoslav–Soviet statement issued in June 1955 which attempted to heal the breach between the two countries since Yugoslavia's 1948 break with the Soviet Union. Soviet leader Khrushchev acknowledged Yugoslavia's integrity and apologised for the policy of his predecessor Stalin. The Declaration was reiterated in 1971 and 1972.

Benelux (acronym)   Agreement on economic collaboration between Belgium, the Netherlands and Luxembourg, which grew out of a convention in London in Sept. 1944 and was manifested in a customs union established on 1 Jan. 1948. In 1954 the three countries agreed that between 1 Mar. 1954 and 1 Mar. 1956 a common policy on trade and payments to non-Benelux countries would be established. A treaty establishing an economic union was concluded at The Hague on 3 Feb. 1958 and came into force on 1 Nov. 1960. This provided for free movement of capital, goods, traffic, services and population between the three member countries, a common trade policy and co-ordination of investment, agricultural and social policies. The union has decreased in importance with the development of policies common to the whole European Union.

Berlin Wall   The East Berlin riots of 1953 and the continuing disparity in living standards encouraged a stream of refugees from East to West Berlin. The communist authorities responded on 13 Aug. 1961 by blocking 68 of 80 border crossing points and constructing a wire and concrete barrier that was to become a permanent feature of the city. All this changed with the revolutions in Eastern Europe in 1989. Dismantling of the wall began, and in Oct. 1990 Berlin became capital of a reunited Germany.

'Big Four'   Representatives of the major victorious powers of the First World War at the Paris Peace Conference of 1919. They were the British Prime Minister Lloyd George (1863–1945); the US President Woodrow Wilson (1856–1924); the French Prime Minister George Clemenceau (1841–1929) and the Italian Prime Minister Vittorio Orlando (1860–1952). Orlando is occasionally omitted from the group which is then known as the 'Big Three'.

Bizonia   Economic union of British and American zones of Germany, 25 June 1947, following disagreement between the four occupying powers. The economic council of Bizonia in Frankfurt am Main had a quasi-governmental role, but remained under the ultimate authority of the occupying powers. France joined Bizonia in July 1948.

Black Berets   Soviet Interior Ministry troops. Used as 'special forces' to suppress nationalism in Lithuania and Latvia in early 1991. The 62,000 OMON, or Black Berets, formed the central corps of troops of the Interior Ministry. Recruited from the Slav population, they were among the fittest, most politically reliable and best-trained troops in the Soviet Union. The failed coup of Aug. 1991 left them discredited.

Black Cloak   The anti-communist guerrillas in Romania after the Second World War.

Black Hand   Popular name of the Serbian secret society (*Ujedinjenje ili Smrt*) formed in Belgrade in May 1911. Led by Col Dragutin Dimitrievič and consisting mainly of army officers, the society's main aim was the unifying of Serb minorities in Austria–Hungary and the Ottoman Empire with the independent state of Serbia. They were responsible for the training of Gavrilo Princip, who assassinated the Austrian Archduke Francis Ferdinand in Sarajevo on 28 June 1914. The society was in conflict with the Serbian government throughout the First World War, culminating in the arrest and execution of Dimitrievič with two others, and the banning of the organisation. These sentences were later quashed by the supreme court of Serbia in 1953 when the country had been incorporated into Yugoslavia.

Black Hundreds   Right-wing extremist groups in Russia which staged pogroms against Jews and attacks on students, intellectuals and revolutionaries. The Black Hundreds, which were anti-Semitic and supporters of Tsarist absolutism, were particularly active from 1906 to 1911.

Blank cheque   The verbal reply given on 5 July 1914 in response to a letter from Emperor Francis Joseph of Austria by Kaiser Wilhelm II to Count Hoyos, an Austrian Foreign Ministry official, guaranteeing German support if Austria attacked Serbia as punishment for the assassination of Archduke Francis Ferdinand in Sarajevo on 28 June 1914.

Blitzkrieg (Ger. 'lightning war') A theory of warfare which involved a rapid attack on a very narrow front to create penetration in depth. The technique involved aerial bombing to reduce enemy resistance and then the deployment of highly mobile armoured columns. Used extensively by the German army in the Second World War and especially by General Guderian in the campaign against France in 1940. Also abbreviated to 'Blitz' in English to describe the heavy bombing and night attacks on British cities by the German air force during the Second World War.

Bloody Sunday A term used to describe a number of events, as follows:

1. In Russia, Sunday 22 Jan. 1905. A procession of workers and their families led by Fr George Gapon was fired on by troops guarding the Winter Palace in St Petersburg. The procession had intended to present a petition to the Tsar calling for an eight-hour day, a constituent assembly and an amnesty for political prisoners. Over one hundred people were killed and several hundred wounded, an event which helped to spark off the 1905 Russian Revolution.
2. In Britain, Sunday 30 Jan. 1972. Thirteen civilians were killed in Londonderry after a demonstration in favour of a united Ireland was broken up by British paratroopers.

Blue Division Volunteers from Spain who fought alongside regular German troops against the Soviet Union on the Eastern Front from Apr. 1942. The Spanish dictator Francisco Bahamonde Franco (1892–1975) was, however, dissuaded by Hitler from joining the war officially on Germany's side.

Blueshirts An interwar Irish fascist movement – originally the Army Comrades Association – which adopted the blue shirt as a uniform in Apr. 1933. Former national police commander General Eoin O'Duffy became leader in July and renamed the organisation the National Guard. The movement was outlawed in Sept. 1933 and merged with the National Centre Party to form the United Ireland Party (Fine Gael) with O'Duffy as President. Disappointed with the movement's progress, the Fine Gael political elements withdrew within a year and O'Duffy established an organisation of Greenshirts. The Blueshirts briefly revived in 1936–37 when O'Duffy led a contingent to support Franco in the Spanish Civil War.

Bokassa Affair Political scandal in France. Amid embarrassing charges made in 1979 that French President Giscard d'Estaing had received gifts of diamonds and a hunting lodge from the self-proclaimed Emperor Bokassa, a corrupt, ostentatious and allegedly cannibalistic dictator of the Central African Republic, a former French colony, French troops were dispatched to hasten the Emperor's removal on 21 Sept. 1979.

Bolshevik (Russ. lit. 'member of the majority') A term applied to the radical faction of the Russian Social Democratic Party which split in 1903. Lenin led the Bolsheviks in opposition to the more moderate Mensheviks. The Bolsheviks came to power in Russia after the Oct. Revolution of 1917, and the name was retained by the Soviet Communist Party until 1952.

Brandt Report   The influential report of Feb. 1980, entitled *North–South: A Programme for Survival*, generated by the Brandt Commission, headed by the former West German Chancellor, which advocated a restructuring of the world economy, financial institutions, and development plans to stimulate growth, trade and confidence to avert divisions between North and South threatening eventual crisis.

Brezhnev Doctrine   The ideological basis of the Warsaw Pact invasion of Czechoslovakia in Aug. 1968. Leonid Brezhnev, General Secretary of the Soviet Communist Party, pronounced a doctrine of 'limited sovereignty', denying East European states the right to diverge widely from the Soviet model, and asserting the legitimacy of intervention. Soviet Party Secretary Mikhail Gorbachev rejected this view in Mar. 1988 and the fall of the Soviet Union made the doctrine outmoded. *See* 'Prague Spring'.

Bund   Russian and Polish Jewish Social Democratic Party founded in Vilna in 1897, advocating a federal Russian empire and an end to anti-Semitic discrimination. The Bund came into conflict with Lenin over its concentration on Jewish interests and withdrew from the Russian Social Democratic Party in 1903. Bundists supported the Mensheviks after 1906 and backed the Provisional Government following the 1917 Feb. Revolution.

Bundesbank   The German central bank, established in 1957 and based in Frankfurt, the country's financial centre. The bank – whose President and board of directors are federal appointees – had a high degree of independence from the government in its role of combating inflation and maintaining the stability of the country's currency.

Bundesrat   Federal council of Germany, consisting of members of the government of the various states or *Länder* and elected by the 10 *Länder* of West Germany (Baden-Württemberg, Bavaria, Bremen, Hamburg, Hessen, Saxony, North Rhine-Westphalia, Rhineland-Palatinate, Saarland and Schleswig-Holstein) and the 6 new *Länder* of the old East Germany.

Bundestag   Federal parliament or Diet of Germany, established by the 'Basic Law' (the constitution) on 23 May 1949. Elected by universal suffrage for a four-year term of office, it passes federal laws and submits them to the Bundesrat.

Bundeswehr   Federal armed forces, the army of Germany. In the immediate postwar period the question of whether Germany should be allowed an army was highly controversial but the threat of the USSR and the obvious acceptance of democracy by Germany finally allayed fears of German militarism.

Butter Mountain   Late 1970s phenomenon in Europe resulting from the Common Agricultural Policy which, by subsidising agricultural producers to protect their interests, encouraged surpluses of butter and grain 'mountains' and wine 'lakes'. Attempts were made in 1983 and 1988 to cut back on subsidies and to reduce production.

Cadres Members of the Communist Party charged with the political education and organisation of the proletariat.

CAP Common Agricultural Policy of the EU with dictates the farming and other primary production policies of the Community and allocates subsidies to the various sectors of European agriculture.

Carnation Revolution *See* **April Revolution.**

Caudillo, El (Sp. lit. 'the leader') Title assumed by Francisco Franco in 1937 as head of the insurgent nationalist forces in the Spanish Civil War, and of the so-called Burgos government. His authority was reinforced in July 1947 with the declaration that he should remain 'Caudillo' or Head of State for life, pending the restoration of the monarchy. He nominated as his successor, Prince Juan Carlos, who became king in 1975.

CEI Central European Initiative, established in Jan. 1992 to encourage cultural and economic co-operation between Eastern and Western Europe. The member states – Austria, Bosnia–Herzegovina, Croatia, Hungary, Slovenia and the former Czechoslovakia – hoped also to balance German dominance in the region.

Central Powers Initially members of the Triple Alliance created by Bismarck in 1882, namely Germany, Austria–Hungary and Italy. As Italy remained neutral at the outbreak of the First World War, the term was applied to Germany, Austria–Hungary, their ally the Ottoman Empire and later also Bulgaria.

CERES Marxist-orientated research body which was one of the main groupings involved in the reformation of the French Socialist Party in 1971. With policies similar to those of the Communist Party, CERES initially had a strong voice in the Party but by the 1980s had lost influence to a new wave of modernisers.

Cetnik *See* **Chetniks**.

CGT (*Confédération Générale du Travail*) The largest French trade union federation, formed in 1906 on a non-political syndicalist platform. A communist minority broke away in 1921, the two sections reuniting in 1935, since when the CGT has been communist-led.

Chancellor Democracy Expression used in West Germany in the 1950s to describe concern at the weakening effect on parliamentary democracy of the autocratic stance taken by Chancellor Konrad Adenauer (1876–1967, Chancellor, 1949–63).

Charter 77 Declaration signed by Czech human rights activists supporting the rights to individual liberties guaranteed by the Soviet Union at the 1975 Helsinki Agreement. 1977 was a Human Rights Year, but the group became subject to persecution and imprisonment by the Czech authorities in spite of protests by the West. One of the original signatories was Vaclav Havel, subsequently President of post-communist Czechoslovakia.

Cheka (Russ.) Extraordinary commission, or secret political police force established by the Bolsheviks in post-revolutionary Russia to defend the regime against internal enemies.

Chernobyl A major accident at a Soviet nuclear reactor complex at Chernobyl in the Ukraine on 26 Apr. 1986. Following a safety experiment which went wrong, a fire and explosion in the Number 4 reactor spread nuclear contamination over a wide area of Russia and northern Europe. Although the immediate death toll was low, the permanent evacuation of the neighbouring town of Pripyat was necessary. The largest nuclear accident in Europe since that at Windscale (Sellafield) in Britain in 1957, the Chernobyl incident did much to highlight concern about the environment and promote Green parties in Europe.

Chetniks Originally Serbian guerrillas seeking liberation from the Ottoman Empire. Active against German supply lines in occupied Balkan states during the First World War. They also opposed German occupation in the Second World War and were aided by the British until 1944. Some commanders collaborated with the Germans and Italians against Tito's partisans. The term was in use again after 1991 to refer to Serbian irregulars fighting the Croats.

Chovevei Zion (Isr. 'Lovers of Zion') Late nineteenth-century movement originating in Russia to encourage Jewish settlement in Palestine, which pre-dated and later joined forces with the Zionist Organisation.

Christian Democracy Anti-communist, moderate political movement formed in many European countries with the development of a mass electorate in the late nineteenth and twentieth centuries. Among the largest was the old Italian Christian Democrat Party founded in 1943 as the successor to the pre-fascist Popular Party, formed in 1919, and until the early 1990s the major representative of Catholic, moderate opinion. The German National People's Party, formed in 1918, and the German Centre Party, formed in 1870, also represent this tradition, latterly taken up by Adenauer's Christian Democratic Union, formed in 1945. Many other European countries have political parties with this or similar labels.

Christian Socialism Name given to the beliefs of many political parties in Europe, founded in response to the challenge of socialism. The first was formed in Austria in the late nineteenth century. Two papal encyclicals (*Rerum novarum* and *Quadragesimo Anno*), anti-socialist but in favour of a Christian corporate state with protection for labour, encouraged their efforts. Today the Christian Socialist parties are essentially conservative but may have quite advanced programmes of social reform. After the Second World War the Austrian Christian Socialist Party was renamed the People's Party.

Christian Social Union The Conservative Party in Bavaria, the traditional ally of the Christian Democrats. Its long-time leader was Franz-Josef Strauss.

Christmas Revolution Term applied to the popular uprising in Romania in Dec. 1989 against the Ceausescu dictatorship. Sometimes called the 'Winter Revolution'.

283

Christmas Truce   The spontaneous ceasefire between British and German troops on the Western Front on Christmas Day 1914. After an exchange of gifts and games of football, the soldiers held their fire for the remainder of the day. The higher command on both sides ensured there was no repetition in following years but in some parts of the line soldiers attempted to keep hostilities at a low level through an unofficial 'live and let live' policy.

CIS   *See* **Commonwealth of Independent States**.

Civic Forum   A Czech party formed in Nov. 1989 by a coalition of human rights and opposition organisations, Civic Forum advocated a return to parliamentary democracy. In the June 1990 elections it won – on a joint ticket with Public Against Violence – 46.3 per cent of the vote and 170 of the 300 legislature seats. In Feb. 1991, the Party split into a moderate and a radical wing. Civic Forum traded heavily upon the prestige of Vaclav Havel and the support of the former communist leader Dubček to become the majority party and form a government.

CNT   (Sp. *Confederación Nacional del Trabajo*)   National Confederation of Labour. Anarcho-syndicalist union federation formed in Oct. 1910, strongest in industrial Catalonia and rural Andalusia, with two million members by the mid-1930s. The CNT resisted Franco's rising in 1936, encouraging industrial and agricultural collectivisation. Weakened by growing communist influence in the Republic and driven underground by nationalist victory in 1939, it re-emerged in the 1980s.

Cod War   Dispute between Britain and Iceland from Sept. 1972 to June 1976 over Iceland's unilateral extension of territorial waters, thereby excluding other fishing fleets, from 12 to 50 miles. Icelandic gunboats attempted to intercept British trawlers and Royal Navy frigates intervened. A compromise agreement allowed a maximum of 24 British trawlers into the area.

Cohabitation   Term used to describe the political situation in France following the 1986 parliamentary election. With two years remaining before the end of President François Mitterrand's term of office, the right won a majority of seats in parliament. The subsequent conservative government and socialist President went on to tolerate and work alongside each other. The term was revived following the left-wing victory in 1997 under Lionel Jospin (with Chirac a right-wing President).

Cold War   *See* p. 177.

Collaboration   The relationship between sections of the population and Second World War German occupation forces in Europe. Collaboration ranged from active political, administrative and economic support for puppet governments, through unavoidable co-operation, to reluctant acquiescence. *See* **Quisling**.

Collective security   Term widely used in international diplomacy between the two world wars, first coined at the 1924 Geneva Conference, denoting a policy whereby the security of individual countries was guaranteed jointly by others. It was the basic principle of the League of Nations and required acceptance by individual members of collective decisions backed up, if necessary, by military action. The term was also applied to attempts to establish a system of multilateral alliances for defence against Nazi Germany in the 1930s. Under the Charter of the UN, power to meet threats to peace is vested in the Security Council of the USA, Russia, Britain, France and China. As the Council cannot act if any member dissents, the principle of collective security is not present in its full form.

Collectivisation The process of transferring land from private to state or collective ownership. Extensively operated in the Soviet Union during the early 1930s when peasants' individual holdings were combined to form agricultural collectives (*Kolkhoz*) or in some cases state-owned farms (*Sovkhoz*) which were run by state employees. Collectivisation altered the whole structure of Soviet agriculture and was to have profound effects. In spite of massive investment under both Khrushchev and Brezhnev, the collectives remained inefficient by Western European or American standards. Gorbachev's more recent campaign to revitalise the Soviet economy failed to find a decisive solution to the legacy bequeathed by Stalin.

Colombey-les-Deux-Églises The village in north-eastern France to which General de Gaulle retired in 1946 following his failure to form a government of national unity. On his subsequent retirement as President of the Fifth Republic in 1969 he lived there until his death in 1970.

Colonels, Greek *See* **Greek Colonels**.

Colons French colonial settlers, particularly used to refer to those in Algeria.

Comecon Council for Mutual Economic Assistance. Organisation established in Moscow in Jan. 1949 to improve trade between the Soviet Union and other East European states. Regarded by Stalin as an instrument to enforce an economic boycott on Yugoslavia, and also used as a Soviet response to growing West European economic interdependence. With the revolutions in Eastern Europe in 1989, Comecon effectively ceased to exist as the former communist states made moves towards creating market economies. In 1991 it was formally dissolved.

Cominform Communist Information Bureau proclaimed in Feb. 1947 to organise Communist activity in Europe, dissolved by Khrushchev in Apr. 1956 as a conciliatory gesture to the West. The nine original members were communist parties of the Soviet Union, Bulgaria, Czechoslovakia, France, Hungary, Italy, Poland, Romania and Yugoslavia (although Yugoslavia was expelled in June 1948).

Comintern   The Communist International, established by Lenin in Mar. 1919 with the aim of promoting revolutionary Marxism. Its stated aim was world revolution but it was always a tool by which the USSR maintained control of the international communist movement. It was formed by the socialist parties which had opposed the war efforts of their national governments between 1914 and 1918, accepting instead Lenin's call for a class war. At the 1920 Congress nationalism was repudiated and adherence to the class war sworn. A structure similar to that of the Soviet Communist Party was adopted, with a small praesidium having the real power. By 1928 it had become a vehicle for Stalinist theory. It was dissolved by Stalin in May 1943 as a good-will gesture towards Russia's Western allies.

Comisco   Committee of the International Socialist Conference which met between 1947 and 1951 and called for socialist unity. In 1948 it declared that socialism was incompatible with suppression of democratic rights and approved the concept of a united Europe. It denounced the socialist parties of Hungary, Bulgaria, Czechoslovakia and Romania for uniting with communists, expelled the pro-communist wing of the Italian Socialists led by Nenni, and admitted exiled social democrats from Eastern Europe, the German Social Democrats and Italians under Saragat and Lombardo. The heir to the 'Second International', it was superseded in 1951 by the 'Socialist International'.

Command economy   A centralised national economy which operates under state control rather than functioning through market forces. Prime examples of command economies were the former Soviet Union and its East European satellites before the collapse of communism in the late 1980s and, to a lesser extent, the Western powers during the Second World War. China, while remaining under Communist Party control, has gradually introduced market mechanisms into its economy.

Commissar   Head of a government department in the former USSR. Political commissars were also attached to the Red Army where they held responsibility for the political education of the armed forces.

Common Agricultural Policy   *See* **CAP**.

Common Market   Popular name for the European Economic Community (*see* pp. 203–5).

Commonwealth of Independent States (CIS)   A voluntary association of 11 (formerly 12) states formed when the Soviet Union disintegrated. Its history to date suggests it is little more than a forum to keep alive some vague form of co-operation after the demise of the old USSR. Early 'agreements' were made at Minsk (14 Feb. 1992, on strategic forces), Kiev (20 Mar. 1992, on state frontiers) and Tashkent (15 May 1992, on collective security). By 1993 the Asian states were drifting away from the CIS.

Concentration camp   Name originally applied to the camps organised by the British under General Kitchener in the Transvaal and Orange River Colonies during the South African War of 1899. In Nazi Germany, after Hitler came to power, camps were established at Dachau and Oranienburg in 1933 for the detention of political and 'racial' enemies. By 1939, six such camps existed in Greater Germany, holding 20,000 prisoners. As part of Hitler's 'Final Solution', these 'preventative detention camps' were increased in number and converted into extermination camps for Jews. Bogus and sadistic medical experiments were often conducted in them and some provided slave labour. Among the most notorious were Belsen, Buchenwald and Ravensbruck in Germany; Auschwitz and Treblinka in Poland. The total number killed in them, both Jews and non-Jews, is believed to be more than five million.

Conducator (Rom. 'leader')   The title used by the Romanian dictator, Nicolae Ceausescu.

Conference on Security and Co-operation in Europe (CSCE)   Major agreement of 19 Nov. 1990, signed in Paris, which marked the formal end of the Cold War. Part of this agreement was the signing of the Conventional Forces in Europe (CFE) Treaty by 22 NATO and Warsaw Pact countries, formalising the biggest cuts in weapons and manpower since the end of the Second World War. Its membership (55 by the end of 2002) acts to provide a forum for co-operation between NATO and the former Warsaw Pact countries. It was originally formed in Helsinki in 1975.

Corfu Declaration   The declaration agreed by Serbia, Croatia, Slovenia and Montenegro on 27 July 1917 to establish a unified state of Yugoslavia following the military defeat of the Austo–Hungarian Empire after the First World War.

Corfu Incident   The shooting of an Italian general and four members of his staff on Greek soil while mapping the Greek–Albanian frontier on 27 Aug. 1923 prompted Mussolini to lodge a claim to compensation and bombard and occupy the Greek island of Corfu four days later. The Greeks appealed to the League of Nations for assistance in what was a flagrant breach of the Covenant of the League. Under pressure from Britain and France, Mussolini withdrew his force from Corfu on 27 Sept. The dispute was referred by the League to the Council of Ambassadors, who persuaded the Greeks to apologise and pay compensation. The incident provides an early example of Mussolini's bullying tactics in foreign policy.

Corporate state   State whose economic and political life is based on trade and professional corporations rather than territorial units. Thus members of parliament would be elected by vocational corporations instead of by geographical constituencies and would regulate industrial production and working conditions. The societies which have come closest to being corporate states were Italy under fascism and Portugal under the dictator Salazar (1928–74). The Catholic Church has tended to favour the idea and Nazi Germany toyed with plans for it.

Cortes Spanish parliament. Suppressed in 1923 by the dictatorship of Primo de Rivera, it was restructured by the Second Republic as a democratically elected institution, only to be swept away by the Civil War (1936–39). Restored again in 1942 as a cypher for Franco's dictatorship, the institution was again restructured in 1978 when the monarchy was restored and free elections took place to the Cortes. This body has two houses, a congress of deputies with 350 members elected every four years by universal suffrage, and an upper house (Senate) with four representatives from each of Spain's provinces and autonomous communities.

Council Communism Influenced by workers' councils activity in the 1917–20 European revolutionary upheavals, Council Communism rejected Bolshevik party-led socialism. Marxist, but with strong anarchist undertones, it advocated economic and social organisation based on a network of factory councils. Its leading theorist was a Dutch astronomer, Anton Pannekoek (1873–1960).

Croatian spring Attempt to introduce communist and moderate nationalist reform in the Yugoslav republic of Croatia in 1969–71, brought to a halt largely through the alienation of Serbs living in the region. A new constitution introduced as a result by Yugoslav President Tito in 1974 attempted to satisfy demands for greater autonomy in the federal republics.

Cult of personality Political phenomenon whereby a leader, usually the Head of State, is elevated above his colleagues to a position where he is seen as responsible for all the nation's or party's achievements but for none of its failures. Such elevation is achieved by a massive propaganda exercise, including posters and statues of the leader, the naming of towns after him, etc. Joseph Stalin (1879–1953) set the pattern as Soviet leader but others have followed, for example Hitler in Germany, Mao Tse-tung in China and Kim Il-sung in North Korea. Such cults appear to flourish only in totalitarian regimes.

DAF *See* **Deutsche Arbeitsfront**.

Decommunisation The process of dismantling the economic, political and social structures of the former communist states by introducing parliamentary democracy and privatisation of state enterprises as a preliminary to building capitalism. In some cases – notably Albania and Bulgaria – this has also involved the imprisonment of high-ranking leaders.

Delors Plan Plan drawn up by the Delors Committee headed by the President of the Commission of the European Economic Community, Jacques Delors, set up in 1988. The plan involved a series of measures to create greater monetary and political unity in the EEC. The first phase created the European Monetary System (EMS). Phase two would set up a European system of central banks to gradually assume greater control over national monetary policy. Much of the plan was opposed by former British Prime Minister Margaret Thatcher.

Democratic centralism The principle of authority of the Soviet and other communist parties, formulated by Lenin. Democratic centralism was fundamentally dictatorial and involved obedience by each section of the Party to decisions reached by superior organs.

Denazification Process undertaken by the Allies after the Second World War of locating Nazis and removing them from private and public positions. Both Party members and those who merely prospered under them were sought, to be punished or requalified for professional work. Special courts, *Spruchkammern*, were established which were empowered to confiscate property, disqualify people from practising professions and impose sentences of up to 10 years' hard labour. The system failed: minor officials were victimised while many leading Nazis escaped.

Destalinisation The overthrowing of the 'cult of personality' that had surrounded Soviet dictator Stalin. Stalin died in 1953, and the process began in 1956 at the Twentieth Party Congress in Russia. The attack on Stalin and his purges was led by Khrushchev. The process included renaming Stalingrad (which became Volgograd). Under Gorbachev's *Glasnost*, there were further revelations of the evils of the Stalin era. Stalin's body was removed from Lenin's mausoleum, statues were taken down and place names changed. Even in Albania, the last outpost of Stalinism, the process was complete by 1991.

Détente Term applied to the improved relations, beginning in Nov. 1969, between the Warsaw Pact countries (led by the USSR) and the West (headed by the USA), which were inaugurated by the Strategic Arms Limitation Talks (SALT). These ended in agreement on arms reductions in May 1973. Further SALT talks began in Nov. 1974 and an agreement was reached in May 1978, but the continued build-up of Soviet arms and the Soviet invasion of Afghanistan in Dec. 1979 called into question the validity of détente. As a result SALT II remained unratified and the détente period was perceived as ended, followed by a period of renewed Cold War under President Reagan and Premier Brezhnev.

Deutsche Arbeitsfront (Ger. 'German labour front') Nazi organisation founded in Nov. 1933 following the dissolution of the trade unions, professing to represent the interests of every German and to unite employers and workers. Wage rises were to be paid only for increased production and 'class warfare' was to be ended. The organisation used the contributions of members (30 million by 1939) and confiscated trade union funds to finance members' holidays and to develop its own industrial and commercial enterprises such as the Volkswagen motor company. *See also* **Kraft durch Freude**.

Deutschmark Originally the currency unit of West Germany and since 1991 of the united Germany. The growing strength of the Deutschmark since its creation in 1948 symbolised the success of the German postwar 'economic miracle' and the currency became the monetary anchor of the European Exchange Rate in 1972.

Dictatorship of the proletariat Marxist description of working-class rule between the collapse of capitalism in revolution and the birth of a classless, communist society. Developed by Lenin after the 1917 Bolshevik seizure of power, dictatorship was exercised by a centralised party. The concept was abandoned by West European communist parties in the 1970s and was replaced in the 1977 Soviet Constitution by the 'state of the whole people'.

Diktat Diplomatic or military settlement forcibly imposed on a defeated enemy, often applied to the 1919 Treaty of Versailles.

Dirigisme Post-Second World War French policy of state intervention in the free enterprise economy without centralised socialist planning.

Displaced persons People estranged from their homelands before and during the Second World War, including those forcibly taken from their own countries to work in another, particularly Germany; those who had fled before invading armies during the war; and those obliged to leave their homes before the war, for example, German Jews and Spanish Republicans. At the end of the war there were some eight million displaced persons in Europe, six million of whom were in Germany. Eventually responsibilities were transferred to the UN High Commission for Refugees which in 1954 had 350,000 refugees on their books. The majority of these, however, were not those originally displaced in the war but persons who had since fled from Soviet-dominated Eastern Europe.

Dissidents Those who refuse to conform with the prevailing political and social mores in their countries. In the USSR the term was used pejoratively of individuals and groups who criticised abuses of human and civil rights. The most famous was probably the Nobel Prize-winning novelist Alexander Solzhenitsyn who was expelled from the USSR in 1974. His works (*One Day in the Life of Ivan Denisovich, The Gulag Archipelago*) highlighted the conditions in which political prisoners were held in 'special' camps in the USSR. The USSR persistently denied Western claims that healthy dissidents were declared mentally ill and incarcerated in mental hospitals.

Doctors' Plot In Jan. 1953 the Soviet leader Stalin alleged that there was a conspiracy among some Moscow doctors (many of whom were Jewish) to kill Soviet officials. The plotters were accused of responsibility for the death of Leningrad party leader Andrei Zhdanov. However, the doctors (who were tortured while in custody) were released following Stalin's death on 5 Mar., ending what had appeared to be a new round of 1930s style purges.

Dopolavoro In Mussolini's fascist Italy the organisation set up to take care of workers' leisure time in such fields as sport, theatre, music, etc.

Drang nach Osten (Ger. 'thrust to the east') German desire to seek territorial gains in Eastern Europe.

Dreadnought The class of 'all-big-gun' battleships whose construction was inaugurated by HMS *Dreadnought*, laid down in Oct. 1905, launched in Feb. 1906 and at sea by Oct. 1906. She carried 10 12-inch guns, whereas no other extant battleship carried more than four; she was the fastest battleship in the world with a speed of 21 knots and the first large battleship to be turbine-powered. Able to outrange and outpace all other battleships, she represented a revolution in naval shipbuilding, sparking an international naval armaments race. In July 1907 Germany began construction of her *Nassau* class ships, similar to the *Dreadnought* class. By 1914 Britain had 19 *Dreadnought* class ships at sea, with a further 13 under construction; Germany had 13 at sea and 7 under construction.

Dreyfus Affair   Scandal in France between 1894 and 1899 involving Alfred Dreyfus (1859–1935), a Jewish army officer who was accused, tried and convicted of passing information to the Germans. Having been sentenced to life imprisonment on Devil's Island, he was found innocent and later exonerated by a second trial in 1899 which proved that many of the documents used to convict him had been forgeries. It became apparent that the authorities had used Dreyfus as a scapegoat to cover up the activities of a Major Esterhazy. During the time taken to convince the authorities of the need for a second trial, many accusations were made, including Zola's letter '*J'accuse*', that anti-Semitism of the authorities and the army had ensured Dreyfus's conviction and delayed his retrial. The 'Dreyfusard' and 'Anti-Dreyfusard' camps displayed many of the characteristic cleavages in the Third Republic.

Dual Alliance   Also known as the Dual Entente. An alliance between Russia and France which lasted from 1893 until the Bolshevik Revolution of Oct. 1917.

Dual Monarchy   Name given to the Austro–Hungarian Empire and, by extension, to its system of government.

Duce (It. lit. 'leader')   Title assumed by Benito Mussolini (*see* p. 260).

Duma   Russian parliament established by the Tsar in 1905 in response to demands which emanated from the abortive revolution of 1905. Free elections to the first two Dumas led to radical demands and rapid dissolution by the government. The Third Duma, elected with much greater government interference, did produce some limited administrative and land reform instigated by premier Stolypin. In spite of government disapproval, the Duma remained a platform for protest and in Nov. 1916 warned the government of impending revolution. As a result of its criticisms of the government, the Duma was suspended for much of the war period. Since the fall of the Soviet Union, the lower house of the Russian parliament has again been known as the Duma.

Dunkirk, Treaty of   Anglo–French agreement signed on 4 Mar. 1947 to provide mutual assistance against German aggression. The treaty also contained provisions for joint consultation over matters of mutual concern. The status of the treaty belongs largely to the postwar era and the re-emergence of France as the major European power, prior to the revival of West Germany, and the development of plans for European unity.

Eastern Bloc   The former communist states of Eastern Europe including the Warsaw Pact countries, Yugoslavia and Albania.

Eastern Front   Battlefront between Russia and Germany in the First and Second World Wars.

Eastern Question   The title given to the various problems of international, and especially European, relations created by the gradual decline of the Ottoman Empire in the late nineteenth and early twentieth centuries. A number of European powers vied for territorial concessions. Austria–Hungary looked to expand into the Balkans, Russia to gain access to the Mediterranean Sea for her Black Sea fleet. Until 1897, the fear of the Russians led Britain to support the Ottoman Empire, but most of this support disappeared after the Armenian massacres. Germany began to play an increasing role in Turkish affairs after a personal visit by the Kaiser in 1898 gave valuable commercial and railway concessions in exchange for a German military mission. The independence of the Balkan states further complicated the issue, especially when Serbia and Romania combined against the Ottoman Empire during the Balkan Wars of 1912. The Empire's alliance with Germany led to its destruction in 1918 and the creation of a Turkish national state.

'Economic Miracle'   *See* **Wirtschaftwunder**.

ECU (European Currency Unit)   A basket of European Community (EC) currencies, composed of amounts of Community members' currencies in proportion to their economic strength. The official ECU was used in the European Monetary System, while a private ECU was used in banking and investment activity.

EEC   *See* pp. 203–5.

EFTA   *See* p. 205.

Einkreisung (Ger. 'encirclement')   Term coined by the German Chancellor Prince Bernhard von Bülow (1849–1929) in 1906 to denote the policy embodied in the Anglo–French–Russian alliance, ascribed to Edward VII of England because of his various visits to European courts. In Germany's opinion her neighbours to east and west were joining hands to encircle her in a hostile alliance aimed at preventing German expansion, thus stopping her from taking a place in the front line of developed nations.

Einsatzgruppen (Ger. 'special service squads')   Task force selected to maintain law and order in German occupied territory between 1941 and 1945 and, more particularly, to murder Jews, partisans, communists and other 'dangerous elements' opposed to Nazi ideology.

ELAS   In wartime Greece, the National People's Army of Liberation, founded by the communist wing of the resistance EAM, after the German army occupied Greece in Apr. 1941. By 1943 it had liberated more than a third of the country. Britain and the USA lent their support to the pro-monarchist resistance groups, the X-bands, led by General Zervas. Clashes between the two sets of partisans led to the expulsion of Zervas in 1943 and the despatch of British troops to Greece in 1944 to prevent a civil war. It was by then clear that ELAS wished to achieve a communist revolution in the way Tito's Yugoslav partisans had done. For the ensuing civil war, *see* p. 178.

Enabling Law   Act passed by the German Reichstag in 1933 giving the Nazi Chancellor Adolf Hitler (1889–1945) the power to pass laws without parliament's consent, signifying the end of the Weimar Republic.

END   European Nuclear Disarmament, a British-based movement formed in 1980 and headed by E. P. Thompson who was also a leading figure on the national council of CND. The initial objective of END was to secure the removal of all nuclear weapons from Europe, but it was later to develop into a pressure-group fighting for a re-united Europe free from domination by either the USSR or the USA. In this capacity END established links with peace groups behind the Iron Curtain, such as the Moscow-based Group to Establish Trust, which had suffered greatly from official persecution. The divergence of approach between END and CND was soon to become apparent.

Enosis (deriv. Gk. 'to unite')   Greek Cypriot movement for the political union of Cyprus and Greece, dating from the late nineteenth century. Until the 1930s the question remained academic, but in 1931 severe rioting broke out between the Greek and Turkish populations of Cyprus and again demands for *enosis* came to the fore. In 1954 the movement was revived under the leadership of Archbishop Makarios III, Patriarch of the Orthodox Church in Cyprus. At the same time demands were made for the right of the island to determine its own future and terrorist activities began, led by EOKA. *See under* Cyprus Emergency (pp. 187–8) for the subsequent conflict.

Entente Cordiale (Fr. 'cordial agreement')   Term first used in the 1840s to describe the special relationship between Britain and France. Revived in the Anglo–French Entente of 8 Apr. 1904 and a similar agreement with Russia in Aug. 1907. These three were known as the Entente Powers until 1917, the agreements being converted to military alliances in Sept. 1911. The basis of the Anglo–French agreement had been the settlement of colonial differences and it survived the First World War, but was strained by the French occupation of the Ruhr in 1923 and the British attack on the French fleet in 1940. Attempts were made after the Second World War to revive the Entente by the Treaty of Dunkirk (1947).

EOKA   Armed movement for the union of Cyprus with Greece (*enosis*) led by Colonel George Grivas (1898–1974) which began a guerrilla campaign against British forces in Cyprus in Apr. 1955, forcing the declaration of a state of emergency on 27 Nov. When a ceasefire came into effect on 13 Mar. 1959, British military and civilian casualties were 142 dead and 684 wounded, with almost 1,000 Greek and Turkish Cypriots killed or injured. When Cyprus became independent under Archbishop Makarios as President on 16 Aug. 1960 without '*enosis*' EOKA members continued their campaign by mounting assassination and coup attempts against Makarios.

Épuration   Purge of collaborators conducted in 1944–45 after liberation of France; 767 were legally executed after trial but 30,000 were believed killed.

Estado Novo   The 'new state' in Portugal. The fascist regime established in 1926 and which was for long ruled after 1932 by António de Oliveira Salazar.

ETA   Militant Basque separatist movement responsible for numerous acts of violence against the government authorities in northern Spain. Its aim is the re-establishment of the short-lived Basque republic, Euzkadi, founded on 7 Oct. 1936 which ceased to exist on 18 June 1937 when the right-wing forces of General Franco (1892–1975) captured Bilbao in the Spanish Civil War.

Ethnic cleansing   Euphemism which emerged in the break-up of the former Yugoslavia in 1992 to describe attempts to remove minority ethnic groups by persuading communities to flee through threats and near-genocidal violence. Most often used to describe Serb actions against the Muslim community in Bosnia.

Euratom   European Atomic Energy Community, established by the Treaty of Rome in Mar. 1957, which came into existence on 1 Jan. 1958. Its original members were Belgium, France, Italy, Luxembourg, the Netherlands and West Germany. Member states are pledged to co-operate in the development and application of nuclear power for peaceful purposes.

Eurocommunism   The policy that individual communist parties in Western European countries would seek and pursue their own political paths, not dominated by or taking orders from the Soviet Union, as had happened under the domination of the Comintern in the interwar period.

European Defence Community   Plan to create a European defence force by a treaty signed on 27 May 1952 between Belgium, France, Italy, Luxembourg, the Netherlands and West Germany. The French National Assembly refused to ratify the treaty on 30 Aug. 1954. At a conference held in London from 28 Sept. to 3 Oct. 1954, Italy and West Germany were invited to accede to the 1948 Treaty of Brussels and the Western European Union was inaugurated on 6 May 1955.

European Economic Community   *See* **EEC**, pp. 203–5.

European Free Trade Association   *See* **EFTA**, p. 205.

European Monetary System   European Economic Community attempt introduced in Mar. 1979 to create currency stability by providing for central bank intervention to keep member states' currencies within $2\frac{1}{4}$ per cent band of the par exchange rate. It was seen as the first move towards European monetary union.

European Nuclear Disarmament   *See* **END**.

European Recovery Programme   Four-year programme presented to the USA on 22 Sept. 1947 by 16 European nations. It called for increased production by each nation, internal financial stability, economic co-operation and planning and a means of rectifying the trade deficit between Europe and the USA by increasing European exports to the latter. These countries formed the Organisation for European Economic Co-operation (OEEC) in response to Truman's offer of 'Marshall Aid', administered by the Economic Co-operation Administration. West Germany joined the OEEC in 1955 and Spain in 1959. On 30 Sept. 1961 it was replaced by the Organisation for Economic Co-operation and Development (OECD).

European Union (EU)   *See* pp. 203–5.

Eurosceptic   Term for opponents of greater European unity via the European Union (former EEC and European Community) brought to a head in Conservative Party debates in the 1990s over the Maastricht Treaty.

Euzkadi   Basque national homeland in north-east Spain, granted autonomy in Oct. 1936. Euzkadi was occupied by Franco's forces in June 1937 and Basque political and cultural nationalism was repressed until his death in 1975. The formation of a Basque parliament in Mar. 1980 has not prevented continued militant agitation, particularly by the ETA terrorist organisation, for full autonomy from Spain.

Evénéments, Les (The events)   *See under* **May Events**.

Évian Agreements   Agreements which ended the Algerian War following talks at Évian in France in Mar. 1962. Prime Minister Pompidou was the principal spokesman for the French government, with Ben Bella, the Algerian leader released from internment, speaking for the *Front de Liberation National* (FLN). Overwhelmingly ratified by referenda in France (Apr.) and Algeria (July), the agreements ended the Algerian war of independence fought against France since 1954 with an immediate ceasefire and a guarantee of French withdrawal by the end of the year. They faced the bitter opposition of Algerian settlers and army officers in the *Organisation de L'Armée Secrète* (OAS).

FAI (Sp., *Federación Anarquista Iberica*)   Iberian Anarchist Federation, formed in July 1927 to maintain anarchist ascendancy in the CNT labour movement. The FAI led resistance to Franco's rising in Barcelona and Valencia and its leaders accepted government posts. Weakened by internal divisions and communist influence in the Republic, the FAI maintained a nominal existence while in exile.

Falange   The only political party permitted in Franco's Spain. Founded by José Antonio Primo de Rivera in 1933 as a right-wing movement opposed to the Republic. José Antonio was assassinated in Nov. 1936 in the early months of the Spanish Civil War. The movement survived his death to be used by Franco when the Grand Council of the Falange replaced the Cortes as the legislative body in Spain between June 1939 and July 1942.

Fasci di Combattimento   The first organisation of the Italian fascist movement under Mussolini. The original group was formed in Milan on 23 Mar. 1919 by an assortment of nationalists, war veterans, etc. The term literally translated means combat group.

Fascist   An Italian nationalist, authoritarian, anti-communist movement developed by Mussolini after 1919 which became the only authorised political party in Italy after the 'March on Rome' in 1922. The movement derived its name from the 'fasces' (bundle of sticks), the symbol of state power in ancient Rome. More generally applied to authoritarian and National Socialist movements in Europe and elsewhere (*see* **Nazi**).

Fashoda Incident   Crisis in Anglo–French relations as a result of rival claims to Sudan. A French detachment under Marchand had marched to the town of Fashoda on the Upper Nile from French West Africa, reaching it in July 1898, just before the arrival of General Kitchener, fresh from his defeat of the Mahdi's forces at Omdurman, with a large Anglo–Egyptian army. France's claim to the area by right of prior conquest was hotly disputed by Britain who wished to retain control of the Nile Valley. A 'war scare' was fanned in both countries by the popular press, but France's distraction by the Dreyfus Affair and lack of support from Russia forced her to back down. Marchand withdrew from Fashoda in Nov. 1898 and France agreed in Mar. 1899 to renounce all claims to the Nile Valley.

February Revolution   First revolution in Russia in 1917. Disenchantment with the war together with food shortages resulted in strikes and riots in St Petersburg on 8 Mar. 1917 (Feb. in the Julian Calendar). Troops joined the rioters and the Duma was obliged to appoint a provisional government under Prince Lvov. On 15 Mar. Tsar Nicholas II was forced to abdicate and real power passed to the liberal intelligentsia inside and outside the Duma. However, the Bolsheviks under Lenin subsequently revived the Soviet that was established in the 1905 Revolution and criticised every act of the provisional government. After an abortive attempt to seize power in July, they subsequently seized power in Oct.

Felipismo   Term for the 13 years of power in modern Spain of Felipe Gonzalez, the socialist leader, until his defeat in the Mar. 1996 election by José María Aznar.

Festung Europa   Term applied to Hitler's plans for an impregnable Reich during the Second World War.

Fifth Column   Secret enemy sympathisers who would rise if necessary to assist attackers. The term was first coined by General Mola during the Spanish Civil War (1936–39). He advanced on Madrid with four military columns but claimed to have a 'fifth column' within the city itself. The term gained wide usage during the Second World War particularly as a popular means of explaining Germany's rapid conquest of the Low Countries and Norway.

Fifth Republic   Established in France on 6 Oct. 1958, it has a strong Presidency and a weak legislature, with the President nominating the Prime Minister, dissolving parliament, and having power to rule by decree and appeal directly to the electorate through referenda. The Republic emphasises independent economic and foreign policies, a commitment to nuclear weapons, and support for the European Union with a vigorous defence of French interests. The National Assembly now has 491 members directly elected for five years (474 from Metropolitan France) and neither the Prime Minister nor any of the cabinet is allowed to hold seats in it.

Final Solution   Euphemism applied by the Nazis to their genocidal policy against the Jews.

Fiume (Rijeka)   Port on the Adriatic, claimed by both Italy and Yugoslavia after 1919. In Jan. 1924 most of Fiume was incorporated into Italy, with Yugoslavia retaining the small port of Susak. Following the Second World War it was eventually ceded to Yugoslavia.

Five Year Plan   System of economic planning first adopted in the Soviet Union between 1928 and 1933. The plan laid down short-term aims and targets for the development of heavy industry and the collectivisation of agriculture. The second plan, 1933–37, aimed at increased production of consumer goods but the third, 1938–43, returned to the primacy of heavy industry, largely directed towards rearmament. The Five Year Plan was adopted as a method of planning by other socialist countries.

Flanders   The largely Flemish-speaking region in the north of Belgium. Increasing demands for devolution (fired by the language issue) culminated in a degree of regional autonomy in 1993.

Flemings   The majority community in Belgium, Roman Catholics speaking a language close to Dutch. A late nineteenth century cultural revival encouraged agitation for Flemish autonomy and German occupation forces in both wars used the grievances in an attempt to divide Belgium. *See* Flanders.

Force de Frappe   The French strategic nuclear strike force.

Forza Italia   The right-wing party formed by Berlusconi to fight the 1994 elections. Anti-immigrant, pro-market forces and populist, it gathered much of the old Christian Democrat vote, but rapidly declined thereafter only to revive for the May 2001 elections.

Fouchet Plan   Attempt proposed by French President de Gaulle (President, 1959–69) to work towards the eventual political unity of the six members of the European Economic Community. The plan, drawn up by Christian Fouchet, was opposed by smaller EEC member states who favoured the prior entry of Britain and Ireland and was abandoned in 1962.

Fourteen Points   A peace programme put forward by President Woodrow Wilson to the US Congress on 8 Jan. 1918 and accepted as the basis for an armistice by Germany and Austria–Hungary. Later it was alleged that the

Allied Powers had violated the principles embodied in the Fourteen Points, especially in relation to the prohibition of *Anschluss*, the union of Germany with Austria. The original points were: the renunciation of secret diplomacy; freedom of the seas; the removal of economic barriers between states; arms reductions; impartial settlement of colonial disputes; evacuation of Russia by Germany and her allies; restoration of Belgium; German withdrawal from France and the return of Alsace–Lorraine; readjustment of the Italian frontiers; autonomous development of nationalities in Austria–Hungary; evacuation of Romania, Serbia and Montenegro and guarantees of Serbian access to the sea; free passage through the Dardanelles and the self-determination of minorities in the Ottoman Empire; creation of an independent Poland with access to the sea; and the creation of a general association of states.

Fourth Republic   Formed on 24 Dec. 1946 in France, its constitution created a figurehead President, a National Assembly and a weak second chamber. It was closely modelled on that of the Third Republic. The Senate was replaced by the Council of the Republic as a purely advisory body, with the Chamber of the National Assembly as the legislative body. The executive had limited power to dissolve parliament, and popular sovereignty was invested in the referendum. The position of the President was similar to that under the Third Republic, except that the President of the Council of Ministers (Prime Minister) had taken over some of his powers, principally the power to propose legislation to parliament and to issue edicts to supplement the law. The programme of the cabinet had to be approved by public vote by an absolute majority of the National Assembly before the Council of Ministers could be appointed. Once appointed they were responsible to the Assembly but not to the Council of the Republic. Despite some economic and industrial success, the Republic was racked by political division and weakness (23 governments in 12 years) and harried by colonial wars in Indo–China and Algeria. It collapsed with France near civil war in Oct. 1958, opening the way to the Gaullist Fifth Republic.

Free City   City under an international administration, not that of one state, such as Danzig between 1919 and 1939 which was under the control of the League of Nations.

French Community, The (La Communauté)   The constitution of the Fifth Republic, promulgated on 6 Oct. 1958, 'offers to the overseas territories which manifest their will to adhere to it new institutions based on the common ideal of liberty, equality and fraternity and conceived with a view to their democratic evolution'. The territories were offered three solutions: they could keep their status; they could become overseas *départements*; they could become, singly or in groups, member states of the Community (Art. 76).

Free French   The *Forces Françaises Libres*, made up of French troops and naval units, who continued the fight against Nazi Germany after the fall of France in the summer of 1940. In opposition to the Vichy regime in France, General de Gaulle established a 'Council for the Defence of the Empire', and later the *Comité National Français*. The Free French were active against Vichy forces in

Syria and Miquelon and St Pierre in 1941. On 19 July 1942 the Free French were renamed the *Forces Françaises Combatantes*, Fighting French Forces (FFC). The FFC represented de Gaulle's main claim as the true representative of French liberation. As the allied forces liberated France in the summer of 1944, the FFC were able to provide the first allied troops to enter Paris after an uprising organised by the *Forces Françaises de L'Intérieur.*

Freikorps (Ger. 'free corps') Counter-revolutionary volunteer forces recruited by the German government in Dec. 1918 to restore internal law and order, to prevent revolution and to protect German frontiers after the collapse of the monarchy and dissolution of the Imperial army. They suppressed left-wing revolutionary movements, including the Spartacist rising of Jan. 1919 and the Bavarian Soviet. Further units fought on the eastern frontiers, mainly against Poland and the Red Army in the Baltic states, until the Allies demanded their disbandment. The involvement of *Freikorps* members such as Erhardt and Lüttwitz in the abortive Kapp Putsch signified the end of the force apart from a brief revival in 1921 due to the war in Upper Silesia. Large numbers of the *Freikorps* who were anti-Semitic and anti-communist later joined the various right-wing paramilitary organisations active in Weimar Germany.

Führer (Ger. lit. 'leader') Title first coined in 1921 to describe Hitler as head of the Nazi Party. After his appointment as Chancellor in 1933, the term was used more widely to describe him as '*Führer*' of Germany.

Führer Prinzip (Ger. 'leadership principle') Basis of Hitler's organisation of the Nazi state, arising from the doctrine of the aristocratic idea of Nature. *Führer Prinzip* was to replace democracy as a system of the authority of every leader downwards and the responsibility upwards, with Hitler at the pinnacle of the system, having supreme authority and ultimate responsibility for Germany's destiny. The *Führer*, and not a parliament, was the ultimate decision-maker in affairs of state.

Gastarbeiter (Ger. 'Guestworker') Overseas labour – predominantly Greek, Turkish and Moroccan – recruited to meet the needs of West German industry in the 1960s and 1970s which was denied citizenship rights and forced to return home when its services were no longer required.

Gauchistes (Fr. 'Leftists') Political groupings to the left of the French Communist Party, including Anarchists, Maoists and Trotskyists, usually with a large proportion of student members, active in the 1968 May Events (*see* p. 308) and the early 1970s.

Gaullists Followers of General Charles de Gaulle (1890–1970), although there is no precise definition of Gaullism. A short-lived mass movement under the Fourth French Republic centred on the *Rassemblement du Peuple Français* (RPF), an authoritarian anti-communist party with fascist tendencies, which enjoyed its greatest success in the late 1940s and early 1950s. The *Union de la Nouvelle République* (UNR) was formed from various Gaullist groups after the establishment of the Fifth French Republic in 1958. Gaullism survived the

299

general's retirement in 1970, and provided a basis for support for his presidential successor, Georges Pompidou.

German Democratic Republic (GDR)   The state formed in 1949 from the postwar Soviet zone of occupation in Germany. Popularly called East Germany. It united with the Federal Republic of Germany on 3 Oct. 1990, following the collapse of communism. At the centre of its constitution was the People's Chamber (*Volkskammer*), which had much greater powers than the West German *Bundestag* and was to be elected through a system of proportional representation at least every four years by all citizens aged 18 or over. The head of government was designated the Minister-President, to be elected by the People's Chamber and requiring a majority in that body. The Head of State was a President elected every four years by a joint session of the People's Chamber and the Chamber of States. Only political parties which accepted democracy were to be allowed to function. With the establishment of the new state in 1949, it rapidly became apparent that real power was to lie not with the elected bodies set up by the constitution but rather with the communist-dominated SED.

Gestapo (Ger. abbreviation of *Geheime Staatspolizei*)   Originally the political police force of the Prussian State Police, the Gestapo was developed as an instrument of internal control in Germany during the Nazi period by Heinrich Himmler as head of the German police. The Gestapo was used extensively to control and suppress opposition to Nazi rule, both inside Germany and later also in occupied territories.

Gibraltar Dispute   The British territory in southern Spain commanding entrance to the Mediterranean, captured by Britain in 1704 and formerly a strategically important naval base, was claimed by Spain in 1939. The UN recognised the claim in 1963, with Britain asserting that the wish of the population expressed overwhelmingly in a referendum was to remain British. The Spanish government closed the frontier in 1969. But, following discussions from 1977, agreement was reached in Apr. 1980 to ease restrictions, and in Jan. 1982 Spain agreed to lift the siege of the colony in return for talks on Gibraltar's future. The border was reopened on 15 Dec. 1982 and the final restrictions lifted in Feb. 1985. In a referendum in Nov. 2002, there was an overwhelming vote to remain British.

Glasnost   The liberalising 'openness' of the Soviet intellectual atmosphere encouraged by Mikhail Gorbachev, following his appointment as Communist Party Secretary in Mar. 1985. *Glasnost* appeared to set few limits on the discussion of contemporary Soviet society and politics and of Soviet history, particularly the Stalin period.

Gleichschaltung (co-ordination)   The term applied to the process of official subordination of all political and social organisations in Germany to Nazi control. The term was first used in Mar. 1933 with the introduction of a law establishing Nazi majorities in the government of each federal state; later it referred to the subordination of many institutions, e.g. trade unions, youth clubs, etc. Its aim was to deprive Germans outside the Nazi Party of a political or social focal point.

Gosplan Soviet State Planning Commission created centrally to control Stalin's economic programmes from 1924 to 1953.

Grand Coalition (Ger. *grosse Koalition*) Term used in Central European politics to denote coalition of two major parties as opposed to a small coalition (*kleine Koalition*) of one major party and a minor party. Such a coalition, between the conservative CDU/CSU and the social democratic SPD governed West Germany from 1966 until 1969. A grand coalition of the conservative ÖVP and the social democratic SPÖ governed Austria from 1945 to 1966.

Great Patriotic War Russian term for the struggle against Nazi Germany following Operation Barbarossa, the German invasion of the Soviet Union in 1941.

Greek Colonels Military junta that seized power in Greece on 21 Apr. 1967. The coup was led by two colonels, George Papadopoulos and Stylianos Pattakos, who suspended the democratic constitution and proclaimed martial law. Claiming to be acting to save Greece from 'internal enemies', Papadopoulos and Pattakos were explicitly anti-communist and traded upon the virulent hatreds which still survived in Greece as a legacy of the Civil War. Although Constantine remained on the throne for six months, he was forced to flee after a botched attempt at a counter-coup on 13 Dec. 1967. His departure allowed the Colonels to convert their regime into a dictatorship. The regime was marked by widespread persecution of left-wing and liberal opponents, with many instances of torture brought before international tribunals. The regime collapsed in July 1974, following its intervention in Cyprus.

Greens Originally and principally the West German ecology party, which first emerged as a political force in Bremen in 1979, when environmentalists and anti-nuclear groups won 5.9 per cent of votes for the *Land* (federal state) parliament. Greens have since been elected to other *Land* parliaments and to the Bundestag, and similar parties have had success in other West European countries. After the defeat of Chancellor Kohl in 1998, Greens participated in government in Germany at national level for the first time. The 2002 elections saw their best performance yet.

Green Socialism A strand within socialism emerging in the 1980s which attempted to reconcile environmentalist concern over the threats of industrialisation to the future of the Earth with the traditional socialist aim of a general improvement in the overall standard of living. *See* Greens.

Grenzgänger Term often used to denote those who escaped from East Germany during the communist era.

Grey Wolves The military wing of the Turkish far-right National Action Party, responsible for killing left-wing opponents. Its best known activist was Mehmet Ali Agca, who made an assassination attempt on Pope John Paul in 1981.

Grundgesetz The postwar constitution (i.e. the Basic Law) of (originally) West Germany. It came into force in 1949.

Guillaume Affair An espionage scandal in West Germany in 1974 which forced the resignation of Chancellor Willy Brandt (1913–92, Chancellor, 1969–74) when his personal assistant Gunter Guillaume was convicted of being a long-term East German spy.

Gulag Russian acronym for the Chief Administration of Corrective Labour Camps, used generally to refer to the Soviet system of penal colonies and labour camps. The term obtained wide currency following the publication in the West in 1972 of the first part of Alexander Solzhenitsyn's *The Gulag Archipelago*, which documented the expansion of forced labour camps under the Bolsheviks and Stalin. He pointedly dedicated the book to 'all those who did not live to tell it'. Publication was followed in 1974 by his arrest and deportation from the Soviet Union.

Habsburgs The house of Habsburg–Lorraine, an Austrian royal dynasty which ruled from 1282 to 1918. The murder of the heir to the Austrian Habsburg throne in 1914, Francis Ferdinand, led to the outbreak of the First World War, and the last Emperor, Charles I, was forced to abdicate in 1918. Attempts to place his son Otto on the Austrian throne in the 1920s and 1930s were ended by the *Anschluss* with Germany in 1938.

Hammer and Sickle Symbol on a red background, the flag of the former USSR, denoting the unity of the peasantry and industrial proletariat and emphasising the equal importance of industry and agriculture to Soviet Russia.

Harpsund democracy Expression used to describe the tri-partite system in Sweden in which government, industry and trade unions jointly formulated policy in an attempt to overcome conflicts of interest. The meetings began in 1939. Sometimes referred to as the 'Third Way'.

Hellenism The desire to bring all the lands once part of Ancient and Byzantine Greece together again under Greek rule. A form of Greek nationalism.

Helsinki Agreement Product of the Helsinki Conference, 1975, between 35 nations concerning European security, proposals for economic collaboration between Eastern and Western blocs, and a reaffirmation of human rights. The last was consistently utilised to raise the cases of dissidents suffering ill-treatment in the Soviet Union.

Herrenvolk (Ger. lit. 'master race') A doctrine expounded by the Nazis who used the supposed superiority of the 'Aryan' race as a justification for German territorial expansion and the enslavement of 'inferior races'.

Hiemuher The Austrian *Freikorps*.

Historic Compromise Term used to describe the support given by the Italian Communist Party (PCI) to the governing Christian Democrats after 1976. The support marked the end of more than a generation of communist exclusion from the governing coalitions of modern Italy and reflected the need to form a strong base with which to deal with growing problems of inflation and terrorism. From 1978 the Communists were virtually unofficial members of the government, largely through the mediation of Aldo Moro, the Christian Democrat Prime Minister. His death in spring 1978 at the hands of terrorists and that of the communist leader Enrico Berlinguer in 1984 undermined a long-term arrangement.

Hohenzollern German royal dynasty which provided the three German emperors, 1871–1918. Originally the Prussian royal house, the monarchy was finally brought to an end by the abdication of Kaiser Wilhelm II in Nov. 1918.

Holocaust, the Term applied to the attempted annihilation of the Jews in Europe by the Nazis in the Second World War. The culmination of centuries of anti-Semitism, the attempted planned extermination was carried into effect in concentration camps and by *Einsatzgruppen* execution squads in conquered Russia. It destroyed an East European Jewish culture 1,000 years old, and carried out the murder of some six million Jews, half of them from Poland. It convinced many Jews that they could no longer live in Europe, or indeed anywhere except in their own state, and was thus the major impetus to Zionism. See p. 231.

Hot Autumn The Italian term (*autunno caldo*) for the period in 1969 of industrial militancy, workers' sit-ins and widespread strikes that had started in 1967.

International Brigades Volunteer brigades formed to support the republican cause in Spain during the Spanish Civil War. Composed mainly of left-wing and communist sympathisers from all parts of Europe and the USA, the volunteers saw the fight against Franco's nationalist insurgents as part of the wider struggle against European fascism.

Iron Curtain Phrase first used in Feb. 1945 by Joseph Goebbels (1897–1945), the Nazi Minister of Enlightenment and Propaganda. However, it was repetition of the phrase in a speech by Winston Churchill at Fulton, Missouri, on 5 Mar. 1946 that first brought it to public attention and made it a term in general use. It denoted the border between Soviet-dominated Eastern Europe and the West and, more specifically, the restraints placed on ideology and movement by communist regimes. With the fall of communism (and the Soviet Union itself) the term is now redundant.

Iron Guard Romanian nationalist and fascist organisation, founded in 1927 as the Legion of the Archangel Michael, becoming known as the Iron Guard in the early 1930s. Founded by Corneliu Codreanu (1899–1938), it combined anti-Semitism, peasant populism, and Christian nationalism in support of right-wing policies. Implicated in the murder of the Liberal premier Ion Duca in 1933, the Legion was reformed as the All-for-the-Fatherland Party which obtained 16 per cent of the vote in the 1937 election. Suppressed by King Carol II's royal dictatorship in 1938, which murdered Codreanu and its leaders, surviving members led the rising which forced Carol's abdication in Sept. 1940 and formed one of the groups supporting the dictatorship of Antonescu (1882–1946). An insurrection led by the Iron Guard, during which it carried out savage massacres of thousands of Jews and other enemies, was crushed with the aid of German troops in Jan. 1941.

Irredentists Italian political party founded about 1878, committed to the incorporation of territories neighbouring the kingdom of Italy (*see* Italia Irredenta).

Italia Irredenta Term applied to the territories of Trentino, Istria and South Tyrol which were acquired by Italy after the Treaty of St Germain (1919). Sometimes regarded as the completion of the *Risorgimento*, the term irredentism has been used to describe any movement committed to the restoration of territory formerly held.

Italian Social Movement Extreme right-wing political party founded in 1946. Its neo-fascist tendencies attracted strongest support in the south of Italy, and particularly in Naples. It became the National Alliance in 1993, fighting the 1994 election with the *Forza Italia.*

July Conspiracy Otherwise known as the Hitler Bomb Plot, this was an attempt by disaffected sections of the German officer corps to assassinate Hitler and end Nazi rule in order that negotiations could take place with the Western Allies. The plot involved a bomb placed in Hitler's East Prussian headquarters by Colonel von Stauffenberg on 20 July 1944 and was assumed to have succeeded by accomplices in Berlin, who thus committed themselves to a new government. Hitler's almost miraculous survival signalled the failure of the plotters and the attempt was used as an excuse by Hitler to purge the army and other high-ranking officials known to oppose the regime. Fifteen of the alleged conspirators committed suicide and 150 others were executed – they included high-ranking army staff, trade unionists, diplomats and politicians.

Kadets In Russia, post-1905 revolution party representing views of the liberal professional and academic classes. Prominent in the Duma, the Kadets were increasingly critical of Tsarism. Favouring a democratic republic after the Feb. 1917 Revolution, the Party was declared an 'enemy of the people' by the Bolsheviks in Jan. 1918 and outlawed.

Kaiser (Ger. 'Caesar', i.e. Emperor) Title assumed by the Prussian King William I following the unification of Germany and the creation of the German Empire. William accepted the crown of a united Germany in Dec. 1870.

Karelia Territory ceded by Finland to the Soviet Union in Mar. 1940, following Finland's defeat in the Winter War. Russian President Boris Yeltsin refused to discuss the possibility of its return, despite Finnish offers of a cash payment and a multi-million pound aid programme.

Kemalism The modernising and secularising nationalism of Kemal Ataturk (1881–1938), President of Turkey 1923–38, who abolished the Sultanate in 1922, and the Caliphate – the religious authority – in 1924. He imposed

Western dress and customs, banned polygamy, encouraged industrialisation, changed from the Arabic to the Latin script, and in 1934 ordered the adoption of surnames, his own – Ataturk – meaning Father of the Turks.

KGB   In Soviet Russia, the Committee of State Security. Title of the Soviet secret police after Mar. 1954. Responsible in the Soviet era for espionage, counter-espionage, internal surveillance, training and funding of terrorist organisations, administration and security of Russian work camps and psychiatric hospitals used to confine dissidents. Its role has changed since the fall of communism.

Kolkhoz   Collective farm in the USSR. In 1930, to aid the 1928–33 Five Year Plan, all individual farms and small-holdings were combined into the *kolkhoz* system. Land is state property and leased back to them: they farm it jointly, using government-run machines and factory centres. In the 1950s there were 250,000 collective farmers (*kolkhozniki*). Members might own a house and a plot of land individually, and keep a few cattle for personal use. *See also* **Sovkhoz**.

Kosovo   Province in the former Yugoslavia which, although over 90 per cent inhabited by ethnic Albanians, is seen by the Serbs as the cradle of their culture. Kosovo was an autonomous region within the Yugoslav federation until direct rule was imposed in 1989, which led to the formation of a Democratic League of Kosovo to agitate peacefully for complete independence. *See* p. 181 for the Kosovo War.

Kraft durch Freude (Ger. 'strength through joy')   Recreational organisation founded by the *Deutsche Arbeitsfront* in Nov. 1933 to perform the social functions of the German trade unions which the Nazi Party had suppressed, e.g. providing cut-price theatre tickets, running adult educational institutes, etc. By 1939, 40 million Germans had taken advantage of its subsidised tourism. It also helped to finance German rearmament by means of the Volkswagen savings swindle, a fraud by which people paid in instalments in advance for new cars which never materialised.

Krajina   Literally frontier or borderland. With the collapse of Yugoslavia, the Serb minority living in Croatia adopted this name for the autonomous republic they attempted to establish in 1991.

Kremlin (Russ. 'citadel')   Refers to the citadel in Moscow occupied by the former Imperial Palace. The administrative headquarters of, and synonymous with, the government of the former USSR.

Kristallnacht (Ger. 'crystal night')   9 Nov. 1938, when the Nazis were organised to destroy Jewish property, littering the streets with glass. A massive amount of damage was done, many thousands of Jews imprisoned and hundreds brutally attacked. *See also* **Anti-Semitism**.

Kulaks (Russ. 'tight-fisted person')   Term used to describe Russian peasants who were able to become landowners as a result of the agrarian reforms of 1906 and were encouraged by Lenin's NEP. Their resistance to collectivisation under the Five Year Plan led to Stalin's order for the liquidation of the *kulak* class. As a result, large numbers were deported to Siberia or executed in their villages. In Aug. 1942, Stalin confessed to Churchill that the numbers killed amounted to some 10 million people.

Länder (Ger.)   Name given to the member states of Germany under the constitution of 1919. The name has remained for the states of the post-1945 Federal Republic of Germany as well as for the nine federal states of Austria.

Lateran treaties   Agreements reached on 11 Feb. 1929 between Mussolini and Pope Pius XI (Pontiff 1922–29), under which the sovereignty of the Vatican City State was recognised and a substantial indemnity paid to it in respect of papal possessions confiscated during Italian unification in 1870. A concordat was established between the Church and the fascist government of Italy under Mussolini.

Lebensraum   (Ger. lit. 'living space') Slogan adopted by German nationalists and especially the Nazi Party in the 1920s and 1930s to justify the need for Germany to expand territorially in the East. The theory was based on the alleged overpopulation of Germany and the need for more territory to ensure their food supplies. Interpreted by some Germans as the desire for a return to the frontiers of 1914, the attack on the Soviet Union suggests that Hitler's interpretation of the concept was much wider.

Little Entente   Pejorative term, first used in the Hungarian newspaper *Pesti Hirlap* on 21 Feb. 1920, for the series of alliances between Yugoslavia and Czechoslovakia (1920), Czechoslovakia and Romania (1921), and Yugoslavia and Romania (1921), which were consolidated by the Treaty of Belgrade in May 1929. Their aim was to provide for mutual assistance in preventing Austria or Hungary from asserting claims to territory lost in the First World War. The alliances were undermined by Yugoslavian co-operation with Germany in 1935–38 and collapsed when France and Britain abandoned support of Czechoslovakia at Munich in 1938.

Louvre Accord   Agreement reached in Paris by the leading Western economies on 21 Feb. 1987 to co-ordinate economic policy in the interests of balanced growth and a reduction of trade imbalances. Against the background of an international exchange crisis, Britain, Canada, France, Japan, the USA and West Germany agreed to foster stability by increasing domestic demand in states with balance of payment surpluses and encouraging growth in those with deficits.

Luftwaffe   German air force, used during the Second World War as the chief instrument of the blitzkrieg.

Luxembourg Accords   Statements issued by the Council of Ministers of the then EEC following agreements reached between the six at meetings on 28 and 29 Jan. 1966. These agreements brought to an end the withdrawal of France (begun on 5 July 1965 under President de Gaulle) from most of the activities of the European Community except some technical groups such as the management groups of the Common Agricultural Policy.

Maastricht Summit held in Dec. 1991 marking a new stage in moves towards European economic and political integration.

Maginot Line French defensive fortifications stretching from Longwy to the Swiss border. Named after French Minister of Defence, André Maginot, the line was constructed between 1929 and 1934 as a means of countering a German attack. Due to the Belgians' refusal to extend the line along their frontier with Germany, and French reluctance to appear to 'abandon' Belgium and build the line along the Franco–Belgian border to the sea, the defensive strategy relied on the Germans' inability to penetrate the Ardennes forest. This hope was seen as misguided when the Germans were able to turn the French flank by an advance through Belgium and the Maginot Line was still virtually intact when France surrendered on 22 July 1940.

Magyar Native name for Hungarians but also a class term meaning one who owned land and was exempt from land tax, attended county assemblies and took part in elections to the Diet. The Austrian Habsburgs attempted to Germanise the Magyars on their territories but Hungarian nationalism provided sufficient pressure to ensure the creation of the Dual Monarchy in 1867 and independence for the state of Hungary after 1918.

Makhnovschtchina Uprising in the Ukraine between 1917 and 1921 led by Nestor Makhno, an anarchist peasant, whose Insurgent Army fought against both the Whites and the Reds, distributed land, organised peasants' and workers' councils on libertarian principles, and which was defeated by the Red Army in Aug. 1921.

Mandates Rights granted to certain states at the end of the First World War by the League of Nations to administer the colonies and dependencies of Germany and the Ottoman Empire. The Mandates came in three forms. Some territories were only under a limited term mandate while they prepared for independence; the British control over Iraq, Palestine and Transjordan, and the French control of Lebanon and Syria came into this category. Others were to be administered indefinitely because of their lack of development. These included all the German colonies in Africa except for South West Africa. The third category were also to be administered indefinitely but could be treated as part of the mandate powers' territory. South West Africa, New Guinea and Samoa were included in these.

Mansholt Plan A series of documents prepared by Sicco Mansholt (EEC Commissioner responsible for Agriculture) proposing reforms of the Common Agricultural Policy. The plan proposed a series of measures – grants, marketing assistance, help and retraining for those who wished to give up farming – to encourage the development of larger and more economic farms and a reform of the structure of agriculture in the EEC. Some proposals based on these ideas were adopted in Mar. 1972 but the overall effect on the structure of farming was small.

Maquis   Name derived from Corsican resistance movements which liberated Corsica in 1943. Maquis groups in mainland France increased greatly in 1943 and 1944, and those in Brittany were particularly effective in hampering German movements prior to D-Day on 6 June 1944.

Mare Nostrum (Lat. 'our sea')   Italian name for the Mediterranean Sea.

Marshall Plan   US Plan for the economic reconstruction of Europe, named after Secretary of State General George C. Marshall. The Organisation for European Economic Co-operation was established to administer the aid in Apr. 1948 but the Soviet rejection of the Plan meant that most of the monetary aid went to Western Europe. Between 1948 and 1952 the US provided some $17,000 million which was a crucial element in European postwar recovery.

Master Race   Race believed by its members to be inherently superior to all others, expressed, for example, in the Nazi ideal of the *Herrenvolk*.

May Events   The events of May 1968 when French students, demonstrating against education cuts in Paris, precipitated a political crisis in France. Police brutality against the students triggered riots and increasingly radical demands. Over 10 million workers also came out on general strike. The strike and riots went on into June, but the government eventually defused the situation by promising educational reform, and wage increases to the workers.

Mein Kampf (Ger. 'My Struggle')   Title of book written by Adolf Hitler while serving a prison sentence following the abortive Munich Putsch of 1923; he was helped in the work by his deputy Rudolf Hess (1894–1987). The book encapsulates his thoughts on Germany's role in world affairs, *Lebensraum* and communism and reflects his anti-Semitism and dislike of democracy.

Menshevik (Russ. 'member of the minority')   Moderate faction of the Russian Social Democratic Party after the Party split in 1903. Opposed to the Bolsheviks, they were formally suppressed from 1922 onwards.

Mitteleuropa (Ger.)   The idea of a German-speaking supranational state in Central Europe which was pioneered by Austrian Minister Schwarzenberg in 1848. The idea was later rejected by Bismarck when it was used to support German domination of south-eastern Europe and the Balkans. In spite of this, the idea was revived in 1915 with the publication of Friedrich Naumann's book *Mitteleuropa*.

Moroccan Crisis   A European crisis precipitated by German attempts to break up the Anglo–French Entente of 1904. Wilhelm II's landing at Tangier and his expression of German support for Moroccan independence led to acrimonious relations between Germany and France and succeeded only in strengthening the bond between France and Britain. The Algeçiras Conference of Jan.–Apr. 1906 recognised French predominance in Morocco and represented a defeat for the German stand.

Morgenthau Plan A proposal at the Quebec Conferences (1944) by US Treasury Secretary Morgenthau that a defeated Germany be stripped of all industry, reverting to an agricultural nation. The Plan was rejected on the grounds of the enormous amount of aid Germany would need to survive, but proved a useful propaganda weapon for the Nazis to urge Germany into fighting harder.

Nassau Agreement Agreement signed between President Kennedy and British Prime Minister Harold Macmillan on 18 Dec. 1962 on nuclear co-operation. The USA agreed to supply Britain with submarine-launched Polaris nuclear missiles to replace her ageing and obsolescent V-bomber force. The agreement was partly the outcome of the good relations enjoyed by Macmillan with Kennedy, but antagonised De Gaulle, who interpreted it as evidence of Britain's continuing relationship with America. He vetoed British entry to the Common Market a month later.

National Salvation Front Romanian political coalition which took power in Romania following the fall of the Ceausescu dictatorship in Dec. 1989. The Front, which initially claimed to be a temporary interim government, organised itself as a party and went on to success in the 1990 election. It was criticised for accepting the membership of important figures from the previous regime. A group of former Communists seceded in 1992.

National schism Term for the bitter division between Constantine I, King of Greece, and his leading Minister, Venizelos, over which side Greece should support in the First World War. Dismissed in Oct. 1915 after a clear election victory in June, the pro-Entente Venizelos set up a rival government in Crete, later moved to Salonika. In June 1917, with British and French support, he engineered the abdication of Constantine in favour of his son Alexander. The death of Alexander in Oct. 1920 and Venizelos's defeat in the elections of Nov. allowed Constantine to return. He was forced into exile again following the disastrous defeats of the Greek armies in Anatolia in 1921–22, abdicating in Sept. 1922.

NATO *See* p. 207.

Nazi Popular contraction of 'National Socialist' and used to describe both the NSDAP as a party and its individual members. The Party was ideologically attached to right-wing authoritarianism (*see* Italian fascism, p. 37) but also included strong anti-Semitism and a belief in the racial supremacy of the 'Aryan' race. The Party was led by Adolf Hitler from 1921 until his death in 1945. It was initially based in Munich and was given a setback by its involvement in the Beer Hall Putsch of Nov. 1923. Nevertheless, the Nazis under Hitler's guidance underwent a resurgence in the late 1920s and achieved a major electoral breakthrough when they captured 107 seats in the Reichstag. Their electoral success continued into 1932 and in an attempt to provide some form of consensus government, Hitler was offered the Chancellorship in 1933. After the 'seizure of power', Nazi Party organisations such as the SS came to dominate many facets of life in Germany. The party organisation collapsed at the end of the Second World War and was made illegal after the German surrender.

Neo-fascism   Expression used to describe the fascist movements that emerged in Europe following the defeat of the German and Italian varieties in the Second World War but which attempt to preserve a democratic image. Among the most significant are the *Front National* in France and the *Movimento Sociale Italiano* in Italy. In Britain, the National Front and the British National Party have remained marginal but the collapse of communist control in Eastern Europe saw a growth of neo-fascist groupings in the 1990s.

New Class   Heretical Marxist theory expounded by the Yugoslav communist Milovan Djilas in his work *The New Class*, published in 1950. Djilas suggested that, contrary to traditional Marxist theory, a political party or bureaucracy with a monopoly of power (such as the Communists in the Soviet bloc) would create a self-perpetuating oligarchy (a new class) intent on retaining power and privilege. Djilas was expelled from the Yugoslav party in 1954.

New Economic Policy   Often shortened to NEP, the New Economic Policy was introduced in Russia by Lenin at the Tenth Party Congress in Mar. 1921. Disturbances and food shortages had made it impossible to impose communism and some amelioration was introduced. Private commerce was permitted and state banks reintroduced. The incentives this provided helped to improve food production and created a more contented peasantry. The NEP was finally abandoned in Jan. 1929 in favour of the Five Year Plan and the collectivisation of agriculture.

'New Imperialism'   Term used to describe the more aggressive colonial policies of West European states in the later nineteenth century. This was epitomised by the 'scramble for Africa' in the 1880s which has been variously attributed to the need for secure markets for domestic manufactures, the need for investment opportunities, the need to assert international standing through the acquisition of colonies, or the need to introduce a foreign policy adventure as a unifying measure in domestic politics.

New Left   A term which emerged in Europe and the USA in the late 1950s to describe a strand of Marxist thought and action which followed the growing disillusion with the Soviet Union's model of socialism, particularly following the suppression of the 1956 Hungarian uprising. Rejecting the Vulgar Marxism of economic determinism, the New Left turned its attention to such concepts as cultural hegemony and alienation. The 1968 events in Europe and anti-Vietnam War activism in the USA marked the peak of New Left influence.

New Nationalism   Term used in the 1990s to describe the revival of nationalism following the collapse of communism. 'New Nationalism' was a major force in the Baltic states, in former Yugoslavia (as in the breakaway of Slovenia and Croatia) and in such conflicts as the Civil War in Bosnia.

'New Order'   Expression denoting Hitler's concept of a Europe integrated under centralised political and economic control. Nazi propaganda was directed towards convincing the world that such a system would benefit all of Europe rather than merely provide the economic resources desired by Germany.

Night of the Long Knives   Night of 29–30 June 1934 when the SS, on Hitler's orders, murdered Captain Ernst Röhm and some 150 other SA leaders. Non-Nazis were also murdered, including the ex-Chancellor General Kurt von Schleicher and his close friend General Kurt von Bredow. The aim of the slaughter was to crush the political power of the SA. In a speech in Berlin on 13 July 1934 Hitler announced that 61 persons, part of an alleged conspiracy, had been shot; a further 13 had died resisting arrest, and 3 had committed suicide. It has been claimed since, however, that more than 1,000 were killed. Hitler first described the episode as 'the Night of the Long Knives' during the speech.

'Nine, the'   Members of the EEC (now EU) between 1973 (when Britain, Ireland and Denmark joined) and 1982 when Greece became the tenth member.

North Atlantic Treaty Organisation   *See* **NATO**.

Northern League   Italian political movement (*Lega Nord*), formed in 1991 which represents the rising populist force of northern Italy. It won 55 seats and 8.7 per cent of the vote in 1992. The Party is anti-Rome, anti-Mafia, anti-immigrant and anti-tax. It is led by Umberto Bossi. Part of the 1994 Berlusconi alliance. In 1996 it declared the 'independent republic of Padania'.

November criminals   Term of abuse commonly used in Germany between 1918 and 1945 to describe those persons who had negotiated the country's surrender in 1918 and the subsequent Treaty of Versailles. They were made scapegoats for the economic and military collapse of Germany in 1918.

Nuremberg Rallies   Mass rallies of hundreds of thousands of people staged by the Nazis at their Party Congresses in Nuremberg between 1933 and 1938. These rallies made great use of oratory and other propaganda devices to appeal to observers and participants.

OAS (*Organisation de l'Armée Secrete*)   French terrorist organisation which posed a serious threat to the Fifth Republic. Most members were ex-Algerian colonists aggrieved at President Charles de Gaulle's desire to end the Algerian War (1954–62), which led to Algerian independence.

October Revolution   Seizure of power in Russia by the Bolsheviks led by Lenin on 6–7 Nov. 1917 (Oct. in the Julian calendar). Their chance came after the failure of the February Revolution to end the war and food shortages. A successful coup was led in the capital, St Petersburg, from Bolshevik headquarters in the Smolny Institute against the Kerensky government in the Winter Palace on the night of 6 Nov. The next day an All-Russian Congress of Soviets authorised the Bolsheviks to establish a Council of the People's Commissars which was to assume executive power. On a promise of 'Peace, Land, Bread' the Bolsheviks were able to take power in other cities. Workers were given control of the factories, private trade was abolished and property belonging to the Church and to 'counter-revolutionaries' was confiscated by the state. For the subsequent Civil War, *see* p. 176.

Octobrist   A section of the Russian liberal constitutional movement. The movement had been divided by the October Manifesto of 1905 into Octobrists and Kadets. The former were right-wing and prepared to co-operate with the government in the Duma. The party was supported by the right-wing of the Zemstvo movement and business classes.

Oder–Neisse Line   Boundary along the rivers Oder and Neisse between Poland and Germany giving to Poland a fifth of Germany's 1938 territory and a sixth of its population, provisionally agreed by the US, UK and USSR at Yalta and Potsdam. Not officially recognised by West Germany until 18 Nov. 1970 as part of Brandt's *Ostpolitik* reconciliation.

OGPU   Soviet security police agency, established in 1922 as the GPU and retitled OGPU after the formation of the USSR in 1923. Founded to suppress counter-revolution and enemies of the system, it was used by the leadership to uncover political dissidents and, after 1928, in enforcing the collectivisation of agriculture. After 1930 it monopolised police activities in the Soviet Union before being absorbed by the NKVD in 1934.

Ossis   West German term for East Germans, in common usage after reunification in 1990.

Ostpolitik   Eastern policy developed in the German Federal Republic by Kurt Kiesinger to normalise relations with those communist countries, other than the Soviet Union, which recognised the German Democratic Republic. It led to the conclusion of peace treaties with the USSR and Poland (1972) and border agreements over traffic and communication between East and West Berlin.

Ottoman (deriv. Turk. *Osman*)   Dynasty, founded by Osman, which ruled the Turkish Empire until the abolition of the sultanate in 1922. In decline throughout the nineteenth century, it finally collapsed under the impact of nationalism from within, and its defeat in the First World War.

Overlord   Codename for the Normandy landings of 1944 by the Allied armies. The name was first used in Aug. 1943 at the conference of Roosevelt and Churchill in Quebec. The logistics of the landings were staggering. On D-Day 4,000 ships left Britain for the coast of Normandy. More than a million and a half American troops had already been transported to Britain for the landings. By 12 June 326,000 men were established in a bridgehead 50 miles wide. By 2 July a million Allied troops were in France. On 15 Aug. another US army landed in the south of France and by the end of 1944 most of France and Belgium had been liberated.

OVRA   Secret police established in fascist Italy in 1927 to reinforce Mussolini's dictatorship.

Paasikivi Line   Term used to describe Finland's postwar foreign policy, particularly in its stance towards the neighbouring Soviet Union, named after Juno Kusti Paasikivi, the country's President from 1946 to 1956.

Pact of Steel   Military alliance concluded between Nazi Germany and fascist Italy in 1939.

Pamyat   A right-wing Russian nationalist movement which emerged in the late 1980s. It contained anti-Semitic and fascist elements.

Pan-Germanism   In German, *Alldeutschtum*, an imperialist movement aimed at uniting all German-speakers in a common empire. It was fostered in the first decade of the twentieth century by the *Alldeutscher Verband* (Pan-Germany Association) headed by a lawyer named Heinrich Class. Its programme included the conquest of territories in Eastern Europe, colonial expansion overseas and naval rearmament. Class was also anti-Semitic. Pan-Germanism was particularly strong in the German-speaking areas of the Austrian empire. Some Pan-Germanists even regarded the Low Countries as German, their Dutch and Belgian inhabitants being termed Lower Germans. They differed from the *Grossdeutsche* (Greater Germans), who also sought unification of German-speaking peoples but were liberal, did not subscribe to extreme racial theories and did not seek an aggressive expansion of territory.

Pan-Slavism   The name given to the various movements for closer union of peoples speaking Slavic languages in the nineteenth and early twentieth centuries. By the 1880s Russia had transformed Pan-Slavism into an instrument to justify its control over Poland and the Ukraine and to spread its influence into the Balkans. Pan-Slavism as an ideology ended with the 1917 Russian Revolution although there have sometimes been suggestions of its revival as, for example, with Russian interest in the fate of Serbia in the 1990s following the break-up of Yugoslavia.

Panzer (Ger. 'armour')   Term used to refer to an individual tank or armoured vehicle, or to denote an armoured division.

Papal Infallibility   Doctrine of the Roman Catholic Church proclaimed at the Vatican Council of 1870 which holds that papal pronouncements on matters of faith and morals are not open to question. The basis of the doctrine is that not all questions are answered by the Bible and that further guidance has to be provided in an authoritative way. It has also been argued that the extension of the Pope's spiritual power was in response to the loss of temporal power over the previous 500 years.

Parteiengesetz   The 1967 Party Law in Germany which regulated the position of political parties and also provided for partial financing by the state.

Partisans   Term originating with the Russians who raided French supply lines on Napoleon's 1812 Moscow campaign; now used generally to refer to armed bands offering resistance behind enemy lines. In the Second World War it took on a specifically left-wing connotation when Stalin urged partisan activities

'Prague Spring' Name given to the period of attempted liberalisation in Czechoslovakia under Dubček as Secretary of the Communist Party in spring 1968. The attempt was brought to an end by the intervention of Warsaw Pact troops in Aug. 1968 and Dubček's replacement by Husak.

Proletkult In Russia, a movement established before the Oct. 1917 Revolution which attempted to create a working-class culture separate, though derived from, bourgeois and peasant culture and, after the Revolution, to remain independent of the Communist Party. By 1920, *Proletkult* had 400,000 members and published 20 journals but Lenin objected to the movement's wish to remain outside the Party's orbit and in Dec. it was absorbed into the People's Commissariat of Education.

Provisional government The government of Russia between Mar. and Oct. 1917. Brought to power after the deposition of the monarchy, the provisional government was made up of members of the Duma but had to share power in Petrograd with the Workers' and Soldiers' Soviet. Rule ended by the Bolshevik Revolution and the creation of a Soviet government.

Purges *See* Yezhovshchina.

Putsch (Ger.) A term used to describe a right-wing *coup d'état* in Germany. Most notable was the Kapp Putsch in 1920 when a journalist, Wolfgang Kapp, and a number of disaffected army officers attempted to overthrow the government in Berlin. The plot was foiled by the indifference of the regular army and the opposition of the trade unions. Also notorious was the ill-fated Beer Hall Putsch, involving Hitler and General Ludendorff in Munich on 9 Nov. 1923.

Quai d'Orsay Embankment of the River Seine in Paris where the French Foreign Office is situated. Term synonymous with the conduct of French foreign affairs.

Quisling Name originating in England during the Second World War to describe a collaborator, Fifth-Columnist or traitor, derived from Vidkun Quisling (1887–1945) leader of the Norwegian *Nasjonal Samling* (National Unity) movement founded in 1933 in imitation of the German Nazi Party. In Dec. 1939 Quisling met Hitler and discussed a possible *coup d'état* in Oslo; in Apr. 1940 he revealed details of Norwegian defences to the Germans. He became head of a puppet government after the German invasion of Apr. 1940 and was executed for treason in Oct. 1945.

Race to the sea, the Term used to describe the attempts from Sept. to Nov. 1914 by the Franco–British forces and the German armies to outflank each other in northern France and reach the Channel. The attempt ended with a line of trenches reaching from the North Sea to Switzerland from which the armies faced one another until 1918.

Rada (Ukrainian/Belorussian, council) A Ukrainian Central Rada was formed in revolutionary Kiev in Mar. 1917 with non-Bolshevik Social Democrats,

Social Revolutionaries and Socialist Federalists having most influence. The Rada's objective of national autonomy aroused little sympathy from the Petrograd provisional government but following the October Revolution the Rada declared a Ukrainian People's Republic in Jan. 1918 and signed the Treaty of Brest-Litovsk with Germany in Mar. However, in Apr. Germany dissolved the Rada and established a puppet government.

Rapacki Plan Plan proposed by Polish Foreign Minister Adam Rapacki (1909–70) in the UN General Assembly on 2 Oct. 1957 and developed and presented to diplomatic representatives in Warsaw on 2 Feb. 1958. It recommended that there should be no manufacturing or stationing of nuclear weapons in Poland, Czechoslovakia, East or West Germany. The USSR approved the plan but the USA and Britain rejected it, partly because it favoured the USSR which had larger numbers of conventional forces, and partly because the USSR wished it to be preceded by direct talks on the future of East and West Germany, a course unacceptable to the latter country.

Rassemblement Pour la République (RPR) Major French political party. The RPR was formed as a successor to the UDR following tensions between the Gaullist and Giscardian wings and the resignation of Jacques Chirac in 1976. It became the largest party in parliament after the 1993 elections with 247 seats. In 1997 it returned 134 members.

Red Army Army of the former USSR, taken from the red flag of socialist revolution. The original communist army in Russia was hastily assembled and organised by Trotsky (1879–1940) as Commissar for War to fight off the counter-revolutionary ('White') armies assembled in Dec. 1917 to crush the Oct. Revolution. Until 1946 the army's official name was 'the Red Army of Workers and Peasants'.

Red Army Faction Radical wing of Baader–Meinhof terrorist group.

Red Brigades Left-wing urban terrorist groups active in Italy, particularly after the economic crisis of the 1970s. The Italian counterpart of the German Baader–Meinhof group.

Red Terror Imprisonment or execution of opponents of the Bolshevik government established by the Oct. Revolution.

Refuseniks Predominantly Jewish citizens who were refused permission to emigrate from the USSR by the authorities during the Soviet era. With the fall of communism there has been a large exodus to Israel.

Reich (Ger.) The term used to describe the German Empire. The First Reich was considered to have been the Holy Roman Empire and thus the unified Germany after 1870 was known as the Second or *Kaiserreich*. This enabled Hitler's ideas of an enlarged Germany to be known as the Third Reich, although this name was officially dropped in the 1930s.

Reichsbanner   An unarmed uniformed defence force attached to the German Social Democratic Party, formed in Feb. 1924, and which collapsed as Hitler consolidated power in 1933.

Reichstag   The German parliament (building) in Berlin. The building was destroyed by fire on 28 Feb. 1933; its destruction was used by the Nazis for propaganda purposes against the left and to pass a number of restrictive decrees.

Rentenmark   New currency introduced into Germany in 1923 by Chancellor Gustav Stresemann (1878–1929). It was necessary to help stabilise the economy after the French had occupied the Ruhr following the German failure to pay reparations.

Reparations   Payments imposed on powers defeated in war to recompense the costs to the victors. Most commonly associated with the payments inflicted on Germany at the end of the First World War, although the actual amount was not fixed until Apr. 1921 when the sum was set at £6,600 million plus interest. The Dawes and Young Plans later reduced the repayments until the effects of the Depression caused reparations payments to be abandoned after Lausanne in 1932. Apart from their international ramifications, reparations payments played an important part in the domestic politics of the Weimar Republic.

Resistance   The popular term for the opposition to the Nazi regime, both inside Germany and in the occupied countries, 1940–45. From Jan. 1942 the Free French began to organise resistance groups and in May 1943 the *Maquis* liberated Corsica. By 1945 resistance groups were active throughout Europe but were often divided among themselves on ideological grounds, providing the basis for postwar political conflicts.

Revisionist   Term applied by orthodox Marxists to one who attempts to re-assess the basic tenets of revolutionary socialism. Originating in Germany in the 1890s and 1900s, its chief exponents were Edouard Bernstein and Karl Kautsky. Regarded as heresy in the Soviet Union, the Cuban, Chinese and Albanian Communists used the same term to describe the Moscow line.

Rexists   Belgian fascist party formed in 1936 by Léon Degrelle and which actively collaborated with the German occupiers from 1940. At the outbreak of the Second World War the Rexists had four parliamentary representatives. The term derived from 'Christus Rex', the slogan of a right-wing Catholic youth group.

Right deviationism   A faction in the Soviet Communist Party in 1927–28 led by Bukharin, Rykov and Tomsky which, while accepting Stalin's proposals for industrialisation, urged a gradual approach and rejected too forceful a move against the Kulaks and the New Economic Policy. Effectively removed from influence in 1929, the three leading spokesmen were later killed in Stalin's purges.

Rocardism   Attempt by the French socialist Prime Minister Michel Rocard to create a progressive consensus after the May 1988 general election by sharing power with centre parties. Non-socialist ministers were allocated half the government posts, but although the policy was encouraged by President Mitterrand it divided socialist supporters.

Rodobrana   A fascist parliamentary body established by the Hlinka Slovak People's Party in Slovakia during the Second World War.

Romanov   The family name of the Russian royal house whose dynasty was ended by the deposition of Tsar Nicholas II in 1917 after the Russian Revolution. He was executed with his family at Ekaterinburg on 16–17 July 1918.

Rome, Treaty of   The founding treaty of 25 Mar. 1957 which established the European Common Market (signed by Belgium, France, Italy, Luxembourg, the Netherlands and West Germany). The treaty created the European Economic Community, a 'Common Market' with the free movement of labour and capital, abolition of internal tariffs and unified external tariffs. *See* pp. 203–4.

Rostock   East German town which gained notoriety on 25 Aug. 1992 for violent disorders directed against asylum-seeking foreign nationals. Neo-Nazi extremists set fire to a reception centre for asylum seekers. Some German residents clearly approved of this action and the local police were slow in stopping the violence. The episode was a dramatic indication of the strength of extremist right-wing support in Germany and of a renascent racism.

Rukh   The name of the nationalist movement in the Ukraine which sought independence from the Soviet Union. Ukraine declared independence on 24 Aug. 1991, confirmed by a referendum on 1 Dec.

Russia's Choice   Russian political party. At one time, the main pro-government, pro-Yeltsin party. Led by Yegor Gaidar, the architect of the Yeltsin economic reforms, it was committed to reduce state involvement in economic management.

Russification   To make Russian in culture, language, customs, etc. Both under the Tsar and communist rule, attempts were made at Russifying the national minorities of the Russian empire and the former USSR to prevent regionalism and a break-up of the state.

SA   Abbreviation of the German *Sturmabteilung* or Storm Battalion, sometimes known as 'Brownshirts' from their uniform. Groups of ex-soldiers organised in quasi-military formations from 1923 to support the Nazis. Under their leader, Röhm, the force grew rapidly to an estimated four and a half million men by June 1934, when both Hitler's and the army's fear of its power prompted Hitler's murder of Röhm and the leaders of the SA in the 'Night of the Long Knives' (30 June 1934). Although it remained in existence, the power of the SA as a political force was broken.

Saar Major German industrial region on the French–German border with rich coal deposits. After the Second World War the Saar was occupied by French troops and incorporated economically into France. A referendum in 1955 voted for reunification with Germany, which was finally achieved in 1959.

Safe havens Term for the UN-protected Bosnian Muslim enclaves established in spring 1993 during the Bosnian Civil War. They included Srebenica, Goradze, Bihac, Sarajevo, etc. The UN frequently proved powerless to protect Muslim communities as the Serbs moved in.

Sahovnica The chequerboard flag of Croatia last used by the Uštaše in the Second World War.

Sajudis The name of the nationalist movement in the Baltic Republic of Lithuania. Led by Vytautas Landsbergis, it declared independence from Russia in 1989. In Jan. 1991, the despatch of Russian paratroops to Vilnius, the Lithuanian capital, caused a political crisis. Landsbergis guided his country to independence in Sept. 1991.

Salami tactics Policy of the postwar Hungarian Communist Party under Matyas Rakosi to undermine its coalition allies. The arrest of Smallholders' Party leader Bela Kovacs in Feb. 1947 was followed in May by the exile of Prime Minister Ferenc Nagy. The Social Democrats and the Democratic Populists were dissolved in 1948. The Communists took control of parliament in rigged elections held in May 1949.

SALT Strategic Arms Limitation Talks between America and the Soviet Union beginning in Nov. 1969 and ending in May 1972 with a treaty restricting anti-ballistic missile development. A second round opened in Nov. 1974 but proved less successful. Renewed talks under Gorbachev led to an outline agreement in 1991.

Samizdat (Russ. 'self-publishing') Secret literature produced by dissidents which circulated in the former Soviet Union as a means of avoiding censorship. Among the most significant productions was the *Chronicle of Current Events*, which began circulating in 1968. The authorities strongly disapproved of it and strict penalties were imposed on those who were caught.

Sanctions Term usually applied to economic boycott of one country by another. Sanctions were the chief weapon of the League of Nations on countries which were not thought to be fulfilling their international obligations. An economic boycott was imposed on Italy in Oct. 1935, following the invasion of Abyssinia, but its terms were limited and largely ineffective. These were finally lifted in July 1936. Similar sanctions were imposed on Rhodesia in 1965 by Britain and the UN but proved ineffective. European nations imposed sanctions on Iraq following its invasion of Kuwait in Aug. 1990. Sanctions were also imposed on Serbia during the Bosnia conflict.

Schengen Agreement An accord signed on 19 June 1990 in Schengen (Luxembourg) by certain EU members on the opening of their common borders.

The original signatories were France, Germany and the Benelux countries. Their borders were to be opened by 1992.

Schlieffen Plan   German military plan for offensive action named after Chief of German General Staff, Count Alfred von Schlieffen, and first produced in 1905. In spite of constant revision, the plan was the basis for the German attack in the west in Aug. 1914. The basic features of the plan were based upon the premise that Germany would have to fight both France and Russia in any future war. The plan therefore provided for a swift 'knock-out' blow against France, while remaining on the defensive against Russia. Crucially, the plan involved an attack through the neutral countries of Holland, Belgium and Luxembourg to avoid the strong defences on the Franco–German border, aiming to encircle Paris and force French surrender. Although modified subsequently, the plan to invade France via Belgium was used in 1914, bringing Great Britain into the war.

Schumann Plan   A key proposal of 9 May 1950 towards European co-operation. It was the step on the road to the creation of the European Economic Community, with the suggestion by French Foreign Minister Schumann that French and German coal and steel production be co-ordinated under a higher authority. The European Coal and Steel Community was created when Italy, Belgium and the Netherlands widened the agreement in 1952.

Scrap of Paper   German Chancellor Bethmann-Hollweg's description of the 1839 Treaty of London, a five-power guarantee of Belgian neutrality which Germany violated by invasion on 4 Aug. 1914, provoking a British declaration of war. He told the British ambassador that 'just for a scrap of paper, Great Britain is going to make war on a kindred nation which desires nothing better than to be friends with her'.

Second Front   Following the German attack on the Soviet Union in June 1941, Stalin asked Britain to launch an invasion in Western Europe to ease the pressure on Russia. Churchill was reluctant to do so without long preparation, despite a vigorous 'Second Front Now' campaign in Britain in 1942. The Second Front – agreed at the Quebec Conference in Aug. 1943 – opened with the Normandy landings on 6 June 1944.

Second International   Formed in Paris in 1889 and based on membership of national parties and trade unions, the Second International was a loose federation which held periodic international congresses. It stood for parliamentary democracy and thus rejected anarchist ideas, but also reaffirmed the commitment to Marxist ideas of the class struggle. Thus there was no question of co-operation with non-socialist parties in power. A main aim was to try to avert war, but the International effectively ended in 1914 although attempts to revive it were made in 1919.

Second Reich   The German Empire 1871–1918, also known as the *Kaiserreich*; the period after German unification when William I, King of Prussia, was offered the throne of the Empire. The last Kaiser, William II, was forced to

321

abdicate after the German army refused to support him at the end of the First World War.

Second Vatican Council   Second ecumenical council of the Roman Catholic Church in modern times, summoned by Pope John XXIII in Jan. 1959. Its purpose was to consider increased collaboration with other churches and renewal of the faith. Over 8,000 bishops attended in Rome when the council opened on 11 Oct. 1962. The council lasted a year and published 16 decrees pointing towards a closer relationship with non-Catholic churches, the use of the vernacular rather than Latin in the liturgy and a greater humanism in Catholic doctrine. The Council marked a major turning-point in the Church's relations with other faiths.

Securitate   The Romanian secret police under the Ceausescu dictatorship. Their brutal suppression of disturbances in Timisoara in Dec. 1989 sparked the Romanian Revolution. Their loyalty and fanaticism caused hundreds of deaths in the Civil War (*see* p. 180). The *Securitate* was disbanded by the new provisional government.

Sèvres   Location of the secret pact between Britain and France when they colluded during the Suez Crisis (*see* p. 179).

SHAPE (Supreme Headquarters, Allied Powers in Europe)   Headquarters of the North Atlantic Treaty Organisation, initially at Fontainebleau, then from 1966 in Brussels.

Show trial   Trial to which great publicity is given for propaganda purposes, held in a way that appears just but with the verdict predetermined. Show trials were numerous in the USSR during the Stalinist purges.

Siegfried Line   Originally, the defences between Lens and Rheims on the German Western Front in Sept. 1918; later, the defences built to emulate the Maginot Line which the Nazis believed invulnerable. American forces reached this German line of defence in the West on 1 Feb. 1945; British and Canadian forces broke through it the same month, crossing the Rhine near Millingen in the northern sector where the line was weaker on 8–9 Feb.

Single European Act   Act agreed in Dec. 1985 at the Luxembourg Summit of European Community leaders and subsequently ratified by the member states. The Act agreed to steps to establish a complete internal market by 31 Dec. 1992. Other proposals included deregulation to help small businesses; the goal of monetary union to be 'progressively realised'; and co-operation in the sphere of foreign policy to promote the development of a European identity. The Act also provided for a system of qualified majority voting in the Council of the EEC. The Act came into force on 1 July 1987.

Sinn Fein   Gaelic for 'Ourselves alone'. Irish Nationalist Party founded in 1902 by Arthur Griffiths (1872–1922) and formed into the Sinn Fein League in 1907–08 when it absorbed other nationalist groups. The group rose to prominence in the 1913–14 Home Rule crisis when many Sinn Feiners joined the Irish

Volunteers and many Dublin workers joined the organisation. Sinn Fein members were involved in the Easter Rising in 1916. Sinn Fein continues to campaign for a United Ireland to include the 'six counties' of Ulster.

Situationism   A left-wing 'critique of everyday life' made by the Situationist International, which was formed in 1957, collapsed in the early 1970s, and had an affinity with Council Communism. Situationism advocated a revolutionary overthrow of capitalism based not on traditional political methods but on total rejection in every sphere of what it saw as consumer society's banality. Situationist slogans were prominent in the May Events (the 1968 student revolt in France) and its rhetoric has widely influenced the European left.

Sitzkrieg   Ironic pun on the German term *Blitzkrieg* to describe the period of military inactivity on the Western Front between Sept. 1939 and May 1940, known in Britain as the 'Phoney War'.

'Six, the' Name given to the members of the EC prior to the entry of Britain, Denmark and Ireland in 1973.

Slansky Trial   The largest Stalinist show trial outside the Soviet Union, with Slansky, the Czech vice-premier and Communist Party Secretary, and thirteen others, eleven of whom were Jews, falsely charged in Nov. 1951 with treason, Zionism, Titoism, Trotskyism and bourgeois nationalism. Eleven were found guilty in Nov. 1952 and Slansky was hanged on 2 Dec. The trial was linked to the obsessive anti-Semitism of Stalin's final years.

Social Chapter   Section of the 1991 Maastricht Treaty giving power to the European Commission to impose the terms of the Social Charter on common standards in employment policy without the possibility of a national veto. The Conservative government in Britain under John Major refused to take part, but the incoming Labour government in 1997 announced its intention to adhere.

Social Charter   The European Community (EC) Charter of Social Rights of Workers, setting out a pattern for a European labour law. Largely the work of Jacques Delors and his colleagues and opposed by right-wing Conservatives, especially in Britain, it guarantees such things as freedom of movement and equal treatment for workers throughout the Community, the right to strike, a guaranteed 'decent standard of living', freedom to join trade unions, the right to collective bargaining, etc. Britain secured an 'opt-out' from this provision (now called the Social Chapter) at Maastricht, but the Labour government elected in 1997 signalled its intention to join.

Social Democracy   Non-doctrinaire, socialist or socialist-inclined political movement of the nineteenth and twentieth centuries, combining concern for greater equality with acceptance of a mixed economy and representing a non-communist left-wing tradition often drawing support from organised labour. Notable examples include the Social Democratic Party of Germany, founded in 1875, and the Swedish Social Democratic Labour Party, formed in 1880.

Social Fascist Communist term of abuse towards Social Democratic and Labour Parties from 1928 to 1934, reflecting the Comintern view that moderate socialists who were rivals for working class support were 'the left wing of fascism'.

Socialism in One Country Doctrine expounded by Lenin in Russia after it became clear that the Revolution of 1917 was not going to affect the other states of Europe. The main task was to create a socialist society without help from outside, either political or economic.

Socialist realism The approved method of art and literature in the Soviet Union under Stalin, enforced by the control of the cultural unions over the origination, production and publication of artistic work. Expulsion from the appropriate union meant an end to publication/exhibition, and during the purges a large number of artists were sent to labour camps or killed. Others were forced to recant publicly after criticism, and conform to the dictates of the artistic unions. While a greater degree of freedom was permitted during the Second World War, Zhdanov reiterated the policy in the postwar era, maintaining an unflinching control over evidence of 'bourgeois individualism' in artistic output. Following Stalin's death there was a thaw under Khrushchev and during his destalinisation campaign the high-water mark came with the publication of Alexander Solzhenitsyn's *A Day in the Life of Ivan Denisovitch* in *Novy mir* in 1962.

Solidarity Polish trade union and reform movement formed in the 1970s to demand liberalisation of the Polish communist regime and the formation of free trade unions. Under its leader, Lech Walesa, the movement won important concessions from the government before the threat of Soviet invasion and the assumption of power by the Polish army led to the banning of the organisation and the imprisonment of its leaders. It survived as a clandestine organisation. The cause of Solidarity was vindicated with the collapse of communism in Poland. Despite divisions within the movement, Walesa was elected President of Poland in Dec. 1990 (although he was defeated in 1995).

Soviet (Russ. 'council') Russian administrative system. Workers' soviets originated in the Oct. Revolution of 1905 and reappeared in 1917 as key organs of the revolution and later of the national administrative machinery. Prior to 1936 a hierarchical system of soviets characterised Russian government, lower soviets electing the higher indirectly, e.g. district soviets chose regional soviets which in turn chose state soviets. The system was held to guarantee the participation of the masses in the political system, which was marked by the unity of executive and legislative power and by close links between state and local authorities. Indirect elections were abolished under the 1936 constitution and all soviets were directly elected by the people, whatever their level.

Sovkhoz State farm in the former USSR, state-owned and run by state employees. In the 1950s there were 4,000 of them and the *Agrogorad* was designed to further the system. *See also* **Kolkhoz**.

Sovnarkom   The Council of People's Commissars in the former Soviet Union.

Spartacists   A group of radical German socialists, active from early summer 1915, who founded the German Communist Party (KPD) in 1918. Following a week of street violence in Berlin in Jan. 1919, their leaders were either imprisoned or murdered by members of the *Freikorps*. The Spartacists were led by Rosa Luxemburg and Karl Liebknecht, both of whom opposed what they saw as the revisionist tendencies of the German Social Democratic Party. Their name was taken from that of Spartacus, leader of a slave revolt against Rome in 73 BC.

Spiegel Affair   West German political crisis of 1962. When the West German magazine *Der Spiegel* published an article critical of the German army, the Defence Minister, Franz-Josef Strauss, had the deputy editor and the writer of the article tried for treason for publishing military secrets. They were acquitted and Strauss was accused of abusing his powers because he had not used the usual legal channels and not informed the Minister of Justice. Strauss eventually resigned. The affair was essentially a confrontation over press freedom and ministerial authoritarianism in West Germany.

'Splendid Isolation'   Phrase used to describe Britain's diplomatic position in the latter part of the nineteenth century and, more generally, during the nineteenth century as a whole when Britain stood aside from entanglement in European alliances. The phrase was used in *The Times* in Jan. 1896 and subsequently (9 Nov.) by Lord Salisbury. The 'isolation' is customarily seen as being ended by the Anglo–Japanese Treaty of 1902.

Squadrismo   The activities of Italian nationalist youths, ex-servicemen and unemployed workers who formed gangs in the early 1920s to attack socialist and Catholic premises and individuals, to break strikes and who occupied the disputed territories of Fiume and Trentino in 1922. They were absorbed into Mussolini's Fascist Militia in 1923.

SS   Abbreviation of German *Schutzstaffel* or Guard Detachment, Hitler's personal bodyguard of dedicated Nazis founded in 1923 as a rival to Röhm's SA. Placed under the command of Heinrich Himmler in 1929, the SS carried out the liquidation of the SA leadership in June 1934 and in July became an independent organisation with its own armed units. *SS-Verfugunstruppe* (Special Task Troops), organised as regular soldiers, were formed from 1935 and as the *Waffen-SS* comprised a group of elite regiments, separate from army control. Other sections of the SS provided concentration camp guards – the *SS-Totenkopfverbande* – and police squads in occupied territory.

Stahlhelm   Paramilitary organisation, active in Weimar Germany, founded by Franz Seldte at Magdeburg in 1918. By 1930 it had 500,000 members. The Seldte wing of the *Stahlhelm* were moderate nationalists on good terms with Stresemann's *Deutsche Volkspartie*. But by 1924 a radical element led by Theodore Duesterberg had become powerful enough to push the *Stahlhelm* into violent

325

anti-republicanism and opposition to the 1929 Young Plan. In 1931 it helped organise the 'Harzburg Front' to unite national opposition to the Weimar Republic. Duesterberg ran for the presidency against Hindenburg and Hitler in 1932 but Seldte entered Hitler's Cabinet in Jan. 1933 and proved a loyal minister. Having initially approved this action, Duesterberg later changed his views and began attempting to obstruct Hitler's chancellorship. In Apr. 1933 he was removed from his post of second *Bündesführer* (league leader) in the *Stahlhelm*. Hitler's order to Seldte to liquidate the organisation was carried out by Nov. 1935.

Stalinism Stalin's revolution from above to build 'Socialism in One Country' forced agricultural collectivisation, laying the basis for rapid heavy industrial development. It was carried out in an atmosphere of intense nationalism and increasingly arbitrary rule exerted through a bureaucracy and was connected with Stalin's 'cult of personality' and the brutal political purges of the 1930s. Latterly, a general description of the regimes in the Soviet Union and its East European satellites during the communist era.

Stasi The name of the security police under the former communist regime in East Germany. They were disbanded in the revolution of 1989.

State capitalism Lenin's description of the compromise made with financial interests in 1918 to ensure Bolshevik survival, while simultaneously reinforcing central control over the economy. More recently, a pejorative description of Soviet socialism in which a privileged bureaucracy is said collectively to dominate economic life with the same relationship to the working class as employers under private capitalism.

Straits Question The issue of rights of passage through the Dardanelles and the Bosphorus which was disputed between the Great Powers and the Ottoman Empire at several points in the nineteenth and twentieth centuries. A series of conventions laid down restrictions on the classes of warships permitted to use the waterway.

Stresa Front Name of agreements made at the Stresa Conference, 11–14 Apr. 1935, attended by the leaders of Italy, Britain and France. They agreed a common front against Hitler's intention to rearm and reform the *Luftwaffe*, condemning Germany's actions and supporting the Locarno Treaties. Britain's separate agreement with Germany on naval matters in June 1935, France's negotiations with Russia to form a pact in May, and Italy's invasion of Ethiopia in Oct. undermined the Front's impact.

Succession states The states formed after the First World War from the territory of the former Austro–Hungarian Empire, or incorporating parts of it. These included Poland, Czechoslovakia, Yugoslavia, Romania, Hungary and Austria. The term can also be applied to the new countries which emerged from the break up of Yugoslavia (Slovenia, Croatia, Bosnia–Herzegovina) and the Soviet Union (Belarus, Ukraine, Moldova, etc.) in the 1990s.

Sudetenland   German-speaking area of northern Bohemia assigned to Czechoslovakia in 1919. Claimed by Hitler for the Reich, the Sudetenland became the centre of an international crisis in 1938 over Germany's attempt to revise the Versailles Treaty by force. The threat of general European war was temporarily averted by the Munich Agreement in which Czechoslovakia was forced to cede the Sudetenland to Germany.

Suez Crisis   *See* p. 179.

Swastika   Ancient religious symbol in the shape of a hooked cross. In European mythology it became linked with the revival of Germanic legends at the end of the nineteenth century. Adopted by a number of extreme right-wing groups in Germany after the First World War, including the Erhardt Brigade, a *Freikorps* unit active in the Kapp Putsch. It was also adopted by Hitler as the symbol of National Socialism and in Sept. 1935 became Nazi Germany's national emblem.

Syndicalism   Theory which advocates the ownership and organisation of industry by workers and their organisations – usually trade unions. This is in contrast to the socialist theory of ownership by the state. Syndicalism is also associated with the belief in the power of trade unionism and the use of the general strike as a weapon to bring about major social and political change. Although often associated with anarchists, many of the syndicalists in the 1920s joined the communist or fascist parties.

Syndicat (Fr. 'trade union')   The basic form of syndicalist activity.

Tangentopoli   The 'City of Bribes' corruption scandal that erupted in Italy in 1992, discrediting the entire political system and threatening to bring down the First Republic which had been founded in 1946. Large numbers of politicians from across the party spectrum were accused of accepting bribes from businessmen in return for contracts and favours.

Test-Ban Treaty   Treaty signed on 5 Aug. 1963 whereby the USA, the USSR and Britain agreed not to test nuclear weapons under the ocean, in outer space or in the atmosphere. Underground testing was not prohibited. The treaty, the conclusion of five years' negotiation, formalised the voluntary restraint from nuclear testing exercised by the signatories between 1958 and 1961. France and China refused to sign and continued nuclear tests.

Third International   Otherwise known as the Communist International or the Comintern. Founded by Lenin in Mar. 1919 to unite revolutionary socialists. Finally disbanded by Stalin in May 1943 as a concession to his Western allies.

Third Reich   Term used to describe the Nazi dictatorship in Germany, 1933–45. Originally coined by the Nazis to describe the expanded Germany of their theories, the term was dropped from official usage in the 1930s.

Third Republic   The term used to describe the government of France from the Franco–Prussian War in 1871 to the fall of France in 1940 and the establishment of the Vichy regime.

327

Titoism   Term for the political philosophy of Josip Tito in Yugoslavia. It was characterised by rejection of Stalinism, and also of nationalism, and an emphasis on economic progress. Above all it was designed to preserve the political stability of Yugoslavia.

Total war   Term of twentieth-century origin meaning a war in which all of a nation's resources (economic, human, ideological, etc.) are mobilised in the effort to win. Applicable, for example, to the war efforts of Germany, the Soviet Union and Britain in the Second World War.

Totenkopfverbände (Ger. 'death's head units')   Paramilitary sub-unit of the SS, who served from 1935 onwards as concentration camp guards. In 1940 the youngest and fittest were formed into an élite fighting division, the Totenkopf Division, and integrated into the Waffen SS.

Tripartism   Name given to the joint governments of Christian Democrats, Socialists and the Communists formed in France and Italy in the immediate aftermath of the Second World War. Tripartism lasted in France until May 1947 when communist ministers were dismissed, while in Italy a Christian Democrat government was formed in Apr. 1947 without communist support. The end of tripartism reflected the hardening of the battle-lines of the Cold War after the temporary co-operation of former resistance partners.

Triple Alliance   Alliance formed between Germany, Austria–Hungary and Italy in 1882.

Triple Entente   Agreement between Britain, France and Russia to resolve their outstanding colonial differences; it became a military alliance in 1914. Sometimes referred to as the Quadruple Entente because of the agreements with Japan.

Trizonia   Term used in the 1940s and 1950s to denote the combined British, French and American zones of occupation in Germany.

Trotskyist   Communist who supports the views of Leon Trotsky, the assumed name of Lev Bronstein (1870–1940), who was ousted from power in the USSR by Stalin in 1924 and later assassinated by Russian agents in Mexico. Trotsky held that the excessive Russian nationalism developed under Stalin was incompatible with genuine international communism, and that Stalin's concentration on the economic development of the USSR could only result in a cumbersome bureaucracy and a purely nationalist outlook. After the Soviet invasion of Hungary in 1956 many members of Western communist parties resigned their allegiance to Soviet communism and turned to Trotskyism.

Truman Doctrine   Policy of the US government announced by President Truman in Mar. 1947 that the USA would not attack the Soviet Union but would rather seek to contain communism within its present limits and actively prevent its extension into new countries. The policy was occasioned by Britain informing the USA that for economic reasons she could no longer support the anti-communist forces in the Greek Civil War, thus requiring Truman to offer American aid to Greece instead. The Doctrine was, however, soon shown to be inadequate by the failure of the Americans to prevent the fall of China to the Communists in Oct. 1949. *See* Cold War.

Tsar (or Czar)   Title of the Russian rulers. It was used until the abdication in 1917 and execution in 1918 of Tsar Nicholas II. The Tsar's eldest son was known as the *Tsarevitch*, and his wife as the *Tsarina*.

Twentieth Party Congress   The landmark 1956 Congress of the Communist Party of the Soviet Union. A secret speech by Soviet Communist Party First Secretary Khrushchev at the proceedings denounced Stalin's 'personality cult', the 1930s purges and other authoritarian excesses; acknowledged legitimacy of alternative roads to socialism than the Soviet model; and argued for 'peaceful coexistence' with the West. The speech had repercussions for communist regimes in Eastern Europe and communist parties in Western Europe.

Twenty-One Conditions   The terms left-wing parties seeking affiliation to the Comintern had to accept. They included organising on the Russian party model and acknowledging ultimate Comintern authority; agitating for a dictatorship of the proletariat; creating an illegal organisation for subversive work; rejecting syndicalism and reformism; conducting revolutionary propaganda in the armed forces; and supporting colonial liberation.

U-2 incident   The shooting down of a US Lockheed U-2 reconnaissance plane over Sverdlovsk in the USSR on 1 May 1960. Its pilot, Gary Powers, was taken prisoner but returned to the USA in Feb. 1962. Such flights had occurred since 1957 but the Russians used the incident for propaganda purposes, demanding an apology from the USA and breaking off the Paris summit conference (16–19 May 1960) when this was refused.

U-boats (Ger. *Untersee*, 'under the sea')   Submarines. In both world wars the German U-boat squadrons posed a serious threat to British merchant ships transporting vital supplies across the Atlantic. Their attacks were countered by the use of convoy tactics, weapons such as depth charges and, in the Second World War, the use of radar.

Ukase (Russ.)   In Russia, originally a decree by the Tsar which, since he was an absolute monarch, had the force of a legal enactment. Such decrees were issued by the Praesidium of the Supreme Soviet of the former USSR and had a similar authority.

Uniates   Catholics of the Eastern Orthodox rite, mainly living in Western Ukraine. Despite their long distinct identity, they were forcibly amalgamated in 1946 into the Russian Orthodox Church in order to suppress national identity in the Ukraine. Following a meeting of Pope John Paul II with Gorbachev in Dec. 1989, the Uniates were promised recognition. With the collapse of the Soviet Union, the Ukraine has regained its political and religious independence.

Unification Treaty   Common term for the treaty uniting East Germany (the German Democratic Republic) with the Federal Republic of Germany. Signed on 31 Oct. 1990.

Union de la Nouvelle République (UNR)   The Gaullist successor to the earlier RPF (*Rassemblement du Peuple Français*). With the establishment of the Fifth Republic in 1958, the UNR was created from various Gaullist movements (including the Union for French Renewal, the Republican Convention and the Workers Committee for the support of General de Gaulle). It won 234 seats in the 1958 election, but soon found itself divided on questions of leadership, organisation and policy, being united only by loyalty to de Gaulle and belief in the need for national renewal. However, during the 1960s it became more homogeneous and developed some of the reflexes of a political party. Gaullism survived the retirement of de Gaulle in 1970.

Union of Democrats for the Republic (UDR)   French political party, founded as a successor to the Gaullist Union for the New Republic (UNR) of 1958. It hoped to form a vehicle for policies that would continue Gaullism after the death of de Gaulle himself.

Union Sacrée (Fr. 'Sacred Union')   Government formed in France at the outbreak of the First World War which included, for the first time and as a symbol of national unity, two socialists among its members.

United Front   A Communist Party tactic which attempted to build temporary alliances with other socialist and working-class parties, ostensibly to face a common enemy, for example fascism. *See* Popular Front.

United Nations, the   *See* p. 208.

UNPROFOR (United Nations Protection Force)   Established in Mar. 1992 and deployed initially in Croatia to create the conditions of peace and security required to permit the negotiations of an overall political settlement of the Yugoslav crisis. Its activities were subsequently extended to Bosnia and Herzegovina, including the supply of relief food convoys and the protection of the Muslim 'safe havens'. By mid-1993 there were over 24,000 UN troops in former Yugoslavia, with France contributing 5,800 men.

Urban guerrillas   Those using terrorist tactics in cities in order to achieve political ends, for example the Red Brigades in Italy, the Red Army in Germany and also the IRA in Ulster.

Uštaše (Serbo–Croatian)   Traditional name employed by Croatian nationalist rebels, specifically adopted in 1929 by a secret terrorist organisation led by the fervent nationalist Ante Pavelić. During the 1930s the Uštaše committed numerous acts of terrorism against Yugoslavia, including the assassination of King Alexander in 1934. They operated from Austria, Hungary and Italy. In 1941 they set up an independent Croatian state, collaborated with the Germans and Italians, and committed atrocities against non-Croats in Yugoslavia, against communists and members of the Serbian Orthodox Church. Pavelić fled to South America after 1945 where he died, but the Uštaše survived as a Croatian separatist and anti-communist organisation.

Vatican 2   *See* **Second Vatican Council**.

Vedel Report   The report of the working party examining the problem of the enlargement of the European Parliament published in Brussels in 1972 by a working group set up by the Commission under the chairmanship of the distinguished French academic and lawyer, Professor Georges Vedel.

Velvet Chancellors   First postwar Chancellors of the Federal Republic of Germany (West Germany), notably Konrad Adenauer (1876–1967), Chancellor from 1949 to 1963.

Velvet Divorce   The division on 1 Jan. 1993 of Czechoslovakia into the separate states of the Czech Republic (10 million population) and Slovakia (5 million). So-called because of the apparent amicable nature of the separation, but also an ironic reference to the 1989 Velvet Revolution which overthrew communist rule.

Velvet Revolution   Title given to the popular uprisings in Prague and other Czech cities in 1989 which overthrew the communist regime.

Versailles Settlement   *See* pp. 192–3.

Vichy   French provincial spa town where the interim autocratic French government was established between July 1940 and July 1944. The Vichy regime was anti-republican, and collaborated extensively with the Germans who occupied the areas it controlled in Nov. 1942. After the liberation of France in 1944, Pétain and the Vichy ministers established a new headquarters inside Germany.

Virgin Lands Campaign   Campaign launched by Khrushchev in 1953 to develop the 'virgin lands' of steppe in Kazakhstan, western Siberia and south-east Russia as grain-growing areas. By 1956, 90 million acres had been brought under cultivation. Early good harvests up to 1956 were followed by declining yields and serious land erosion, all of which severely dented Khrushchev's reputation.

Vlasovites   Russian prisoners of war in the Second World War who fought on the German side under the leadership of General A. A. Vlasov.

Völkisch (Ger.)   Militant, aggressive nationalism, used particularly with reference to Nazi policies.

Volksgerichten   The so-called 'People's Courts' established in Nazi Germany to try political offences. The accused were not allowed to produce evidence in their defence. Over 7,000 people were brought before the courts and of these 2,000 were sentenced to death.

Volkskammer   The parliament of the former German Democratic Republic (East Germany) in East Berlin.

Waffen SS   Elitist military organisation, a sub-unit of the SS, with intense loyalty to Hitler. Waffen troops were all Aryans, but not necessarily German: they included volunteers from France, the Netherlands, Belgium, Hungary, Lithuania and Romania who joined primarily to fight against Bolsheviks.

There were 40 Waffen divisions in the field in the Second World War; the organisation helped put down the Warsaw Uprising in Apr. 1943.

Walloons   The French-speaking minority which inhabits industrial southern Belgium, comprising 45 per cent of the population. Although the constitution guarantees the protection of cultural and political rights, a *Mouvement Populaire Walloon* agitates for more autonomy within Belgium. *See* **Flemings**.

War Communism   Bolshevik policy in 1918 to meet the pressures of civil war and economic collapse, including nationalisation of larger enterprises and a state monopoly of exchange, the partial militarisation of labour, and the forced requisition of agricultural produce. War Communism's unpopularity and failure led to the New Economic Policy in Mar. 1921.

War criminal   A concept first enunciated in the 'Hang the Kaiser' campaign at the end of the First World War. In the 1946 Nuremberg Trials, 177 Nazis were indicted as war criminals for genocide and planning aggressive war, new and controversial concepts in international law. Ten were sentenced to death. Some of those accused of crimes in the wars of the 1990s in Yugoslavia have been brought to trial at The Hague as war criminals.

War Guilt Clause   Article 231 of the Versailles Treaty, compelling Germany to accept responsibility for the First World War and its ensuing damage. Intended to provide a legal basis for reparations claims made by the victors, it encouraged a bitterness which added to the difficulties of the Weimar Republic.

Warsaw Pact   Military alliance of the USSR and East European satellites formed when the Eastern European Mutual Assistance Treaty was signed in 1955 by the communist states in Europe (except Albania and Yugoslavia). The treaty made joint provision for mutual defence for 20 years and represented the communist, especially Russian, response to the formation of NATO in 1949 and the rearming of the Federal Republic of Germany. The Pact permitted the USSR to keep forces in the satellite states and had a united command structure, reinforced by regular exercises and manoeuvres. Following the collapse of communism in Eastern Europe, by late 1990 the Warsaw Pact had effectively ceased to exist as a military alliance.

Warsaw Uprising   As the Soviets approached Warsaw in 1944, the Polish Home Army rose up against the Germans on 1 Aug. The Red Army halted its advance, leaving the Poles to fight on alone. All appeals for help were ignored and reinforcements disarmed. The Poles could not resist unaided and surrendered on 2 Oct. 1944. Warsaw was liberated on 17 Jan. 1945.

Weimar   Town where the German National Constituent Assembly met in Feb. 1919. It gave its name to the German Republic of 1918–33. The town was chosen to allay fears of the Allied Powers and the other German states about Prussian domination in Berlin, and also to escape from the associations attached to the former capital city. The economic problems which beset the Weimar Republic and the concomitant unemployment facilitated the rise of Hitler, and in Mar. 1933 he suspended the Weimar Constitution of July 1919 to make way for the Third Reich.

Welfare capitalism   Post-Second World War West European mixed economies in which free enterprise capitalism co-existed with a state commitment to low unemployment, extensive social security and the provision of health and other social services. Called into question by the ascendancy of right-wing conservatism and the pressures of economic depression in the 1970s and 1980s.

Weltpolitik (Ger. lit. 'world politics')   A new trend in German foreign policy at the end of the nineteenth century. The Kaiser, Wilhelm II, determined to transform Germany into a first-rank global power. Ultra-nationalistic pressure combined with social and economic forces to support new interest in colonial expansion, the scramble for territory in China and Africa, and the establishment of a powerful navy.

Wende   German term for a major political turning point or landmark event (e.g. the fall of communist East Germany and the subsequent reunification of Germany).

Werner Report   Report prepared in 1970 by a committee set up by the Finance Ministers of the European Community, and chaired by the Prime Minister of Luxembourg, Pierre Werner. It set out a plan for increased economic integration between the member states of the European Community, intended to lead to economic and monetary union by 1980. Subsequent economic crises prevented the full implementation of the report.

White Armies   Most frequently used of the opponents of the Bolshevik Revolution of 1917 in Russia. The anti-Communists organised the White Armies, who took part in the White Terror.

White House   The site of the Russian Parliament in Moscow. It was at the heart of the August coup of 1991.

White March   Name of the protest demonstration in Oct. 1996 by 325,000 Belgian citizens in Brussels to show their outrage at political patronage and corruption in the country. The march was sparked by the paedophile scandal at Charleroi.

White Russians   Term for Russians living on the western border of the Soviet Union (now the independent state of Belarus) but used generally to describe counter-revolutionary forces in the aftermath of the Bolshevik Revolution of 1917.

Winter Revolution   *See* Christmas Revolution.

Winter War   The invasion of Finland by the USSR. Intensive fighting in harsh conditions took place between 30 Nov. 1939 and 12 Mar. 1940. *See* p. 177.

Wirtschaftswunder   The rapid recovery of the West German economy after 1945. The term means economic miracle.

Yaoundé, Convention(s) of   The agreements which pre-dated the Lomé Convention with the EC. The first Yaoundé Convention was signed on 1 July 1963 at Yaoundé, the capital of Cameroon and was in effect from 1 June 1964 for five years; the second Yaoundé Convention was signed on 29 July 1969 to run from 1 Jan. 1971 to 31 Jan. 1975. The Conventions were made between the then EEC and 18 independent African states under Part IV of the Treaty of Rome. The first Convention provided for the abolition of tariffs between the associated states and the EEC, and made provisions to ease trade in agricultural goods. It also covered the provision of aid. The second Convention increased this aid.

Year of Martyrdom   Term used by the Romanian fascist movement, the Iron Guard, of the cycle of murder and revenge during 1938–39. The period began with the arrest and murder 'while attempting to escape' of Codreanu and other Iron Guard leaders in 1938. The Iron Guard assassinated Prime Minister Calinescu in Oct. 1939.

Yezhovshchina (Russ.)   A word used to describe the Stalinist purges of the 1920s and 1930s. The name derives from the head of the Soviet secret police, N. I. Yezhov.

Young Pioneers   Communist youth organisation in former USSR.

Young Plan   Plan proposed by US businessman Owen D. Young (1874–1962) on 7 June 1929 as a means of settling German reparations. He suggested that the level of reparations should be reduced by 75 per cent and that remaining payments should be made in the form of annuities paid into an international bank until 1988. Germany accepted the plan in Aug. 1929, but when Hitler became Chancellor in 1933 he refused to pay and thus ended the plan.

Young Turks   Liberal reform movement among young army officers in the Ottoman Empire, active between 1903 and 1909. The rebellion of 1908 led to the creation of a 'Committee of Union and Progress', headed by Enver Bey, Ahmed Djemel and Mehmed Talaat. They persuaded the Sultan to re-establish constitutional rule and convene a parliament. Splits arose between the three leaders (who went on to achieve prominence in the Balkan Wars and through their encouragement of the German alliance), and other radicals. Their influence lasted throughout the First World War.

Zemstvo   Russian provincial or district councils first established by Tsar Alexander II in Jan. 1864. They were active between 1865–66 and 1917 in the fields of public health, agricultural development, road building and primary education. Although dominated by the gentry they became a genuinely liberal force.

Zentrum   The conservative Roman Catholic Centre Party in Germany from 1871 to 1933. Developed in response to Bismarck's anti-Catholic policies, it was influential in early twentieth-century coalitions and again in the post-First World War Weimar Republic. Dissolved by the Nazis in July 1933.

Zimmermann telegram   Coded message of 19 Jan. 1917 from the German Foreign Minister, Arthur Zimmermann, to the German minister in Mexico, urging the conclusion of a German–Mexican alliance in the event of a declaration of war on Germany by America when Germany resumed unrestricted submarine warfare against shipping on 1 Feb. Mexico would be offered the recapture of her 'lost territories' in New Mexico, Arizona and Texas. Intercepted by British Naval Intelligence, the telegram was released to the American press on 1 Mar., greatly inflaming feeling against Germany, and helping to precipitate the American declaration of war against Germany on 6 Apr. 1917.

Zionism   Belief in the need to establish an autonomous Jewish homeland in Palestine which in its modern form originated with Theodor Herzl (1860–1904), a Hungarian journalist living in Vienna. The Dreyfus Affair and the pogroms of Eastern Europe convinced him that the Jews could have no real safety until they had a state of their own. They had always regarded Palestine as a spiritual homeland but had not up to then considered forming an actual state there. Herzl faced opposition from assimilated Jews who felt safe in the countries where they lived. Even after the 1917 Balfour Declaration supporting a Jewish homeland in Palestine, few Jews went to Palestine before the horrors of the Nazi regime and the Holocaust.

TOPIC BIBLIOGRAPHY

List of abbreviations

A.H.R.   *American Historical Review*
C.E.H.   *Central European History*
C.H.J.   *Cambridge Historical Journal (later, Historical Journal)*
Ec.H.R.   *Economic History Review*
E.H.Q.   *European History Quarterly*
E.H.R.   *English Historical Review*
E.S.R.   *European Studies Review (later, European History Quarterly)*
F.H.S.   *French Historical Studies*
H.   *History*
H.J.   *Historical Journal*
H.T.   *History Today*
H.W.J.   *History Workshop Journal*
I.R.S.H. *International Review of Social History*
J.C.E.A. *Journal of Central European Affairs*
J.C.H.   *Journal of Contemporary History*
J.Ec.H.   *Journal of Economic History*
J.H.I.   *Journal of the History of Ideas*
J.M.H.   *Journal of Modern History*
P.P.   *Past and Present*
R.P.   *Review of Politics*
S.E.E.R. *Slavonic and East European Review*
S.H.   *Slavic History*
S.R.   *Slavic Review*
T.R.H.S. *Transactions of the Royal Historical Society*

Topics

1. European diplomacy, 1871–1914.
2. The First World War, 1914–18.
3. The Russian Revolution and Lenin, 1917–24.
4. Italy from unification to Mussolini, 1871–1943.
5. The Weimar Republic, 1919–33.
6. Nazi Germany, 1933–45.
7. Stalin's Russia, 1923–53.
8. Eastern Europe between the wars, 1918–39.
9. The Spanish Civil War, 1936–39.
10. France, 1918–44.
11. Interwar diplomacy, 1919–39.
12. The Second World War, 1939–45.
13. The Holocaust.
14. The Cold War.
15. Western European democracy since 1945.
16. Decolonisation.
17. The movement for European unity.
18. Eastern Europe since 1945.

Introductory note

There are several general histories which include the twentieth century as part of their broad coverage of European history as a whole, notably N. Davies, *Europe: A History* (1996), J. M. Roberts, *A History of Europe* (1996), and J. Stevenson, *The History of Europe* (2002). For the twentieth century see J. Joll, *Europe since 1870: An International History* (1973), M. Mazower, *Dark Continent* (1998), J. M. Roberts, *Europe, 1880–1945* (3rd edn, 2000) and J. W. Young, *Cold War Europe, 1945–1989* (1989). Europe's role as part of the larger world history of the twentieth century is discussed in P. Calvocoressi, *World Politics Since 1945* (new edn, 2001), P. M. H. Bell, *The World Since 1945: an international history* (2001), E. Hobsbawm, *The Age of Extremes: The Short Twentieth Century, 1914–1991* (1994), W. R. Keylor, *The Twentieth Century: An International History* (1984), and G. Lundestad, *East, West, North, South: Major Developments in International Politics, 1945–1990* (1991).

International relations are considered in E. H. Carr, *The Twenty Years Crisis, 1919–1939: An Introduction to the Study of International Relations* (1961), G. Ross, *The Great Powers and the Decline of the European States System, 1914–1945* (1983), and J. P. Dunbabin, *International Relations Since 1945* (1994). Other themes are considered in C. and R. Tilly, *The Rebellious Century, 1830–1930* (1978), on protest movements, P. Flora and A. J. Heidenheimer (eds), *Development of Welfare States in America and Europe* (1981), G. Luebert, *Liberalism, Fascism or Social Democracy: Social Classes and the Political Origins of Regimes in Inter-War Europe* (1991), and S. Salter and J. Stevenson (eds), *The Working Class and Politics in Europe and America, 1929–1945* (1989).

For general reference on European affairs, see J. Stevenson, *Macmillan Dictionary of British and European History since 1914* (1991), and on specific parts of Europe, A. Webb, *The Longman Companion to Central and Eastern Europe since 1919* (2002), M. McCaulay, *The Longman Companion to Russia since 1914* (1998), A. Blair, *The Longman Companion to the European Union since 1945* (2000), and R. and B. Crampton, *Atlas of Eastern Europe in the Twentieth Century* (1996). For statistical information see B. R. Mitchell, *European Historical Statistics, 1750–1970* (1975) and for a wide-ranging compendium of facts and figures, see C. Cook and J. Paxton, *European Political Facts of the Twentieth Century* (2002).

1. European diplomacy, 1871–1914

The European diplomatic scene after the Franco–Prussian War was dominated by Bismarck's attempts to ensure the lasting security of the new German Empire. At first he tried to achieve this through the '*Dreikaiserbund*', a conservative alliance with Austria–Hungary and Russia in the 1870s, but this was increasingly undermined by Austrian and Russian ambitions in the Balkans, where the decline of the Ottoman Empire created a power vacuum. In 1879 Bismarck decided to ally with Austria–Hungary alone in the Dual Alliance, while in 1894 Russia made an alliance with France. Tension between the two blocs grew, notably over the Bosnian Crisis in 1908, and Britain too became suspicious of German ambitions. In 1914 another crisis in the Balkans brought the two sides to war. Various interpretations of the origins of the war have been put forward; from early anti-Germanism, there was a swing towards blaming the alliance systems in general. More recently, Fischer has revived interest in Germany's responsibility for the war and the wider factors affecting Europeans' readiness to go to war have to be considered.

Essay topics

- How stable was the European diplomatic system created by Bismarck?
- Why did a crisis in the Balkans lead to a general European war in 1914?

Sources and documents

M. Hurst (ed.), *Key Treaties for the Great Powers, vol. II, 1870–1914* (1972) covers the whole period, though mere treaty texts are rather unexciting sources. To be preferred perhaps is I. Geiss, *July, 1914: Selected Documents* (1967) and G. Martel, *The Origins of the First World War* (1987) which provides both an overview of the historical debate and a selection of documents. C. Nicolson, *The Longman Companion to the First World War: Europe 1914–1918* (2001) is a mine of information on both diplomacy and home fronts.

Secondary works

A. J. P. Taylor, *The Struggle for Mastery in Europe, 1848–1918* (1954) remains a remarkably thorough analysis of the diplomatic struggles, while R. Albrecht-Carrié, *A Diplomatic History of Europe from the Congress of Vienna* (1961) provides the wider background. Another well-established but essential account is W. L. Langer, *European Alliances and Alignments, 1871–90* (1956), which he followed with *The Diplomacy of Imperialism, 1890–1902* (1951). See also F. R. Bridge and R. Bullen, *The Great Powers and the European States System* (1980). On individual countries see C. Andrew, *Théophile Delcassé and the Making of the Entente Cordiale* (1968) and P. V. Rolo, *Entente Cordiale* (1969).

The origins of the First World War have attracted a vast literature. J. Joll, *The Origins of the First World War* (1985) is a recent modern overview. The decision by individual countries to go to war is examined in K. Wilson (ed.), *Decisions for War, 1914* (1995) and R. J. W. Evans and H. Pogge von Strandmann (eds), *The Coming of the First World War* (1988). B. Schmitt, *The Outbreak of War in 1914* (Historical Association pamphlet, 1964) analyses the role of the Alliance systems in the outbreak of war, which is more fully related in his study, *The Coming of the War* (2 vols, 1930). The great classic of the 'diplomatic' school of thinking is L. Albertini, *The Origins of the War of 1914* (3 vols, 1952–57).

More recent accounts are L. C. F. Turner, *The Origins of the First World War* (1970) and H. W. Koch, *The Origins of the First World War* (1984 edn). Also useful is the short account of the break-up of the nineteenth-century international system, R. Langhorne, *The Collapse of the Concert of Europe, 1890–1914* (1981), while M. S. Anderson, *The Eastern Question, 1774–1923* (1966) provides a wider perspective on that particular problem. Among the most important later interpretations has been F. Fischer, *Germany's War Aims in the First World War* (1967) which sees the war as a result of Germany's prewar expansionism. See also his *War of Illusion* (1972) and *From Kaiserreich to Third Reich* (1986). On Germany, see V. Berghahn, *Germany and the Approach of War in 1914* (1973), I. Geiss, *German Foreign Policy, 1871–1914* (1976), and G. Ritter, *The Schlieffen Plan* (1958). J. C. G. Rohl (ed.), *1914: Delusion or Design? The Testimony of Two German Diplomats* (1973) has important material on attitudes in German ruling circles. Austria–Hungary's role is considered in R. Bridge, *From Sadowa to Sarajevo* (1972) and A. S. Williamson, *Austria–Hungary and the Origins of the First World War* (1991); France in J. Keiger, *France and the Origins of the First World War* (1983); Russia in D. Lieven, *Russia and the Origins of the First World War* (1983); and Britain in Z. S. Steiner, *Britain and the Origins of the First World War* (1977). The specific rivalry of Britain and Germany is considered in the classic E. L. Woodward, *Great Britain and the German Navy* (1935), but is now updated on the naval side by A. J. Marder, *From the Dreadnought to Scapa Flow, vol. I: The Road to War, 1904–14* (1961) and on the political side by P. Kennedy, *The Rise of the Anglo–German Antagonism, 1860–1914* (1980). The arms build-up in general is considered in D. Stevenson, *Armaments and the Coming of War in Europe, 1904–1914* (1996). M. Howard discusses the 'climate' of 1914 in Evans and Pogge von Strandmann (eds), *The Coming of the First World War* (above), and Europe's readiness for war is considered in his 'Reflections on the Great War' in his *Studies in War and Peace* (1970). The commercially published units of the Open University course on *War, Peace and Social Change: Europe, 1900–1955* have, in A. Marwick, B. Waites, C. Emsley and I. Donnachie, *Book I: Europe on the Eve of War* (1990), Unit 6, a useful step-by-step guide to the debates.

Articles

Two articles which take up the theme of the relationship between domestic and foreign policy are W. J. Mommsen, 'Domestic factors in German foreign policy before 1914', *C.E.H.* (1973), reprinted in J. Sheehan (ed.), *Imperial Germany* (1976), and M. R. Gordon, 'Domestic conflict and the origins of the First World War: the British and German cases', *J.M.H.* (1974). An appraisal of the Fischer thesis and its critics can be found in R. J. Evans, 'From Hitler to Bismarck: Third Reich to Kaiserreich in recent historiography', *H.J.* (1984).

2. The First World War, 1914–18

When war broke out in August 1914 it was widely expected to be 'over by Christmas'. Instead, in the West at least, the situation soon became one of trench warfare and deadlock. Modern weapons, especially the machine gun, barbed wire and heavy artillery, ensured huge casualties, concentrated among men aged between about twenty and forty. Armies numbering millions of men were mobilised, while behind them 'home fronts' were established: economies were geared to war production, women went to work in factories, propaganda machines ensured loyalty to the war effort and hatred of the enemy. The strain on European society was enormous. Governments were changed in France and Britain, revolutions broke out in Russia and Germany, and the Austro–Hungarian and Ottoman Empires were finally shattered. The world would never be the same again.

Essay topics

- Why did the First World War not end until November 1918?
- Why did Western democratic regimes tend to survive the war more successfully than the Eastern autocracies?

Sources and documents

P. Vansittart, *Voices from the Great War* (1983) draws together eye-witness evidence on the war from all levels of society. Of the memoirs, see D. Lloyd George, *War Memoirs* (2 vols, 1928) and W. S. Churchill, *The World Crisis* (1928). Of the literature produced by the war, H. Barbusse's *Le Feu* (*Under Fire*) (1917), E. Junger, *The Storm of Steel* (1929), R. Graves, *Goodbye to All That* (1929), and E. M. Remarque, *All Quiet on the Western Front* (1929) are outstanding.

Secondary works

There are numerous general histories of the war but among the most approachable are A. J. P. Taylor, *The First World War: An Illustrated History* (1966), invaluable because of its illustrations, C. Falls, *The First World War* (1966) and B. H. Liddell-Hart, *History of the First World War* (1970). M. Ferro, *The Great War* (1963) is another short, readable introduction. See also J. Terraine, *The Western Front, 1914–18* (1964). For works which place the military aspects of the war in a broader context see K. Robbins, *The First World War* (Oxford, 1984), B. Bond, *War and Society in Europe, 1870–1970* (1984), and G. Hardach, *The First World War* (1977).

Of more recent accounts see J. Keegan, *The First World War* (1998) and H. Strachan's *Oxford Illustrated History of the First World War* (1998). N. Ferguson, *The Pity of War* (1998) offers a stimulating set of fresh perspectives. H. Herwig, *The First World War: Germany and Austria-Hungary* (1997), although concerned with only two of the combatants, is vitally concerned with the war's conduct and conclusion.

The nature of the new warfare is discussed in J. Ellis, *Eye-Deep in Hell* (1976) and A. E. Ashworth, *The Trench Warfare* (1980), while A. Horne, *The Price of Glory: Verdun, 1916* (1964), L. Macdonald, *They Called it Passchendaele* (1983) and M. Middlebrook, *The First Day on the Somme* (1971) and *The Kaiser's Battle* (1983) (on Germany's 1918 offensive) give full treatment of individual battles, as does J. Keegan, *The Face of Battle* (1979).

The effect of the war on individual societies can be traced in J. Kocka, *Facing Total War: German Society, 1914–1918* (1985), A. Rosenberg, *Imperial Germany: the birth of the German Republic* (1931), A. Marwick, *The Deluge: British Society and the First World War* (1965), A. J. May, *The Passing of the Habsburg Monarchy* (2 vols, 1966), L. Kochan, *Russia in Revolution, 1890–1918* (1966), J. J. Becker,

The Great War and the French People (1983), and N. Stone, *The Eastern Front* (1978). General coverage of such issues is provided by A. Marwick, *War and Social Change in the Twentieth Century* (1974). For a cultural history, see P. Fussell, *The Great War and Modern Memory* (1975).

The revolutionary effects of the war are discussed in C. L. Bertrand (ed.), *Revolutionary Situations in Europe, 1917–1922* (1977) and F. L. Carsten, *Revolution in Central Europe, 1918–1919* (1972). For Germany, see A. J. Ryder, *The German Revolution* (1966) and D. Geary, 'Radicalism and the worker: metalworkers and revolution, 1914–1923', in R. J. Evans (ed.), *Society and Politics in Wilhelmine Germany* (1978).

War aims and the failure of early peace attempts are discussed in F. Fischer, *Germany's War Aims in the First World War* (1987), V. Rothwell, *British War Aims and Peace Diplomacy* (1971), C. Andrew and A. Kanya-Forstner, *France Overseas* (1981), as well as A. J. P. Taylor, *The Struggle for Mastery in Europe, 1848–1918* (1954). See also M. Kitchen, *The Silent Dictatorship* (1976) on the growing role of the German General Staff.

For the Versailles Treaty see pp. 359–60.

Articles

The thesis that sections of the German lower middle classes were radicalised by the war is raised in J. Kocka, 'The First World War and the "Mittelstand": German artisans and white-collar workers', *J.C.H.* (1973), and for a review of these views, see W. J. Mommsen, 'Society and war: two new analyses of the First World War', *J.M.H.* (1977). D. Geary, 'The German labour movement, 1848–1918', *E.S.R.* (1976) is also useful for German reactions.

3. The Russian Revolution and Lenin, 1917–24

Under the pressures of war the Tsarist autocracy finally collapsed early in 1917 and power was given to a more democratic regime of elected representatives. The change of government unleashed forces that were difficult to control, however: soldiers deserted from the army, factory workers adopted militant political views, and the peasants began to seize land for themselves from the great estates. In the 'October Revolution' the communist 'Bolsheviks' seized power under Lenin, and established a radically reformist but authoritarian regime. They made peace with Germany, overcame their conservative opponents and defeated the attempts of the Western powers to overthrow them. Historians debate about the kind of regime Lenin might have created had he not become increasingly ill and died in 1924.

Essay topics

- Was the Bolshevik seizure of power in 1917 primarily the result of their own strengths and abilities?
- What were the main achievements and failings of Lenin in power, 1917–24?

Sources and documents

M. McCauley (ed.), *The Russian Revolution and the Soviet State, 1917–21* (1980) provides a full set of documents, while L. Trotsky, *The History of the Russian Revolution* (1977) is an account by a leading revolutionary. H. Shukman (ed.), *The Blackwell Encyclopedia of the Russian Revolution* (1988) is a mine of information with a good, short introduction on the historiography of the Revolution. There are memoirs by N. Sukhanov, *The Russian Revolution, 1917* (1955), J. Reed, *Ten Days that Shook the World* (1961) (the latter an American observer of the October Revolution), and A. Kerensky, *The Kerensky Memoirs* (1966). For this and the later period of Soviet history, see M. McCauley, *The Longman Companion to Russia since 1914* (2000).

Secondary works

The basic account of the events of 1917–24 can be traced in the excellent general histories by R. Service, *A History of Twentieth-Century Russia* (1997) and by G. Hosking, *A History of the Soviet Union* (1990); see also McCauley (as above).

There are good starting points in R. Pipes, *The Russian Revolution, 1899–1919* (1990), O. Figes, *A People' Tragedy: The Russian Revolution, 1891–1924* (1996), J. D. White, *The Russian Revolution, 1917–1921* (1994), and E. Acton, *Rethinking the Russian Revolution* (1990). Among the national histories which deal with the breakdown of the regime, see H. Seton-Watson, *The Russian Empire, 1801–1917* (1967), J. N. Westwood, *Endurance and Endeavour: Russian History, 1812–1971* (1973), and L. Kochan and P. Abraham, *The Making of Modern Russia* (1983). R. B. McKean, *The Russian Constitutional Monarchy, 1907–1917* (Historical Association pamphlet, 1977) synthesises much recent research. There are also useful essays in R. Pipes (ed.), *Revolutionary Russia* (1968) and a useful, short interpretative essay in J. Dunn, *Modern Revolutions* (1972), ch. 1.

E. H. Carr, *A History of Soviet Russia: The Bolshevik Revolution* (3 vols, 1966) provides the standard account of these years, although his *The Russian Revolution from Lenin to Stalin* (1980) is shorter. See also G. Hosking, *A History of the Soviet Union* (1990). Other accounts on aspects of this period are provided by G. Katkov, *Russia, 1917: The February Revolution* (1967), R. Pipes, *The Formation of the Soviet Union* (1954), and M. Ferro, *October 1917: A Social History of the Russian Revolution* (1980).

Several works approach the period from a biographical viewpoint, including B. Wolfe, *Three Who Made a Revolution* (1966), on Lenin, Trotsky and Stalin, D. Shub, *Lenin* (1966), C. Hill, *Lenin and the Russian Revolution* (1971), A. B. Ulam, *Lenin and the Bolsheviks* (1965), I. Deutscher, *Stalin* (1966), and I. Deutscher, *The Prophet Armed: Trotsky, 1879–1921* (1963). On the Marxist background to Bolshevik thinking, see E. Wilson, *To the Finland Station* (1947).

The civil war period and allied intervention are discussed in G. Swain, *The Origins of the Russian Civil War* (1995), J. Bradley, *Allied Intervention in Russia* (1968), R. Ullman, *Intervention and the War: Anglo–Soviet Relations, 1917–21* (1961), while R. Service, *The Bolshevik Party in Revolution, 1917–23* (1979) and T. Rigby, *Lenin's Government* (1979) look at Soviet institutions in this period.

A work looking beyond 1924, towards Stalinism, is S. Fitzpatrick, *The Russian Revolution, 1917–32* (1982). The long-term development of foreign policy is considered in A. B. Ulam, *Expansion and Coexistence, Soviet Foreign Policy, 1917–27* (1968).

4. Italy from unification to Mussolini, 1871–1943

The final unification of Italy in 1871 failed to fulfil the great hopes of the 'risorgimento' period. Deep economic and social divisions between north and south, the alienation of the Catholic Church from the new Italian monarchy, and the narrow electoral franchise left a picture of division and weakness in the late nineteenth century. Around 1900 there was increasing violence in the countryside and factories. The 'Giolitti era' marked a return to relative calm but the strains of the First World War and the effects of electoral reform created the conditions for Mussolini's rise to power in the 1920s. His fascist regime was characterised by authoritarian rule and bold foreign adventures, but it failed to tackle Italy's deeper social problems and brought defeat, and Mussolini's overthrow, in the Second World War. The weaknesses of Italian democracy and the nature of Mussolini's brand of fascism are common areas of interest.

Essay topics

- Why was Mussolini able to overthrow Italian democracy?
- What were the main successes and failings of Mussolini in office, 1922–43?

Sources and documents

Ciano's Diaries, 1937–8 (1952) and *1939–43* (1947) cover the later Fascist period from within the government, while the views of opponents can be found in G. Salvemini, *The Fascist Dictatorship in Italy* (1928) and *Under the Axe of Fascism* (1936).

Secondary works

For a general background to Italian history see D. Mack Smith, *Italy: A Modern History* (1959) and M. Clark, *Modern Italy, 1871–1982* (1984). Helpful short introductions to the Fascist era are M. Blinkhorn, *Mussolini and Fascist Italy* (1984) and J. Whittam, *Fascist Italy* (1996).

On the pre-fascist period, C. Seton-Watson, *Italy from Liberalism to Fascism* (1967) is the standard work. Relations between church and state are examined in A. Jemolo, *Church and State in Italy, 1850–1950* (1960) and R. A. Webster, *The Cross and the Fasces: Christian Democracy in Italy, 1860–1960* (1960). Popular disorder is considered in J. A. Davis, *Conflict and Control: Law and Order in Nineteenth Century Italy* (1988). For the continuation of unrest up to the fascist era, see F. M. Snowden, *Violence and the Great Estates in the South of Italy: Apulia, 1900–1922* (1986), and on the role of the army, J. Gooch, *Army, State and Society in Italy, 1870–1915* (1989). R. Bosworth, *Italy and the Approach of the First*

World War (1983) covers foreign policy. See also C. Tilly, L. Tilly, and R. Tilly, *The Rebellious Century, 1830–1930* (1975), ch. 3. For postwar events see P. Spriano, *The Occupation of the Factories* (trans. edn, 1975), M. Clark, *Antonio Gramsci and the Revolution that Failed* (1977), and G. Williams, *Proletarian Order* (1975). The best overall study of the fascist takeover is A. Lyttleton, *The Seizure of Power, 1919–29* (1973), while the local dimension is considered in P. Corner, *Fascism in Ferrara* (1975) and F. Snowden, *The Fascist Revolution in Tuscany, 1919–1922* (1989). The position of the monarchy, crucial in 1922 and thereafter, has received admirable treatment in D. Mack Smith, *Italy and its Monarchy* (1990). General treatments of the period include A. Cassels, *Fascist Italy* (1985) and A. De Grand, *Italian Fascism: Its Origins and Development* (1989). Intellectual aspects of fascism are considered in A. Lyttleton, *Italian Fascism from Pareto to Gentile* (1973), while features of fascist policy are considered in C. Duggan, *Fascism and the Mafia* (1989) and V. de Grazia, *The Culture of Consent: Mass Organisation of Leisure in Fascist Italy* (1981). Working-class responses are treated in P. Corner 'Italy', in S. Salter and J. Stevenson (eds), *The Working Class and Politics in Europe and America, 1929–1945* (1990).

Of the biographies of Mussolini, R. Bosworth, *Mussolini* (2002) is a reliable recent account; see also L. Fermi, *Mussolini* (1961). D. Mack Smith, *Mussolini's Roman Empire* (1977) and E. M. Robertson, *Mussolini as Empire Builder* (1977), which concentrates on 1932–36, and surveys foreign policy, while E. Wiskemann, *The Rome–Berlin Axis* (1949) concentrates on the German alliance, as does F. W. Deakin, *The Brutal Friendship* (2 vols, 1966). The economic performance of Fascist Italy is examined in W. G. Welk, *Fascist Economic Policy: An Analysis of Italy's Economic Experiment* (1938) and R. Sarti, *Fascism and Industrial Leadership in Italy, 1919–1940* (1971).

Articles

On the unrest of wartime, see G. Procacci, 'Popular protest and labour conflict in Italy, 1915–18', *S.H.* (1989). On Mussolini, see S. Woolf, 'Mussolini as revolutionary', *J.C.H.* (1966) and on the economy, A. Albertoz, 'The crisis of the corporative state', *J.C.H.* (1969) and R. Sarti, 'Mussolini and the Italian industrial leadership in the battle of the lira, 1925–27', *P.P.* (1970).

5. The Weimar Republic, 1919–33

The Weimar Republic was established in the wake of military defeat in the First World War and the overthrow of the Kaiser, and soon faced even greater problems – the harsh peace of Versailles, enforced by the Allies, and the massive inflation of the early 1920s. It was in this difficult period that the Nazi Party, under Adolf Hitler, came into being and attempted to overthrow the government in the Munich Putsch of 1923. In the years after this the Republic staged something of a recovery, achieving economic growth, political stability and even, thanks to Stresemann, international standing. Historians argue whether, but for the effects of the 'slump' after 1929, and the bankruptcies and political extremism which it created, Weimar could have survived. The appeal of Nazism and the role of army, business and churches under Weimar have all received attention.

Essay topics

- Did the possession of 'the most democratic constitution in the world' tend to help or hinder the Weimar Republic in its search for political stability?
- Assess the contribution of Hitler to the Nazi rise to power.

Sources and documents

For excellent selections of documents on Weimar and the rise of Nazism, see J. Noakes and G. Pridham (eds), *Documents on Nazism, 1919–1945* (1974) and J. Noakes and G. Pridham (eds), *Nazism, 1919–1945. Vol. I. The Rise to Power, 1919–1934* (1983). J. Hiden, *The Weimar Republic* (2nd edn, 1996) has useful material specifically on Weimar. Hitler's *Mein Kampf* (1925–26) is available in translation (ed. D. C. Watt, 1969); see also N. H. Baynes, *The Speeches of Adolf Hitler, April 1922–August 1939* (1942).

Secondary works

Introductions include D. Bookbinder, *Weimar Germany* (1996), C. Fischer, *The Rise of the Nazis* (2nd edn, 2002), J. Hiden, *The Weimar Republic* (2nd edn, 1996), and *Republican and Fascist Germany: Themes and Variations in the History of the Third Reich, 1918–1945* (1996). More substantial works are H. Heiber, *The Weimar Republic: Germany, 1918–1933* (1993) and E. Kolb, *The Weimar Republic* (1988). E. Eyck, *History of the Weimar Republic* (2 vols, 1962, 1963) is a full and useful study of the period. A. J. Nicholls, *Weimar and the Rise of Hitler* (1968) is shorter and more analytical, while R. J. Bessel and E. J. Feuchtwanger (eds), *Social Change and Political Development in the Weimar Republic* (1981) is an important group of essays.

There is another group of excellent essays in M. Fulbrook, *Twentieth Century Germany: Politics, Culture and Society, 1918–1990* (2001), Pt. I, chs. 1–4. For Hitler's early years, the standard treatment is now I. Kershaw, *Hitler, 1889–1936: Hubris* (1998), though the older A. Bullock, *Hitler, A Study in Tyranny* (1964) and W. A. Carr, *Hitler: A Study in Personality and Politics* (1978) remain valuable. See also I. Kershaw (ed.), *Weimar: Why did German Democracy Fail?* (1990).

The revolution of 1918–19 and the birth of Weimar has received quite full treatment. A. Rosenberg, *Imperial Germany: The Birth of the German Republic* (1931) remains a useful, if old, account; A. J. Ryder, *The German Revolution* (1967) concentrates on the Socialists (see also the shorter account in his Historical Association pamphlet of the same title, published in 1959). F. L. Carsten, *Revolution in Central Europe, 1918–19* (1971) is excellent on the 'grass roots' establishment of workers' and soldiers' councils, and J. P. Nettl, *Rosa Luxemburg* (1969) provides a biography of a leading revolutionary. R. Cooper, *Failure of a Revolution: Germany in 1918–19* (1955) criticises the Social Democrats, for whom see also R. N. Hunt, *German Social Democracy, 1918–1933* (1970) and W. L. Guttsman, *The German Social Democratic Party, 1875–1933* (1981).

E. J. Hobsbawm, 'Confronting defeat: the German Communist Party' in *Revolutionaries* (1977) looks at the KPD.

Two important studies of inflation of the early 1920s and its impact are G. D. Feldman, *The Great Disorder: Politics, Economics and Society in the German Inflation, 1914–24* (1996) and N. Ferguson, *Paper and Iron: Hamburg Business and German Politics in the Era of Inflation, 1897–1927* (1995); on the economy, see H. James, *The German Slump* (1988). Two of the leading politicians of the Weimar era are examined in H. A. Turner, *Stresemann and the Politics of the Weimar Republic* (1963), H. W. Gatzke, *Stresemann and the Rearmament of Germany* (1954), and A. Dorpalen, *Hindenburg and the Weimar Republic* (1964).

J. W. Wheeler-Bennett, *The Nemesis of Power: The German Army in Politics, 1918–45* (1980 edn) is critical of the military under Weimar. The same theme is covered by F. L. Carsten, *The Reichswehr and German Politics, 1918–33* (1966) and the older and more general, G. Craig, *The Politics of the Prussian Army, 1640–1945* (1955). The political rise of the Nazis at 'grass roots' level can be traced in M. Kater, *The Nazi Party, 1919–45* (1984), W. S. Allen, *The Nazi Seizure of Power* (1966), and J. Noakes, *The Nazi Party in Lower Saxony* (1971). There is a useful set of essays in E. Matthias and A. J. Nicholls (eds), *German Democracy and the Triumph of Hitler* (1971) and P. D. Stachura (ed.), *The Nazi Machtergreifung* (1983). On Nazi support, see also T. Childers, *The Nazi Voter, The Social Foundations of Fascism in Germany 1919–1933* (1983). The effects of the Depression are recorded in K. Hardach, *The Political Economy of Germany in the Twentieth Century* (1980); also D. Geary, 'Unemployment and Working Class Solidarity, 1929–33', in R. J. Evans and D. Geary (eds), *The German Unemployed* (1987), P. D. Stachura (ed.), *Unemployment and the Great Depression in Weimar Germany* (1986); and M. Kele, *Nazis and Workers* (1972).

Articles

On the role of the KPD in assisting the Nazis' rise, see C. Fischer, 'Class enemies or class brothers? Communist–Nazi relations in Germany, 1929–33' and D. Geary, 'Nazis and workers, a response to Conan Fischer's "Class enemies or class brothers"', *E.H.Q.* (1985). On the role of business in the rise of the Nazis, see H. Ashby Turner, 'Big business and the rise of Hitler', *A.H.R.* (1969), G. D. Fieldman, 'The social and economic policies of German big business, 1918–1929', *A.H.R.* (1969), and E. Nolte, 'Big business and German politics', *A.H.R.* (1969). More generally on Nazi support, see T. Childers, 'The social basis of the National Socialist vote', *J.C.H.* (1976), J. Noakes, 'Nazi voters', *H.T.* (1980), and K. O'Lessker, 'Who voted for Hitler: a new look at the class basis of Nazism', *American Journal of Sociology* (1969).

6. Nazi Germany, 1933–45

Having obtained power by what, on the surface, could be portrayed as 'constitutional' means, Hitler overthrew the Weimar Republic and enforced authoritarian government, with himself as Führer and the Nazi Party as the only legitimate political force. At first, despite rigged elections, the imprisonment of opponents, and the enforcement of strict controls on the people, he had successes, reducing unemployment and increasing Germany's international standing. But in 1939 his expansionist foreign policy brought conflict with Britain and France. Already Hitler had inspired anti-Semitic outrages, blaming the Jews for Germany's past misfortunes, and during the war the 'Final Solution', involving the slaughter of millions of Jews, was adopted. Meanwhile, however, the strain of 'total war' proved too much for Germany. Hitler, increasingly deranged, committed suicide in the midst of defeat in 1945. Exactly how such a man could gain and wield such power has concerned historians ever since.

Essay topics

- Why did the German people not overthrow Hitler?
- What were the main facets of Nazi political ideology?

Sources and documents

J. Noakes and G. Pridham (eds), *Documents on Nazism, 1919–1945* (1974) presents a good selection of documents on the whole era, and on the Hitlerite period see their *Nazism, 1919–1945: Vol. II. State, Economy and Society, 1933– 1939* (1984). Hitler's *Mein Kampf* (1925–26, ed. D. C. Watt, 1969) and Goebbel's *Diaries* (1948) provide a valuable insight into the Nazi mind. More accessible and compelling on the war period is A. Speer, *Inside the Third Reich* (1970), though it should be approached with care, while H. Rauschning, *Germany's Revolution of Destruction* (1939) is remarkably perceptive on the revolutionary strand in Hitler's make-up. D. G. Williamson, *The Third Reich* (1982) is a short modern selection of documents with introductory chapters. G. Bielenberg, *The Past is Myself* (1968) is a remarkable inside account of life in the Third Reich by a British woman. T. Kirk, *Longman Companion to Nazi Germany* (1995) has extensive factual and reference information, while M. Freeman, *Atlas of Nazi Germany* (1995) also has valuable material.

Secondary works

There is an enormous amount of work on Hitler and the Nazis. H. R. Trevor-Roper's introduction to *The Last Days of Hitler* (1978 edn) remains impressively perceptive. Of the biographies of Hitler, the standard work is now I. Kershaw's two-volume study, *Hitler, 1889–1936: Hubris* (1998) and *Hitler, 1937–1945: Nemesis* (2001). Among a number of other studies, A. Bullock, *Hitler* (1964) remains a readable but full account, J. C. Fest, *Hitler* (1974) and J. Toland, *Adolf Hitler* (1976) are long and detailed, while N. Stone, *Hitler* (1980) is short but stimulating. J. C. Fest, *The Face of the Third Reich* (1970) looks at Hitler's deputies, one of whom receives full coverage in E. K. Bramsted, *Goebbels and National Socialist Propaganda* (1965). Two interesting attempts at 'psychohistory' can be found in W. Langer, *The Mind of Adolf Hitler* (1972) and W. Carr, *Hitler: A Study in Personality and Politics* (1978).

Up-to-date and succinct accounts of the rise of the Nazis can be found in C. Fischer, *The Rise of the Nazis* (2nd edn, 2002) and in the chapter by J. Stephenson in M. Fulbrook (ed.), *Twentieth Century Germany: Politics, Culture and Society, 1918–1990* (2001), which also contains excellent short accounts of the main features of the Nazi state, by I. Kershaw (the Nazi dictatorship), O. Bartov (on the Germans at war) and N. Stargardt (on the 'final solution').

The best single account is I. Kershaw, *The Nazi Dictatorship* (3rd edn, 1993), but see also M. Brozat, *The Hitler State* (1981), N. Frei, *National Socialist Rule in Germany: The Führer State* (1993), J. Dulffer, *Nazi Germany, 1933–1945* (1995), K. Bracher, *The German Dictatorship* (1973), and K. Hilderbrand, *The Third Reich* (1984). D. Orlow, *A History of the Nazi Party, 1933–45* (1973), D. Welch, *The Third Reich: Politics and Propaganda* (1994), G. C. Browder, *Hitler's Enforcers: The Gestapo and the SS Security Service in the Nazi Revolution* (1996), D. F. Crew, *Nazism and German Society, 1933–1945* (1994), R. Gruenberger, *A Social History of the Third Reich* (1974), and J. P. Stern, *The Führer and the People* (1975) cover various aspects of the Third Reich, while J. Hiden and J. Farquharson, *Explaining Hitler's Germany* (1983) looks at historical views of the Nazi regime. J. Noakes (ed.), *Government, Party and People in Nazi Germany* (1980) has several good essays and a detailed bibliography. On other aspects of German society, see A. Schweitzer, *Big Business in the Third Reich* (1964), D. Guerin, *Fascism and Big Business* (1979), R. J. O'Neill, *The German Army and the Nazi Party, 1933–1939* (1966), Z. A. B. Zeman, *Nazi Propaganda* (1964), E. K. Bramsted, *Goebbels and National Socialist Propaganda 1925–1945* (1965), J. S. Conway, *The Nazi Persecution of the Churches* (1968), and G. Lewy, *The Catholic Church and Nazi Germany* (1964). On the economy, see H. James, *The German Slump* (1988).

Hitler's opponents are considered in H. Graml (ed.), *The German Resistance to Hitler* (1970) and I. Kershaw, *Popular Opinion and Political Dissent in the Third Reich: Bavaria, 1933–1945* (1986). On the position of the working class, see S. Salter, 'Germany', in S. Salter and J. Stevenson (eds), *The Working Class and Politics in Europe and America, 1929–1945* (1989); also useful is D. J. K. Peukert, *Inside Nazi Germany: Conformity, Opposition and Racism in Everyday Life* (1987). Hitler's anti-Semitism is considered in Kershaw, *Nazi Dictatorship*, ch. 5 (see above) and H. Krausnick, 'The persecution of the Jews', in H. Krausnick and M. Broszat, *Anatomy of the SS State* (1968), but see also L. Dawidowicz, *The War against the Jews, 1933–45* (1975), D. J. Goldhagen, *Hitler's Willing Executioners* (1996). K. Schleunes, *The Twisted Road to Auschwitz* (1970). More recent treatments include M. Burleigh and W. Wippermann, *The Racial State: Germany, 1933–45* (1991), J. Burrin, *Hitler and the Jews* (1994) and on the euthanasia programme, M. Burleigh, *Death and Deliverance: Euthanasia in Germany, c. 1900–1945* (1994).

Foreign policy is considered in G. I. Weinberg, *The Foreign Policy of Hitler's Germany: Diplomatic Revolution in Europe, 1933–1936* (1970) and *The Foreign Policy of Hitler's Germany: Starting World War II* (1980). K. Hildebrand, *The Foreign Policy of the Third Reich* (1973) stresses Hitler's pragmatism, while W. Carr, *Arms, Autarky and Aggression: A Study in German Foreign Policy, 1933–1939* (1972) relates economic policy to foreign policy. Two important recent studies of the outbreak of war in 1939 are D. Cameron Watt, *How War Came* (1989), and R. Overy and A. Wheatcroft, *The Road to War* (1989); see also P. M. Bell, *The*

Origins of the Second World War in Europe (1986) and V. Rothwell, *The Origins of the Second World War* (1995).

On Hitler's economic policies, see W. Carr, *Arms, Autarky and Aggression*, B. A. Caroll, *Design for Total War: Arms and Economics in the Third Reich* (1968), and B. H. Klein, *Germany's Economic Preparations for War* (1959). T. Mason, 'The primacy of politics: politics and economics in National Socialist Germany', in S. J. Woolf (ed.), *The Nature of Fascism* (1968) discusses the Nazi attitude to economics, a view taken up by A. Milward in W. Laqueur (ed.), *Fascism: A Readers' Guide* (1979). For the German economy at war, see A. Milward, *The German Economy at War* (1965) and his wider *War, Economy and Society 1939–1945* (1977).

Articles

R. Bessel, 'Living with the Nazis: some recent writing on the social history of the Third Reich', *E.H.Q.* (1984) comments on German domestic reactions. See also T. Mason, 'Labour in the Third Reich', *P.P.* (1966), 'Women in Germany, 1925–40: family, welfare and work', *H.W.J.* (1974), and 'The workers' opposition in Nazi Germany', *H.W.J.* (1981), and L. D. Stokes, 'The German people and the destruction of the European Jews', *C.E.H.* (1973). Two articles linking domestic politics and foreign policy are R. J. Overy, 'Hitler's war and the German economy: a reinterpretation', *Ec.H.R.* (1982), and 'Germany, "Domestic Crisis" and war in 1939', *P.P.* (1987).

7. Stalin's Russia, 1923–53

In the aftermath of Lenin's death Joseph Stalin gradually asserted himself in power, defeating even the able Leon Trotsky. Stalin's concept of 'socialism in one country' by arguing that Russia could achieve communism herself, without the 'world revolution' predicted by other Marxists, gave Russia new faith in herself. After 1928 the 'Stalinisation' programme was pursued to industrialise Russia, by strict control of agriculture and strong central direction, and a series of 'five-year plans'. This was accompanied in the 1930s by increasingly totalitarian methods and the elimination of all possible opposition to Stalin. Nevertheless in 1941–45 the communist regime survived Hitler's invasion intact and Stalin's control remained secure down to his death in 1953. His totalitarian legacy has troubled his successors, but he had seen Russia become the world's second greatest power.

Essay topics

- Was the 'Stalinisation' programme justified?
- What factors helped Stalin to establish and maintain his personal authority in Russia?

Sources and documents

M. McCauley, *Stalin and Stalinism* (1983) has some useful documents, but M. Fainsod, *Smolensk under Soviet Rule* (1959) remains a vivid account from

Soviet archives of the realities of the collectivisation process. On the purges, see the experiences of V. Serge, *Memoirs of a Revolutionary* (1963) and E. Ginsberg, *Into the Whirlwind* (1968). M. Djilas, *Conversations with Stalin* (1969) shows the later Stalin; see also N. Khrushchev, *Khrushchev Remembers* (1970) and A. Solzhenitsyn, *The Gulag Archipelago 1918–56* (1974).

Secondary works

For introductions see R. Service, *A History of Twentieth Century Russia* (1997), M. Maudsley, *Stalin and Stalinism* (1990), and G. Hosking, *A History of the Soviet Union* (1985). Stalin's place as legatee of the Revolution, whether fulfilling or betraying it, is raised in A. B. Ulam, *The New Face of Soviet Totalitarianism* (1963) and S. Fitzpatrick, *The Russian Revolution* (1982); the classic 'betrayal' view is L. Trotsky, *The Revolution Betrayed* (1937). There are several good biographies, notably I. Deutscher, *Stalin* (1966), A. B. Ulam, *Stalin* (1973), and R. H. McNeal, *Stalin: Man and Ruler* (1988). Recent general treatments include G. Ward, *Stalin's Russia* (1993), M. McCauley, *Stalin and Stalinism* (2nd edn, 1995), and C. Gill, *The Origins of the Stalinist Political System* (1990). Also helpful are R. Tucker, *Stalin in Power: the Revolution from Above, 1928–1941* (1990) and I. Kershaw and M. Lewin (eds), *Stalinism and Nazism. Dictatorships in Comparison* (1997).

For the background to collectivisation and industrialisation, see Hosking, *History of the Soviet Union* (above) and A. Nove, *An Economic History of the U.S.S.R.* (1972). For collectivisation, see R. W. Davies, *The Socialist Offensive* (1976) and on industrialisation his *The Industrialisation of the Soviet Union* (1980). The political dimension of modernisation is considered by H. Kuromiya, *Stalin's Industrial Revolution: Politics and Workers, 1928–1932* (1988) and his essay on the USSR. in S. Salter and J. Stevenson (eds), *The Working Class and Politics in Europe and North America, 1929–45* (1989). Soviet claims to have avoided the world depression are examined in R. W. Davies, 'The Ending of Mass Unemployment in the USSR', in D. Lane (ed.), *Labour and Employment in the U.S.S.R.* (1986). Factors assisting support for the Stalinist regime are considered in S. Fitzpatrick, *Education and Social Mobility in the U.S.S.R., 1921–1934* (1979). On the Terror, see R. Conquest, *The Great Terror* (1968; rev. edn 1990) and J. Arch Getty, *Origins of the Great Purges: The Soviet Communist Party Reconsidered, 1933–1938* (1985). R. Medvedev, *Let History Judge: The Origins and Consequences of Stalinism* (2nd edn, 1989) is a view from a leading Soviet historian, reflecting the post-Gorbachev openness about the Stalinist past. For the development of the party, see L. Schapiro, *The Communist Party of the Soviet Union* (1970) and the early sections of his *The Government and Politics of the Soviet Union* (rev. edn, 1967). The new working-class 'vanguard' is considered in L. Viola, *The Best Sons of the Fatherland* (1987), while the military is examined in J. Erickson, *The Soviet High Command. A Military–Political History, 1918–1941* (1962). The position of the peasantry is put in long-term perspective in J. Channon, *The Russian and Soviet Peasantry, 1880–1991* (1997), but see also S. Fitzpatrick, *Stalin's Peasants: Resistance and Survival in the Russian Village after Collectivization* (1996) and L. Viola, *Peasant Rebels under Stalin* (1996).

For Russia at war, see A. Werth, *Russia at War* (1965), A. Dallin, *German Rule in Russia, 1941–5* (1957), J. Barber and M. Harrison (eds), *The Soviet Home Front, 1941–1945* (1991), and S. J. Main, *The USSR and the Defeat of Nazi Germany, 1941–45* (1997). Stalin's foreign policy is discussed in G. F. Kennan, *Russia and the West under Lenin and Stalin* (1961), A. B. Ulam, *Expansion and Co-existence* (1967), J. Haslam, *Soviet Foreign Policy, 1930–33* (1983) and *The Soviet Union and the Struggle for Collective Security* (1984), R. C. Raack, *Stalin's Drive to the West, 1938–1945* (1995), G. Mastny, *Soviet Insecurity and the Cold War* (1994), and S. Goncharov, J. Lewis and X. Litai, *Uncertain Partners: Stalin, Mao, and the Korean War* (1995).

Articles

On the Stalin era between the wars, see S. Cohen, 'Stalin's Revolution reconsidered', *S.R.* (1973), D. R. Brower, 'Collectivised agriculture in Smolensk: the Party, the peasantry and the crisis of 1932', *The Russian Review* (1977), S. Fitzpatrick, 'The Russian Revolution and social mobility', *Politics and Society* (1984), M. Lewin, 'Society and the Stalinist state in the period of the Five Year Plans', *S.H.* (1976); and M. R. Dohan, 'The Economic Origins of Soviet Autarky, 1927/8–1934', *S.R.* (1976).

8. Eastern Europe between the wars, 1918–39

The break-up of Austria–Hungary at the end of the First World War, together with the defeats of Russia, Germany and Turkey, allowed the various nationalities of Eastern Europe to assert their independence. Many, impressed by the victory of the Western powers in 1918, established democratic regimes. Unfortunately, these states soon faced enormous problems. Political inexperience, limited industry, illiteracy and inflation all took their toll; certain nationalities (such as the Slovaks and Ukrainians) still sought independent rights, while the defeated powers, like Hungary, resented the victors, like Romania. In most states democracy simply collapsed from within and with the coming of the 'slump' Eastern Europe fell prey to foreign domination, largely by Germany. In 1938 Hitler absorbed Austria and much of Czechoslovakia. In 1939 events in Eastern Europe became the cause of a world war.

Essay topics

* Why were the states of Eastern Europe generally unable to establish stable, democratic regimes between the wars?
* Why was Czechoslovakia unable to resist Hitler's annexationist pressures in 1938?

Sources and documents

Eastern Europe was the stamping ground for many intellectuals and historians who sought to identify and, if possible, solve the problems of Eastern Europe's kaleidoscope of cultures, nationalities and prejudices. Many of their contemporary writings are historical documents in themselves. See, for example, E. Wiskemann, *Czechs and Germans* (1938) and *The Europe I Saw* (1968), E. Beneš, *My War Memoirs* (1928), C. A. Macartney, *Hungary and her Successors* (1937), and R. W. Seton-Watson, *A History of the Czechs and Slovaks* (1943).

Secondary works

General introductions to the period are provided by H. Seton-Watson, *Eastern Europe between the Wars* (1962) and J. Rothschild, *East Central Europe between the Two World Wars* (1974), while a wider perspective is given in A. Palmer, *The Lands Between: A History of East Central Europe since the Congress of Vienna* (1970). C. A. Macartney and A. Palmer, *Independent Eastern Europe* (1962) and H. and C. Seton-Watson, *The Making of New Europe* (1981) are also helpful.

A. Polonsky, *The Little Dictators* (1975) covers each East European state since 1918 in turn, and there are various individual works on East European states, notably R. Clogg, *A Short History of Modern Greece* (1979), M. Macdermott, *A History of Bulgaria* (1962), S. Pollo and A. Puto, *The History of Albania* (1981), S. Fischer-Galati, *Twentieth Century Rumania* (1970), and A. Polonsky, *Politics in Independent Poland 1921–39* (1972). With regard to German expansion in the 1930s, Austria is discussed in J. Gehl, *Austria, Germany and the Anschluss, 1931–9* (1963) and G. Brook-Shepherd, *Anschluss* (1963). On the more complex Czechoslovakian issue, see I. Lukes, *Czechoslovakia between Stalin and Hitler* (1996), J. W. Bruegel, *Czechoslovakia before Munich* (1973), E. M. Smelser, *The Sudeten Problem 1933–8* (1975), and, for background, J. Korbel, *Twentieth Century Czechoslovakia* (1977).

9. The Spanish Civil War, 1936–39

In 1931 the Second Republic was established in Spain, following a period of right-wing dictatorship and inept monarchical rule. But it soon fell victim to the deep, historical divisions in Spanish politics, and in July 1936 an army uprising led by General Franco and General Mola began the Civil War. Internally, this represented a struggle between conservative groups, such as the army, Church, landowners and fascist elements, against republicans, socialists, communists and anarchists. However, the war soon gained a wider European significance, representing to many the struggle against fascism by democratic and left-wing ideologies. Foreign volunteers, as 'International Brigades', fought for the Republic and it received important assistance from the Soviet Union. Franco received support from Mussolini and Hitler, while the Western democracies pursued a controversial policy of 'non-intervention'. Franco gradually conquered most of Spain and achieved victory in 1939, establishing a personal dictatorship which was to last until the 1970s. The origins of the war and the relative significance of historic as opposed to short-term factors in its outbreak and character are major issues, particularly in regard to the conduct of the Popular Front government prior to the outbreak of the war. The extent to which the war was, in fact, one between fascism and democracy, as opposed to one drawing on primarily Spanish issues, is important, as is the role of foreign intervention and the influence of the war on international relations.

Essay topics

- To what extent was the Spanish Republic established in 1931 the author of its own downfall?
- How important to the outcome of the Spanish Civil War were the policies of the major European powers?
- Was the Spanish Civil War primarily a war of rival ideologies?

Sources and documents

R. Fraser, *Blood of Spain* (1979) has eye-witness accounts of the conflict, while George Orwell, *Homage to Catalonia* (1938) and J. Gurney, *Crusade in Spain* (1974) are two accounts from British volunteers who fought for the Republic. See, too, P. Toynbee, *The Distant Drum: Reflections on the Spanish Civil War* (1979). Two contemporary novels which breathe something of the atmosphere of the conflict are E. Hemingway, *For Whom the Bell Tolls* (1940) and A. Malraux, *Days of Hope* (1938). F. Borkenau, *The Spanish Cockpit* (1937) was an influential tract for the times.

Secondary works

R. Carr, *Spain, 1808–1939* (1966; rev. edn, *Spain, 1808–1975,* 1982) is an essential starting point, rooting the Civil War in Spanish development, as does his *The Spanish Tragedy* (1977). G. Brenan, *The Spanish Labyrinth* (1943) is widely recognised as a modern classic for its deep understanding of the Spanish context. P. Preston (ed.), *Revolution and War in Spain, 1931–1939* (1984) has an extremely useful historiographical essay by the editor. See also F. R. de Meneses, *Franco and the Spanish Civil War* (2001).

H. Thomas, *The Spanish Civil War* (rev. edn, 1977) remains a well-balanced narrative, but see also G. Jackson, *The Spanish Republic and the Civil War* (1965). On the origins of the war, P. Preston, *The Coming of the Spanish Civil War* (2nd edn, 1994) gives emphasis to the land question, as does E. E. Malefakis, *Agrarian Reform and Peasant Revolution* (1970). R. Carr (ed.), *The Republic and the Civil War in Spain* (1971) is another useful collection of essays, as is M. Blinkhorn (ed.), *Spain in Conflict 1931–1939: Democracy and Its Enemies* (1986).

On the right-wing forces, see P. Preston, *The Politics of Revenge: Fascism and the Military in 20th Century Spain* (1995), F. Lannon, *Privilege, Persecution and Prophecy: The Catholic Church in Spain, 1875–1975* (1987), M. Vincent, 'Spain', in T. Buchanan and M. Conway (eds), *Political Catholicism in Europe, 1918–1965* (1996), R. Robinson, *The Origins of Franco's Spain* (1970), S. Payne, *Falange* (1961), and the biographies of Franco by P. Preston, *Franco* (1993), B. Crozier, *Franco* (1967), and J. Trythall, *Franco* (1970). On the left, see S. Payne, *The Spanish Revolution* (1970) and P. Broué and E. Témine, *The Revolution and the Civil War in Spain* (1972), the latter critical of the communists' role. Two books sympathetic to the anarchists are V. Richards, *Lessons of the Spanish*

356

Revolution (1957) and M. Bookchin, *The Spanish Anarchists* (1977). The role of the communists is also considered in D. T. Cattell, *Communism and the Spanish Civil War* (1955) and B. Balloten, *The Grand Camouflage* (1961), reissued as *The Spanish Revolution: The Left and the Struggle for Power during the Civil War* (1979). A fascinating case study of a group which exemplifies the complexities of Spanish politics is M. Blinkhorn, *Carlism and Crisis in Spain 1931–1939* (1975); see also M. Blinkhorn, 'Spain', in S. Salter and J. Stevenson (eds), *The Working Class and Politics in Europe and North America, 1929–1945* (1990).

Interventionism is discussed in D. Puzzo, *Spain and the Great Powers, 1936–41* (1962), V. Brome, *The International Brigades* (1965), J. F. Coverdale, *Italian Intervention in the Spanish Civil War* (1977), J. Edwards, *Britain and the Spanish Civil War* (1979), and E. H. Carr, *The Comintern and the Spanish Civil War* (1984). G. Weintraub, *The Last Great Cause* (1976) is an exposé of the war of propaganda carried out by both sides to enlist support. On the most famous episode – the bombing of Guernica – see G. Thomas and M. Witts, *Guernica* (1975) and H. R. Southworth, *Guernica! Guernica! A Study of Journalism, Diplomacy, Propaganda and History* (1977).

10. France, 1918–44

Although the Third Republic emerged victorious from the First World War, the interwar period was one of increasing self-doubt and division for France. Unstable governments, industrial and demographic weaknesses, and economic problems (especially the 'slump') were compounded by increasing extremism on the left and right, with the emergence of the communist party and fascist groups. In the 1930s the Stavisky riots and failure of the 'Popular Front' government, alongside the growing Nazi menace, created grave disillusion. Even so, the Third Republic retained many of its prewar strengths, including social stability and widespread sympathy for the regime, and historians question whether the Republic would have collapsed but for the overwhelming military defeat at German hands in 1940. In 1940 Marshal Pétain made peace with Germany and established a collaborationist regime at Vichy. France did not recover her independence for four years.

Essay topics

- How close did France come to civil war in the interwar period?
- Why was France defeated in 1940?
- To what extent did the Vichy regime represent what most of the French wanted between 1940 and 1944?

Sources and documents

J.-P. Sartre's novel, *Iron in the Soul* (1949, trans. 1950) and M. Bloch, *Strange Defeat* (1940) represent different reactions to France's defeat. P. Laval, *The Unpublished Diary of Pierre Laval* (1948) and S. M. Osgood (ed.), *The Fall of France, 1940* (1965) are also helpful.

Secondary works

J. F. McMillan, *Dreyfus to de Gaulle: Politics and Society in France, 1898–1969* (1985) and *Twentieth Century France: Politics and Society in France, 1898–1991* (1992), and M. Larkin, *France since the Popular Front: Government and People, 1936–1986* (1988) are good general accounts, but see also P. Bernard and H. Dubieff, *The Decline of the Third Republic, 1914–38* (1985), R. Vinen, *France, 1934–70* (1996), and M. Agulhon, *The French Republic, 1879–1992* (1993).

The important Popular Front era is discussed in J. Jackson, *The Popular Front in France: Defending Democracy, 1934–1938* (1988) and its leading figure in J. Coulton, *Léon Blum* (1974). The most important party of the interwar years is examined in P. Larmour, *The French Radical Party in the 1930s* (1964), while there is a useful survey of the right in R. Austin, 'The Conservative right and the far right in France: the search for power, 1934–44', in M. Blinkhorn (ed.), *Fascists and Conservatives* (1990); see also W. D. Irvine, *French Conservatism in Crisis* (1979) and C. A. Micaval, *The French Right and Nazi Germany, 1933–9* (1972). For the left see the survey essay by R. McGraw, 'France', in S. Salter and J. Stevenson (eds), *The Working Class and Politics in Europe and North America, 1929–45* (1990), R. Tiersky, *The French Communist Party, 1920–1970* (1974), and E. Mortimer, *The Rise of the French Communist Party, 1920–1947* (1984). The role of the army is considered in A. Horne, *The French Army in Politics* (1984).

On the approach to war, see A. Adamthwaite, *France and the Coming of the Second World War* (1977), while the fall of France is discussed in A. Horne, *To Lose a Battle: France, 1940* (1979) and R. Collier, *1940: the World in Flames* (1980). The politicians involved in the collapse are considered in H. R. Lottman, *Pétain: Hero or Traitor?* (1985), R. Griffiths, *Marshal Petain* (1970), S. Hoffman, 'The Vichy circle of French conservatives' in his *Decline or Renewal? France since the 1930s* (1974), and G. Warner, *Pierre Laval and the Eclipse of France* (1968), and J. Lacouture, *De Gaulle: The Rebel: 1890–1944* (trans. edn, 1990). The Vichy regime is examined in R. Aron, *The Vichy Régime, 1940–4* (1958), R. Paxton, *Vichy France* (1972), and R. Kedward, *Occupied France: Collaboration and Resistance, 1940–44* (1985). R. Cobb, *French and Germans, Germans and French* (1983) and R. Kedward and R. Austin (eds), *Vichy France and the Resistance: Ideology and Culture* (1985) examine aspects of the interaction. The resistance is the subject of P. Burrin, *Occupied France: Collaboration and Resistance, 1940–44* (1996), R. Kedward, *Resistance in Vichy France* (1978), M. Dank, *The French against the French* (1978), and M. R. D. Foot, *Resistance* (1976). The specific issue of anti-Semitism is set out in P. Kingston, *Anti-Semitism in France during the 1930s* (1983) and R. Paxton and M. Marrus, *Vichy France and the Jews* (1981).

Articles

For an overview, see K. Passmore, 'The French Third Republic: Stalemate Society or Cradle of Fascism?', *French History* (1993). For important, more specialised aspects, D. R. Watson, 'The politics of electoral reform in France during the Third Republic, 1900–40', *P.P.* (1966), A. Sauvy, 'The economic crisis of the 1930s in France', *J.C.H.* (1969), and D. Johnson, 'Léon Blum and the Popular Front', *H.* (1970) are all helpful. W. D. Irvine, 'French conservatives and the "New Right" during the 1930s', *F.H.S.* (1974) and K.-J. Muller, 'French fascism and modernization', *J.C.H.* (1976) are useful on the right.

11. Interwar diplomacy, 1919–39

Despite the enormous casualties of the First World War, the peacemakers who gathered in Paris in 1919 failed to achieve a stable diplomatic framework in Europe. The Treaty of Versailles with Germany seemed vindictive in retrospect and many powers came away from Paris determined to alter the settlement. The new international peacekeeping body, the League of Nations, proved weak and in the 1920s even Britain and France fell out over the treatment of Germany and colonial problems. In the 1930s Hitler's Germany and Mussolini's Italy adopted expansionist policies, which the Western democracies at first tried to end by 'appeasement'. By September 1939, however, Hitler had already established domination over much of Eastern Europe, and his invasion of Poland finally led to a European war.

Essay topics

- To what extent should the Versailles Peace Conference be described as a failure?
- Was there any point before 1939 when Hitler could have been more effectively opposed?
- 'The Second World War was Hitler's war.' Discuss.

Sources and documents

A. Adamthwaite, *The Lost Peace* (1980) provides an invaluable documentary source on the whole period. J. M. Keynes's *The Economic Consequences of the Peace* (1919) represents one of the most influential critiques of the peace. See also H. Nicholson, *Peacemaking, 1919* (1933). For the later period, see on German foreign policy, N. H. Baynes, *The Speeches of Adolf Hitler, April 1922–August 1939* (1942), and on Italy, *Ciano's Diaries, 1937–8* (1952) and *1939–43* (1947). For Britain, see Lord Avon, *Facing the Dictators* (1962) and *The Reckoning* (1965), and W. S. Churchill, *The Second World War, vol. I, The Gathering Storm* (1949). For Russia, see I. Maisky, *Who Helped Hitler?* (1964).

Secondary works

E. H. Carr, *The Twenty Years Crisis* (new edn, 1981) remains a stimulating account of the period. G. N. Gathorne-Hardy, *A Short History of International Affairs, 1920–39* (1950) has aged less well. Among general accounts, H. Gatzke, *European Diplomacy between the Two World Wars* (1972) is to be preferred, and once again R. Albrecht-Carrié, *A Diplomatic History of Europe from the Congress of Vienna* (1961) provides the wider background. R. A. C. Parker, *Europe, 1919–45* (1969) is also a good general introduction.

On 1919 and its immediate aftermath A. J. Mayer, *The Policy and Diplomacy of Peacemaking* (1968), G. Schulz, *Revolution and Peace Treaties* (1972), and S. Marks, *The Illusion of Peace* (1976) are useful, while F. P. Walters, *A History of the League of Nations* (1960) remains the most thorough account of that body.

On the origins of war in 1939, A. J. P. Taylor, *The Origins of the Second World War* (1961) is still exciting and very readable, though its arguments have been undermined. E. M. Robertson, *The Origins of the Second World War* (1976) is more recent and, on the 1930s especially, see also C. Thorne, *The Approach of War* (1967), D. C. Watt, *Too Serious a Business* (1975), and A. Adamthwaite, *The Making of the Second World War* (1977). A recent overview is P. Bell, *The Origins of the Second World War in Europe* (1986). The definitive study of the immediate crisis is now D. Cameron Watt, *How War Came: The Immediate Origins of the Second World War, 1938–9* (1989); also valuable is R. Overy and A. Wheatcroft, *The Road to War* (1989) and V. Rothwell, *The Origins of the Second World War* (1995).

On specific events and issues, N. Rostow, *Anglo–French Relations, 1934–6* (1984) analyses Western policies at a key period, while K. Robbins, *Munich* (1968) and T. Taylor, *Munich* (1979) look at the most criticised episode in 1930s diplomacy. S. Newman, *March, 1939* (1976) concentrates on the British guarantee to Poland, which was so vital in the outbreak of war. On French policy, see especially A. Adamthwaite, *France and the Coming of the Second World War* (1977), and on Germany, G. L. Weinberg, *The Foreign Policy of Hitler's Germany* (1970) and W. Carr, *Arms, Autarky and Aggression* (1972). On British appeasement in general, see especially M. Gilbert, *The Roots of Appeasement* (1966), K. Middlemas, *Diplomacy of Illusion* (1972), and W. R. Rock, *British Appeasement in the 1930s* (1976). See also the essays by N. Medlicott and M. Howard in D. Dilks (ed.), *Retreat from Power: Studies of Britain's Foreign Policy of the Twentieth Century: Vol. One, 1906–1939* (1981).

Articles

On the Versailles Treaty see W. A. McDougall, M. Trachtenberg, and C. S. Maier, *J.M.H.* (1979), Special issue on Versailles; A. Lentin, 'What Really Happened at Paris?', *Diplomacy and Statecraft* (1990); D. Stevenson, 'French War Aims and the American Challenge', *H.J.* (1979). On the reparations issue, see S. Marks, 'Reparations Reconsidered: A Reminder', *C.E.H.* (1969); D. Felix, 'Reparations Considered with a Vengeance', *C.E.H.* (1971); S. Marks, 'The Myths of Reparations', *C.E.H.* (1978); and M. Trachtenberg, 'Reparation at the Paris Peace Conference', *J.M.H.* (1979).

Among the numerous articles on the various crises of the 1930s, see especially R. A. C. Parker, 'Great Britain, France and the Ethiopian Crisis, 1935–6', *E.H.R.* (1974), C. A. Macdonald, 'Britain, France and the April Crisis of 1939', *E.S.R.* (1972), and M. Newman, 'The origins of Munich', *H.J.* (1978).

12. The Second World War, 1939–45

Although Hitler was able to overrun Poland, Norway, Denmark, the Low Countries and France in 1939–40, Britain survived and in 1941 was joined by Russia and America. In the air the Germans lost the 'Battle of Britain' and were soon faced with Anglo–American bombing of their own cities; at sea, the Allied use of radar helped defeat the U-boat menace; while on land the German army proved unable to break Russian resistance. Economic factors, notably American industrial production and manpower, began to tell in the Allies' favour, and from 1943 Hitler's defeat was clearly inevitable. The use of German technology to produce the snorkel, jet aircraft and rockets came too late to affect the outcome. Nonetheless, many would argue that it was Hitler's own ambition which ultimately proved his greatest enemy. The social and political repercussions of 'total war' with mass civilian involvement have also become important areas of discussion.

Essay topics

- To what extent did economic considerations dictate the course of the Second World War in Europe?
- How far did European experience of 'total war' affect its conduct and its outcome?
- Why were the campaigns of the Second World War more mobile than those of the First?

Sources and documents

H. Jacobsen and A. Smith (eds), *World War II* (1980) has documents on military policy and strategy, and there are numerous collections of memoirs. W. S. Churchill, *The Second World War* (6 vols, 1948–54) and C. de Gaulle, *War Memoirs* (3 vols, 1955–59) are perhaps the best from European statesmen and, from the generals, Lord Alanbrooke, *War Diaries 1939–1945* (2001) and Montgomery of Alamein, *Memoirs* (1958). A. Speer, *Inside the Third Reich* (1970) remains a telling account of the resilience of the German war machine. On the civilian side, see on Holland O. Frank, *The Diary of Anne Frank* (1947), on Britain R. Broad and S. Fleming (eds), *Nella Last's Diary* (1981), and on the concentration camps O. Lengyel, *Five Chimneys* (1959). Two English language accounts of life within Germany are C. Bielenberg, *The Past is Myself* (1968) and *The Berlin Diaries, 1940–1945, of Marie 'Missie' Vassiltchikov* (1985).

Secondary works

Of the general introductions see especially R. A. C. Parker, *Struggle for Survival: The History of the Second World War* (1990), R. Overy, *Why the Allies Won* (1995), G. Weinberg, *A World at Arms: a Global History of World War II* (1994), P. Calvocoressi and G. Wint, *Total War* (1974), B. Liddell Hart, *The Second World War* (1970), and A. J. P. Taylor, *The Second World War: An Illustrated History* (1976). For the impact of the war on the combatants, A. Marwick, *War and Social Change in the Twentieth Century* (1974) concentrates on the social effects. D. Irving, *Hitler's War* (1983) gives an account of the war from the German perspective, for which see also O. Bartov, 'From blitzkrieg to total war' in M. Fulbrook (ed.), *Twentieth Century Germany* (2001). On Russia, see A. Werth,

Russia at War (1965), J. D. Barber and M. Harrison, *The Soviet Home Front, 1941–1945: A Social and Economic History of the USSR in World War II* (1991), and S. Bialer (ed.), *Stalin and his Generals* (1971). For Britain, see A. Calder, *The People's War* (1969). On the economic conduct of the war, see A. S. Milward, *War, Economy and Society, 1939–1945* (1977), also his *The German Economy at War* (1965) and R. Overy, *War and Economy in the Third Reich* (1995).

The opening phase of the war is covered by B. Collier, *1940: The World in Flames* (1980) and *1941: Armageddon* (1982). The controversy over the effectiveness and morality of the bombing offensive against Germany is considered in N. Frankland, *The Bombing Offensive against Germany* (1965) and M. Hastings, *Bomber Command* (1979). For the German side of the air war, see D. Irving, *The Rise and Fall of the Luftwaffe* (1973). For the war at sea, see D. Macintyre, *The Battle of the Atlantic* (1961), J. Costello and T. Hughes, *The Battle of the Atlantic* (1977), and W. Frank, *The Sea Wolves* (1955). The decisive struggle on the Eastern Front is considered in A. Clark, *Barbarossa* (1965), and J. Erickson, *The Road to Stalingrad: Stalin's War with Germany* (1975) and *The Road to Berlin* (1983).

For the final phase of the war, see E. Belfield and H. Essame, *The Battle for Normandy* (1965) and C. Ryan, *The Last Battle* (1974). Specifically on the new form of mobile warfare, see H. Guderian, *Panzer Leader* (1952) and F. W. von Mellenthin, *Panzer Battles* (1955). Technical developments affecting the conduct of the war are discussed in R. V. Jones, *Most Secret War* (1978) and B. Johnson, *The Secret War* (1978). Increasing attention has been given to the conduct of the war and its effects upon those engaged in it. O. Bartov, *The Eastern Front, 1941–45: German troops and the barbarisation of warfare* (1986) and *Hitler's Army. Soldiers, Nazis and War in the Third Reich* (1991) is a brilliant analysis of the conduct of the war in the east, but see also C. Browning, *Ordinary Men; Reserve Police Battalion 101 and the Final Solution in Poland* (1992), T. Schulte, *The German Army and Nazi Policies in Occupied Russia* (1989) and, more generally, P. Addison and A. Calder (eds), *Time to Kill* (1995) on servicemen.

The fate of areas conquered by the Germans is considered in W. Warmbrunn, *The Dutch under German Occupation* (1963), G. Hirschfield, *Nazi Rule and Dutch Collaboration* (1988), A. K. Hoidal, *Quisling: A Study in Treason* (1989), A. Dallin, *German Rule in Russia, 1941–5* (1957), and on France see especially P. Burrin, *Occupied France: Collaboration and Resistance* (1996), H. R. Kedward and R. Austin (eds), *Vichy France and Resistance* (1985), J. Sweets, *Choices in Vichy France: the French under German Occupation* (1986), H. R. Kedward and N. Wood (eds), *The Liberation of France* (1995) and R. O. Paxton, *Vichy France* (1973), while the resistance movements are analysed in H. Michel, *The Shadow War: Resistance in Europe, 1939–45* (1972), S. Haves and R. White (eds), *Resistance in Europe, 1939–1945* (1975), and M. R. D. Foot, *Resistance* (1976). On the fate of the Jews, see M. Marrus, *The Holocaust in History* (1989), L. S. Dawidowicz, *The War against the Jews* (1975), and G. Fleming, *Hitler and the Final Solution* (1984).

On diplomacy during the war, see H. Feis, *Churchill, Roosevelt, Stalin* (1957), W. H. McNeill, *America, Britain and Russia* (1953), and G. Kolko, *The Politics of War* (1968). D. Carlton, *Churchill and Stalin* (1999), examines a key 'big power' relationship and the Soviet view is discussed in V. Mastny, *Russia's Road to the Cold War* (1979) and R. C. Raack, *Stalin's Drive to the West, 1938–1945: The Origins of the Cold War* (1995). For the origins of the Cold War see J. Young, *The Cold War in Europe, 1945–91* (2nd edn, 1996).

13. The Holocaust

The fate of European Jewry at the hands of the Nazis has given rise to an enormous literature which seeks to understand the processes which led from the often prevalent anti-Semitism of many European states to the industrialised mass slaughter carried out by the Nazis from 1941. The question of whether there was a particular German trait of anti-Semitism and why the Nazis of all fascist movements took a particularly virulent policy against the Jews has attracted attention. In particular there is considerable debate about the intentions of the Nazis and whether the 'Final Solution' was Hitler's objective from the outset or the product of the particular circumstances in which the Nazis found themselves from 1941, when millions of European Jews were under their control as a result of the conquests in the East. The link of the destruction of the European Jews with the euthanasia policy and other aspects of racial purity, such as the killing of gypsies, homosexuals and the unfit, has come under scrutiny. The collusion of other groups in Nazi policy, both in the occupied territories in the East and in the governments of collaborationist and allied countries, has also been examined. Questions remain about whether more could have been done by the Allies, the occupied powers or by Jews themselves to resist Nazi policy. A trickle of Holocaust memoirs in the aftermath of the war has given way to a flood of material in recent years more fully documenting Nazi policies and their consequences.

Essay topics

- Why did the Nazis persecute the Jews?
- To what extent was the 'Final Solution' the outcome of the circumstances Nazi Germany faced in 1941 rather than the result of long-term policy?
- Why did the Allied governments not act more directly to interfere with the 'Final Solution'?

Sources and documents

Hitler's *Mein Kampf* (1925–26) is available edited by D. C. Watt (1969) and there is considerable factual material in M. Freeman, *Atlas of Nazi Germany* (new edn, 1995) and W. Laqueur (ed.), *The Holocaust Encyclopedia* (2001). Participant accounts include O. Frank, *The Diary of Anne Frank* (1947), Primo Levi, *If This is Man* (1979), O. Lengyel, *Five Chimneys* (1959), E. Kogon, *The Theory and Practice of Hell* (1950), H. Kruk, *The Last Days of the Jerusalem of Lithuania: Chronicles from the Vilna Ghetto and the camps, 1939–1944* (ed. B. Harshav, 2002), and H. Fried, *The Road to Auschwitz: fragments of a life* (ed. M. Meyer, 1990). Recently available in English is V. Klemperer, *I Shall Bear Witness: Diaries, 1933–41* and *Till the Bitter End, 1942–45* (1998–9).

Secondary works

For general perspectives see M. Marrus, *The Holocaust in History* (1989), Y. Bauer, *Rethinking the Holocaust* (2002), C. Browning, *The Path to Genocide* (1992), P. Burrin, *Hitler and the Jews: The Genesis of the Holocaust* (1994), and R. Hilberg, *The Destruction of the European Jews* (3 vols, 1985). Older accounts include L. S. Dawidowicz, *The War against the Jews* (1975), K. Schleunes, *The Twisted Road to Auschwitz* (1970), and G. Fleming, *Hitler and the Final Solution* (1984). The latter tend to follow the view that the Holocaust was the outcome of long-term policy, the so-called 'intentionalist' view, which is usefully discussed in I. Kershaw, *The Nazi Dictatorship* (1989), especially ch. 5; see also N. Stargardt, 'The Holocaust' in M. Fulbrook, *Twentieth Century Germany* (2001). Recent collections of essays which examine aspects of the debate over Nazi policy are O. Bartov (ed.), *The Holocaust: Origins, Implementation, Aftermath* (2000), D. Cesarani (ed.), *The Final Solution: Origins and Implementation* (1994), G. Hirschfield (ed.), *The Policies of Genocide: Jews and Soviet Prisoners of War in Nazi Germany* (1986) and W. Pehle (ed.), *November 1938: From Reichkristallnacht to Genocide* (1991).

On non-Jewish victims, see Hirschfield (above), G. Grau (ed.), *Hidden Holocaust? Gay and Lesbian Persecution in Germany, 1933–1945* (1995), D. Kenrick and G. Puxon, *The Destiny of European Gypsies* (1972), and M. Burleigh, *Death and Deliverance: 'Euthanasia' in Germany, c. 1900–1945* (1994), B. Muller-Hill, *Murderous Science: Elimination by Scientific Selection of Jews, Gypsies and others, Germany, 1933–1945* (1988), and U. Herbert, *A History of Foreign Labour in Germany, 1880–1980* (1990).

On the complicity or conformity of Germans with the Holocaust, see the controversial view of D. Goldhagen, *Hitler's Willing Executioners: Ordinary Germans and the Holocaust* (1996), but see also C. Browning, *Ordinary Men: Reserve Police Battalion 101 and the Final Solution in Poland* (1992) and his *Nazi Policy, Jewish Workers, German Killers* (2000), S. Friedlander, *Nazi Germany and the Jews: The Years of Persecution, 1933–1939* (1997), M. Burleigh and W. Wippermann, *The Racial State: Germany, 1933–1945* (1991), T. Schulte, *The German Army and Nazi Policies in Occupied Russia* (1989), O. Bartov, *Hitler's Army: Soldiers, Nazis, and War in the Third Reich* (1991), and D. Peukert, *Inside Nazi Germany: Conformity, Opposition and Racism in Everyday Life* (1993). See also D. Bankier, *The Germans and the Final Solution: Public Opinion under Nazism* (1992) and Ulrich Herbert, *Forced Foreign Labour in the Third Reich* (1997). The 'denial' of one leading Nazi is considered in G. Sereny, *Albert Speer: His Struggle with Truth* (1995).

The complicity of other states is considered in M. Marrus and R. Paxton, *Vichy France and the Jews* (1981) and G. Hirschfield and P. Marsh (eds), *Collaboration in France: Politics and Culture During the Occupation, 1940–44* (1989), P. F. Sugar (ed.), *Native Fascism in the Successor States, 1918–45* (1971), E. Mendelsohn, *The Jews of East Central Europe between the World Wars* (1987), M. Michaelis, *Mussolini and the Jews* (1978), J. Steinberg, *All or Nothing: the Axis and the Holocaust* (1990), and M. Dean, *Collaboration in the Holocaust: Crimes of the Local Police in*

Belorussia and Ukraine, 1941–44 (2000). On the failure of the Allies to assist the Jews more decisively, see L. D. Rubinstein, *The Myth of Rescue* (1999).

Reactions to the Holocaust by its victims are considered in E. Cohen, *Human Behaviour in the Concentration Camp* (1998) and P. Levi, *The Drowned and the Saved* (1980). The wider question of how the Holocaust is perceived and commemorated is examined in J. E. Young, *Holocaust Remembrance: The Shapes of Memory* (1994) and his *The Texture of Memory: Holocaust Memorials and Meaning* (1993). See also Z. Amishai-Maisels, *Depiction and Interpretation: The Influence of the Holocaust on the Visual Arts* (1993), T. Cole, *Images of the Holocaust: The Myth of the Shoah Business* (1999) and Y. Eliach, 'Documenting the Landscape of Death: The Politics of Commemoration and Holocaust Studies' in Y. Bauer (ed.), *Remembering the Future*, vol. III (1989).

Articles

On the often considered crucial Wannsee Conference, see C. Gerlach, 'The Wannsee Conference, the Fate of the Jews and Hitler's decision in principle to exterminate all the Jews', *J.M.H.* (1998).

14. The Cold War

Despite their wartime alliance, the Soviet Union and the Western powers, America and Britain, soon differed over the shape of the postwar world. The Russian takeover in Eastern Europe and enforcement of communist regimes, together with Soviet pressures in Germany and the Middle East, led to the Truman Doctrine in 1947, by which the Americans undertook to resist communist pressure. America and the West Europeans joined together in NATO in 1949, and the following years were characterised by deep-seated tension, known as the Cold War, with notable crises over the Korean War, the future of Berlin and Cuba.

Essay topics

- To what extent may Russia be blamed for beginning the Cold War?
- Why did the Cold War end?

Sources and documents

A readily accessible selection can be found in M. McCauley, *The Origins of the Cold War* (1983), but the early period is well covered from the documentary side by W. Lafeber, *The Origins of the Cold War* (1977) and M. Carlyle (ed.), *Documents on International Affairs, 1947–8* (1952) and *1949–50* (1953). There are numerous memoirs on the Cold War theme but among the best are H. S. Truman, *Year of Decisions, 1945* (1955) and *Years of Trial and Hope, 1946–53* (1956), and D. Acheson, *Present at the Creation* (1970). See also J. Young, *The Longman Companion to Cold War and Detente, 1941–91* (1993) for a compendium of factual material and full bibliography, and T. S. Arms, *Encyclopedia of the Cold War* (1994).

Secondary works

Good introductions to the present state of knowledge can be found in
J. L. Gaddis, *We Now Know: Rethinking Cold War History* (1997) and J. Young,
The Cold War in Europe, 1945–91 (new edn, 1996). J. Isaacs and T. Downing,
Cold War (1998) is a good popular account with documents and illustrations
to accompany a television series. Soviet policy is now better understood with
the partial opening of the Soviet archives; see especially R. C. Raack, *Stalin's
Drive to the West, 1938–1945: The Origins of the Cold War* (1995) and V. Mastny,
The Cold War and Soviet Insecurity: The Stalin Years (1996). The older studies by
A. B. Ulam, *Expansion and Coexistence* (1968) and T. W. Wolfe, *Soviet Power and
Europe, 1945–70* (1970) have to be seen in the light of more recent work. There
are other general works, most being American: J. W. Spanier, *American Foreign
Policy since the Second World War* (1980) is pro-American, S. E. Ambrose, *Rise to
Globalism* (1983) and W. Lafeber, *America, Russia and the Cold War* (1982) are
more questioning of US policy, while L. J. Halle, *The Cold War as History* (1967)
is still a useful, balanced account on part of the period.

The early years of the Cold War have received most coverage. Again there
are conservative accounts, such as G. F. Hudson, *The Hard and Bitter Peace* (1966)
and H. L. Feis, *From Trust to Terror* (1970), criticisms of America in G. and
J. Kolko, *The Limits of Power* (1972) and D. Yergin, *Shattered Peace* (1977).
J. L. Gaddis, *The United States and the Origins of the Cold War* (1973) is good,
and on the British, see V. Rothwell, *Britain and the Cold War, 1941–7* (1983)
and A. Deighton (ed.), *Britain and the First Cold War* (1989). Coverage of the
continental states is slight, but on France, see G. de Carmoy, *The Foreign Policies
of France* (1970) and, on the early years, E. Furniss, *France, Troubled Ally* (1960).

Articles

Two useful articles are J. L. Gaddis, 'The emerging post-revisionist synthesis',
Diplomatic History (1983) and D. Reynolds, 'The Big Three and the division of
Europe 1945–8: an overview', *Diplomacy and Statecraft* (1990). R. Ovendale,
'Britain, the U.S.A. and the European Cold War, 1945–8', *H.* (1982) is a
discussion of the major issues in the early postwar years, and G. Warner,
'The Truman Doctrine and the Marshall Plan', *International Affairs* (1974) dis-
cusses what was perhaps the key year. Of vital importance to the framing of
America's anti-communist policy was G. F. Kennan, 'The sources of Soviet
conduct', *Foreign Affairs* (1947), while A. Schlesinger, 'Origins of the Cold War',
Foreign Affairs (1967) gives an intelligent, short discussion.

15. Western European democracy since 1945

Western Europe in the aftermath of the Second World War proved far more
stable and wealthy than after the First. Despite the reconstruction problems
left by war, economic recovery, helped by the American Marshall Aid programme, was quite rapid, while democracy was re-established in France, Germany, Italy and elsewhere. The NATO alliance and extension of European

unity created a feeling of security and solidarity, which helped make the 1950s and 1960s decades of relative calm. There were problems, however. In France, political instability and the difficulties of decolonisation brought the fall of the Fourth Republic in 1958. Italian political life was characterised by rapid government changes and extremist pressures, and in the 1970s, despite the restoration of democracy in Spain, Portugal and Greece, all Europe was faced with the problems of inflation and unemployment.

Essay topics

- Why did West Germany prove more politically stable than Italy as a postwar democracy?
- To what extent can de Gaulle's period in office after 1958 be seen as a turning point in French history?

Sources and documents

For a wide-ranging set of documents, see P. Lane, *Europe since 1945* (1985) and for factual material on specific parts of Europe, A. Webb, *The Longman Companion to Germany since 1945* (1998) and A. Webb, *The Longman Companion to Central and Eastern Europe since 1919* (2002).

Secondary works

For general coverage of events see W. Laqueur, *Europe since Hitler* (1970), D. Urwin, *Western Europe since 1945* (1981), and P. Calvocoressi, *World Politics since 1945* (1982 edn). Also good are R. Mayne, *The Recovery of Europe* (1970), M. Crouzet, *The European Renaissance since 1945* (1970), and R. Morgan, *West European Politics since 1945* (1972). Rather narrower in interest is F. R. Willis, *France, Germany and the New Europe, 1945–67* (1969), while F. Fry and G. Raymond, *The Other Western Europe* (1980) looks at the smaller democracies. On economic reconstruction, see A. S. Milward, *The Reconstruction of Western Europe 1945–51* (1984), and M. J. Hogan, *The Marshall Plan* (1988).

On France in this period, see R. Gildea, *France since 1945* (1996), R. Vinen, *Bourgeois Politics in France, 1945–1951* (1995), and on the Fourth and Fifth Republics, see P. M. Williams, *Crisis and Compromise: Politics in the Fourth Republic* (1964 edn), P. M. Williams and M. Harrison, *Politics and Compromise: Politics and Society in de Gaulle's Republic* (1971), J. Ardagh, *The New France* (1978), and M. Anderson, *Conservative Politics in France* (1974). See also the studies of de Gaulle by D. Cook, *Charles de Gaulle* (1984), S. Berstein, *The Republic of de Gaulle, 1958–69* (1993), H. Gough and J. Hone, *De Gaulle and 20th Century France* (1994). For Germany, see as introduction M. Fulbrook (ed.), *Twentieth Century Germany: Politics, Culture, and Society, 1918–1990* (2001), Pt. II, which has synoptic essays on both West and East Germany, and on unification, L. Kattenacker, *Germany since 1945* (1997), I. Derbyshire, *Politics in Germany from Division to Unification* (1991), D. Childs, *The Fall of the GDR: Germany's Road to Unity* (2001), and K. H. Jarausch, *The Rush to German Unity* (1994) There are also valuable studies available in the following: A. J. Nicholls, *The Bonn Republic: West*

German Democracy, 1945–91 (1997), P. Pulzer, *German Politics, 1945–1995* (1995), D. L. Bark and D. R. Gress, *A History of West Germany, 1945–90* (2nd edn, 1993), and K. Larres and P. Panayi (eds), *The Federal Republic of Germany since 1949* (1996). On personalities, see T. Prittie, *The Velvet Chancellors* (1979) and *Adenauer* (1971).

On Italy, see M. Clark, *Modern Italy, 1871–1982* (1984), P. Ginsborg, *A History of Contemporary Italy: Society and Politics, 1943–1988* (1990), and also his *Italy and its Discontents: Family, Civil Society, State, 1980–2001* (2001). S. Tarrow, *Democracy and Disorder: Protest and Politics in Italy, 1965–75* (1989), and in the short Oxford History series, see P. McCarthy, *Italy since 1945* (2000) with a current bibliography. See also J. Dunnage, *Twentieth Century Italy: a social history* (2003).

Among other countries, Spain provides an interesting barometer of the spread of democracy in Western Europe: see R. Carr, *A History of Spain, 1808–1980* (rev. edn, 1980), R. Carr and J. P. Fusi, *Spain: Dictatorship to Democracy* (1979), D. Gilmour, *The Transformation of Spain* (1985), and P. Preston, *The Triumph of Democracy in Spain* (1986).

16. Decolonisation

Decolonisation was one of the great transformations of the postwar world, with immense repercussions for both the new states that arose from the European empires and for the European powers themselves. Theories of imperialism and its causes are inevitably linked with those for its demise, with an early fashion for Marxist theories of neo-colonialism giving way to more complex interpretations of European withdrawal and the processes of state formation that followed. The period covered was very long, from before the Second World War to the 1970s (in the case of Portugal) and even later in the destruction of 'white only' and apartheid regimes in Africa. Decolonisation also overlapped with the Cold War, making the struggles in South-East Asia and parts of Africa particularly protracted and bloody.

Essay topics

- Why did the European powers decolonise so rapidly after 1945?
- To what extent did the colonising powers merely replace political control with economic ties when they gave independence?
- Why did the experience of decolonisation prove so bitter and protracted for some countries but relatively painless for others?
- Examine the impact of decolonisation on any one Western colonial power.

Sources and documents

See D. K. Fieldhouse, *The Theory of Capitalist Imperialism* (1967) with texts and introduction. For chronologies, facts and figures and extensive bibliography, see M. Chamberlain, *The Longman Companion to European Decolonisation in the Twentieth Century* (1998); see also R. B. Smith and J. Stockwell (eds), *British Policy and the Transfer of Power in Asia: Documentary Perspectives* (1988).

Secondary works

See M. E. Chamberlain, *Decolonisation* (2nd edn, 1990), R. Holland, *European Decolonization, 1918–1981: An Introductory Survey* (1985), H. Grimal, *Decolonisation: The British, French, Dutch and Belgian Empires, 1919–1963* (1980), and W. Mommsen and J. Osterhammel, *Imperialism and After: Continuities and Discontinuities* (1986). For Africa, see J. D. Hargreaves, *Decolonisation in Africa* (1988), P. Gifford and W. R. Louis (eds), *The Transfer of Power in Africa: Decolonisation, 1940–1960* (1982), and on the French experience in Africa, A. Horne, *A Savage War of Peace: Algeria, 1954–1962* (1977) and D. S. White, *Black Africa and De Gaulle: From the French Empire to Independence* (1979). Asian independence is considered in R. Jeffrey, *Asia: The Winning of Independence* (1981), J. Stockwell in N. Tarling (ed.), *The Cambridge History of South East Asia*, vol. 2 (1992), A. Short, *The Communist Insurrection in Malaya, 1948–1960* (1975), H. Tinker, *Burma: The Struggle for Independence, 1944–48* (1983–4), A. Reid, *The Indonesian National Revolution, 1945–1950* (1974), A. Short, *The Origins of the Vietnam War* (1990), S. Karnow, *Vietnam: A History* (1994), and M. Shipway, *The Road to War: France and Vietnam, 1944–47* (1996).

Specifically on Britain, see J. Darwin, *The End of the British Empire* (1991) and *Britain and Decolonisation* (1988). On France see R. F. Betts, *France and Decolonisation, 1900–1960* (1991) and A. Clayton, *The Wars of French Decolonisation* (1994). F. Feredi, *Colonial Wars and the Politics of Third World Nationalism* (1994) and J. P. D. Dunbabin, *International Relations since 1945, Vol. II: The Post-imperial Age* (1994) put decolonisation in international perspective. The domestic impact is considered in M. Kahler, *Decolonisation in Britain and France: The Domestic Consequences of International Relations* (1984).

17. The movement for European unity

One of the most remarkable occurrences in Western Europe in the aftermath of the Second World War was the move towards some form of European unity. This was first seen in the Organization for European Economic Co-operation (1948) and the Council of Europe (1949). More far-reaching pressures of a 'supranational' kind led to the Schuman Plan (1950) and eventually the European Economic Community or Common Market (1957). Originally, these supranational bodies included only six states but after 1973 they were gradually extended. There were many strong reasons for such greater unity to come about, not least the experiences of war. Doubts about 'supranationalism' from both Britain (down to the present) and France's President de Gaulle (during the 1960s) were a major challenge to the European movement.

Essay topics

- Account for the rise of the European unity movement in the postwar period.
- To what extent was the move towards greater European unity shaped by French policy, 1950–69?

Sources and documents

Two very useful 'inside' accounts of the European unity movement can be found in the *Memoirs* (1978) of Jean Monnet, the 'father of European unity' and P.-H. Spaak, *The Continuing Battle* (1971). Relevant documents can be found in R. Vaughan, *Post-war Integration in Europe* (1976), and, on Britain and the Community, in U. Kitzinger (ed.), *The Second Try: Labour and the E.E.C.* (1968). For a wide-ranging set of material on the European Union, see A. Blair, *The Longman Companion to the European Union since 1945* (1999).

Secondary works

There are general discussions of the European unity movement in W. Laqueur, *Europe since Hitler* (1970) and D. Urwin, *Western Europe since 1945* (1981 edn). The fullest account of the early years of the unity movement can be found in W. Lipgens, *A History of European Integration, 1945–7* (1982), though this is very detailed. J. W. Young, *Britain, France and the Unity of Europe, 1945–51* (1984) is shorter and more analytical, while on the early 1950s, see E. Fursdon, *The European Defence Community* (1981), on the vain bid to create a 'European Army'. On the Common Market itself, see R. Pryce, *The Politics of the European Community* (1973) and A. M. Williams, *The European Community* (1994).

American relations with the European unity movement are discussed by M. Beloff, *The United States and the Unity of Europe* (1963) and R. Manderson-Jones, *Special Relationship* (1972), while British relations are discussed in M. Camps, *Britain and the European Community, 1955–63* (1964) and U. Kitzinger, *Diplomacy and Persuasion* (1974).

For the development of the European Community in the 1970s, see W. Feld, *The European Community in World Affairs* (1976), J. Fitzmaurice, *The European Parliament* (1978), and V. Herman and J. Lodge, *The European Parliament and the European Community* (1978).

18. Eastern Europe since 1945

Although Britain and France went to war to defend Eastern Europe in 1939, the end of the Second World War largely saw German domination of the area replaced by that of Russia. Between 1944 and 1948 communist parties established themselves in power, removed their democratic and rightist opponents and carried out Soviet-style reforms. But although these states became linked to the USSR through the Warsaw Pact and COMECON, it became apparent that Russian control in the Eastern bloc had limitations. Yugoslavia and Albania managed to escape the Soviet orbit, and although Moscow crushed opposition in East Germany, Hungary and Czechoslovakia, the communist states of the region managed to achieve differing degrees of independence prior to the collapse of communism in 1989.

Essay topics

- How important was the presence of the Red Army as a factor in creating communist states in Eastern Europe, 1944–48?

- Why did the Soviet Union intervene militarily in Hungary (1956) and Czechoslovakia (1968) but not in Yugoslavia (1948)?
- Account for the collapse of the communist regimes in Eastern Europe in 1989.

Sources and documents

M. McCauley, *The Origins of the Cold War* (1983) has some relevance; see also V. Dedijer, *Tito Speaks* (1954) on Yugoslavia. T. Garton Ash, *We the People: The Revolution of 1989* (1990) and L. Jones, *States of Change* (1990) are two reports on the events of 1989. Russian views are collected in C. Cerf and M. Albee, *Voices of Glasnost* (1989), letters to the Soviet magazine *Ogonyok*; see also M. Gorbachev, *Perestroika* (1986) and G. Stokes, *From Stalinism to Pluralism: A Documentary History of Eastern Europe since 1945* (2nd edn, 1996). For factual information on Eastern Europe spanning the communist era to the present, see A. Webb, *The Longman Companion to Central and Eastern Europe since 1919* (2002).

Secondary works

The essential background can be found in J. L. H. Keep, *Last of the Empires: A History of the Soviet Union, 1945–1991* (1996) and P. G. Lewis, *Central Europe since 1945* (1994); also F. Fejto, *A History of the People's Democracies* (1971), R. Okey, *Eastern Europe, 1740–1985* (2nd edn, 1986), and H. Seton-Watson, *The East European Revolution* (1985). On the early background to postwar Eastern Europe, see M. McCauley (ed.), *Communist Power in Europe, 1944–49* (1977), and on the general decay of Soviet influence, see G. Ionescu, *The Break-up of the Soviet Empire in Eastern Europe* (1965), Z. Brezezinski, *The Soviet Bloc* (1974), L. Labedz (ed.), *Revisionism* (1962), and H. Seton-Watson, *Nationalism and Communism, Essays, 1946–63* (1964); the impact of Gorbachev is considered in K. Dawisha, *Eastern Europe, Gorbachev and Reform: The Great Challenge* (1988).

For individual countries, see M. Fulbrook, *Anatomy of a Dictatorship: Inside the GDR, 1949–1989* (1995), M. McCauley, *The German Democratic Republic* (1983), M. Fulbrook's collection *Twentieth Century Germany: Politics, Culture, and Society, 1918–1990* (2001), Pt. II, which has synoptic essays on both East Germany and unification, L. Kattenacker, *Germany since 1945* (1997), I. Derbyshire, *Politics in Germany from Division to Unification* (1991), D. Childs, *The Fall of the GDR: Germany's Road to Unity* (2001), and K. H. Jarausch, *The Rush to German Unity* (1994). There are also valuable studies available in D. Childs (ed.), *Honecker's Germany* (1985), and *The GDR, Moscow's German Ally* (1983), J. P. Nettl, *The Eastern Zone and Soviet Policy in Germany, 1945–50* (1951), and J. Stele, *Socialism with a German Face* (1977). On Yugoslavia, see D. Rusinow, *Yugoslav Experiment, 1948–1974* (1977), P. Auty, *Tito* (1974) and, more generally, F. Singleton, *Twentieth Century Yugoslavia* (1976). On Hungary, see G. Litvan, *The Hungarian Revolution of 1956* (1996), F. Vali, *Rift and Revolt in Hungary* (1961), and M. Molnar, *Budapest 1956: A History of the Hungarian Revolution* (1971). On Czechoslovakia, see V. V. Kusin, *Intellectual Origins of the Prague Spring* (1971), G. Golan,

Reform Rule in Czechoslovakia (1973), and H. G. Skilling, *Czechoslovakia: The Interrupted Revolution* (1976). For Poland, see generally R. F. Leslie (ed.), *A History of Poland since 1863* (1983), N. Bethell, *Gomulka* (1969), N. Ascherson, *The Polish August* (1981), and T. Garton Ash, *Polish Revolution: Solidarity 1980–82* (1983).

Longer-term views of the events of 1989 are G. Stokes, *The Walls Came Tumbling Down* (1993), A. Heller and F. Feher, *From Yalta to Glasnost: The Dismantling of Stalin's Empire* (1990), and D. Selbourne, *Death of the Dark Hero: Eastern Europe, 1987–9* (1990). G. Prins (ed.), *Spring in Winter: The 1989 Revolutions* (1990), M. Frankland, *The Patriot's Revolution: How Eastern Europe Won Its Freedom* (1990), and M. Glenny, *The Rebirth of History* (1990) are all freshly drawn views of the momentous events of 1989. An analysis of Russian developments can be found in H. Smith, *The New Russians* (1990), M. Galeotti, *The Age of Anxiety: Society and Politics in Soviet and post-Soviet Russia* (1995), and G. Smith (ed.), *Nationalities of the Former Soviet Union* (1995). See also P. Desai, *Perestroika in Perspective: The Design and Dilemmas of Soviet Reform* (1989), S. Kull, *Burying Lenin: The Revolution in Soviet Ideology and Foreign Policy* (1992), and S. Sakwa, *Gorbachev and his Reforms, 1985–1990* (1991).

First-hand information is available now in M. Gorbachev, *Memoirs* (1997) and slightly greater distance from the events has sustained more considered accounts, such as R. K. Daniels, *Russia's Transformation: Snapshots of a Crumbling System* (1998), M. Galeotti, *Gorbachev and his Revolution* (1997), and M. McCauley, *Gorbachev* (1998).

MAPS

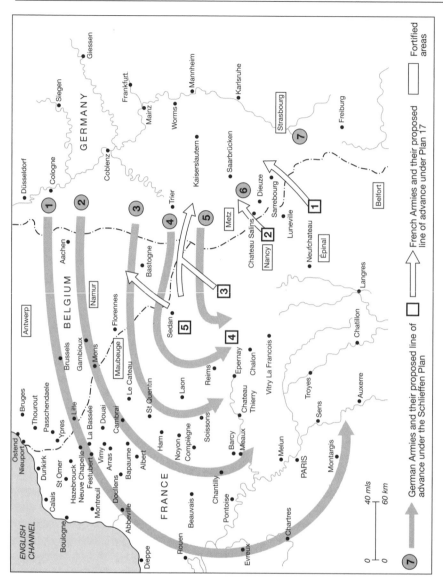

French and German war plans in 1914

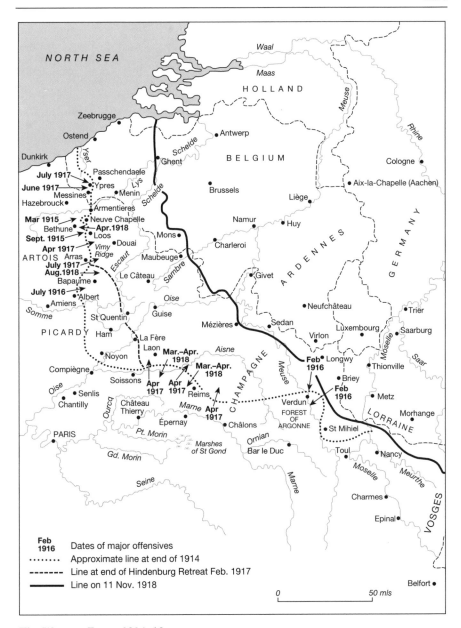

The Western Front: 1914–18

375

The Eastern Front: 1914–18

Lost by Germany 1919

Saar: League of Nations control 1919-35

Demilitarised Rhineland 1919-36

Austria-Hungary until 1918

Plebiscite Areas

Former territory of Imperial Russia

European frontiers, 1919–37

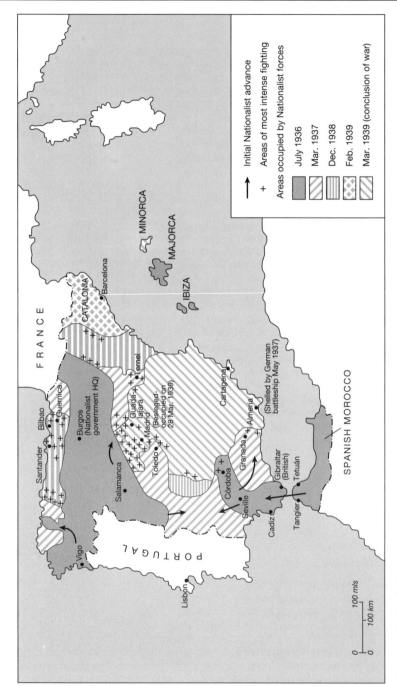

The Spanish Civil War

Legend:
- Initial Nationalist advance (arrow)
- Areas of most intense fighting (+)
- Areas occupied by Nationalist forces
  - July 1936
  - Mar. 1937
  - Dec. 1938
  - Feb. 1939
  - Mar. 1939 (conclusion of war)

FRANCE

PORTUGAL

SPANISH MOROCCO

MINORCA
MAJORCA
IBIZA

CATALONIA
Barcelona
Teruel
Guadalajara
Madrid (Besieged-occupied on 28 Mar. 1939)
Toledo
Burgos (Nationalist government HQ)
Guernica
Santander
Bilbao
Salamanca
Vigo
Lisbon
Córdoba
Seville
Cadiz
Tangier
Tetuán
Gibraltar (British)
Granada
Almeria
Cartagena (Shelled by German battleship May 1937)

0   100 mls
0   100 km

378

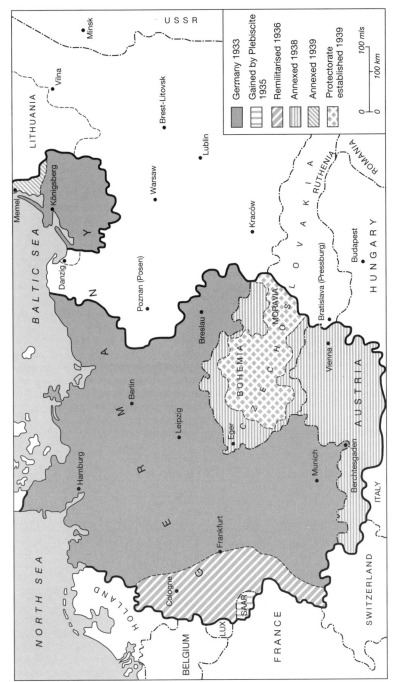

The expansion of Germany, 1935–39

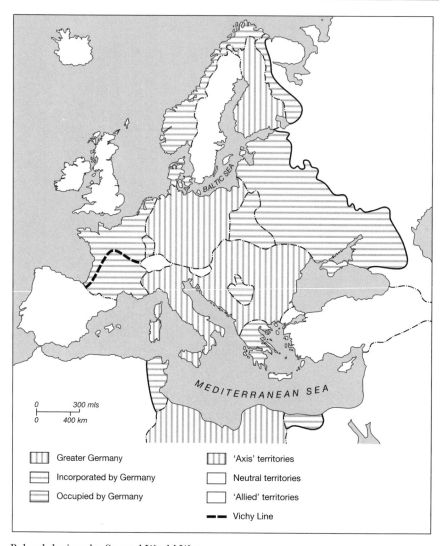

Poland during the Second World War

Nazi Germany and Europe, 1942

* Part of the Russian
  Federation

† Not a unitary state, but
  partitioned into Bosnian Serb,
  Croat and Muslim areas

Eastern Europe since communism

The European Union, 1997

INDEX

Note: References to tables, maps and the topic bibliography are given as '11*t*', '374*map*' and '342–4*bib*'.